ANNUAL EDITIONS

Global Issues 09/10

Twenty-Fifth Edition

EDITOR

Robert M. Jackson
California State University, Chico

Robert M. Jackson is a professor emeritus of political science and past dean of the School of Graduate, International and Sponsored Programs at California State University, Chico. In addition to teaching courses on third world politics and globalization, he has published articles on the international political economy, international relations simulations, and political behavior. Dr. Jackson has been responsible for numerous international training programs for professionals throughout the world. International educational exchanges and study abroad programs also have been an area of special interest. His research and professional travels include China, Japan, Hong Kong, Taiwan, Singapore, Malaysia, Spain, Portugal, Morocco, Belgium, Germany, the Czech Republic, the Netherlands, Russia, Mexico, Guatemala, Honduras, Costa Rica, El Salvador, Brazil, Chile, and Argentina.

McGraw-Hill Higher Education

Boston   Burr Ridge, IL   Dubuque, IA   New York   San Francisco   St. Louis
Bangkok   Bogotá   Caracas   Kuala Lumpur   Lisbon   London   Madrid   Mexico City
Milan   Montreal   New Delhi   Santiago   Seoul   Singapore   Sydney   Taipei   Toronto

Higher Education

ANNUAL EDITIONS: GLOBAL ISSUES, TWENTY-FIFTH EDITION

Annual Editions® is a registered trademark of The McGraw-Hill Companies, Inc.

Annual Editions is published by the **Contemporary Learning Series** group within the McGraw-Hill Higher Education division.

1 2 3 4 5 6 7 8 9 0 QPD/QPD 0 9

ISBN 978–0–07–812770–0
MHID 0–07–812770–X
ISSN 1093–278X

Managing Editor: *Larry Loeppke*
Senior Managing Editor: *Faye Schilling*
Developmental Editor: *Debra A. Henricks*
Editorial Coordinator: *Mary Foust*
Editorial Assistant: *Nancy Meissner*
Production Service Assistant: *Rita Hingtgen*
Permissions Coordinator: *Lenny J. Behnke*
Senior Marketing Manager: *Julie Keck*
Marketing Communications Specialist: *Mary Klein*
Marketing Coordinator: *Alice Link*
Project Manager: *Sandy Wille*
Design Specialist: *Tara McDermott*
Senior Production Supervisor: *Laura Fuller*
Cover Graphics: *Kristine Jubeck*

Compositor: Laserwords Private Limited
Cover Images: © Comstock Images/PictureQuest/RF (inset); © PhotoLink/Getty Images/RF (background)

Library in Congress Cataloging-in-Publication Data
Main entry under title: Annual Editions: Global Issues. 2009/2010.
  1. Global Issues—Periodicals by Jackson, Robert M., *comp*. II. Title: Global Issues
658 '.05

www.mhhe.com

Editors/Advisory Board

Members of the Advisory Board are instrumental in the final selection of articles for each edition of ANNUAL EDITIONS. Their review of articles for content, level, currentness, and appropriateness provides critical direction to the editor and staff. We think that you will find their careful consideration well reflected in this volume.

EDITOR

Robert M. Jackson
California State University, Chico

ADVISORY BOARD

Preface

In publishing ANNUAL EDITIONS we recognize the enormous role played by the magazines, newspapers, and journals of the public press in providing current, first-rate educational information in a broad spectrum of interest areas. Many of these articles are appropriate for students, researchers, and professionals seeking accurate, current material to help bridge the gap between principles and theories and the real world. These articles, however, become more useful for study when those of lasting value are carefully collected, organized, indexed, and reproduced in a low-cost format, which provides easy and permanent access when the material is needed. That is the role played by ANNUAL EDITIONS.

The beginning of the new millennium was celebrated with considerable fanfare. The prevailing mood in much of the world was that there was a great deal for which we could congratulate ourselves. The very act of sequentially watching on television live celebrations from one time zone to the next was proclaimed as a testimonial to globalization and the benefits of modern technology. The tragic events of September 11, 2001, however, were a stark reminder of the intense emotions and methods of destruction available to those determined to challenge the status quo. The subsequent wars in Afghanistan and Iraq along with continuing acts of terror have dampened the optimism that was expressed at the outset of the twenty-first century.

While the mass media may focus on the latest crisis for a few weeks or months, the broad forces that are shaping the world are seldom given the in-depth analysis that they warrant. Scholarly research about these historic forces of change can be found in a wide variety of publications, but these are not readily accessible. In addition, students just beginning to study global issues can be discouraged by the terminology and abstract concepts that characterize much of the scholarly literature. In selecting and organizing the materials for this book, we have been mindful of the needs of beginning students and have, thus, selected articles that invite the student into the subject matter.

Each unit begins with an introductory article(s) providing a broad overview of the subject area to be studied. The following articles examine in more detail specific case studies that often identify the positive steps being taken to remedy problems. Recent events are a continual reminder that the world faces many serious challenges, the magnitude of which would discourage even the most stouthearted individual. While identifying problems is easier than solving them, it is encouraging to know that many are being addressed.

Perhaps the most striking feature of the study of contemporary global issues is the absence of any single, widely held theory that explains what is taking place.

As a result, we have made a conscious effort to present a wide variety of points of view. The most important consideration has been to present global issues from an international perspective, rather than from a purely American or Western point of view. By encompassing materials originally published in different countries and written by authors of various nationalities, the anthology represents the great diversity of opinions that people hold. Two writers examining the same phenomenon may reach very different conclusions. It is not just a question of who is right or wrong, but rather understanding that people from different vantage points can have differing perspectives on an issue.

Another major consideration when organizing these materials was to explore the complex interrelationship of factors that produce social problems such as poverty. Too often, discussions of this problem (and others like it) are reduced to arguments about the fallacies of not following the correct economic policy or not having the correct form of government. As a result, many people overlook the interplay of historic, cultural, environmental, economic, and political factors that form complex webs that bring about many different problems. Every effort has been made to select materials that illustrate this complex interaction of factors, stimulating the beginning student to consider realistic rather than overly simplistic approaches to the pressing problems that threaten the existence of civilization.

In addition to an annotated table of contents and a topic guide, included in this edition of *Annual Editions: Global Issues* are Internet references that can be used to further explore topics addressed in the articles.

This is the twentieth-fifth edition of *Annual Editions: Global Issues*. When looking back over more than two decades of work, a great deal has taken place in world affairs, and the contents and organization of the book reflect these changes. Nonetheless there is one underlying constant. It is my continuing goal to work with the editors and staff at McGraw-Hill Contemporary Learning Series to provide materials that encourage the readers of this book to develop a life-long appreciation of the complex and rapidly changing world in which we live. I want to thank Jared Meyer for his timely research assistance. This collection of articles is an invitation to further explore the global issues of the twenty-first century and become personally involved in the great issues of our time.

Finally, materials in this book were selected for both their intellectual insights and readability. Timely and well-written materials should stimulate good classroom lectures and discussions. I hope that students and teachers will enjoy using this book. Readers can have input into the next edition by completing and returning the postage-paid article rating form in the back of the book.

Robert M. Jackson
Editor

Contents

Preface   iv
Correlation Guide   xii
Topic Guide   xiii
Internet References   xvi

UNIT 1
Global Issues in the Twenty-First Century: An Overview

Unit Overview   xx

1. **A Special Moment in History,** Bill McKibben, *The Atlantic,*
   May 1998

   The interconnected dangers of **overpopulation, climate change, and pollution** have
   been in the headlines for years, but doomsday has not yet arrived. Bill McKibben examines two important questions: What if we have already inflicted serious damage on the
   planet? And what if there are only a few decades left to salvage a stable environment?   3

2. **Can Extreme Poverty Be Eliminated?,** Jeffrey D. Sachs,
   Scientific American, September 2005

   One of the United Nations Millennium Project's goals was reducing by half the level of
   extreme **poverty** by 2015. The director of the project describes how business as usual
   has to be replaced with programs that address the underlying causes of poverty by improving **health, education, water, sanitation, food production, and roads.**   7

3. **The Ideology of Development,** William Easterly, *Foreign Policy,*
   July/August 2007

   The author critically evaluates both the **economic and political assumptions** of **development** theorists such as Jeffrey Sachs and Thomas Friedman. Easterly argues that
   the top down approach managed by international bureaucrats has done little to alleviate
   poverty while at the same time minimizing local solutions to economic challenges. This
   article is an excellent companion piece to other articles in this section, for it presents a
   distinctly different perspective.   12

4. **The Rise of the Rest,** Fareed Zakaria, *Newsweek,* May 12, 2008

   There is considerable speculation about the **future** role of the United States in the **international economic system.** The author discusses the growing political and economic
   importance of other countries and how the United States must learn to adapt if it is going
   to maintain its ability to lead.   15

5. **Feminists and Fundamentalists,** Kavita Ramdas, *Current History,*
   March 2006

   The **women's movement** had great success during the twentieth century. Today, it
   faces a backlash. The new challenges facing women are discussed along with strategies to meet them.   20

The concepts in bold italics are developed in the article. For further expansion, please refer to the Topic Guide.

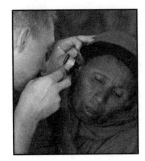

UNIT 2
Population and Food Production

Unit Overview   **24**

6. **The Century Ahead,** Chris Wilson, *Daedalus,* Winter 2006
   Rapid **population** growth was the dominant demographic trend in the twentieth century. The author argues that the twenty-first century is likely to be the century of aging. The implications of this demographic transition are examined in different regions of the world.   **26**

7. **Africa's Restless Youth,** Michelle Gavin, *Current History,* May 2007
   While much of the world's population is aging, Africa is in the midst of a **demographic youth bulge.** The **social and political consequences** of this are described in this article.   **29**

8. **Still Hungry: One Eighth of the World's People Do Not Have Enough to Eat,** Per Pinstrup-Andersen and Fuzhi Cheng, *Scientific American,* September 2007
   The cause of **hunger** is not insufficient **food production.** Factors contributing to hunger are discussed along with identifying who is hungry and where they are located.   **35**

9. **Pandemic Pandemonium,** Josh N. Ruxin, *National Journal,* July/August 2008
   A broad discussion of various diseases and the potential for **pandemics** is presented here. The article describes the efforts and challenges facing national and **international health organizations** as they confront the age-old threat to civilization.   **40**

UNIT 3
The Global Environment and Natural Resources Utilization

Unit Overview   **44**

10. **Deflating the World's Bubble Economy,** Lester R. Brown, *USA Today Magazine,* November 2003
    Lester Brown is one of the leading commentators on global **environmental issues.** In this article, he argues that unless damaging trends are reversed, depleted aquifers and exhausted soils could lead to the abandonment of rich **agricultural areas.** Brown also provides case studies of a number of successful transitions to sustainable practices.   **46**

11. **The Great Leap Backward?,** Elizabeth C. Economy, *Foreign Affairs,* September/October 2007
    China's rapid **economic growth** is resulting in deteriorating environmental conditions. These consequences are described along with the government's ambitious targets for **environmental protection,** which are often ignored by local officials.   **49**

12. **Water of Life in Peril,** Sharon Palmer, *Today's Dietitian,* October 2007
    The author provides a comprehensive discussion of the strain on fresh water supplies, including inefficient, wasteful irrigation and **food** production systems. The article examines different efforts to increase efficiency, including **recycling** waste water.   **57**

The concepts in bold italics are developed in the article. For further expansion, please refer to the Topic Guide.

13. **Ocean 'Dead Zones' Spreading Worldwide,** Randolph E. Schmid, *The Sacramento Bee,* August 15, 2008

The number of known areas of the **oceans** and coastal waters where life has been snuffed out due to oxygen depletion has doubled in the last two years. The article summarizes the **research** related to this problem.　　60

14. **Cry of the Wild,** Sharon Begley, *Newsweek,* August 6, 2007

Hunting, including protected animals, is a **multimillion-dollar business.** The impact of hunting on **endangered species** is described along with the efforts to protect the world's vanishing wildlife.　　62

UNIT 4
Political Economy

Unit Overview　　64

Part A.　Globalization Debate

15. **Globalization and Its Contents,** Peter Marber, *World Policy Journal,* Winter 2004/05

The term **globalization** has different meanings for different people, often depending on their political perspective. The debate about the positive and negative impacts of this situation is reviewed from a broad historical perspective. The author concludes that the evidence strongly suggests that **human prosperity** is improving as boundaries between people are lowered.　　67

16. **It's a Flat World, After All,** Thomas L. Friedman, *The New York Times,* April 3, 2005

Thomas Friedman is a well-known commentator who has contributed significantly to the debate about **globalization.** This article summarizes his latest book, *The World Is Flat.* He discusses a number of **technological trends** that are not only involving new participants in the global economy but also fundamentally changing the way people do business.　　73

17. **Why the World Isn't Flat,** Pankaj Ghemawat, *Foreign Policy,* March/April 2007

The concept of **globalization** has defined much of the debate about international **economic activity** for the past twenty years. The author critically examines the basic assumptions of those that argue that this trend is dominant, and concludes that "the champions of globalization are describing a world that doesn't exist."　　78

Part B.　General Case Studies

18. **The Case against the West: America and Europe in the Asian Century,** Kishore Mahbubani, *Foreign Affairs,* May/June 2008

The changing international, **economic** roles of both Asian and Western countries is described along with an evaluation of how the West is resisting the rise of the Asian countries. There is specific focus on the issues of **nuclear nonproliferation,** the Middle East, and **trade.**　　81

19. **A Bigger World,** *The Economist,* September 20, 2008

Globalization is entering a new phase, one in which companies from **emerging markets** are competing against rich-country corporations. The article discusses the implications of this trend to the **future** of capitalism.　　86

The concepts in bold italics are developed in the article. For further expansion, please refer to the Topic Guide.

20. **The Lost Continent,** Moisés Naím, *Foreign Policy,* November/December 2006

The author observes that the role of **Latin America** in the world has been declining for decades. He examines the reasons for this diminished role with a special focus on **political culture.**   **89**

21. **Promises and Poverty,** Tom Knudson, *Sacramento Bee,* September 23, 2007

Companies often market their products by boasting about what they do for the **environment.** Starbuck's eco-friendly approach is examined with a special focus on the complex story of **coffee** in East Africa.   **93**

22. **Drugs,** Ethan Nadelmann, *Foreign Policy,* September/October 2007

The author challenges the basic assumptions of the **war on drugs.** He describes the **financial** and **criminal** dimensions of illegal drug trafficking. He asserts that prohibition has failed. A smarter drug-control **policy** is emerging, which focuses on results rather than on rhetoric.   **99**

Part C. Global Energy Case Studies

23. **Ensuring Energy Security,** Daniel Yergin, *Foreign Affairs,* March/April 2006

Daniel Yergin is a leading expert on global **energy** politics. He provides a comprehensive overview of the changing energy markets and U.S. national **security.** New consumers, such as India and China, have changed the supply and demand equation. Increasingly complex systems of oil shipping have further compounded the **political economy** of global energy.   **102**

24. **The Power and the Glory,** Geoffrey Carr, *The Economist,* June 21, 2008

The article provides comprehensive review of the changing patterns of **energy** consumption as the price of oil increases and efforts to reduce **greenhouse gases** accelerate. The article focuses on **new technologies** and the **economic** dimensions of developing new sources of clean, renewable energy.   **108**

25. **Nuclear Now!: How Clean, Green Atomic Energy Can Stop Global Warming,** Peter Schwartz and Spencer Reiss, *Wired,* February 2005

The argument that nuclear power is an **environmentally friendly** alternative to **oil and coal** is presented along with a discussion of "interim storage" and the recycling of nuclear waste. Numerous references are made to the role of nuclear power in Europe and Japan, which provides an international context to the discussion.   **111**

26. **Life After Peak Oil,** Gregory Clark, *The Sacramento Bee,* December 23, 2007

The author argues that after an initial period of painful adaptation, Americans can lead happy and healthy lives in a world with high energy costs.   **116**

UNIT 5
Conflict

Unit Overview   **118**

27. **Terrorist Rivals: Beyond the State-Centric Model,** Louise Richardson, *Harvard International Review,* Spring 2007

An examination of the traditional way of viewing international politics reveals an interesting conclusion: "That a country with secure borders, a formidable nuclear deterrent, and no military rivals . . . feels vulnerable, speaks to the inadequacies of the traditional formulation of the **balance of power.** " In addressing the threat of **terrorism,** the author offers six principles for guiding U.S. policy in the **future.**   **120**

The concepts in bold italics are developed in the article. For further expansion, please refer to the Topic Guide.

28. **The Long March to Be a Superpower,** *The Economist,* August 4, 2007

The Chinese military is rapidly modernizing itself by purchasing Russian equipment and developing new missiles and other weapons systems. The capability of the People's Liberation Army to challenge the United States is assessed along with a discussion of the ability to wage asymmetrical **warfare.**

124

29. **What Russia Wants,** Ivan Krastev, *Foreign Policy,* May/June 2008

The author examines the **foreign policy** of Russia and its assumptions about the **future** of the United States and Europe.

127

30. **Lifting the Veil: Understanding the Roots of Islamic Militancy,**
Henry Munson, *Harvard International Review,* Winter 2004

This article explores the question, "Why do they hate us?" Using public opinion polls to examine attitudes in the Middle East, Professor Munson identifies two sources of **anti-American militancy:** U.S. support of Israel and a backlash to the strategy and tactics of the **war on terrorism.**

130

31. **A Mideast Nuclear Chain Reaction?,** Joseph Cirincione, *Current History,* December 2008

As Iran develops the technology to enrich **uranium** suitable for building a nuclear weapon, other countries in the Middle East are beginning to pursue this technology as well. The author discusses the potential for a regional **nuclear arms race** which could significantly increase the possibility of a **nuclear war.**

133

32. **The Politics of Death in Darfur,** Gérard Prunier, *Current History,* May 2006

A complex mix **of tribal, ethnic, and religious cross-currents** forms the backdrop for the unfolding crisis in the **drought-prone** Darfur region of Sudan. The French author describes the national and international political maneuvering that impedes a meaningful response to this **humanitarian crisis.**

136

33. **Banning the Bomb: A New Approach,** Ward Wilson, *Dissent,* Winter 2007

The military utility of **nuclear weapons** is challenged along with the doctrine that has supported their development. The author argues that nuclear weapons have no real military value and proposes that they be banned, thereby eliminating the danger of them falling into the hands of **terrorists** and unstable leaders.

144

UNIT 6
Cooperation

Unit Overview

148

34. **Europe as a Global Player: A Parliamentary Perspective,**
Hans-Gert Poettering, *Harvard International Review,* Spring 2007

The evolution of the European Parliament is chronicled in this article. This expansion of the **legislative power** and responsibility has resulted in significant changes in both the scope of **European Union** policy and the integration of member countries.

150

35. **The Grameen Bank,** Muhammad Yunus, *Scientific American,* November 1999

A small experiment, begun in Bangladesh to loan money to poor people as a way of helping them become more productive, has turned into **a major, new concept in the eradication of poverty.**

153

36. **Geneva Conventions,** Steven R. Ratner, *Foreign Policy,* March/April 2008

The author discusses the **international law** governing the treatment of soldiers and civilians during **war** with a focus on 21st century issues, including the War on Terror.

157

37. **Is Bigger Better?,** David Armstrong, *Forbes,* June 2, 2008

Using **market incentives,** the world's largest **antipoverty** group helped pull Bangladesh out of the ashes. Now it wants to take on Africa.

160

The concepts in bold italics are developed in the article. For further expansion, please refer to the Topic Guide.

UNIT 7
Values and Visions

Unit Overview   **162**

38. Humanity's Common Values: Seeking a Positive Future, Wendell Bell,
The Futurist, September/October 2004

The author argues that, "there is an emerging global ethic, a set of shared values."
These have evolved and now shape and constrain behavior. Specific principles along
with behavior that supports the development of ***legal and ethical norms*** necessary for
a positive global ***future*** are described here.   **164**

39. And the Winner Is . . ., Alan Wolfe, *The Atlantic,* March 2008

The article is a comprehensive discussion of the relationship between ***religious practices*** and per capita ***income.*** The author argues that "the secular underpinning of today's religious growth" is directly affecting beliefs and practices. The overall trend is for
greater understanding between ***religions*** and not an expansion of extremism.   **170**

40. Life, Religion and Everything, Laura Sevier, *The Ecologist,*
September 2007

The author examines the renewed focus of all, major ***religious*** groups to view the land
as alive and ***sacred*** with value beyond ***economic*** terms.   **175**

Test-Your-Knowledge From   **180**
Article Rating Form   **181**

The concepts in bold italics are developed in the article. For further expansion, please refer to the Topic Guide.

Correlation Guide

The *Annual Editions* series provides students with convenient, inexpensive access to current, carefully selected articles from the public press. **Annual Editions: Global Issues 09/10** is an easy-to-use reader that presents articles on important topics such as *population, environment, political economy,* and many more. For more information on *Annual Editions* and other *McGraw-Hill Contemporary Learning Series* titles, visit www.mhcls.com.

This convenient guide matches the units in **Annual Editions: Global Issues 09/10** with the corresponding chapters in two of our best-selling McGraw-Hill Political Science textbooks by Rourke and Boyer.

Annual Editions: Global Issues 09/10	**International Politics on the World Stage, Brief, 8/e by Rourke/Boyer**	**International Politics on the World Stage, 12/e by Rourke**
Unit 1: Global Issues in the Twenty-First Century: An Overview	**Chapter 1:** Thinking and Caring about World Politics **Chapter 2:** The Evolution of World Politics **Chapter 5:** Globalization and Transnationalism: The Alternative Orientation	**Chapter 1:** Thinking and Caring about World Politics **Chapter 2:** The Evolution of World Politics **Chapter 5:** Globalism: The Alternative Orientation
Unit 2: Population and Food Production	**Chapter 8:** International Law and Human Rights: An Alternative Approach	**Chapter 14:** Preserving and Enhancing Human Rights and Dignity
Unit 3: The Global Environment and Natural Resources Utilization	**Chapter 12:** Preserving and Enhancing the Global Commons	**Chapter 15:** Preserving and Enhancing the Biosphere
Unit 4: Political Economy	**Chapter 6:** Power and the National States: The Traditional Structure **Chapter 7:** International Organization: An Alternative Structure **Chapter 10:** Globalization in the World Economy **Chapter 11:** Global Economic Competition and Cooperation	**Chapter 7:** Intergovernmental Organization: Alternative Governance **Chapter 8:** National Power and Statecraft: The Traditional Approach **Chapter 12:** National Economic Competition: The Traditional Road
Unit 5: Conflict	**Chapter 6:** Power and the National States: The Traditional Structure **Chapter 9:** Pursuing Security	**Chapter 8:** National Power and Statecraft: The Traditional Approach **Chapter 10:** National Security: The Traditional Road **Chapter 11:** International Security: The Alternative Road
Unit 6: Cooperation	**Chapter 8:** International Law and Human Rights: An Alternative Approach **Chapter 11:** Global Economic Competition and Cooperation	**Chapter 9:** International Law and Justice: An Alternative Approach **Chapter 13:** International Economic Cooperation: The Alternative Road
Unit 7: Values and Visions	**Chapter 3:** Level of Analysis **Chapter 8:** International Law and Human Rights: An Alternative Approach	**Chapter 3:** Levels of Analysis and Foreign Policy **Chapter 14:** Preserving and Enhancing Human Rights and Dignity

Topic Guide

This topic guide suggests how the selections in this book relate to the subjects covered in your course. You may want to use the topics listed on these pages to search the Web more easily.

On the following pages a number of Web sites have been gathered specifically for this book. They are arranged to reflect the units of this Annual Editions reader. You can link to these sites by going to *http://www.mhcls.com*.

All the articles that relate to each topic are listed below the bold-faced term.

Agriculture

1. A Special Moment in History
2. Can Extreme Poverty Be Eliminated?
3. The Ideology of Development
8. Still Hungry: One Eighth of the World's People Do Not Have Enough to Eat
10. Deflating the World's Bubble Economy
12. Water of Life in Peril

Communication

1. A Special Moment in History
16. It's a Flat World, After All
17. Why the World Isn't Flat

Conservation

1. A Special Moment in History
10. Deflating the World's Bubble Economy
11. The Great Leap Backward?
12. Water of Life in Peril
13. Ocean 'Dead Zones' Spreading Worldwide
14. Cry of the Wild
23. Ensuring Energy Security
24. The Power and the Glory
25. Nuclear Now!: How Clean, Green Atomic Energy Can Stop Global Warming
26. Life After Peak Oil

Cultural customs and values

2. Can Extreme Poverty Be Eliminated?
3. The Ideology of Development
4. The Rise of the Rest
5. Feminists and Fundamentalists
6. The Century Ahead
15. Globalization and Its Contents
16. It's a Flat World, After All
17. Why the World Isn't Flat
18. The Case against the West: America and Europe in the Asian Century
20. The Lost Continent
26. Life After Peak Oil
30. Lifting the Veil: Understanding the Roots of Islamic Militancy
36. Geneva Conventions
37. Is Bigger Better?
38. Humanity's Common Values: Seeking a Positive Future
39. And the Winner Is . . .
40. Life, Religion and Everything

Demographics

1. A Special Moment in History
6. The Century Ahead
7. Africa's Restless Youth
9. Pandemic Pandemonium

Dependencies, international

4. The Rise of the Rest
15. Globalization and Its Contents
16. It's a Flat World, After All
17. Why the World Isn't Flat

18. The Case against the West: America and Europe in the Asian Century
19. A Bigger World
21. Promises and Poverty
22. Drugs
23. Ensuring Energy Security

Development, economic

2. Can Extreme Poverty Be Eliminated?
3. The Ideology of Development
4. The Rise of the Rest
5. Feminists and Fundamentalists
8. Still Hungry: One Eighth of the World's People Do Not Have Enough to Eat
9. Pandemic Pandemonium
11. The Great Leap Backward?
15. Globalization and Its Contents
16. It's a Flat World, After All
17. Why the World Isn't Flat
18. The Case against the West: America and Europe in the Asian Century
19. A Bigger World
20. The Lost Continent
21. Promises and Poverty
37. Is Bigger Better?

Development, social

2. Can Extreme Poverty Be Eliminated?
3. The Ideology of Development
5. Feminists and Fundamentalists
7. Africa's Restless Youth
18. The Case against the West: America and Europe in the Asian Century
20. The Lost Continent
21. Promises and Poverty
36. Geneva Conventions
37. Is Bigger Better?
38. Humanity's Common Values: Seeking a Positive Future
39. And the Winner Is . . .
40. Life, Religion and Everything

Ecology

1. A Special Moment in History
2. Can Extreme Poverty Be Eliminated?
10. Deflating the World's Bubble Economy
11. The Great Leap Backward?
12. Water of Life in Peril
13. Ocean 'Dead Zones' Spreading Worldwide
14. Cry of the Wild
16. It's a Flat World, After All
23. Ensuring Energy Security
24. The Power and the Glory
25. Nuclear Now!: How Clean, Green Atomic Energy Can Stop Global Warming
40. Life, Religion and Everything

Economics

1. A Special Moment in History
2. Can Extreme Poverty Be Eliminated?
3. The Ideology of Development

4. The Rise of the Rest
8. Still Hungry: One Eighth of the World's People Do Not Have Enough to Eat
10. Deflating the World's Bubble Economy
11. The Great Leap Backward?
15. Globalization and Its Contents
16. It's a Flat World, After All
17. Why the World Isn't Flat
18. The Case against the West: America and Europe in the Asian Century
19. A Bigger World
20. The Lost Continent
21. Promises and Poverty
22. Drugs
23. Ensuring Energy Security
24. The Power and the Glory
25. Nuclear Now!: How Clean, Green Atomic Energy Can Stop Global Warming
39. And the Winner Is . . .

Energy: Exploration, production, research, and politics

10. Deflating the World's Bubble Economy
11. The Great Leap Backward?
23. Ensuring Energy Security
24. The Power and the Glory
25. Nuclear Now!: How Clean, Green Atomic Energy Can Stop Global Warming
26. Life After Peak Oil

Environment

1. A Special Moment in History
10. Deflating the World's Bubble Economy
11. The Great Leap Backward?
12. Water of Life in Peril
13. Ocean 'Dead Zones' Spreading Worldwide
14. Cry of the Wild
21. Promises and Poverty
23. Ensuring Energy Security
24. The Power and the Glory
25. Nuclear Now!: How Clean, Green Atomic Energy Can Stop Global Warming

Food

1. A Special Moment in History
3. The Ideology of Development
8. Still Hungry: One Eighth of the World's People Do Not Have Enough to Eat
10. Deflating the World's Bubble Economy
12. Water of Life in Peril
21. Promises and Poverty

Future

1. A Special Moment in History
2. Can Extreme Poverty Be Eliminated?
4. The Rise of the Rest
5. Feminists and Fundamentalists
6. The Century Ahead
7. Africa's Restless Youth
8. Still Hungry: One Eighth of the World's People Do Not Have Enough to Eat
9. Pandemic Pandemonium
10. Deflating the World's Bubble Economy
11. The Great Leap Backward?
14. Cry of the Wild
18. The Case against the West: America and Europe in the Asian Century
23. Ensuring Energy Security
24. The Power and the Glory
25. Nuclear Now!: How Clean, Green Atomic Energy Can Stop Global Warming
26. Life After Peak Oil

27. Terrorist Rivals: Beyond the State-Centric Model
28. The Long March to Be a Superpower
29. What Russia Wants
31. A Mideast Nuclear Chain Reaction?
33. Banning the Bomb: A New Approach
34. Europe as a Global Player: A Parliamentary Perspective

Global political issues

4. The Rise of the Rest
18. The Case against the West: America and Europe in the Asian Century
27. Terrorist Rivals: Beyond the State-Centric Model
29. What Russia Wants
31. A Mideast Nuclear Chain Reaction?
32. The Politics of Death in Darfur
33. Banning the Bomb: A New Approach
34. Europe as a Global Player: A Parliamentary Perspective
36. Geneva Conventions

Hunger

1. A Special Moment in History
8. Still Hungry: One Eighth of the World's People Do Not Have Enough to Eat
10. Deflating the World's Bubble Economy
12. Water of Life in Peril

International aid

2. Can Extreme Poverty Be Eliminated?
3. The Ideology of Development
37. Is Bigger Better?

International economics

1. A Special Moment in History
2. Can Extreme Poverty Be Eliminated?
3. The Ideology of Development
4. The Rise of the Rest
8. Still Hungry: One Eighth of the World's People Do Not Have Enough to Eat
10. Deflating the World's Bubble Economy
11. The Great Leap Backward?
15. Globalization and Its Contents
16. It's a Flat World, After All
17. Why the World Isn't Flat
18. The Case against the West: America and Europe in the Asian Century
19. A Bigger World
20. The Lost Continent
21. Promises and Poverty
22. Drugs
23. Ensuring Energy Security
24. The Power and the Glory
26. Life After Peak Oil
37. Is Bigger Better?
39. And the Winner Is . . .

Legal global issues

14. Cry of the Wild
18. The Case against the West: America and Europe in the Asian Century
33. Banning the Bomb: A New Approach
34. Europe as a Global Player: A Parliamentary Perspective
36. Geneva Conventions

Military: Warfare and terrorism

27. Terrorist Rivals: Beyond the State-Centric Model
28. The Long March to Be a Superpower
29. What Russia Wants
30. Lifting the Veil: Understanding the Roots of Islamic Militancy
31. A Mideast Nuclear Chain Reaction?

32. The Politics of Death in Darfur
33. Banning the Bomb: A New Approach

Natural Resources

8. Still Hungry: One Eighth of the World's People Do Not Have Enough to Eat
10. Deflating the World's Bubble Economy
11. The Great Leap Backward?
12. Water of Life in Peril
13. Ocean 'Dead Zones' Spreading Worldwide
14. Cry of the Wild
23. Ensuring Energy Security
24. The Power and the Glory
40. Life, Religion and Everything

Political global issues

2. Can Extreme Poverty Be Eliminated?
3. The Ideology of Development
5. Feminists and Fundamentalists
9. Pandemic Pandemonium
10. Deflating the World's Bubble Economy
16. It's a Flat World, After All
17. Why the World Isn't Flat
18. The Case against the West: America and Europe in the Asian Century
22. Drugs
27. Terrorist Rivals: Beyond the State-Centric Model
29. What Russia Wants
31. A Mideast Nuclear Chain Reaction?
33. Banning the Bomb: A New Approach
34. Europe as a Global Player: A Parliamentary Perspective
39. And the Winner Is . . .

Population

1. A Special Moment in History
6. The Century Ahead
7. Africa's Restless Youth
9. Pandemic Pandemonium

Poverty

2. Can Extreme Poverty Be Eliminated?
3. The Ideology of Development
8. Still Hungry: One Eighth of the World's People Do Not Have Enough to Eat
15. Globalization and Its Contents
17. Why the World Isn't Flat
21. Promises and Poverty
37. Is Bigger Better?

Science, technology, and research and development

1. A Special Moment in History
10. Deflating the World's Bubble Economy
13. Ocean 'Dead Zones' Spreading Worldwide
16. It's a Flat World, After All
23. Ensuring Energy Security
24. The Power and the Glory
25. Nuclear Now!: How Clean, Green Atomic Energy Can Stop Global Warming

Terrorism

27. Terrorist Rivals: Beyond the State-Centric Model
30. Lifting the Veil: Understanding the Roots of Islamic Militancy
32. The Politics of Death in Darfur

Trade

4. The Rise of the Rest
15. Globalization and Its Contents
16. It's a Flat World, After All
17. Why the World Isn't Flat
18. The Case against the West: America and Europe in the Asian Century
21. Promises and Poverty

Underdeveloped countries

2. Can Extreme Poverty Be Eliminated?
3. The Ideology of Development
4. The Rise of the Rest
7. Africa's Restless Youth
10. Deflating the World's Bubble Economy
17. Why the World Isn't Flat
21. Promises and Poverty
22. Drugs
32. The Politics of Death in Darfur
37. Is Bigger Better?

Values

3. The Ideology of Development
5. Feminists and Fundamentalists
18. The Case against the West: America and Europe in the Asian Century
33. Banning the Bomb: A New Approach
36. Geneva Conventions
38. Humanity's Common Values: Seeking a Positive Future

Internet References

The following Internet sites have been selected to support the articles found in this reader. These sites were available at the time of publication. However, because Web sites often change their structure and content, the information listed may no longer be available. We invite you to visit http://www.mhcls.com for easy access to these sites.

Annual Editions: Global Issues 09/10

General Sources

U.S. Information Agency (USIA)
http://www.america.gov/

USIA's home page provides definitions, related documentation, and discussions of topics of concern to students of global issues. The site addresses today's Hot Topics as well as ongoing issues that form the foundation of the field.

World Wide Web Virtual Library: International Affairs Resources
http://www.etown.edu/vl/

Surf this site and its extensive links to learn about specific countries and regions, to research various think tanks and international organizations, and to study such vital topics as international law, development, the international economy, human rights, and peacekeeping.

UNIT 1: Global Issues in the Twenty-First Century: An Overview

The Henry L. Stimson Center
http://www.stimson.org

The Stimson Center, a nonpartisan organization, focuses on issues where policy, technology, and politics intersect. Use this site to find varying assessments of U.S. foreign policy in the post–cold war world and to research other topics.

The Heritage Foundation
http://www.heritage.org

This page offers discussion about and links to many sites having to do with foreign policy and foreign affairs, including news and commentary, policy review, events, and a resource bank.

IISDnet
http://www.nsi-ins.ca/

The International Institute for Sustainable Development presents information through links to business, sustainable development, and developing ideas. "Linkages" is its multimedia resource for policymakers.

The North-South Institute
http://www.nsi-ins.ca/ensi/index.htm

Searching this site of the North-South Institute, which works to strengthen international development cooperation and enhance gender and social equity, will help you find information and debates on a variety of global issues.

UNIT 2: Population and Food Production

The Hunger Project
http://www.thp.org

Browse through this nonprofit organization's site, whose goal is the sustainable end to global hunger through leadership at all levels of society. The Hunger Project contends that the persistence of hunger is at the heart of the major security issues threatening our planet.

Penn Library: Resources by Subject
http://www.library.upenn.edu/cgi-bin/res/sr.cgi

This vast site is rich in links to information about subjects of interest to students of global issues. Its extensive population and demography resources address such concerns as migration, family planning, and health and nutrition in various world regions.

World Health Organization
http://www.who.int

This home page of the World Health Organization will provide you with links to a wealth of statistical and analytical information about health and the environment in the developing world.

WWW Virtual Library: Demography & Population Studies
http://demography.anu.edu.au/VirtualLibrary/

A definitive guide to demography and population studies can be found at this site. It contains a multitude of important links to information about global poverty and hunger.

UNIT 3: The Global Environment and Natural Resources Utilization

National Geographic Society
http://www.nationalgeographic.com

This site provides links to material related to the atmosphere, the oceans, and other environmental topics.

National Oceanic and Atmospheric Administration (NOAA)
http://www.noaa.gov

Through this home page of NOAA, part of the U.S. Department of Commerce, you can find information about coastal issues, fisheries, climate, and more. The site provides many links to research materials and to other Web resources.

SocioSite: Sociological Subject Areas
http://www.pscw.uva.nl/sociosite/TOPICS/

This huge site provides many references of interest to those interested in global issues, such as links to information on ecology and the impact of consumerism.

United Nations Environment Programme (UNEP)
http://www.unep.ch

Consult this home page of UNEP for links to critical topics of concern to students of global issues, including desertification, migratory species, and the impact of trade on the environment.

UNIT 4: Political Economy

Belfer Center for Science and International Affairs (BCSIA)
http://ksgwww.harvard.edu/csia/

BCSIA is the hub of Harvard University's John F. Kennedy School of Government's research, teaching, and training in international affairs related to security, environment, and technology.

Internet References

U.S. Agency for International Development

http://www.usaid.gov

Broad and overlapping issues such as democracy, population and health, economic growth, and development are covered on this Web site. It provides specific information about different regions and countries.

The World Bank Group

http://www.worldbank.org

News, press releases, summaries of new projects, speeches, publications, and coverage of numerous topics regarding development, countries, and regions are provided at this World Bank site. It also contains links to other important global financial organizations.

UNIT 5: Conflict

DefenseLINK

http://www.defenselink.mil

Learn about security news and research-related publications at this U.S. Department of Defense site. Links to related sites of interest are provided. The information systems BosniaLINK and GulfLINK can also be found here. Use the search function to investigate such issues as land mines.

Federation of American Scientists (FAS)

http://www.fas.org

FAS, a nonprofit policy organization, maintains this site to provide coverage of and links to such topics as global security, peace, and governance in the post–cold war world. It notes a variety of resources of value to students of global issues.

ISN International Relations and Security Network

http://www.isn.ethz.ch

This site, maintained by the Center for Security Studies and Conflict Research, is a clearinghouse for information on international relations and security policy. Topics are listed by category (Traditional Dimensions of Security, New Dimensions of Security, and Related Fields) and by major world region.

The NATO Integrated Data Service (NIDS)

http://www.nato.int/structur/nids/nids.htm

NIDS was created to bring information on security-related matters to within easy reach of the widest possible audience. Check out this Web site to review North Atlantic Treaty Organization documentation of all kinds, to read *NATO Review,* and to explore key issues in the field of European security and transatlantic cooperation.

UNIT 6: Cooperation

Carnegie Endowment for International Peace

http://www.ceip.org

An important goal of this organization is to stimulate discussion and learning among both experts and the public at large on a wide range of international issues. The site provides links to *Foreign Policy,* to the Moscow Center, to descriptions of various programs, and much more.

OECD/FDI Statistics

http://www.oecd.org/statistics/

Explore world trade and investment trends and statistics on this site from the Organization for Economic Cooperation and Development. It provides links to many related topics and addresses the issues on a country-by-country basis.

U.S. Institute of Peace

http://www.usip.org

USIP, which was created by the U.S. Congress to promote peaceful resolution of international conflicts, seeks to educate people and to disseminate information on how to achieve peace. Click on Highlights, Publications, Events, Research Areas, and Library and Links.

UNIT 7: Values and Visions

Human Rights Web

http://www.hrweb.org

The history of the human rights movement, text on seminal figures, landmark legal and political documents, and ideas on how individuals can get involved in helping to protect human rights around the world can be found in this valuable site.

InterAction

http://www.interaction.org

InterAction encourages grassroots action and engages government policymakers on advocacy issues. The organization's Advocacy Committee provides this site to inform people on its initiatives to expand international humanitarian relief, refugee, and development-assistance programs.

World Map

N
W · E
S

U.S.

CANADA

NORTH
PACIFIC
OCEAN

UNITED STATES

NORTH
ATLANTIC
OCEAN

Tropic of Cancer

U.S.

MEXICO

GUYANA
SURINAME
FRENCH
GUIANA
(FR)

COLOMBIA

Equator

ECUADOR

VENEZUELA

P
E
R
U

B R A Z I L

WESTERN
SAMOA

BOLIVIA

TONGA

PARAGUAY

Tropic of Capricorn

CHILE

URUGUAY

ARGENTINA

SOUTH
ATLANTIC
OCEAN

SOUTH
PACIFIC
OCEAN

Antarctic Circle

90°   U.S.   70°

THE
BAHAMAS

CUBA

MEXICO

DOMINICAN
REPUBLIC

JAMAICA   HAITI   PUERTO RICO

BELIZE

ST. KITTS AND NEVIS
ANTIGUA AND BARBUDA
DOMINICA

GUATEMALA   HONDURAS   CARIBBEAN
SEA

MARTINIQUE

ST. LUCIA

EL
SALVADOR   NICARAGUA   ST. VINCENT AND THE GRENADINES

BARBADOS
GRENADA

COSTA RICA

TRINIDAD AND TOBAGO

PANAMA

COLOMBIA   VENEZUELA

Scale: 1 to 125,000,000

0   1000   2000 Miles

0   1000   2000   3000 Kilometers

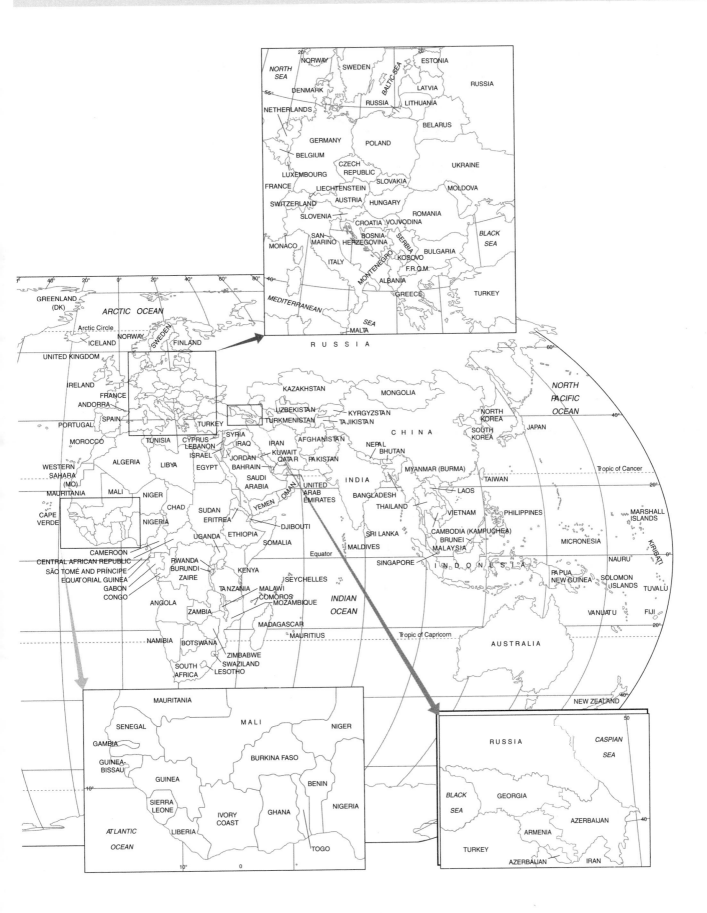

UNIT 1

Global Issues in the Twenty-First Century: An Overview

Unit Selections

1. **A Special Moment in History,** Bill McKibben
2. **Can Extreme Poverty Be Eliminated?,** Jeffrey D. Sachs
3. **The Ideology of Development,** William Easterly
4. **The Rise of the Rest,** Fareed Zakaria
5. **Feminists and Fundamentalists,** Kavita Ramdas

Key Points to Consider

- Do the analyses of any of the authors in this section employ the assumptions implicit in the allegory of the balloon? If so, how? If not, how are the assumptions of the authors different?

- All the authors point to interactions among different factors. What are some of the relationships that they cite? How do the authors differ in terms of the relationships they emphasize?

- What assets that did not exist 100 years ago do people have now to solve problems?

- What events during the past 60 years have had the greatest impact on shaping the realities of contemporary international affairs?

- What do you consider to be the five most pressing global problems of today? How do your answers compare to those of your family, friends, and classmates?

- Describe how international affairs might be different in the year 2050. Why do you think these differences will come about?

Student Web Site
www.mhcls.com

Internet References

The Henry L. Stimson Center
http://www.stimson.org
The Heritage Foundation
http://www.heritage.org
IISDnet
http://www.nsi-ins.ca/
The North-South Institute
http://www.nsi-ins.ca/ensi/index.html

Imagine yellow paint being brushed onto an inflated, clear balloon. The yellow color, for purposes of this allegory, represents people. In many ways the study of global issues is first and foremost the study of people. Today, there are more human beings occupying Earth than ever before. In addition, we are in the midst of a period of unprecedented population growth. Not only are there many countries where the majority of people are under age 16, but also, due to improved health care, there are more older people alive than ever before. The effect of a growing global population, however, goes beyond sheer numbers, for this trend has unprecedented impact on natural resources and social services. An examination of population trends and the related topic of food production is a good place to begin an in-depth study of global issues.

Imagine that our fictional artist next dips the brush into a container of blue paint to represent nature. The natural world plays an important role in setting the international agenda. Shortages of raw materials, climate change, regional droughts,

and pollution of waterways are just a few examples of how natural resources can have global implications.

Adding blue paint to the balloon reveals one of the most important underlying concepts found in this book. Although the balloon originally was covered by both yellow and blue paint (people and nature as separate conceptual entities), the two combined produce an entirely different color: green. Talking about nature as a separate entity or people as though they were somehow removed from the forces of the natural world is a serious intellectual error. The people–nature relationship is one of the keys to understanding many of today's most important global issues.

The third color to be added to the balloon is red. This color represents social structures. Factors falling into this category include whether a society is urban or rural, industrial or agrarian, and consumer-oriented or dedicated to the needs of the state. The relationship between this component and the others is extremely important. The impact of political decisions on the

1

environment, for example, is one of the most significant features of the contemporary world. Will the whales or bald eagles survive? Historically, the forces of nature determined which species survived or perished. Today, survival depends on political decisions or indecision. Understanding the complex relationship between social structure and nature (known as "ecopolitics") is central to the study of global issues.

Added to the three primary colors is the fourth and final color of white. It represents the *meta* component (i.e., those qualities that make human beings different from other life forms). These include new ideas and inventions, culture and values, religion and spirituality, and art and literature. The addition of the white paint immediately changes the intensity and shade of the mixture of colors, again emphasizing the relationship among all four factors.

If the painter continues to ply the paintbrush over the miniature globe, a marbled effect becomes evident. From one area to the next, the shading varies because one element is more dominant than another. Further, the miniature system appears dynamic. Nothing is static; relationships are continually changing. This leads to a number of important insights: (1) there are no such things as separate elements, only connections or relationships; (2) changes in one area (such as the climate) will result in changes in all other areas; and (3) complex and dynamic relationships make it difficult to predict events accurately, so observers and policymakers are often surprised by unexpected events.

This book is organized along the basic lines of the balloon allegory. The first unit provides a broad overview of a variety of perspectives on the major forces that are shaping the world of the twenty-first century. From this "big picture" perspective more in-depth analyses follow. Unit 2, for example, focuses on population, disease, and hunger. Unit 3 examines the environment and related natural resource issues. The next three units look at different aspects of the world's social structures. They explore issues of economics, national security, conflict, and

international cooperation. In the final unit, a number of "meta" factors are presented.

The reader should keep in mind that, just as it was impossible to keep the individual colors from blending into new colors on the balloon, it is also impossible to separate global issues into discrete chapters in a book. Any discussion of agriculture, for example, must take into account the impact of a growing population on soil and water resources, as well as new scientific breakthroughs in food production. Therefore, the organization of this book focuses attention on issue areas; it does not mean to imply that these factors are somehow separate.

With the collapse of the Soviet Empire and the end of the cold war, the outlines of a new global agenda emerged. Rather than being based on the ideology and interests of the two superpowers, new political, economic, environmental, cultural, and security issues began to interact in an unprecedented fashion. Rapid population growth, environmental decline, uneven economic progress, and global terrorist networks are all parts of a complex state of affairs for which there is no historic parallel. As we proceed through the first decade of the twenty-first century, signs abound that we are entering a new era. In the words of Abraham Lincoln, "As our case is new, so we must think anew." Compounding this situation, however, is a whole series of old problems such as ethnic and religious rivalries.

The authors in this first unit provide a variety of perspectives on the trends that they believe are the most important to understand the historic changes at work at the global level. This discussion is then pursued in greater detail in the following units.

Although the authors look at the same world, they often come to different conclusions. This raises an important issue of values and beliefs, for it can be argued that there is no objective reality, only differing perspectives. In short, the study of global issues will challenge each thoughtful reader to examine her or his own values and beliefs.

A Special Moment in History

BILL MCKIBBEN

We may live in the strangest, most thoroughly different moment since human beings took up farming, 10,000 years ago, and time more or less commenced. Since then time has flowed in one direction—toward *more*, which we have taken to be progress. At first the momentum was gradual, almost imperceptible, checked by wars and the Dark Ages and plagues and taboos; but in recent centuries it has accelerated, the curve of every graph steepening like the Himalayas rising from the Asian steppe. . . .

But now—now may be the special time. So special that in the Western world we might each of us consider, among many other things, having only one child—that is, reproducing at a rate as low as that at which human beings have ever voluntarily reproduced. Is this really necessary? Are we finally running up against some limits?

To try to answer this question, we need to ask another: *How many of us will there be in the near future?* Here is a piece of news that may alter the way we see the planet—an indication that we live at a special moment. At least at first blush the news is hopeful. *New demographic evidence shows that it is at least possible that a child born today will live long enough to see the peak of human population.*

Around the world people are choosing to have fewer and fewer children—not just in China, where the government forces it on them, but in almost every nation outside the poorest parts of Africa. . . . If this keeps up, the population of the world will not quite double again; United Nations analysts offer as their mid-range projection that it will top out at 10 to 11 billion, up from just under six billion at the moment. . . .

The good news is that we won't grow forever. The bad news is that there are six billion of us already, a number the world strains to support. One more near-doubling—four or five billion more people—will nearly double that strain. Will these be the five billion straws that break the camel's back? . . .

Looking at Limits

The case that the next doubling, the one we're now experiencing, might be the difficult one can begin as readily with the Stanford biologist Peter Vitousek as with anyone else. In 1986 Vitousek decided to calculate how much of the earth's "primary productivity" went to support human beings. He added together the grain we ate, the corn we fed our cows, and the forests we cut for timber and paper; he added the losses in food as we overgrazed grassland and turned it into desert. And when he was finished adding, the number he came up with was 38.8 percent. We use 38.8 percent of everything the world's plants don't need to keep themselves alive; directly or indirectly, we consume 38.8 percent of what it is possible to eat. "That's a relatively large number," Vitousek says. "It should give pause to people who think we are far from any limits." Though he never drops the measured tone of an academic, Vitousek speaks with considerable emphasis: "There's a sense among some economists that we're *so* far from any biophysical limits. I think that's not supported by the evidence."

For another antidote to the good cheer of someone like Julian Simon, sit down with the Cornell biologist David Pimentel. He believes that we're in big trouble. Odd facts stud his conversation—for example, a nice head of iceberg lettuce is 95 percent water and contains just fifty calories of energy, but it takes 400 calories of energy to grow that head of lettuce in California's Central Valley, and another 1,800 to ship it east. ("There's practically no nutrition in the damn stuff anyway," Pimentel says. "Cabbage is a lot better, and we can grow it in upstate New York.") Pimentel has devoted the past three decades to tracking the planet's capacity, and he believes that we're already too crowded—that the earth can support only two billion people over the long run at a middle-class standard of living, and that trying to support more is doing damage. He has spent considerable time studying soil erosion, for instance. Every raindrop that hits exposed ground is like a small explosion, launching soil particles into the air. On a slope, more than half of the soil contained in those splashes is carried downhill. If crop residue—cornstalks, say—is left in the field after harvest, it helps to shield the soil: the raindrop doesn't hit hard. But in the developing world, where firewood is scarce, peasants burn those cornstalks for cooking fuel. About 60 percent of crop residues in China and 90 percent in Bangladesh are removed and burned, Pimentel says. When planting season comes, dry soils simply blow away. "Our measuring stations pick up African soils in the wind when they start to plough."

The very things that made the Green Revolution so stunning—that made the last doubling possible—now cause trouble. Irrigation ditches, for instance, water 27 percent of all arable land and help to produce a third of all crops. But when flooded soils are baked by the sun, the water evaporates and the minerals in the irrigation water are deposited on the land. A hectare (2.47 acres) can accumulate two to five tons of salt annually, and eventually plants won't grow there. Maybe 10 percent of all irrigated land is affected.

. . . [F]ood production grew even faster than population after the Second World War. Year after year the yield of wheat and corn and rice rocketed up about three percent annually. It's a favorite statistic of the eternal optimists. In Julian Simon's book *The Ultimate Resource* (1981), charts show just how fast the growth was, and how it continually cut the cost of food. Simon wrote, "The obvious implication of this historical trend toward cheaper food—a trend that probably extends back to the beginning of agriculture—is that real prices for food will continue to drop. . . . It is a fact that portends more drops in price and even less scarcity in the future."

A few years after Simon's book was published, however, the data curve began to change. That rocketing growth in grain production ceased; now the gains were coming in tiny increments, too small to keep pace with population growth. The world reaped its largest harvest of grain per capita in 1984; since then the amount of corn and wheat and rice per person has fallen by six percent. Grain stockpiles have shrunk to less than two months' supply.

No one knows quite why. The collapse of the Soviet Union contributed to the trend—cooperative farms suddenly found the fertilizer supply shut off and spare parts for the tractor hard to come by. But there were other causes, too, all around the world—the salinization of irrigated fields, the erosion of topsoil, and all the other things that environmentalists had been warning about for years. It's possible that we'll still turn production around and start it rocketing again. Charles C. Mann, writing in *Science*, quotes experts who believe that in the future a "gigantic, multi-year, multi-billion-dollar scientific effort, a kind of agricultural 'person-on the-moon project,'" might do the trick. The next great hope of the optimists is genetic engineering, and scientists have indeed managed to induce resistance to pests and disease in some plants. To get more yield, though, a cornstalk must be made to put out another ear, and conventional breeding may have exhausted the possibilities. There's a sense that we're running into walls.

. . . What we are running out of is what the scientists call "sinks"—places to put the by-products of our large appetites. Not garbage dumps (we could go on using Pampers till the end of time and still have empty space left to toss them away) but the atmospheric equivalent of garbage dumps.

It wasn't hard to figure out that there were limits on how much coal smoke we could pour into the air of a single city. It took a while longer to figure out that building ever higher smokestacks merely lofted the haze farther afield, raining down acid on whatever mountain range lay to the east. Even that, however, we are slowly fixing, with scrubbers and different mixtures of fuel. We can't so easily repair the new kinds of pollution. These do not come from something going wrong—some engine without a catalytic converter, some waste-water pipe without a filter, some smokestack without a scrubber. New kinds of pollution come instead from things going as they're supposed to go—but at such a high volume that they overwhelm the planet. They come from normal human life—but there are so many of us living those normal lives that something abnormal is

happening. And that something is different from the old forms of pollution that it confuses the issue even to use the word.

Consider nitrogen, for instance. But before plants can absorb it, it must become "fixed"—bonded with carbon, hydrogen, or oxygen. Nature does this trick with certain kinds of algae and soil bacteria, and with lightning. Before human beings began to alter the nitrogen cycle, these mechanisms provided 90–150 million metric tons of nitrogen a year. Now human activity adds 130–150 million more tons. Nitrogen isn't pollution—it's essential. And we are using more of it all the time. Half the industrial nitrogen fertilizer used in human history has been applied since 1984. As a result, coastal waters and estuaries bloom with toxic algae while oxygen concentrations dwindle, killing fish; as a result, nitrous oxide traps solar heat. And once the gas is in the air, it stays there for a century or more.

Or consider methane, which comes out of the back of a cow or the top of a termite mound or the bottom of a rice paddy. As a result of our determination to raise more cattle, cut down more tropical forest (thereby causing termite populations to explode), and grow more rice, methane concentrations in the atmosphere are more than twice as high as they have been for most of the past 160,000 years. And methane traps heat—very efficiently.

Or consider carbon dioxide. In fact, concentrate on carbon dioxide. If we had to pick one problem to obsess about over the next fifty years, we'd do well to make it CO_2—which is not pollution either. Carbon *mon*oxide is pollution: it kills you if you breathe enough of it. But carbon *di*oxide, carbon with two oxygen atoms, can't do a blessed thing to you. If you're reading this indoors, you're breathing more CO_2 than you'll ever get outside. For generations, in fact, engineers said that an engine burned clean if it produced only water vapor and carbon dioxide.

Here's the catch: that engine produces a *lot* of CO_2. A gallon of gas weighs about eight pounds. When it's burned in a car, about five and a half pounds of carbon, in the form of carbon dioxide, come spewing out the back. It doesn't matter if the car is a 1958 Chevy or a 1998 Saab. And no filter can reduce that flow—it's an inevitable by-product of fossil-fuel combustion, which is why CO_2 has been piling up in the atmosphere ever since the Industrial Revolution. Before we started burning oil and coal and gas, the atmosphere contained about 280 parts CO_2 per million. Now the figure is about 360. Unless we do everything we can think of to eliminate fossil fuels from our diet, the air will test out at more than 500 parts per million fifty or sixty years from now, whether it's sampled in the South Bronx or at the South Pole.

This matters because, as we all know by now, the molecular structure of this clean, natural, common element that we are adding to every cubic foot of the atmosphere surrounding us traps heat that would otherwise radiate back out to space. Far more than even methane and nitrous oxide, CO_2 causes global warming—the greenhouse effect—and climate change. Far more than any other single factor, it is turning the earth we were born on into a new planet.

. . . For ten years, with heavy funding from governments around the world, scientists launched satellites, monitored weather balloons, studied clouds. Their work culminated in a long-awaited report from the UN's Intergovernmental Panel on

Climate Change, released in the fall of 1995. The panel's 2,000 scientists, from every corner of the globe, summed up their findings in this dry but historic bit of understatement: "The balance of evidence suggests that there is a discernible human influence on global climate." That is to say, we are heating up the planet—substantially. If we don't reduce emissions of carbon dioxide and other gases, the panel warned, temperatures will probably rise 3.6° Fahrenheit by 2100, and perhaps as much as 6.3°.

You may think you've already heard a lot about global warming. But most of our sense of the problem is behind the curve. Here's the current news: the changes are already well under way. When politicians and businessmen talk about "future risks," their rhetoric is outdated. This is not a problem for the distant future, or even for the near future. The planet has already heated up by a degree or more. We are perhaps a quarter of the way into the greenhouse era, and the effects are already being felt. From a new heaven, filled with nitrogen, methane, and carbon, a new earth is being born. If some alien astronomer is watching us, she's doubtless puzzled. This is the most obvious effect of our numbers and our appetites, and the key to understanding why the size of our population suddenly poses such a risk.

Stormy and Warm

What does this new world feel like? For one thing, it's stormier than the old one. Data analyzed last year by Thomas Karl, of the National Oceanic and Atmospheric Administration, showed that total winter precipitation in the United States has increased by 10 percent since 1900 and that "extreme precipitation events"—rainstorms that dumped more than two inches of water in twenty-four hours and blizzards—had increased by 20 percent. That's because warmer air holds more water vapor than the colder atmosphere of the old earth; more water evaporates from the ocean, meaning more clouds, more rain, more snow. Engineers designing storm sewers, bridges, and culverts used to plan for what they called the "hundred-year storm." That is, they built to withstand the worst flooding or wind that history led them to expect in the course of a century. Since that history no longer applies, Karl says, "there isn't really a hundred-year event anymore . . . we seem to be getting these storms of the century every couple of years." When Grand Forks, North Dakota, disappeared beneath the Red River in Spring, 1997, some meteorologists referred to it as "a 500-year flood"—meaning, essentially, that all bets are off. Meaning that these aren't acts of God. "If you look out your window, part of what you see in terms of weather is produced by ourselves," Karl says. "If you look out the window fifty years from now, we're going to be responsible for more of it."

Twenty percent more bad storms, 10 percent more winter precipitation—these are enormous numbers. It's like opening the newspaper to read that the average American is smarter by 30 IQ points. And the same data showed increases in drought, too. With more water in the atmosphere, there's less in the soil, according to Kevin Trenberth, of the National Center for Atmospheric Research. Those parts of the continent that are normally dry—the eastern sides of mountains, the plains and deserts—are even drier, as the higher average temperatures evaporate more

of what rain does fall. "You get wilting plants and eventually drought faster than you would otherwise," Trenberth says. And when the rain does come, it's often so intense that much of it runs off before it can soak into the soil.

So—wetter and drier. *Different.* . . .

The effects of . . . warming can be found in the largest phenomena. The oceans that cover most of the planet's surface are clearly rising, both because of melting glaciers and because water expands as it warms. As a result, low-lying Pacific islands already report surges of water washing across the atolls. "It's nice weather and all of a sudden water is pouring into your living room," one Marshall Islands resident told a newspaper reporter. "It's very clear that something is happening in the Pacific, and these islands are feeling it." Global warming will be like a much more powerful version of El Niño that covers the entire globe and lasts forever, or at least until the next big asteroid strikes.

If you want to scare yourself with guesses about what might happen in the near future, there's no shortage of possibilities. Scientists have already observed large-scale shifts in the duration of the El Niño ocean warming, for instance. The Arctic tundra has warmed so much that in some places it now gives off more carbon dioxide than it absorbs—a switch that could trigger a potent feedback loop, making warming ever worse. And researchers studying glacial cores from the Greenland Ice Sheet recently concluded that local climate shifts have occurred with incredible rapidity in the past—18° in one three-year stretch. Other scientists worry that such a shift might be enough to flood the oceans with fresh water and reroute or shut off currents like the Gulf Stream and the North Atlantic, which keep Europe far warmer than it would otherwise be. (See "The Great Climate Flip-flop," by William H. Calvin, January (*Atlantic*.) In the words of Wallace Broecker, of Columbia University, a pioneer in the field, "Climate is an angry beast, and we are poking it with sticks."

But we don't need worst-case scenarios: best-case scenarios make the point. The population of the earth is going to nearly double one more time. That will bring it to a level that even the reliable old earth we were born on would be hard-pressed to support. Just at the moment when we need everything to be working as smoothly as possible, we find ourselves inhabiting a new planet, whose carrying capacity we cannot conceivably estimate. We have no idea how much wheat this planet can grow. We don't know what its politics will be like: not if there are going to be heat waves like the one that killed more than 700 Chicagoans in 1995; not if rising sea levels and other effects of climate change create tens of millions of environmental refugees; not if a 1.5° jump in India's temperature could reduce the country's wheat crop by 10 percent or divert its monsoons. . . .

We have gotten very large and very powerful, and for the foreseeable future we're stuck with the results. The glaciers won't grow back again anytime soon; the oceans won't drop. We've already done deep and systemic damage. To use a human analogy, we've already said the angry and unforgivable words that will haunt our marriage till its end. And yet we can't simply walk out the door. There's no place to go. We have to salvage what we can of our relationship with the earth, to keep things from getting any worse than they have to be.

If we can bring our various emissions quickly and sharply under control, we *can* limit the damage, reduce dramatically the chance of horrible surprises, preserve more of the biology we were born into. But do not underestimate the task. The UN's Intergovernmental Panel on Climate Change projects that an immediate 60 percent reduction in fossil-fuel use is necessary just to stabilize climate at the current level of disruption. Nature may still meet us halfway, but halfway is a long way from where we are now. What's more, we can't delay. If we wait a few decades to get started, we may as well not even begin. It's not like poverty, a concern that's always there for civilizations to address. This is a timed test, like the SAT: two or three decades, and we lay our pencils down. It's *the* test for our generations, and population is a part of the answer. . . .

The numbers are so daunting that they're almost unimaginable. Say, just for argument's sake, that we decided to cut world fossil-fuel use by 60 percent—the amount that the UN panel says would stabilize world climate. And then say that we shared the remaining fossil fuel equally. Each human being would get to produce 1.69 metric tons of carbon dioxide annually—which would allow you to drive an average American car nine miles a day. By the time the population increased to 8.5 billion, in about 2025, you'd be down to six miles a day. If you carpooled, you'd have about three pounds of CO_2 left in your daily ration—enough to run a highly efficient refrigerator. Forget your computer, your TV, your stereo, your stove, your dishwasher, your water heater, your microwave, your water pump, your clock. Forget your light bulbs, compact fluorescent or not.

I'm not trying to say that conservation, efficiency, and new technology won't help. They will—but the help will be slow and expensive. The tremendous momentum of growth will work against it. Say that someone invented a new furnace tomorrow that used half as much oil as old furnaces. How many years would it be before a substantial number of American homes had the new device? And what if it cost more? And if oil stays cheaper per gallon than bottled water? Changing basic fuels—to hydrogen, say—would be even more expensive. It's not like running out of white wine and switching to red. Yes, we'll get new technologies. One day last fall *The New York Times* ran a special section on energy, featuring many up-and-coming improvements: solar shingles, basement fuel cells. But the same day, on the front page, William K. Stevens reported that international negotiators had all but given up on preventing a

doubling of the atmospheric concentration of CO_2. The momentum of growth was so great, the negotiators said, that making the changes required to slow global warming significantly would be like "trying to turn a supertanker in a sea of syrup."

There are no silver bullets to take care of a problem like this. Electric cars won't by themselves save us, though they would help. We simply won't live efficiently enough soon enough to solve the problem. Vegetarianism won't cure our ills, though it would help. We simply won't live simply enough soon enough to solve the problem.

Reducing the birth rate won't end all our troubles either. That, too, is no silver bullet. But it would help. There's no more practical decision than how many children to have. (And no more mystical decision, either.)

The bottom-line argument goes like this: The next fifty years are a special time. They will decide how strong and healthy the planet will be for centuries to come. Between now and 2050 we'll see the zenith, or very nearly, of human population. With luck we'll never see any greater production of carbon dioxide or toxic chemicals. We'll never see more species extinction or soil erosion. Greenpeace recently announced a campaign to phase out fossil fuels entirely by mid-century, which sounds utterly quixotic but could—if everything went just right—happen.

So it's the task of those of us alive right now to deal with this special phase, to squeeze us through these next fifty years. That's not fair—any more than it was fair that earlier generations had to deal with the Second World War or the Civil War or the Revolution or the Depression or slavery. It's just reality. We need in these fifty years to be working simultaneously on all parts of the equation—on our ways of life, on our technologies, and on our population.

As Gregg Easterbrook pointed out in his book *A Moment on the Earth* (1995), if the planet does manage to reduce its fertility, "the period in which human numbers threaten the biosphere on a general scale will turn out to have been much, much more brief" than periods of natural threats like the Ice Ages. True enough. But the period in question happens to be our time. That's what makes this moment special, and what makes this moment hard.

BILL McKIBBEN is the author of several books about the environment, including *The End of Nature* (1989) and *Hope, Human and Wild* (1995). His article in this issue appears in somewhat different form in his book *Maybe One: A Personal and Environmental Argument for Single-Child Families*, published in 1998 by Simon & Schuster.

Can Extreme Poverty Be Eliminated?

Market economics and globalization are lifting the bulk of humanity out of extreme poverty, but special measures are needed to help the poorest of the poor.

JEFFREY D. SACHS

Almost everyone who ever lived was wretchedly poor. Famine, death from childbirth, infectious disease and countless other hazards were the norm for most of history. Humanity's sad plight started to change with the Industrial Revolution, beginning around 1750. New scientific insights and technological innovations enabled a growing proportion of the global population to break free of extreme poverty.

Two and a half centuries later more than five billion of the world's 6.5 billion people can reliably meet their basic living needs and thus can be said to have escaped from the precarious conditions that once governed everyday life. One out of six inhabitants of this planet, however, still struggles daily to meet some or all of such critical requirements as adequate nutrition, uncontaminated drinking water, safe shelter and sanitation as well as access to basic health care. These people get by on $1 a day or less and are overlooked by public services for health, education and infrastructure. Every day more than 20,000 die of dire poverty, for want of food, safe drinking water, medicine or other essential needs.

For the first time in history, global economic prosperity, brought on by continuing scientific and technological progress and the self-reinforcing accumulation of wealth, has placed the world within reach of eliminating extreme poverty altogether. This prospect will seem fanciful to some, but the dramatic economic progress made by China, India and other low-income parts of Asia over the past 25 years demonstrates that it is realistic. Moreover, the predicted stabilization of the world's population toward the middle of this century will help by easing pressures on Earth's climate, ecosystems and natural resources—pressures that might otherwise undo economic gains.

EXTREME POVERTY could become a thing of the past in a few decades if the affluent countries of the world pony up a small percentage of their wealth to help the planet's 1.1 billion indigent populations out of conditions of dire poverty.

Although economic growth has shown a remarkable capacity to lift vast numbers of people out of extreme poverty, progress is neither automatic nor inevitable. Market forces and free trade are not enough. Many of the poorest regions are ensnared in a poverty trap: they lack the financial means to make the necessary investments in infrastructure, education, health care systems and other vital needs. Yet the end of such poverty is feasible if a concerted global effort is undertaken, as the nations of the world promised when they adopted the Millennium Development Goals at the United Nations Millennium Summit in 2000. A dedicated cadre of development agencies, international financial institutions, nongovernmental organizations and communities throughout the developing world already constitute a global network of expertise and goodwill to help achieve this objective.

This past January my colleagues and I on the U.N. Millennium Project published a plan to halve the rate of extreme poverty by 2015 (compared with 1990) and to achieve other quantitative targets for reducing hunger, disease and environmental degradation. In my recent book, *The End of Poverty,* I argue that a large-scale and targeted public investment effort could in fact eliminate this problem by 2025, much as smallpox was eradicated globally. This hypothesis is controversial, so I am pleased to have the opportunity to clarify its main arguments and to respond to various concerns that have been raised about it.

Beyond Business as Usual

Economists have learned a great deal during the past few years about how countries develop and what roadblocks can stand in their way. A new kind of development economics needs to emerge, one that is better grounded in science—a "clinical economics" akin to modern medicine. Today's medical professionals understand that disease results from a vast array of interacting factors and conditions: pathogens, nutrition, environment, aging, individual and population genetics, lifestyle. They also know that one key to proper treatment is the ability

Crossroads for Poverty

The Problem

- Much of humankind has succeeded in dragging itself out of severe poverty since the onset of the Industrial Revolution in the mid-18th century, but about 1.1 billion out of today's 6.5 billion global inhabitants are utterly destitute in a world of plenty.
- These unfortunates, who get by on less than $1 a day, have little access to adequate nutrition, safe drinking water and shelter, as well as basic sanitation and health care services. What can the developed world do to lift this huge segment of the human population out of extreme poverty?

The Plan

- Doubling affluent nations' international poverty assistance to about $160 billion a year would go a long way toward ameliorating the terrible predicament faced by one in six humans. This figure would constitute about 0.5 percent of the gross national product (GNP) of the planet's rich countries. Because these investments do not include other categories of aid, such as spending on major infrastructure projects, climate change mitigation or post conflict reconstruction, donors should commit to reaching the long stand target of 0.7 percent of GNP by 2015.
- These donations, often provided to local groups, would need to be closely monitored and audited to ensure that they are correctly targeted toward those truly in need.

to make an individualized diagnosis of the source of illness. Likewise, development economists need better diagnostic skills to recognize that economic pathologies have a wide variety of causes, including many outside the traditional ken of economic practice.

Public opinion in affluent countries often attributes extreme poverty to faults with the poor themselves—or at least with their governments. Race was once thought the deciding factor. Then it was culture: religious divisions and taboos, caste systems, a lack of entrepreneurship, gender inequities. Such theories have waned as societies of an ever widening range of religions and cultures have achieved relative prosperity. Moreover, certain supposedly immutable aspects of culture (such as fertility choices and gender and caste roles) in fact change, often dramatically, as societies become urban and develop economically.

Most recently, commentators have zeroed in on "poor governance," often code words for corruption. They argue that extreme poverty persists because governments fail to open up their markets, provide public services and clamp down on bribe taking. It is said that if these regimes cleaned up their acts, they, too, would flourish. Development assistance efforts have become largely a series of good governance lectures.

The availability of cross-country and time-series data now allows experts to make much more systematic analyses. Although debate continues, the weight of the evidence indicates that governance makes a difference but is not the sole determinant of economic growth. According to surveys conducted by Transparency International, business leaders actually perceive many fast-growing Asian countries to be more corrupt than some slow-growing African ones.

Geography—including natural resources, climate, topography, and proximity to trade routes and major markets—is at least as important as good governance. As early as 1776, Adam Smith argued that high transport costs inhibited development in the inland areas of Africa and Asia. Other geographic features, such as the heavy disease burden of the tropics, also interfere. One recent study by my Columbia University colleague Xavier Sala-i-Martin demonstrated once again that tropical countries saddled with malaria have experienced slower growth than those free from the disease. The good news is that geographic factors shape, but do not decide, a country's economic fate. Technology can offset them: drought can be fought with irrigation systems, isolation with roads and mobile telephones, diseases with preventive and therapeutic measures.

The other major insight is that although the most powerful mechanism for reducing extreme poverty is to encourage overall economic growth, a rising tide does not necessarily lift all boats. Average income can rise, but if the income is distributed unevenly the poor may benefit little, and pockets of extreme poverty may persist (especially in geographically disadvantaged regions). Moreover, growth is not simply a free-market phenomenon. It requires basic government services: infrastructure, health, education, and scientific and technological innovation. Thus, many of the recommendations of the past two decades emanating from Washington—that governments in low-income countries should cut back on their spending to make room for the private sector—miss the point. Government spending, directed at investment in critical areas, is itself a vital spur to growth, especially if its effects are to reach the poorest of the poor.

The Poverty Trap

So what do these insights tell us about the region most afflicted by poverty today, Africa? Fifty years ago tropical Africa was roughly as rich as subtropical and tropical Asia. As Asia boomed, Africa stagnated. Special geographic factors have played a crucial role.

Foremost among these is the existence of the Himalaya Mountains, which produce southern Asia's monsoon climate and vast river systems. Well-watered farmlands served as the starting points for Asia's rapid escape from extreme poverty during the past five decades. The Green Revolution of the 1960s and 1970s introduced high-yield grains, irrigation and fertilizers, which ended the cycle of famine, disease and despair.

It also freed a significant proportion of the labor force to seek manufacturing jobs in the cities. Urbanization, in turn, spurred growth, not only by providing a home for industry and innovation but also by prompting greater investment in a healthy and skilled labor force. Urban residents cut their fertility rates and

Globalization, Poverty and Foreign Aid

Average citizens in affluent nations often have many questions about the effects of economic globalization on rich and poor nations and about how developing countries spend the aid they receive. Here are a few brief answers:

Is Globalization Making the Rich Richer and the Poor Poorer?

Generally, the answer is no. Economic globalization is supporting very rapid advances of many impoverished economies, notably in Asia. International trade and foreign investment inflows have been major factors in China's remarkable economic growth during the past quarter century and in India's fast economic growth since the early 1990s. The poorest of the poor, notably in sub-Saharan Africa, are not held back by globalization; they are largely bypassed by it.

Is Poverty the Result of Exploitation of the Poor by the Rich?

Affluent nations have repeatedly plundered and exploited poor countries through slavery, colonial rule and unfair trade practices. Yet it is perhaps more accurate to say that exploitation is the result of poverty (which leaves impoverished countries vulnerable to abuse) rather than the cause of it. Poverty is generally the result of low productivity per worker, which reflects poor health, lack of job-market skills, patchiness of infrastructure (roads, power plants, utility lines, shipping ports), chronic malnutrition and the like. Exploitation has played a role in producing some of these conditions, but deeper factors [geographic isolation, endemic disease, ecological destruction, challenging conditions for food production] have tended to be more important and difficult to overcome without external help.

Will Higher Incomes in Poor Countries Mean Lower Incomes in Rich Countries?

By and large, economic development is a positive-sum process, meaning that all can partake in it without causing some to suffer. In the past 200 years, the world as a whole has achieved a massive increase in economic output rather than a shift in economic output to one region at the expense of another. To be sure, global environmental constraints are already starting to impose themselves. As today's poor countries develop, the climate, fisheries and forests are coming under increased strain. Overall global economic growth is compatible with sustainable management of the ecosystems on which all humans depend—indeed, wealth can be good for the environment—but only if public policy and technologies encourage sound practices and the necessary investments are made in environmental sustainability.

Do U.S. Private Contributions Make Up for the Low Levels of U.S. Official Aid?

Some have claimed that while the U.S. government budget provides relatively little assistance to the poorest countries, the private sector makes up the gap. In fact, the Organization for Economic Cooperation and Development has estimated that private foundations and nongovernmental organizations give roughly $6 billion a year in international assistance, or 0.05 percent of U.S. gross national product (GNP). In that case, total U.S. international aid is around 0.21 percent of GNP—still among the lowest ratios of all donor nations.

—J.D.S.

thus were able to spend more for the health, nutrition and education of each child. City kids went to school at a higher rate than their rural cousins. And with the emergence of urban infrastructure and public health systems, city populations became less disease-prone than their counterparts in the countryside, where people typically lack safe drinking water, modern sanitation, professional health care and protection from vector-borne ailments such as malaria.

Africa did not experience a green revolution. Tropical Africa lacks the massive floodplains that facilitate the large-scale and low-cost irrigation found in Asia. Also, its rainfall is highly variable, and impoverished farmers have been unable to purchase fertilizer. The initial Green Revolution research featured crops, especially paddy rice and wheat, not widely grown in Africa (high-yield varieties suitable for it have been developed in recent years, but they have not yet been disseminated sufficiently). The continent's food production per person has actually been falling, and Africans' caloric intake is the lowest in the world; food insecurity is rampant. Its labor force has remained tethered to subsistence agriculture.

Compounding its agricultural woes, Africa bears an overwhelming burden of tropical diseases. Because of climate and the endemic mosquito species, malaria is more intensively transmitted in Africa than anywhere else. And high transport costs isolate Africa economically. In East Africa, for example, the rainfall is greatest in the interior of the continent, so most people live there, far from ports and international trade routes.

Much the same situation applies to other impoverished parts of the world, notably the Andean and Central American highlands and the landlocked countries of Central Asia. Being economically isolated, they are unable to attract much foreign investment (other than for the extraction of oil, gas and precious minerals). Investors tend to be dissuaded by the high transport costs associated with the interior regions. Rural areas therefore remain stuck in a vicious cycle of poverty, hunger, illness and illiteracy. Impoverished areas lack adequate internal savings to make the needed investments because most households live hand to mouth. The few high-income families, who do accumulate savings, park them overseas rather than at home. This capital flight includes not only financial capital but also the human variety, in the form of skilled workers—doctors, nurses, scientists and engineers, who frequently leave in search of improved economic opportunities abroad. The poorest countries are often, perversely, net exporters of capital.

Put Money Where Mouths Are

The technology to overcome these handicaps and jump-start economic development exists. Malaria can be controlled using bed nets, indoor pesticide spraying and improved medicines. Drought-prone countries in Africa with nutrient depleted soils can benefit enormously from drip irrigation and greater use of fertilizers. Landlocked countries can be connected by paved highway networks, airports and fiber-optic cables. All these projects cost money, of course.

Many larger countries, such as China, have prosperous regions that can help support their own lagging areas. Coastal eastern China, for instance, is now financing massive public investments in western China. Most of today's successfully developing countries, especially smaller ones, received at least some backing from external donors at crucial times. The critical scientific innovations that formed the underpinnings of the Green Revolution were bankrolled by the Rockefeller Foundation, and the spread of these technologies in India and elsewhere in Asia was funded by the U.S. and other donor governments and international development institutions.

We in the U.N. Millennium Project have listed the investments required to help today's impoverished regions cover basic needs in health, education, water, sanitation, food production, roads and other key areas. We have put an approximate price tag on that assistance and estimated how much could be financed by poor households themselves and by domestic institutions. The remaining cost is the "financing gap" that international donors need to make up.

For tropical Africa, the total investment comes to $110 per person a year. To place this into context, the average income in this part of the world is $350 per annum, most or all of which is required just to stay alive. The full cost of the total investment is clearly beyond the funding reach of these countries. Of the $110, perhaps $40 could be financed domestically, so that $70 per capita would be required in the form of international aid.

Adding it all up, the total requirement for assistance across the globe is around $160 billion a year, double the current rich-country aid budget of $80 billion. This figure amounts to approximately 0.5 percent of the combined gross national product (GNP) of the affluent donor nations. It does not include other humanitarian projects such as postwar Iraqi reconstruction or Indian Ocean tsunami relief. To meet these needs as well, a reasonable figure would be 0.7 percent of GNP, which is what all donor countries have long promised but few have fulfilled. Other organizations, including the International Monetary Fund, the World Bank and the British government, have reached much the same conclusion.

When polled, Americans greatly overestimate how much foreign aid the U.S. gives—by as much as 30 times.

Foreign Aid: How Should the Money Be Spent?

Here is a breakdown of the needed investment for three typical low-income African countries to help them achieve the Millennium Development Goals. For all nations given aid, the average total annual assistance per person would come to around $110 a year. These investments would be financed by both foreign aid and the countries themselves.

Investment Area	Average per Year between 2005–2015 ($ per capita)		
	Ghana	Tanzania	Uganda
Hunger	7	8	6
Education	19	14	5
Gender equality	3	3	3
Health	25	35	34
Water supply and sanitation	8	7	5
Improving slum conditions	2	3	2
Energy	15	16	12
Roads	10	22	20
Other	10	10	10
Total	100	117	106

Calculated from data from Investing in Development [U.N. Millennium Project, Earth Scan Publications, 2005]. Numbers do not sum to totals because of rounding.

We believe these investments would enable the poorest countries to cut poverty by half by 2015 and, if continued, to eliminate it altogether by 2025. They would not be "welfare payments" from rich to poor but instead something far more important and durable. People living above mere subsistence levels would be able to save for their futures; they could join the virtuous cycle of rising incomes, savings and technological inflows. We would be giving a billion people a hand up instead of a handout.

If rich nations fail to make these investments, they will be called on to provide emergency assistance more or less indefinitely. They will face famine, epidemics, regional conflicts and the spread of terrorist havens. And they will condemn not only the impoverished countries but themselves as well to chronic political instability, humanitarian emergencies and security risks.

The debate is now shifting from the basic diagnosis of extreme poverty and the calculations of financing needs to the practical matter of how assistance can best be delivered. Many people believe that aid efforts failed in the past and that care is needed to avoid the repetition of failure. Some of these concerns are well grounded, but others are fueled by misunderstandings.

When pollsters ask Americans how much foreign aid they think the U.S. gives, they greatly overestimate the amount by as much as 30 times. Believing that so much money has been donated and so little has been done with it, the public concludes that these programs have "failed." The reality is rather different.

U.S. official assistance to sub-Saharan Africa has been running at $2 billion to $4 billion a year, or roughly $3 to $6 for every African. Most of this aid has come in the form of "technical cooperation" (which goes into the pockets of consultants), food contributions for famine victims and the cancellation of unpaid debts. Little of this support has come in a form that can be invested in systems that improve health, nutrition, food production and transport. We should give foreign aid a fair chance before deciding whether it works or not.

A second common misunderstanding concerns the extent to which corruption is likely to eat up the donated money. Some foreign aid in the past has indeed ended up in the equivalent of Swiss bank accounts. That happened when the funds were provided for geopolitical reasons rather than development; a good example was U.S. support for the corrupt regime of Mobutu Sese Seko of Zaire (now the Democratic Republic of the Congo) during part of the cold war. When assistance has been targeted at development rather than political goals, the outcomes have been favorable, ranging from the Green Revolution to the eradication of smallpox and the recent near-eradication of polio.

The aid package we advocate would be directed toward those countries with a reasonable degree of good governance and operational transparency. In Africa, these countries include Ethiopia, Ghana, Mali, Mozambique, Senegal and Tanzania. The money would not be merely thrown at them. It would be provided according to a detailed and monitored plan, and new rounds of financing would be delivered only as the work actually got done. Much of the funds would be given directly to villages and towns to minimize the chances of their getting diverted by central governments. All these programs should be closely audited.

Western society tends to think of foreign aid as money lost. But if supplied properly, it is an investment that will one day yield huge returns, much as U.S. assistance to Western Europe and East Asia after World War II did. By prospering, today's impoverished countries will wean themselves from endless charity. They will contribute to the international advance of science, technology and trade. They will escape political instability, which leaves many of them vulnerable to violence, narcotics trafficking, civil war and even terrorist takeover. Our own security will be bolstered as well. As U.N. Secretary-General Kofi Annan wrote earlier this year: "There will be no development without security, and no security without development."

The author, **JEFFREY D. SACHS,** directs the Earth Institute at Columbia University and the United Nations Millennium Project. An economist, Sachs is well known for advising governments in Latin America, Eastern Europe, the former Soviet Union, Asia and Africa on economic reforms and for his work with international agencies to promote poverty reduction, disease control and debt reduction in poor countries. A native of Detroit, he received his BA, MA and PhD degrees from Harvard University.

The Ideology of Development

WILLIAM EASTERLY

A dark ideological specter is haunting the world. It is almost as deadly as the tired ideologies of the last century—communism, fascism, and socialism—that failed so miserably. It feeds some of the most dangerous trends of our time, including religious fundamentalism. It is the half-century-old ideology of Developmentalism. And it is thriving.

Like all ideologies, Development promises a comprehensive final answer to all of society's problems, from poverty and illiteracy to violence and despotic rulers. It shares the common ideological characteristic of suggesting there is only one correct answer, and it tolerates little dissent. It deduces this unique answer for everyone from a general theory that purports to apply to everyone, everywhere. There's no need to involve local actors who reap its costs and benefits. Development even has its own intelligentsia, made up of experts at the International Monetary Fund (IMF), World Bank, and United Nations.

The power of Developmentalism is disheartening, because the failure of all the previous ideologies might have laid the groundwork for the opposite of ideology—the freedom of individuals and societies to choose their destinies. Yet, since the fall of communism, the West has managed to snatch defeat from the jaws of victory, and with disastrous results. Development ideology is sparking a dangerous counterreaction. The "one correct answer" came to mean "free markets," and, for the poor world, it was defined as doing whatever the IMF and the World Bank tell you to do. But the reaction in Africa, Central Asia, Latin America, the Middle East, and Russia has been to fight against free markets. So, one of the best economic ideas of our time, the genius of free markets, was presented in one of the worst possible ways, with unelected outsiders imposing rigid doctrines on the xenophobic unwilling.

The backlash has been so severe that other failed ideologies are gaining new adherents throughout these regions. In Nicaragua, for instance, IMF and World Bank structural adjustments failed so conspicuously that the pitiful Sandinista regime of the 1980s now looks good by comparison. Its leader, Daniel Ortega, is back in power. The IMF's actions during the Argentine financial crisis of 2001 now reverberate a half decade later with Hugo Chavez, Venezuela's illiberal leader, being welcomed with open arms in Buenos Aires. The heavy-handed directives of the World Bank and IMF in Bolivia provided the soil from which that country's neosocialist president, Evo Morales, sprung. The disappointing payoff following eight structural adjustment loans to Zimbabwe and $8 billion in foreign aid during the 1980s and 1990s helped Robert Mugabe launch a vicious counterattack on democracy. The IMF-World Bank—Jeffrey Sachs application of "shock therapy" to the former Soviet Union has created a lasting nostalgia for communism. In the Middle East, $154 billion in foreign aid between 1980 and 2001, 45 structural adjustment loans, and "expert" advice produced zero per capita GDP growth that helped create a breeding ground for Islamic fundamentalism.

This blowback against "globalization from above" has spread to every corner of the Earth. It now threatens to kill sensible, moderate steps toward the freer movement of goods, ideas, capital, and people.

Development's Politburo

The ideology of Development is not only about having experts design your free market for you; it is about having the experts design a comprehensive, technical plan to solve all the problems of the poor. These experts see poverty as a purely technological problem, to be solved by engineering and the natural sciences, ignoring messy social sciences such as economics, politics, and sociology.

Sachs, Columbia University's celebrity economist, is one of its main proprietors. He is now recycling his theories of overnight shock therapy, which failed so miserably in Russia, into promises of overnight global poverty reduction. "Africa's problems," he has said, "are . . . solvable with practical and proven technologies." His own plan features hundreds of expert interventions to solve every last problem of the poor—from green manure, breast-feeding education, and bicycles to solar-energy systems, school uniforms for AIDS orphans, and windmills. Not to mention such critical interventions as "counseling and information services for men to address their reproductive health needs." All this will be done, Sachs says, by "a united and effective United Nations country team, which coordinates in one place the work of the U.N. specialized agencies, the IMF, and the World Bank."

So the admirable concern of rich countries for the tragedies of world poverty is thus channeled into fattening the international aid bureaucracy, the self-appointed priesthood of Development. Like other ideologies, this thinking favors collective goals such as national poverty reduction, national economic growth, and the global Millennium Development Goals, over the aspirations of individuals. Bureaucrats who write poverty-reduction frameworks outrank individuals who actually reduce poverty by, say, starting a business. Just as Marxists favored world revolution and socialist internationalism, Development stresses world goals over the autonomy of societies to choose their own path. It favors doctrinaire abstractions such as "market-friendly policies," "good investment climate," and "pro-poor globalization" over the freedom of individuals.

Development also shares another Marxist trait: It aspires to be scientific. Finding the one correct solution to poverty is seen as a scientific problem to be solved by the experts. They are always sure they know the answer, vehemently reject disagreement, and then later change their answers. In psychiatry, this is known as Borderline Personality Disorder. For the Development Experts, it's a way of life. The answer at first was aid-financed investment and industrialization in poor countries, then it was market-oriented government policy reform, then it was fixing institutional problems such as corruption, then it was globalization, then it was the Poverty Reduction Strategy to achieve the Millennium Development Goals.

One reason the answers keep changing is because, in reality, high-growth countries follow a bewildering variety of paths to development, and the countries with high growth rates are constantly changing from decade to decade. Who could be more different than successful developers such as China and Chile, Botswana and Singapore, Taiwan and Turkey, or Hong Kong and Vietnam? What about the many countries who tried to emulate these rising stars and failed? What about the former stars who have fallen on hard times, like the Ivory Coast, which was one of the fastest developers of the 1960s and 1970s, only to become mired in a civil war? What about Mexico, which saw rapid growth until 1980 and has had slow growth ever since, despite embracing the experts' reforms?

The experts in Developmentalism's Politburo don't bother themselves with such questions. All the previous answers were right; they were just missing one more "necessary condition" that the experts have only just now added to the list. Like all ideologies, Development is at the same time too rigid to predict what will work in the messy real world and yet flexible enough to forever escape falsification by real-world events. The high church of Development, the World Bank, has guaranteed it can never be wrong by making statements such as, "different policies can yield the same result, and the same policy can yield different results, depending on country institutional contexts and underlying growth strategies." Of course, you still need experts to figure out the contexts and strategies.

Resistance is Futile

Perhaps more hypocritical yet is Development's simple theory of historical inevitability. Poor societies are not just poor, the experts tell us, they are "developing" until they reach the final stage of history, or "development," in which poverty will soon end. Under this historiography, an end to starvation, tyranny, and war are thrown in like a free toaster on an infomercial. The experts judge all societies on a straight line, per capita income,

with the superior countries showing the inferior countries the image of their own future. And the experts heap scorn on those who resist the inevitabilities on the path to development.

One of today's leading Developmentalists, *New York Times* columnist Thomas Friedman, can hardly conceal his mockery of those who resist the march of history, or "the flattening of the world." "When you are Mexico," Friedman has written, "and your claim to fame is that you are a low-wage manufacturing country, and some of your people are importing statuettes of your own patron saint from China, because China can make them and ship them all the way across the Pacific more cheaply than you can produce them . . . you have got a problem. [T]he only way for Mexico to thrive is with a strategy of reform . . . the more Mexico just sits there, the more it is going to get run over." Friedman seems blissfully unaware that poor Mexico, so far from God yet so close to American pundits, has already tried much harder than China to implement the experts' "strategy of reform."

The self-confidence of Developmentalists like Friedman is so strong that they impose themselves even on those who accept their strategies. This year, for instance, Ghana celebrated its 50th anniversary as the first black African nation to gain independence. Official international aid donors to Ghana told its allegedly independent government, in the words of the World Bank: "We Partners are here giving you our pledge to give our best to make lives easier for you in running your country." Among the things they will do to make your life easier is to run your country for you.

Unfortunately, Development ideology has a dismal record of helping any country actually develop. The regions where the ideology has been most influential, Latin America and Africa, have done the worst. Luckless Latins and Africans are left chasing yesterday's formulas for success while those who ignored the Developmentalists found homegrown paths to success. The nations that have been the most successful in the past 40 years did so in such a variety of different ways that it would be hard to argue that they discovered the "correct answer" from development ideology. In fact, they often conspicuously violated whatever it was the experts said at the time. The East Asian tigers, for instance, chose outward orientation on their own in the 1960s, when the experts' conventional wisdom was industrialization for the home market. The rapid growth of China over the past quarter century came when it was hardly a poster child for either the 1980s Washington Consensus or the 1990s institutionalism of democracy and cracking down on corruption.

What explains the appeal of development ideology despite its dismal track record? Ideologies usually arise in response to tragic situations in which people are hungry for clear and comprehensive solutions. The inequality of the Industrial Revolution bred Marxism, and the backwardness of Russia its Leninist offshoot. Germany's defeat and demoralization in World War I birthed Nazism. Economic hardship accompanied by threats to identity led to both Christian and Islamic fundamentalism. Similarly, development ideology appeals to those who want a definitive, complete answer to the tragedy of world poverty and inequality. It answers the question, "What is to be done?" to borrow the title of Lenin's 1902 tract. It stresses collective social outcomes that must be remedied by collective, top-down action by the intelligentsia, the revolutionary vanguard, the development expert. As Sachs explains, "I have . . . gradually come to understand through my scientific research and on the ground advisory work the awesome power in our generation's hands to end the massive suffering of the extreme poor . . . although introductory economics textbooks preach individualism and decentralized markets, our safety and prosperity depend at least as much on collective decisions."

Freeing the Poor

Few realize that Americans in 1776 had the same income level as the average African today. Yet, like all the present-day developed nations, the United States was lucky enough to escape poverty before there were Developmentalists. In the words of former IMF First Deputy Managing Director Anne Krueger, development in the rich nations "just happened." George Washington did not have to deal with aid partners, getting structurally adjusted by them, or preparing poverty-reduction strategy papers for them. Abraham Lincoln did not celebrate a government of the donors, by the donors, and for the donors. Today's developed nations were free to experiment with their own pragmatic paths toward more government accountability and freer markets. Individualism and decentralized markets were good enough to give rise to penicillin, air conditioning, high-yield corn, and the automobile—not to mention better living standards, lower mortality, and the iPod.

The opposite of ideology is freedom, the ability of societies to be unchained from foreign control. The only "answer" to poverty reduction is freedom from being told the answer. Free

societies and individuals are not guaranteed to succeed. They will make bad choices. But at least they bear the cost of those mistakes, and learn from them. That stands in stark contrast to accountability-free Developmentalism. This process of learning from mistakes is what produced the repositories of common sense that make up mainstream economics. The opposite of Development ideology is not anything goes, but the pragmatic use of time-tested economic ideas—the benefits of specialization, comparative advantage, gains from trade, market-clearing prices, trade-offs, budget constraints—by individuals, firms, governments, and societies as they find their own success.

History proves just how much good can come from individuals who both bear the costs and reap the benefits of their own choices when they are free to make them. That includes local politicians, activists, and businesspeople who are groping their way toward greater freedom, contrary to the Developmentalists who oxymoronically impose freedom of choice on other people. Those who best understood the lessons of the 20th century were not the ideologues asking, "What is to be done?" They were those asking, "How can people be more free to find their own solutions?"

The ideology of Development should be packed up in crates and sent off to the Museum of Dead Ideologies, just down the hall from Communism, Socialism, and Fascism. It's time to recognize that the attempt to impose a rigid development ideology on the world's poor has failed miserably. Fortunately, many poor societies are forging their own path toward greater freedom and prosperity anyway. That is how true revolutions happen.

WILLIAM EASTERLY is professor of economics at New York University.

The Rise of the Rest

It's true China is booming, Russia is growing more assertive, terrorism is a threat. But if America is losing the ability to dictate to this new world, it has not lost the ability to lead.

FAREED ZAKARIA

Americans are glum at the moment. No, I mean really glum. In April, a new poll revealed that 81 percent of the American people believe that the country is on the "wrong track." In the 25 years that pollsters have asked this question, last month's response was by far the most negative. Other polls, asking similar questions, found levels of gloom that were even more alarming, often at 30- and 40-year highs. There are reasons to be pessimistic—a financial panic and looming recession, a seemingly endless war in Iraq, and the ongoing threat of terrorism. But the facts on the ground—unemployment numbers, foreclosure rates, deaths from terror attacks—are simply not dire enough to explain the present atmosphere of malaise.

American anxiety springs from something much deeper, a sense that large and disruptive forces are coursing through the world. In almost every industry, in every aspect of life, it feels like the patterns of the past are being scrambled. "Whirl is king, having driven out Zeus," wrote Aristophanes 2,400 years ago. And—for the first time in living memory—the United States does not seem to be leading the charge. Americans see that a new world is coming into being, but fear it is one being shaped in distant lands and by foreign people.

Look around. The world's tallest building is in Taipei, and will soon be in Dubai. Its largest publicly traded company is in Beijing. Its biggest refinery is being constructed in India. Its largest passenger airplane is built in Europe. The largest investment fund on the planet is in Abu Dhabi; the biggest movie industry is Bollywood, not Hollywood. Once quintessentially American icons have been usurped by the natives. The largest Ferris wheel is in Singapore. The largest casino is in Macao, which overtook Las Vegas in gambling revenues last year. America no longer dominates even its favorite sport, shopping. The Mall of America in Minnesota once boasted that it was the largest shopping mall in the world. Today it wouldn't make the top ten. In the most recent rankings, only two of the world's ten richest people are American. These lists are arbitrary and a bit silly, but consider that only ten years ago, the United States would have serenely topped almost every one of these categories.

These factoids reflect a seismic shift in power and attitudes. It is one that I sense when I travel around the world. In America, we are still debating the nature and extent of anti-Americanism. One side says that the problem is real and worrying and that we must woo the world back. The other says this is the inevitable price of power and that many of these countries are envious—and vaguely French—so we can safely ignore their griping. But while we argue over why they hate us, "they" have moved on, and are now far more interested in other, more dynamic parts of the globe. The world has shifted from anti-Americanism to *post*-Americanism.

I. The End of Pax Americana

During the 1980s, when I would visit India—where I grew up—most Indians were fascinated by the United States. Their interest, I have to confess, was not in the important power players in Washington or the great intellectuals in Cambridge. People would often ask me about . . . Donald Trump. He was the very symbol of the United States—brassy, rich, and modern. He symbolized the feeling that if you wanted to find the biggest and largest anything, you had to look to America. Today, outside of entertainment figures, there is no comparable interest in American personalities. If you wonder why, read India's newspapers or watch its television. There are dozens of Indian businessmen who are now wealthier than the Donald. Indians are obsessed by their own vulgar real estate billionaires. And that newfound interest in *their own* story is being replicated across much of the world.

How much? Well, consider this fact. In 2006 and 2007, 124 countries grew their economies at over 4 percent a year. That includes more than 30 countries in Africa. Over the last two decades, lands outside the industrialized West have been growing at rates that were once unthinkable. While there have been booms and busts, the overall trend has been unambiguously upward. Antoine van Agtmael, the fund manager who coined the term "emerging markets," has identified the 25 companies most likely to be the world's next great multinationals. His list includes four companies each from Brazil, Mexico, South Korea, and Taiwan; three from India, two from China, and one each from Argentina, Chile, Malaysia, and South Africa. This is something much broader than the much-ballyhooed rise of China or even Asia. It is the rise of the rest—the rest of the world.

We are living through the third great power shift in modern history. The first was the rise of the Western world, around the 15th century. It produced the world as we know it now—science and technology, commerce and capitalism, the industrial and agricultural revolutions. It also led to the prolonged political dominance of the nations of the Western world. The second shift, which took place in the closing years of the 19th century, was the rise of the United States. Once it industrialized, it soon became the most powerful nation in the world, stronger than any likely combination of other nations. For the last 20 years, America's superpower status in every realm has been largely unchallenged—something that's never happened before in history, at least since the Roman Empire dominated the known world 2,000 years ago. During this Pax Americana, the global economy has accelerated dramatically. And that expansion is the driver behind the third great power shift of the modern age—the rise of the rest.

At the military and political level, we still live in a unipolar world. But along every other dimension—industrial, financial, social, cultural—the distribution of power is shifting, moving away from American dominance. In terms of war and peace, economics and business, ideas and art, this will produce a landscape that is quite different from the one we have lived in until now—one defined and directed from many places and by many peoples.

The post-American world is naturally an unsettling prospect for Americans, but it should not be. This will not be a world defined by the decline of America but rather the rise of everyone else. It is the result of a series of positive trends that have been progressing over the last 20 years, trends that have created an international climate of unprecedented peace and prosperity.

I know. That's not the world that people perceive. We are told that we live in dark, dangerous times. Terrorism, rogue states, nuclear proliferation, financial panics, recession, outsourcing, and illegal immigrants all loom large in the national discourse. Al Qaeda, Iran, North Korea, China, Russia are all threats in some way or another. But just how violent is today's world, really?

A team of scholars at the University of Maryland has been tracking deaths caused by organized violence. Their data show that wars of all kinds have been declining since the mid-1980s and that we are now at the lowest levels of global violence since the 1950s. Deaths from terrorism are reported to have risen in recent years. But on closer examination, 80 percent of those casualties come from Afghanistan and Iraq, which are really war zones with ongoing insurgencies—and the overall numbers remain small. Looking at the evidence, Harvard's polymath professor Steven Pinker has ventured to speculate that we are probably living "in the most peaceful time of our species' existence."

Why does it not feel that way? Why do we think we live in scary times? Part of the problem is that as violence has been ebbing, information has been exploding. The last 20 years have produced an information revolution that brings us news and, most crucially, images from around the world all the time. The immediacy of the images and the intensity of the 24-hour news cycle combine to produce constant hype. Every weather disturbance is the "storm of the decade." Every bomb that explodes is BREAKING NEWS. Because the information revolution is so new, we—reporters, writers, readers, viewers—are all just now figuring out how to put everything in context.

We didn't watch daily footage of the two million people who died in Indochina in the 1970s, or the million who perished in the sands of the Iran-Iraq war ten years later. We saw little of the civil war in the Congo in the 1990s, where millions died. But today any bomb that goes off, any rocket that is fired, any death that results, is documented by someone, somewhere and ricochets instantly across the world. Add to this terrorist attacks, which are random and brutal. "That could have been me," you think. Actually, your chances of being killed in a terrorist attack are tiny—for an American, smaller than drowning in your bathtub. But it doesn't feel like that.

The threats we face are real. Islamic jihadists are a nasty bunch—they do want to attack civilians everywhere. But it is increasingly clear that militants and suicide bombers make up a tiny portion of the world's 1.3 billion Muslims. They can do real damage, especially if they get their hands on nuclear weapons. But the combined efforts of the world's governments have effectively put them on the run and continue to track them and their money. Jihad persists, but the jihadists have had to scatter, work in small local cells, and use simple and undetectable weapons. They have not been able to hit big, symbolic targets, especially ones involving Americans. So they blow up bombs in cafés, marketplaces, and subway stations. The problem is that in doing so, they kill locals and alienate ordinary Muslims. Look at the polls. Support for violence of any kind has dropped dramatically over the last five years in all Muslim countries.

Militant groups have reconstituted in certain areas where they exploit a particular local issue or have support from a local ethnic group or sect, most worryingly in Pakistan and Afghanistan where Islamic radicalism has become associated with Pashtun identity politics. But as a result, these groups are becoming more local and less global. Al Qaeda in Iraq, for example, has turned into a group that is more anti-Shiite than anti-American. The bottom line is this: since 9/11, Al Qaeda Central, the gang run by Osama bin Laden, has not been able to launch a single major terror attack in the West or any Arab country—its original targets. They used to do terrorism, now they make videotapes. Of course one day they will get lucky again, but that they have been stymied for almost seven years points out that in this battle between governments and terror groups, the former need not despair.

Some point to the dangers posed by countries like Iran. These rogue states present real problems, but look at them in context. The American economy is 68 times the size of Iran's. Its military budget is 110 times that of the mullahs. Were Iran to attain a nuclear capacity, it would complicate the geopolitics of the Middle East. But none of the problems we face compare with the dangers posed by a rising Germany in the first half of the 20th century or an expansionist Soviet Union in the second half. Those were great global powers bent on world domination. If this is 1938, as some neoconservatives tell us, then Iran is Romania, not Germany.

Others paint a dark picture of a world in which dictators are on the march. China and Russia and assorted other oil potentates are surging. We must draw the battle lines now, they warn, and engage in a great Manichean struggle that will define the next century. Some of John McCain's rhetoric has suggested that he adheres to this dire, dyspeptic view. But before we all sign on for a new Cold War, let's take a deep breath and gain some perspective. Today's rising great powers are relatively benign by historical measure. In the past, when countries grew rich they've wanted to become great military powers, overturn the existing order, and create their own empires or spheres of influence. But since the rise of Japan and Germany in the 1960s and 1970s, none have done this, choosing instead to get rich within the existing international order. China and India are clearly moving in this direction. Even Russia, the most aggressive and revanchist great power today, has done little that compares with past aggressors. The fact that for the first time in history, the United States can contest Russian influence in Ukraine—a country 4,800 miles away from Washington that Russia has dominated or ruled for 350 years—tells us something about the balance of power between the West and Russia.

Compare Russia and China with where they were 35 years ago. At the time both (particularly Russia) were great power threats, actively conspiring against the United States, arming guerrilla movement across the globe, funding insurgencies and civil wars, blocking every American plan in the United Nations. Now they are more integrated into the global economy and society than at any point in at least 100 years. They occupy an uncomfortable gray zone, neither friends nor foes, cooperating with the United States and the West on some issues, obstructing others. But how large is their potential for trouble? Russia's military spending is $35 billion, or 1/20th of the Pentagon's. China has about 20 nuclear missiles that can reach the United States. We have 830 missiles, most with multiple warheads, that can reach China. Who should be worried about whom? Other rising autocracies like Saudi Arabia and the Gulf states are close U.S. allies that shelter under America's military protection, buy its weapons, invest in its companies, and follow many of its diktats. With Iran's ambitions growing in the region, these countries are likely to become even closer allies, unless America gratuitously alienates them.

II. The Good News

In July 2006, I spoke with a senior member of the Israeli government, a few days after Israel's war with Hezbollah had ended. He was genuinely worried about his country's physical security. Hezbollah's rockets had reached farther into Israel than people had believed possible. The military response had clearly been ineffectual: Hezbollah launched as many rockets on the last day of the war as on the first. Then I asked him about the economy— the area in which he worked. His response was striking. "That's puzzled all of us," he said. "The stock market was higher on the

last day of the war than on the first! The same with the shekel." The government was spooked, but the market wasn't.

Or consider the Iraq War, which has produced deep, lasting chaos and dysfunction in that country. Over two million refugees have crowded into neighboring lands. That would seem to be the kind of political crisis guaranteed to spill over. But as I've traveled in the Middle East over the last few years, I've been struck by how little Iraq's troubles have destabilized the region. Everywhere you go, people angrily denounce American foreign policy. But most Middle Eastern countries are booming. Iraq's neighbors—Turkey, Jordan, and Saudi Arabia—are enjoying unprecedented prosperity. The Gulf states are busy modernizing their economies and societies, asking the Louvre, New York University, and Cornell Medical School to set up remote branches in the desert. There's little evidence of chaos, instability, and rampant Islamic fundamentalism.

The underlying reality across the globe is of enormous vitality. For the first time ever, most countries around the world are practicing sensible economics. Consider inflation. Over the past 20 years hyperinflation, a problem that used to bedevil large swaths of the world from Turkey to Brazil to Indonesia, has largely vanished, tamed by successful fiscal and monetary policies. The results are clear and stunning. The share of people living on $1 a day has plummeted from 40 percent in 1981 to 18 percent in 2004 and is estimated to drop to 12 percent by 2015. Poverty is falling in countries that house 80 percent of the world's population. There remains real poverty in the world—most worryingly in 50 basket-case countries that contain 1 billion people—but the overall trend has never been more encouraging. The global economy has more than doubled in size over the last 15 years and is now approaching $54 trillion! Global trade has grown by 133 percent in the same period. The expansion of the global economic pie has been so large, with so many countries participating, that it has become the dominating force of the current era. Wars, terrorism, and civil strife cause disruptions temporarily but eventually they are overwhelmed by the waves of globalization. These circumstances may not last, but it is worth understanding what the world has looked like for the past few decades.

III. A New Nationalism

Of course, global growth is also responsible for some of the biggest problems in the world right now. It has produced tons of money—what businesspeople call liquidity—that moves around the world. The combination of low inflation and lots of cash has meant low interest rates, which in turn have made people act greedily and/or stupidly. So we have witnessed over the last two decades a series of bubbles—in East Asian countries, technology stocks, housing, subprime mortgages, and emerging market equities. Growth also explains one of the signature events of our times—soaring commodity prices. $100 oil is just the tip of the barrel. Almost all commodities are at 200-year highs. Food, only a few decades ago in danger of price collapse, is now in the midst of a scary rise. None of this is due to dramatic fall-offs in supply. It is demand, growing global demand, that is fueling these prices. The effect of more and more people eating, drinking, washing, driving, and consuming will have seismic effects on the global system. These may be high-quality problems, but they are deep problems nonetheless.

The most immediate effect of global growth is the appearance of new economic powerhouses on the scene. It is an accident of history that for the last several centuries, the richest countries in the world have all been very small in terms of population. Denmark has 5.5 million people, the Netherlands has 16.6 million. The United States is the biggest of the bunch and has dominated the advanced industrial world. But the real giants—China, India, Brazil—have been sleeping, unable or unwilling to join the world of functioning economies. Now they are on the move and naturally, given their size, they will have a large footprint on the map of the future. Even if people in these countries remain relatively poor, as nations their total wealth will be massive. Or to put it another way, any number, no matter how small, when multiplied by 2.5 billion becomes a very big number. (2.5 billion is the population of China plus India.)

The rise of China and India is really just the most obvious manifestation of a rising world. In dozens of big countries, one can see the same set of forces at work—a growing economy, a resurgent society, a vibrant culture, and a rising sense of national pride. That pride can morph into something uglier. For me, this was vividly illustrated a few years ago when I was chatting with a young Chinese executive in an Internet café in Shanghai. He wore Western clothes, spoke fluent English, and was immersed in global pop culture. He was a product of globalization and spoke its language of bridge building and cosmopolitan values. At least, he did so until we began talking about Taiwan, Japan, and even the United States. (We did not discuss Tibet, but I'm sure had we done so, I could have added it to this list.) His responses were filled with passion, bellicosity, and intolerance. I felt as if I were in Germany in 1910, speaking to a young German professional, who would have been equally modern and yet also a staunch nationalist.

As economic fortunes rise, so inevitably does nationalism. Imagine that your country has been poor and marginal for centuries. Finally, things turn around and it becomes a symbol of economic progress and success. You would be proud, and anxious that your people win recognition and respect throughout the world.

In many countries such nationalism arises from a pent-up frustration over having to accept an entirely Western, or American, narrative of world history—one in which they are miscast or remain bit players. Russians have long chafed over the manner in which Western countries remember World War II. The American narrative is one in which the United States and Britain heroically defeat the forces of fascism. The Normandy landings are the climactic highpoint of the war—the beginning of the end. The Russians point out, however, that in fact the entire Western front was a sideshow. Three quarters of all German forces were engaged on the Eastern front fighting Russian troops, and Germany suffered 70 percent of its casualties there. The Eastern front involved more land combat than all other theaters of World War II put together.

Such divergent national perspectives always existed. But today, thanks to the information revolution, they are amplified, echoed, and disseminated. Where once there were only the narratives laid out by *The New York Times, Time, Newsweek,* the BBC, and CNN, there are now dozens of indigenous networks and channels—from Al Jazeera to New Delhi's NDTV to Latin America's Telesur. The result is that the "rest" are now dissecting the assumptions and narratives of the West and providing alternative views. A young Chinese diplomat told me in 2006, "When you tell us that we support a dictatorship in Sudan to have access to its oil, what I want to say is, 'And how is that different from your support of a medieval monarchy in Saudi Arabia?' We see the hypocrisy, we just don't say anything—yet."

The fact that newly rising nations are more strongly asserting their ideas and interests is inevitable in a post-American world. This raises a conundrum—how to get a world of many actors to work together. The traditional mechanisms of international cooperation are fraying. The U.N. Security Council has as its permanent members the victors of a war that ended more than 60 years ago. The G8 does not include China, India or Brazil—the three fastest-growing large economies in the world—and yet claims to represent the movers and shakers of the world economy. By tradition, the IMF is always headed by a European and the World Bank by an American. This "tradition," like the segregated customs of an old country club, might be charming to an insider. But to the majority who live outside the West, it seems bigoted. Our challenge is this: Whether the problem is a trade dispute or a human rights tragedy like Darfur or climate change, the only solutions that will work are those involving many nations. But arriving at solutions when more countries and more non-governmental players are feeling empowered will be harder than ever.

IV. The Next American Century

Many look at the vitality of this emerging world and conclude that the United States has had its day. "Globalization is striking back," Gabor Steingart, an editor at Germany's leading news magazine, Der Spiegel, writes in a best-selling book. As others prosper, he argues, the United States has lost key industries, its people have stopped saving money, and its government has become increasingly indebted to Asian central banks. The current financial crisis has only given greater force to such fears.

But take a step back. Over the last 20 years, globalization has been gaining depth and breadth. America has benefited massively from these trends. It has enjoyed unusually robust growth, low unemployment and inflation, and received hundreds of billions of dollars in investment. These are not signs of economic collapse. Its companies have entered new countries and industries with great success, using global supply chains and technology to stay in the vanguard of efficiency. U.S. exports and manufacturing have actually held their ground and services have boomed.

The United States is currently ranked as the globe's most competitive economy by the World Economic Forum. It remains dominant in many industries of the future like nanotechnology, biotechnology, and dozens of smaller high-tech fields. Its universities are the finest in the world, making up 8 of the top ten and 37 of the top fifty, according to a prominent ranking produced by Shanghai Jiao Tong University. A few years ago the National Science Foundation put out a scary and much-discussed statistic. In 2004, the group said, 950,000 engineers graduated from China and India, while only 70,000 graduated from the United States. But those numbers are wildly off the mark. If you exclude the car mechanics and repairmen—who are all counted as engineers in Chinese and Indian statistics—the numbers look quite different. Per capita, it turns out, the United States trains more engineers than either of the Asian giants.

But America's hidden secret is that most of these engineers are immigrants. Foreign students and immigrants account for almost 50 percent of all science researchers in the country. In 2006 they received 40 percent of all PhDs. By 2010, 75 percent of all science PhDs in this country will be awarded to foreign students. When these graduates settle in the country, they create economic opportunity. Half of all Silicon Valley start-ups have one founder who is an immigrant or first generation American. The potential for a new burst of American productivity depends not on our education system or R&D spending, but on our immigration policies. If these people are allowed and encouraged to stay, then innovation will happen here. If they leave, they'll take it with them.

More broadly, this is America's great—and potentially insurmountable—strength. It remains the most open, flexible society in the world, able to absorb other people, cultures, ideas, goods, and services. The country thrives on the hunger and energy of poor immigrants. Faced with the new technologies of foreign companies, or growing markets overseas, it adapts and adjusts. When you compare this dynamism with the closed and hierarchical nations that were once superpowers, you sense that the United States is different and may not fall into the trap of becoming rich, and fat, and lazy.

American society can adapt to this new world. But can the American government? Washington has gotten used to a world in which all roads led to its doorstep. America has rarely had to worry about benchmarking to the rest of the world—it was always so far ahead. But the natives have gotten good at capitalism and the gap is narrowing. Look at the rise of London. It's now the world's leading financial center—less because of things that the United States did badly than those London did well, like improving regulation and becoming friendlier to foreign capital. Or take the U.S. health care system, which has become a huge liability for American companies. U.S. carmakers now employ more people in Ontario, Canada, than Michigan because in Canada their health care costs are lower. Twenty years ago, the United States had the lowest corporate taxes in the world. Today they are the second-highest. It's not that ours went up. Those of others went down.

American parochialism is particularly evident in foreign policy. Economically, as other countries grow, for the most part the pie expands and everyone wins. But geopolitics is a struggle for influence: as other nations become more active internationally, they will seek greater freedom of action. This necessarily means that America's unimpeded influence will decline. But if the world that's being created has more power centers, nearly all are invested in order, stability and progress. Rather than narrowly obsessing about our own short-term interests and interest groups, our chief priority should be to bring these rising forces into the global system, to integrate them so that they in turn broaden and deepen global economic, political, and cultural ties. If China, India, Russia, Brazil all feel that they have a stake in the existing global order, there will be less danger of war, depression, panics, and breakdowns. There will be lots of problems, crisis, and tensions, but they will occur against a backdrop of systemic stability. This benefits them but also us. It's the ultimate win-win.

To bring others into this world, the United States needs to make its own commitment to the system clear. So far, America has been able to have it both ways. It is the global rule-maker but doesn't always play by the rules. And forget about standards created by others. Only three countries in the world don't use the metric system—Liberia, Myanmar, and the United States. For America to continue to lead the world, we will have to first join it.

Americans—particularly the American government—have not really understood the rise of the rest. This is one of the most thrilling stories in history. Billions of people are escaping from abject poverty. The world will be enriched and ennobled as they become consumers, producers, inventors, thinkers, dreamers, and doers. This is all happening because of American ideas and actions. For 60 years, the United States has pushed countries to open their markets, free up their politics, and embrace trade and technology. American diplomats, businessmen, and intellectuals have urged people in distant lands to be unafraid of change, to join the advanced world, to learn the secrets of our success. Yet just as they are beginning to do so, we are losing faith in such ideas. We have become suspicious of trade, openness, immigration, and investment because now it's not Americans going abroad but foreigners coming to America. Just as the world is opening up, we are closing down.

Generations from now, when historians write about these times, they might note that by the turn of the 21st century, the United States had succeeded in its great, historical mission—globalizing the world. We don't want them to write that along the way, we forgot to globalize ourselves.

Adapted from *The Post-American World* by **Fareed Zakaria.** © 2008 by Fareed Zakaria. With permission of the publisher, W.W. Norton & Company, Inc.

Feminists and Fundamentalists

Reassertions of an idealized past and a restored 'women's place' are occurring, from Kabul to Cambridge, at a time when the international community has concurred that women's rights are a global good.

KAVITA RAMDAS

The women's movement, as we refer to it now, was one of the most successful movements of the past century. It has been successful in many ways. Perhaps the most tangible evidence is that women's rights have become a desirable commodity, something that in the company of civilized nations people are proud to hold up as a model of what they have achieved, much in the way that democracy has become a global good.

In 1995, 189 countries signed a pact accepting the Beijing Declaration and Platform for Action as an expression of their goals. The platform called itself "an agenda for women's empowerment. It aims at removing obstacles to women's active participation in all spheres of public and private life, through a full and equal share in economic, social, cultural, and political decision making. This means the principle of shared power and responsibility should be established at home, in the workplace, and in wider national and international communities. Equality between women and men is a matter of human rights and a condition for social justice. It is also a necessary and fundamental prerequisite for equality, development, and peace."

These are, indeed, the ideals to which we as an international community should aspire. And in achieving this recognition of women's rights as a global good, we have arguably accomplished one of the most essential outcomes for any social movement: a broad and diverse constituency now concurs that it shares certain values and that we should all collectively promote them.

The women's movement has also been successful, maybe a little less so, with respect to a narrower definition of accomplishment: legal progress in a variety of areas. Today we see—and we sometimes take it for granted—that women are admitted to educational institutions where years ago they were not accepted; that women enjoy opportunities to pursue careers in fields formerly closed to them; that they have inheritance rights, the right to open their own bank accounts, and so forth.

Of course, women still have a long way to go in achieving the narrower legal definition of equality, even in America. Something that seems fairly basic—equal pay for equal work—has not been and probably will not be approved. The Equal Rights Amendment languishes still in the halls of the US Congress. And the United States remains one of the few countries that has not signed the Convention on the Elimination of All Forms of Discrimination against Women.

It does seem, however, that most of the world's nations have accepted women's rights as a global good. And yet the question arises: Is this achievement permanent? Is there some development that might threaten this and future advances of the women's movement?

Social Insecurity

While many of us have arrived at an apparent consensus about the good sense of making women's rights central to our enterprise as forward-looking communities, we are also seeing that the world is coping with unprecedented and unbelievably rapid change—change in science and technology, in social structures, in the movement of people and ideas across borders. As a consequence, all kinds of relationships that once were given are today up for grabs: relationships between individuals and communities, between citizens and states, between parents and children, between husbands and wives. Because of this, millions of people at some fundamental level feel less secure.

Now, the world as we know it has been run to this point by men. Therefore, today's pervasive insecurity is also challenging the prevailing structures in which men set the rules, including the rules of public discourse and political engagement. So what we are seeing is a reaction. The world has mostly agreed that women's rights are a good thing. But, at the same time, this frightening sense of change is condensing into one particular evidence of that change. And that evidence is the transformed position of women in our societies.

The result is a variety of efforts to reassert idealized notions of the past. Islamic fundamentalism is one example that attracts considerable attention. But the assertion of an idealized past is happening across the world, across cultures, within different religious traditions, in different countries and languages, and at all levels of society.

Sistani and Summers

Consider the cases of Iraq's Ali al-Sistani and America's Lawrence Summers. Obviously, these are very different men. They do not share a similar worldview, and they come from very different contexts. Grand Ayatollah Sistani, who wants to impose fundamentalist Islamic constraints on Iraqi women, lives in a rapidly transforming postcolonial society. His is a Muslim country, where the past is alive. Summers—the president of Harvard University who infamously wondered aloud whether women have the same innate abilities in math and science as men—lives in a highly developed capitalist society.

Yet America is also a society in which women increasingly challenge academia and male privilege within academia. Both Iraq and the United States are attempting to respond to where women are located within their social structures. I would argue that both Sistani and Summers are trying, at some level, to place boundaries around what women's roles ought to be.

They are doing so because these roles are up for grabs, and because the aspirations of women pose a widespread dilemma. Having more or less signed on in general to the global good of women's rights, many people around the world feel insecure about what women's advances might mean for their own lives, for their own relationships, for decision making in their own institutions.

This is the global threat: the feeling that somehow, if we let women just take off with this idea about women's rights, who knows where it could go? The last US presidential election highlighted a classic example of this fear, with a number of state ballot referendums drawing voters determined to defend the institution of marriage against perceived erosion.

Indeed, for some the very relevance of men to the reproductive process seems under assault. State governments in America continue to impose restrictions on abortion. But what significance do male partners retain if, outside of marriage between "man and wife," a woman can go to a sperm bank and make an independent choice to have a child? And what does this mean for society? And how do you begin to control this?

The Way We Were

It is not an accident that mass rapes became a symbol of the Bosnian war during the 1990s. An estimated 20,000 to 50,000 Bosnian women were raped during that genocidal conflict. Indeed, mass rape has become a feature of modern warfare—a strange phenomenon, when you consider that warfare has also become so highly technologically developed. We have all these amazing smart bombs, yet we also witness one of the most medieval forms of exerting power. What does this represent, in a society, more broadly?

And how do we think about this reassertion of an idealized past, these "fundamentalisms?" They are certainly not unique to one religion; I have watched Hindu fundamentalists in India spend the past eight years eulogizing one male god in a society that has long prided itself on worshipping numerous goddesses as well as gods.

Predictably, the idealized tradition, the fundamentalist challenge, is borne everywhere on the backs of women, and there is widespread reluctance to oppose it. This is what we found in

Afghanistan under the Taliban, a brutal form of gender apartheid that was allowed to exist until the United States invaded in the aftermath of 9-11. Even today, we hear many arguments for why we should not impose human rights on societies that have other cultural traditions—why, if women are treated badly, we ought to be careful about making demands because that may be how things are done in those societies.

The kind of violence that women and girls experience on a day-to-day basis around the world, the kind of entrenched discrimination they face—if this behavior were applied against almost any ethnic or national minority, there would be loud and persistent calls for intervention. After the US invasion of Afghanistan, some rhetoric was heard about the liberation of that country's women. But, as Afghan women would point out, that liberation did not happen until two edifices, two towers, were attacked in the United States.

The variety of fundamentalisms notwithstanding, the one thread they share is the attempt to control women's bodies, the ability of women to move freely, and their ability to speak with any kind of free voice within their societies. It is ironic but telling that these reassertions of an idealized past and a restored "women's place" are occurring, from Kabul to Cambridge, at a time when the international community has concurred that women's rights are a global good. They are occurring at a time when every major international foundation and financial institution has agreed that no development goals—whether in economics, political development, or social development—can be achieved without investing in girls' education and the full and equal participation of women.

The Feminist Vanguard

Fortunately, while there is a threat, there is also hope. The hope is that the women's movement and the advancement of women's rights will be the vanguard in the international community's struggle to overcome fundamentalisms.

You can see this hope in the dilemma the US government is struggling with right now. The Bush administration is caught in a tricky contradiction. Because we have all agreed that women's rights are a global good, the administration cannot say that women's rights do not matter. Yet it is deeply beholden to a Christian fundamentalist movement within the United States that truly believes we must return to an idealized notion of the past.

The Southern Baptist Church, for example, has decided to put the word "obey" back in marriage vows; a woman should obey her husband (it is not in the man's vows). Promise Keepers is another movement that harkens back to eighteenth- and nineteenth-century definitions of husbands as hunter-gatherers and women as loyal wives who stay at home and raise the family. President Bush himself has made a number of speeches that evoke idealized images of a time when, as my husband would say, "men were men, and women were women."

The harkening back to a more constrictive order for women continues while the United States claims to be liberating women overseas from uncivilized nations that do not support women's equality. Human rights are held up as a global good even as they are undermined in the everyday lives of women. At the level of implementation, what you actually see are increasing restrictions on the freedom and control that women have—over their reproductive choices and access to contraception, for example—along with cutbacks in spending on health and education that harm women the most.

This is the global threat: the feeling that somehow, if we let women just take off with this idea about women's rights, who knows where it could go?

Some think Title IX has gone too far and want to turn it back. When many hear the term "Title IX," they think it has to do with women in sports. In fact, it has everything to do with President Summers' comments about women in the sciences. Title IX of the 1972 Education Amendments to the 1964 Civil Rights Act required fair access to a wide variety of educational resources—from soccer playing fields to science laboratories.

There are many levels at which, in the face of rhetorical acceptance of women's rights, policies and proposals are being pursued that would undermine achievements that took decades to accomplish. The women's movement has a vital role in resisting rollbacks.

Changing Culture

I work in the international arena, and people often ask me, "Why do other cultures not value women's rights?" And I like to remind them that there is nothing unique about cultures, and that there is no culture I can think of that intrinsically values women's rights.

Reformers in the United States fought for a very long time for women to be recognized as more than just the property of men, just as they struggled for the rights of black people to be recognized as human beings. Cultures are not static. There is nothing that says Western culture is inherently thoughtful and considerate and inclusive of women, minorities, or anyone else.

Why have some cultures evolved to a place where equal rights are regarded as desirable? Because those who have been most oppressed within these cultures have chosen to fight for the right to be treated with equality and dignity. And this is the same thing that is happening today in most of the world. In India, in Afghanistan, in Iraq, in Peru, in the indigenous communities of Mexico, people are struggling to have their culture evolve as a living, breathing thing, and to have women and girls who have not traditionally had voice in those cultures to now have voice.

There is hope in this—in women's rights as a fulcrum on which societies can tip toward modernity, not in the narrowly defined sense of Westernization, but true modernity, in terms of imagining a different conception of how the world can be organized. Women's movements struggle precisely at this fulcrum between modernity and the fundamentalist pressures to regress, and here there is promise.

In my work I have seen women in the most oppressive and closed societies take extraordinary risks and truly challenge the status quo. I have seen them find ways to make their culture more inclusive, more accepting, and more fundamentally equal for all people within their societies.

My organization, the Global Fund for Women, worked with Afghan women's groups during the Taliban's rule, both in refugee camps in Pakistan and in secret schools for girls—and for boys, I might add, inside Afghanistan. (One of the things people often do not think about is that the success of the women's movement accrues to both women and men. When the Taliban pulled women out of schools in Afghanistan, 65 percent of primary school teachers in the country were women. The government's action jeopardized the education of a whole generation of Afghan boys, who then had no alternative but to go to Islamic religious schools.)

What we found in our work over those years with a number of Afghan women's groups is that they are incredibly strategic about building alliances with male allies within their communities. They do not see their fight as a struggle against men. They see it as a struggle against the patriarchal system. They have been extraordinarily creative about choosing their priorities.

I was in Afghanistan in 2003 after the Taliban had been toppled. Like everyone else, I had seen the pictures of women throwing off their burqas, which everyone in the United States was very excited about (but which most women in Afghanistan, in fact, have not done; while in Iraq many more women have put them back on). To me, far more a sign of liberation in Afghanistan was a scene I witnessed in a small classroom in Kabul, where three women taught a class of 45 male teachers—village school teachers from different provinces around Afghanistan.

These three women, their heads covered in scarves, were discussing the pedagogy of successful education. Amid building blocks made out of recycled cigarette cartons, they were talking to the male teachers about how educators need to make learning joyful and pleasurable, something that children can be enthused about.

When it was time for questions and answers, I asked, "What does it feel like to be sitting in a classroom and listening to three women teachers teaching you?" One man raised his hand and said, "I'm a professor of mathematics and science, and for 25 years, Afghan schoolchildren are boys who have learned how to hold an AK-47 before they learned how to do basic math. I haven't been in a school that has had a science laboratory for 25 years." He said, "During these 25 years, it was women who kept education alive in our country, and I think it's time we should be learning from the women." It was an extraordinary statement, and to me, more powerful than any picture of a woman pulling off her burqa.

"Equal to What?"

Across much of the world the leadership of the women's movement has shifted from the kinds of experiences that Western feminists underwent in the 1960s and 1970s, which were very important and in many ways necessary, but which were very much filled with conflict. There is a willingness now in the developing world to be more inclusive, an approach born out of necessity and also from a sense that this is a struggle we have to be in together.

Women's groups in different parts of the world are showing an increasing ability to build on the notion that their states and the international institutions have all signed onto—this idea that women's rights are a global good—while at the same time finding a way to make it real in their own communities, finding a way to say, "Well, so what happens when the old traditions die?"

In Ethiopia, for example, over 90 percent of women go through female genital mutilation (FGM) as a rite of passage, and women's organizations are challenging the practice. But they are not challenging it from the perspective of "this is an evil, ancient, tribal tradition." Rather, they are looking to the root causes of the tradition.

As I heard an Ethiopian mother explain it, "If you know that the only economic security for your daughter is to ensure that she gets married, and if you know that no one will marry her unless she has gone through the process of FGM, because you cannot assure her purity otherwise, then you have no choice as a mother but to make your daughter go through it, even though you don't have to explain to us how painful it is and what the health consequences are, because each of us has lived those experiences."

If, however, we create an environment in which girls can go to school and stay in school longer, and women have opportunities to earn an income and contribute to their families, then girls will not have to depend for their economic prospects on being married off at age 12 or 13. And if we look at the status of widows in Ethiopia and attend to their security, we can also make a difference, because it turns out that it is the widows who get paid for performing the circumcision ceremony. They depend on this ritual as a means of support because people abandon them at the edges of villages.

The environment fostered by educational and microenterprise initiatives is one that emphasizes joint efforts among men and women within a community. It is not one that says men are the problem. Indeed, women often are just as much the perpetrators of traditional values and practices as men are. What has come through clearly for women's organizations in the rest of the world is that we are struggling against a system, and this system oppresses both women and men who are caught within it.

In the 1960s and 1970s, feminists in the United States were saying, "We want to be equal to you, we want to play on your playing fields, we want to play the same game." Today the women's movement internationally is saying something very different. It is asking the question: "Equal to what?" What do we want to be equal to? And what is the game we should be playing together, men and women, to ensure a freer, more just world that offers more opportunities for all of us?

KAVITA RAMDAS is president and CEO of the Global Fund for Women.

UNIT 2

Population and Food Production

Unit Selections

6. **The Century Ahead,** Chris Wilson
7. **Africa's Restless Youth,** Michelle Gavin
8. **Still Hungry: One Eighth of the World's People Do Not Have Enough to Eat,** Per Pinstrup-Andersen and Fuzhi Cheng
9. **Pandemic Pandemonium,** Josh N. Ruxin

Key Points to Consider

- What are the basic characteristics and trends of the world's population? How many people are there? How long do people typically live?

- How fast is the world's population growing? What are the reasons for this growth? How do population dynamics vary from one region to the next?

- In many regions of the world, the graying of the population is an important trend. What are some of the political implications of this trend?

- How does rapid population growth affect the quality of the environment, social structures, and the ways in which humanity views itself?

- In an era of global interdependence, how much impact can individual governments have on demographic changes?

- What are the causes of hunger in the world? Are agricultural resources sufficient to feed a growing population?

- What are some of the infectious diseases that threaten the human population? Are organizational resources, both national and international, sufficient to meet this timeless challenge?

- How can economic and social policies be changed in order to reduce the impact of population growth on environmental quality?

Student Web Site

www.mhcls.com

Internet References

The Hunger Project
  http://www.thp.org
Penn Library: Resources by Subject
  http://www.library.upenn.edu/cgi-bin/res/sr.cgi
World Health Organization
  http://www.who.int
WWW Virtual Library: Demography & Population Studies
  http://demography.anu.edu.au/VirtualLibrary/

Affter World War II, the world's population reached an estimated 2 billion people. It had taken 250 years to triple to that level. In the six decades following World War II, the population tripled again to 6 billion. When the typical reader of this book reaches the age of 50, demographers estimate that the global population will have reached 8 1/2 billion! By 2050, or about 100 years after World War II, some experts forecast that 10 to 12 billion people may populate the world. A person born in 1946 (a so-called baby boomer) who lives to be 100 could see a six-fold increase in population.

Nothing like this has ever occurred before. To state this in a different way: In the next 50 years, there will have to be twice as much food grown, twice as many schools and hospitals available, and twice as much of everything else just to maintain the current and rather uneven standard of living. We live in an unprecedented time in human history.

One of the most interesting aspects of this population growth is that there is little agreement about whether this situation is good or bad. The government of China, for example, has a policy that encourages couples to have only one child. In contrast, there are a few governments that use various financial incentives to promote large families.

In the first decade of the new millennium, there are many population issues that transcend numerical or economic considerations. The disappearance of indigenous cultures is a good example of the pressures of population growth on people who live on the margins of modern society. Finally, while demographers develop various scenarios forecasting population growth, it is important to remember that there are circumstances that could lead not to growth but to a significant decline in global population. The spread of AIDS and other infectious diseases reveals that confidence in modern medicine's ability to control these scourges may be premature. Nature has its own checks and balances for the population dynamic. This factor is often overlooked in an age of technological optimism.

The lead article in this section provides an overview of the general demographic trends in the contemporary world, with a

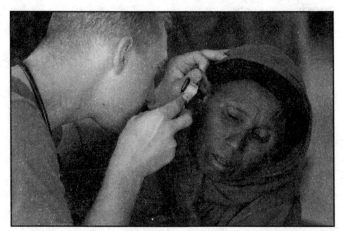

© U.S. Air Force photo by Staff Sgt. Stephen Schester

special focus on issues related to aging. In the second article, the African demographic youth bulge (which is a trend much different than found in most other regions of the world) is described along with its social and political implications. There are, of course, no greater checks on population growth than the ability an adequate food supply and contain the spread of infectious disease. Some experts question whether current technologies are sustainable over the long run. How much food are we going to need, and how are farmers and fishermen going to provide it? Will markets deliver food to those in greatest need? Finally, the continuous threat of the spread of disease and the ability of national and international public health organizations to contain it are issues directly related to population issues.

Making predictions about the future of the world's population is a complicated task, for there are a variety of forces at work and considerable variation from region to region. The danger of oversimplification must be overcome if governments and international organizations are going to respond with meaningful policies. Perhaps one could say that there is not a global population problem but rather many population challenges that vary from country to country and region to region.

The Century Ahead

Chris Wilson

The twentieth century was, above all else, a century of population growth; the twenty-first century will be a century of aging. Between 1900 and 2000 the world's population quadrupled, from around 1.5 billion to over 6 billion. Most of this increase occurred after World War II. At present, it seems unlikely that the population will grow by more than about a further 50 percent. The most plausible forecasts see a population numbering between 9 and 10 billion by about 2050, with stability or decline in total population thereafter.

However, the population at older ages will increase far more quickly in the coming century than in the last. Indeed, the end of population growth and its replacement by aging are logically related. All rapidly growing populations are young. If each birth cohort is larger than the one before, there will always be plenty of young people.

Population growth was so characteristic of the recent past that we tend to regard it as the norm. However, for most of human history the long-run rate of population growth has been very close to zero. From the biblical Adam and Eve, it would have taken only thirty-two doublings of the population to reach over 8 billion. At the rate of population growth seen in the 1960s and early 1970s—over 2 percent a year, implying a doubling time of around thirty years—and given that the gap between generations is also usually about thirty years—such an increase could have taken place inside a millennium. Even James Ussher's 1650 estimate of October 23, 4004 B.C. as the date of creation implies we have been around much longer than that. And since *Homo sapiens* actually emerged one hundred and fifty thousand or so years ago, the rate of growth has obviously been close to zero.

Similarly, extrapolating the growth rates of the recent past into the future soon yields logically impossible figures. Ansley Coale once calculated that a growth rate of 2 percent a year sustained for five thousand years would lead to the sheer volume of human beings exceeding that of the solar system.

The absence of growth is a necessary but not sufficient condition for aging; we also need long life expectancy. In populations before the modern medical era, relatively few people survived to reach three score years and ten. Thus, population aging is a novelty requiring both long lives and a low growth rate (i.e., low fertility). Though rare in the past, these conditions are now becoming the norm around the world.

When demographers try to understand the determinants of aging, they use one of social science's great generalizing models: the demographic transition. When a population modernizes, it undergoes, along with many other aspects of development, a set of interconnected changes called the demographic transition. According to this model, every population at some point has high fertility (mostly between four and six children per woman) and low life expectancy (mostly between twenty-five and forty years). With the spread of modern medicine and public health, mortality improves; as family planning and contraceptive use become the norm, fertility falls. Usually life expectancy rises first, with a delay before fertility declines. This difference in timing leads to substantial population growth before the two processes come back into balance.

This process of transition began in the late eighteenth and nineteenth centuries in Europe, the United States, and the other neo-Europes; it became a global phenomenon after World War II. Today, more than half of the world's people live in places where fertility is at or below the level needed for long-run intergenerational replacement (about 2.1 children per woman), and global life expectancy is approaching seventy years.

Trends in mortality can be followed in considerable detail for many European countries from the mid-nineteenth century, and for a few especially well-documented cases, as far back as the late 1700s. For Japan and the United States detailed information dates back to the early twentieth century. What these statistics reveal is both simple and striking. There has been an enormous reduction in mortality, with life expectancy for the two sexes combined now approaching, or even exceeding, eighty in most developed countries. Even more remarkably, this progress has been very regular for many decades. Jim Oeppen and James Vaupel have shown, for example, that the trend in "best-practice" life expectancy (i.e., the country with the longest life expectancy in each year) has been linear for more than 150 years.[1] In each decade the "state of the art" has increased about 2.5 years. Moreover, although there has been some variation at the national level, most developed countries have demonstrated strongly linear trends in life expectancy for the whole of the twentieth century.

Paradoxically, although this trend has been evident in mortality statistics for many decades, it is only in the last few years that it has been recognized. Demographers, actuaries, and others concerned with forecasting mortality had always hitherto assumed that life expectancy was approaching some asymptotic limit and would thus level off in the near future. But if there is some biological limit to extending longevity, there is no sign of it yet. As Oeppen and Vaupel point out, estimates of the maximum possible life expectancy made throughout the twentieth century were, on average, surpassed within five years of being made. This consistent error is of more than purely academic interest—pension- and health-care systems have been funded on the basis of large underestimates of the number of elderly people in the future.

The linearity of the upward climb in life expectancy has occurred in spite of the fact that very different age groups and causes of death have been involved in different eras. Before World War II, almost all progress took place in reducing infectious diseases, with the biggest impact for infants and children. In contrast, today much of the improvement is concentrated at old ages. Perhaps the best analogy for these remarkable changes is to be found in models of economic growth. Just as modern theory hypothesizes the existence of an endogenous rate of growth that is in some sense built into our economic system, so too there may be an endogenous rate of improvement in health, as measured by life expectancy. In any event, we have every reason to expect that continued increases in the average length of life will augment population aging.

There are, of course, exceptions to this optimistic picture. In the Soviet Union and its client states in Eastern and Central Europe, life expectancy stagnated from the 1960s until the end of Communism. It then worsened still further in many cases, in the immediate aftermath of the revolution. In Russia and many of the post-Soviet states it remains low, especially for men. Male life expectancy in Russia today is roughly the same as it was in 1950: about sixty years. To put this stagnation into perspective, the equivalent figure for the United States has increased since 1950 by almost ten years from sixty-six to seventy-six.

In the post-Communist countries further west, however, the last decade has seen rapid improvements; life expectancy there will likely converge to levels seen in Western Europe within a few decades. The origins of the health crisis under Communism and its persistence in Russia, Ukraine, and the other post-Soviet states is a matter of heated debate in both the scientific and general literature. Whatever the cause, the crisis serves as a warning against unqualified Panglossian optimism. Likewise, the emergence of HIV/AIDS and the associated reemergence of tuberculosis make clear that all future estimates of improvement in public health must take into account the potential for severe reversals.

Overall, however, the last half-century has seen unprecedented convergence in mortality patterns around the world. While rich countries still lead in life expectancy, the gap between these leaders and most developing countries has shrunk substantially. In fact, there has been more convergence in demography than in any other aspect of modernization. For example, consider Latin America as a whole, where the United Nations estimates current life expectancy is seventy-two years, and GDP per head (adjusted for inflation and other factors) is below $4,000, according to the Organization for Economic Cooperation and Development. Now consider the United States. Life expectancy in the United States was seventy-two years as recently as the early 1970s. In contrast, the U.S. GDP per head exceeded $4,000 by 1900. Latin America is a century behind the United States in income growth, but only thirty to thirty-five years behind in life expectancy. We can make similar comparisons for most developing countries. And though the gaps in educational attainment or urbanization are somewhat smaller than in GDP per head, none of the other conventional quantitative indices of development has converged as rapidly as demography.

In recent decades there has also been a striking convergence in fertility, which has declined rapidly in most countries. More than half of the world's population now lives in countries or regions in which fertility is below the level needed for intergenerational replacement.[2] In most of Southern Europe (including Italy and Spain) and in most of Central and Eastern Europe, the total fertility rate (the number of children born per woman) is below 1.3. Similar values are now seen in Japan, South Korea, and many of the more developed parts of China. Even some countries that might seem unlikely candidates have experienced rapid fertility decline. In Iran, for example, fertility fell from over six children per woman to just over two between the mid-1980s and mid-1990s. In contrast, fertility in the United States has seemed to defy gravity, staying close to or even above the replacement level for the last two decades. Among the developing countries in which fertility is now lower than in the United States are China, Brazil, Thailand, and Tunisia. If the trends of the last twenty-five years continue for another decade or so, the U.S. fertility level will be well above the median for the human population as a whole.

The very speed of fertility decline in many countries will produce an exaggerated form of aging. While aging is an inevitable and global phenomenon, countries in which fertility has fallen rapidly will experience a form of 'super aging' in the middle decades of this century. The baby boom cohorts of Southern Europe or the pretransition cohorts in China are very large compared to those that followed, and their getting old will greatly exacerbate any problems that aging generates.

There is also a sense in which aging can be 'locked in' as part of a country's demographic regime through a form of negative momentum. For example, in Southern Europe, the large number of baby boomers moving through the childbearing ages has disguised the very low fertility rate of recent decades. The largest age groups at present are those ages 25 to 39. In the coming decades, however, the much smaller cohorts born since the mid-1980s will be in the reproductive ages. Unless these cohorts (currently ages 0 to 19) have much higher fertility than their parents, the number of births in countries such as Italy and Spain will shrink even more rapidly in the future than it has so far. In contrast, the United States and other countries in which fertility has stabilized at close to the replacement level (in Europe, they include France and the Nordic countries) will face much less severe challenges from demographic disruption.

The future is always uncertain to some degree, but when trends have been so clear and so consistent for decades, they form a solid basis for prediction. It is very close to certain that aging will be one of the defining global phenomena in the twenty-first century. The ways in which societies choose to adapt to this new reality will test the old adage that "demography is destiny." Fatalism, however, is uncalled for—to a substantial degree we can still choose our future. However, demography does impose strong constraints on the range of feasible options. Taking these constraints into account is the basis for informed reactions to the challenges posed by aging.

Notes

1. Jim Oeppen and James W. Vaupel, "Broken Limits to Life Expectancy," *Science 296* (2002): 1030–1031.
2. Chris Wilson, "Fertility Below Replacement Level," *Science 304* (2004): 207–209.

CHRIS WILSON is a staff member of the World Population Program at the International Institute for Applied Systems Analysis in Laxenberg, Austria. One of Europe's most widely cited demographers, he is currently researching the causes and consequences of global demographic convergence.

From *Daedalus*, 135:1, Winter 2006, pp. 5–9. Copyright © 2006 by the American Academy of Arts and Sciences. Reprinted by permission of MIT Press Journals.

Africa's Restless Youth

People interested in Africa's future ought to concern themselves not just with potential conflict, but also potential political change. Youth populations are at the heart of these possibilities.

MICHELLE GAVIN

Scanning the horizon for insight as to what will influence the future of sub-Saharan Africa, one can immediately point to several broad baskets of important indicators. Obviously contributing to the picture are economic growth (or the lack thereof), insecure borders, increasing resource scarcity, the HIV/AIDS pandemic, and the balance of power within nations among ethnic and regional groups. However, a close look at the political engagement and political agendas of youth should also be included in the mix. Young Africans' quest for empowerment will make them significant catalysts for change.

Africa is currently in the midst of what demographers call a youth bulge. A youth bulge typically occurs when less-developed countries, with both high fertility and high mortality rates, begin to bring infant and child mortality rates down. Eventually, development gains tend to bring fertility rates down as well. But in the lag time before this occurs, a population boom of children who survive to adulthood reshapes the demographic landscape.

In Africa today, this dynamic translates into some startling figures. More than 70 percent of all Zimbabweans, for example, are now under 30; the same is true in Kenya, Uganda, Ethiopia, Liberia, and Nigeria, among other countries. Over one-third of the entire population of Zimbabwe, and over 56 percent of the adult (over 15) population, is between 15 and 29 years old. In fact, young adults (aged 15 to 29) make up 40 percent or more of the total adult population in the vast majority of sub-Saharan countries; in roughly 30 African countries, they constitute more than half of the adult population. In contrast, approximately 40 percent of the population in the United States is under 30, and young adults constitute less than 30 percent of the adult population as a whole.

Any discussion of the youth bulge in Africa risks veering into the land of breathless alarmism—*young men and street gangs and guns, oh my!*—or overcorrecting and wandering into the territory of commencement-speech clichés about how the children are indeed the future. But there is room for a closer examination of African youth that emphasizes their political role, and this should be a priority in future research. The young are more inclined to take risks, but vast youthful populations are not going to engage in violence simply for its own sake. On the other hand, violence may be a symptom of clashing political agendas.

In a region where the state has been the source of most power and economic opportunity, but governing institutions are often weak, the desires and grievances of youth are very likely to have political implications. Governments and international actors probably cannot control the degree to which youth bulges shape societies for good or for ill, but they can at least influence outcomes. Focusing too narrowly on violence and conflict rather than on underlying political tensions tends to yield a fairly sickly crop of policy prescriptions, all variations on the theme of "brace yourself." By seeking to understand youth political engagement more clearly, policy makers may be able to create conditions conducive to youth movements that do not leave a legacy of trauma and dysfunction in their wake.

Forever Young?

For the purposes of this article, I am defining youth as anyone from 15 to 29 years old. However, definitions of youth are tricky and often culturally specific. They are also subject to revision and even manipulation. Sierra Leone's National Youth Policy, for instance, targets citizens ages 15 to 35, and Sierra Leoneans sometimes use the term "youth" to describe people in their 40s—this in a country where average life expectancy for males is about 38. Last November, Zimbabwe's *Financial Gazette* questioned the youth credentials of Absolom Sikhosana, the ruling party's Youth League Secretary, suggesting that he was masquerading as a member of the 35-and-under set and that he might in fact be "past his sell-by date." In 2002, South Africa's National Youth Development Policy Framework included a youth definition of 15 to 28, but the National Youth Policy adopted in 1997 had targeted the 14-to-35 range. In any case, according to the International Council on National Youth Policy, various South African government departments use different definitions, which rarely correspond to either of the official policies.

These variable and amorphous definitions point to an interesting phenomenon: in some African countries it is getting increasingly difficult to make the transition from youth to adulthood. Inadequate education systems combine with stratospheric unemployment rates to foreclose the possibility of securing a job that could provide financial security. This in turn makes it unfeasible to marry and start one's own family. Meanwhile, population growth has contributed to a land squeeze, and as desirable land has been divided many times over to accommodate heirs, younger siblings in particular are cut off from the prospect of inheriting workable plots.

Youths are pushed into the continent's urban centers seeking a pathway to a viable future, only to find themselves among the unemployed and alienated masses of young people already looking for the same thing. Here, they are increasingly exposed to many of the same media images of material success that bombard young people in the most developed countries—messages often crafted by marketers to explicitly target the youth demographic. The contrast between these images and their own circumstances and prospects is hard to ignore, amplifying a sense of relative deprivation.

Some young people continue their quest for opportunity by leaving their country and even the continent altogether, risking their lives by placing themselves in the hands of sophisticated and dangerous human smuggling networks that profit from the vast divide between the prospects for African and European youth. But practical and legal constraints ensure that this pathway, like the others, is often blocked. In these situations, many of Africa's youth are caught in a Peter Pan scenario gone terribly wrong. Try as they might, they cannot seem to become adults.

Many African cultures place an extremely high premium on respect for elders. Young people are expected to know their place and to abide by the wisdom of those rich in life experience. Yet, if youth are trapped—indefinitely—in some sort of preparatory state, awaiting the time when they are accorded the respect, responsibility, and opportunity associated with being full-fledged adults in their society, it seems unreasonable to assume that they will wait patiently for a day that is nowhere in sight.

Youths have something to prove, and given opportunity, they will assert themselves. Just how violently or constructively that might happen depends on a range of factors, including the existence and nature of manipulation from older elites, the amount of political space available for civic action, and the capacity of the state and the private sector to hear and understand youth aspirations and to deliver opportunities in a relatively timely fashion.

In one way or another, young Africans are in the market for alternatives to the status quo.

Of course, no country's youth is monolithic. Ethnic, religious, and regional schisms can split demographic cohorts just as they can split a population at large. Also, it is often hard to discern where young women fit into the picture. This is so in part because many become mothers during this period of life, culturally moving into adulthood and a lifetime of domestic responsibility. In addition, young women's leadership and civic engagement opportunities, even within the context of youth movements, often are limited on the basis of gender alone.

Even among young men, agitation for power and respect—be it peaceful or violent—will not be the preoccupation of all youth in any setting. Nevertheless, a vocal, visible, organized segment of the youth population, particularly if it is concentrated in Africa's urban centers, can make for a movement with profound political consequences, and these political actors will be on the stage for many years to come.

Change Agents

In Africa's independence movements and struggles against colonial powers, young people played an important role in case after case. The party that governed Somalia on independence was even called the Somali Youth League. More recently, youth were pivotal in the anti-apartheid struggle in South Africa. Nelson Mandela was 26 when he and other young leaders came together to form the African National Congress Youth League in 1944; their work transformed the ANC. Later, in 1968, 22-year-old Steve Biko led the newly formed and highly influential South African Students Organization. The Soweto uprising of 1976 was grounded in secondary school students' resistance to apartheid policies, and students mobilized en masse to demand change throughout the rest of the struggle.

But today, when their demographic weight is much greater relative to older Africans' than it has been in the past, young people are most often cast in the role of a diffusely destabilizing threat, rather than as potential agents of political and social transformation. The strain of analysis that sees the youth bulge as a fundamentally threatening phenomenon often points to research that suggests a strong relationship between the likelihood of civil conflict and the existence of an urbanized youth bulge. In 2001, the U.S. Central Intelligence Agency released a report on global demographic trends, saying of the projected youth bulges in Africa and parts of the Middle East that:

> "The failure to adequately integrate youth populations is likely to perpetuate the cycle of political instability, ethnic wars, revolutions, and anti-regime activities. . . . Increases in youth populations will aggravate problems with trade, terrorism, anti-regime activities, warfare, and crime and add to the many existing factors that already are making the region's problems increasingly difficult to surmount."

In an influential 2003 report titled *The Security Demographic*, researchers with the nongovernmental organization Population Action International found that countries experiencing a youth bulge were more than twice as likely as other countries to experience civil strife. The numbers are compelling, and so are the recent histories of devastating conflict in states like Liberia and Sierra Leone, where youth were both perpetrators and victims of appalling violence on a massive scale. It is easy to develop a generalized sense that "youth bulge" is code for marauding, angry young men.

Certainly it is not hard to understand why many African youths might have a highly developed sense of grievance. In addition to the frustrating struggle for adult status, shocking numbers of young Africans have at some point in their short lives fallen into one or more of the following unhappy categories: combatants, victims of atrocities, refugees, internally displaced persons, forced laborers, or street children.

AIDS orphans are expected to number 18 million in sub-Saharan Africa in 2010. In the worst-affected areas, their numbers are already overwhelming the capacity of extended family networks to care for them, and alternative support structures are weak or non-existent. According to UNAIDS, 6.2 million Africans 15 to 24 years old are already HIV-positive, and half of all new infections in the region occur in this age group.

There is a strong temptation to write off a "lost generation," but there is no avoiding the fact that those currently holding power will not be able to wield it forever.

The vast majority of Africa's young people have an intimate knowledge of poverty. Even elite youths are faced with a shortage of jobs in which to apply the skills they may have acquired at tremendously overcrowded, underfunded universities. Overall, according to the International Labor Organization (ILO), there are more than 17.4 million unemployed 15- to 24-year-olds in Africa, leading to a regional youth unemployment rate of 18 percent. And even the young people who do have jobs are hardly financially secure: the ILO notes that over 57 percent of African youth are working at the $1-per-day level. One can easily imagine that this cohort as a whole would be quick to blame someone or something—a governing regime or an ethnic group—for a rough past and an uncertain future.

The relationship between youth bulges and violence is important, but it speaks to just one manifestation of youth frustrations and desires. Other avenues for affecting the future include partisan political action, participation in civil society organizations, student activism, and engagement in transnational religious movements. Regardless of whether these manifold forms of expression are accompanied by violent tactics, in light of youths' demographic dominance, all of them will affect the region's future. In one way or another, young Africans are in the market for alternatives to the status quo.

This could mean significant change. In many African countries, the actors dominating the political scene have been on stage (if not in power) for quite some time. President Mwai Kibaki of Kenya is over 75 years old. President Abdoulaye Wade of Senegal is over 80. President Robert Mugabe of Zimbabwe is 83. Most existing state structures, such as party youth wings, do not actually function as entry points to party leadership. The nearly ubiquitous ministries of "youth and sports" are marginal and marginalizing institutions. They are ill-equipped to function as sustainable mechanisms for accommodating and responding to the size and potential strength of youth political activism. When voters under 29 constitute 40 percent of all registered voters, as they did in the last Liberian election, their issues and demands cry out to be mainstream priorities, not sideshows.

Tools of the Elite

Building a capacity to respond to youth demands for empowerment, rather than simply trying to keep a lid on unrest, starts with understanding the dynamics of contemporary youth's political engagement. African youth in the market for alternatives to their current situation will either generate their own vision, or adopt ones supplied by others.

Instances in which youth are manipulated and mobilized to serve an elite agenda are all too easy to come by. Military movements throughout the continent have recruited children and youth on a massive scale. Vast numbers of young Rwandans complied with the most hideous instructions during the 1994 genocide. In Zimbabwe, the ruling party established brutal camps to indoctrinate young people in the party's ideology and to train the party's youth militia.

The camps were organized in 2001 under the auspices of the National Youth Service Training Program, an initiative ostensibly aimed at improving job skills and awareness of civic responsibility. In fact, young Zimbabweans were coerced into attending training camps that taught torture techniques and exposed them to beatings and rapes in the course of molding them into new party loyalists. As the main opposition force in the country, the Movement for Democratic Change, has faltered and split, factions of it, too, have deployed young thugs to intimidate rivals. Meanwhile, the outlook for young Zimbabweans grows increasingly dim, as the national unemployment rate soars to an estimated 80 percent and the economy continues to shrink.

In 2004, disturbing reports emerged from the city of Mbuji-Mayi in the Democratic Republic of Congo. Street children and youths eager for any kind of employment had been mobilized by political elites to demonstrate in rallies and protests and to intimidate opposition figures and supporters in exchange for payment. But these young people went from being political militants for hire to becoming the victims of a massacre. Angry mobs, fed up with the crimes being committed by young people who felt empowered by their political patrons, rampaged through the city, beating and in many instances killing street children and youths.

These horrifying incidents speak to the time-honored tradition of rounding up young people and, by offering short-term opportunity (payment, license to loot, and so forth) and some proximity to power, convincing them to act as violent, visible backers of a given political power. Youth often are enlisted to support political repression and to occupy political space so as to deny it to others. From Kenya to Cameroon, the recruitment of young people to reinforce ethnic divisions, intimidate voices of dissent, and send signals about who possesses strength and power—whatever is most useful for the elites doing the recruiting—has been a regular feature of Africa's political landscape. In some cases, the formation of militant party youth wings is explicit. In other cases, direct ties to the party are less formal, perhaps protecting the party from being held accountable for disruptive youth action.

In the Driver's Seat

But instances in which youth pursue their own agendas can be found as well, and the nature of these efforts ranges from non-threatening to extremely confrontational. The sub-Saharan region is rich in dynamic, creative youth groups with a public service focus, from theater troupes dramatizing HIV/AIDS prevention techniques in Uganda to peace-building programs sustained by Tutsi and Hutu youth in Burundi. Some student groups are clearly co-opted by elites. But others, like the Kenyan University Students Organization that existed in the mid-1990s to demand democratic change, challenge the ruling class and operate as independent civil society actors.

Consider the action of some Sierra Leonean youths, including ex-combatants, in the wake of that country's devastating civil war. These youths wanted power, but rather than focusing exclusively on personal enrichment, the Movement of Concerned Kono Youth, or MOCKY, tried to stand in for what its members perceived to be an absent or ineffective law enforcement presence. As the country's civil war wound down, MOCKY tried to fill roles one would normally associate with government—conducting patrols, monitoring mining activity, and attempting to negotiate with a multinational mining company operating in the region in an effort to secure community development commitments. Dissatisfied by what the state had to offer and longing to assert themselves in positions of leadership and authority, these youths tried to organize an alternative.

Some youth-dominated armed groups in the Niger Delta claim to have a similar agenda. Interestingly, former Nigerian dictator Sani Abacha's "two million man march" in 1998 was a turning point for youth activism. A group calling itself Youths Earnestly Ask for Abacha ostensibly organized this display of support for the regime, although the government clearly directed the entire affair. Young people from around the country were bussed to the gleaming capital city of Abuja to participate, where they saw state-of-the-art infrastructure and facilities presumably financed with Nigeria's oil wealth. The contrast between the wealth on display in Abuja and the desperately poor oil-producing communities in the Niger Delta helped to radicalize a generation.

Being used as Abacha's instruments drove the young people to develop and pursue their own agenda. No longer content to let local chiefs negotiate with the government or oil companies on behalf of communities, youth formed pressure groups and, in many cases, armed militias. Some groups remain available for hire to politicians around election time, but it is clear that these armed youth movements cannot be controlled by the state. Today, media-savvy, youth-dominated militant groups like the Movement for the Emancipation of the Niger Delta (MEND) engage in operations ranging from kidnapping foreign oil workers to hosting CNN correspondents. Their actions have consequences not only for local security, but also for international oil markets.

The Case of Ivory Coast

The distinction between youth acting as instruments and youth acting as agents is not always clear, and power between elites and youth leaders can ebb and flow. Perhaps nowhere are the lines as blurry today as they are in Ivory Coast. Once a proud island of stability and economic growth, over the past decade the country has descended into a toxic mix of civil conflict, violent xenophobia, and political stalemate—with youth as major actors throughout.

When longtime President Felix Houphouet Boigny died in 1993, he was replaced by Henri Konan Bedie, who sought to consolidate his power by marginalizing his primary political rival, Alassane Ouattara. Bedie's method was to promote *"ivoirité"*—an ultranationalist vision of the country's identity that excluded many of the migrant workers from Burkina Faso, Mali, and Guinea who had long labored in Ivory Coast's northern agricultural fields. Not coincidentally, it also excluded Ouattara, whose main base of support was in the north, because of complicated questions about where his parents were born.

Bedie was soon overthrown in a coup, but his formula for neutralizing any political threat from Ouattara was later embraced by the current president, Laurent Gbagbo, who came to power in 2000 in a dubious election in which the two major parties' candidates were prevented from participating. A rebellion broke out in 2002, eventually splitting the country into two parts—the north and west controlled by rebels known as the *Forces Nouvelles,* and the south and east under the control of the Gbagbo government, state security forces, and their militia allies. Notably, both sides' ranks were strengthened by former combatants hardened by youth-dominated conflict in Liberia and Sierra Leone. These roving soldiers-for-hire are a new part of the regional youth landscape.

While these political machinations and the resulting conflict unfolded, global economic conditions that had been squeezing the Ivorian economy throughout the 1980s and 1990s—particularly falling prices for coffee and cocoa—began to bite ferociously. *Ivoirité* fed many elite youths' hunger for someone to blame for the scarcity of jobs, land, and opportunities. Meanwhile, northern youth became increasingly agitated about the prospect of being systematically excluded from the few opportunities available within the country. Both youth groups acted on their anxieties, led by young men who had risen to prominence as students in Ivory Coast's highly political university setting.

In fact, Guillaume Soro, the leader of the *Forces Nouvelles,* and Charles Ble Goude, leader of the pro-Gbagbo Young Patriots militia, were consecutive secretaries general of the Student Federation of Ivory Coast (FESCI) in the period from 1995 to 2001. Other militia leaders also have backgrounds as FESCI officers. FESCI was founded in the early 1990s to advocate for improved conditions at increasingly overcrowded and under-resourced university campuses; it was a movement of youth resisting the shrinking opportunities presented to them and protesting favoritism in the distribution of scholarship funds. In those early days, FESCI's dissatisfaction with government policies aligned it with the movement that advocated for multiparty politics—a movement in which the political party founded by Gbagbo (a former university lecturer himself) played an important part.

Today, the Young Patriots and allied youth militias are among the primary enforcement arms of Gbagbo's state. They can mobilize masses of youth with astonishing speed, and their activities range from the conventionally political (collecting signatures on petitions calling for the *Forces Nouvelles* to be disarmed) to the clearly repressive (prohibiting the distribution of newspapers deemed insufficiently loyal to the ruling party) to the extremely violent (brutally beating opposition supporters or simply those who appear to be of Burkinabe or Malian descent).

The International Crisis Group has documented how rural youth, some of whom had left the city after finding no employment despite having attained university degrees, have been inspired by intense state-controlled media coverage of the Young Patriots' activities to take actions that give them their own social and economic power. They set up barricades to monitor movement in and out of villages, enabling them to collect fees and attempt to reform the land tenure system according to the dictates of *ivoirité*. For their part, the *Forces Nouvelles* act as a de facto government in the territory they control, and profit from trade in cotton and arms, maintaining their own trans-boundary economic networks.

Meanwhile, FESCI lives on, allied to the Young Patriots and the Gbagbo regime. It dominates campus life by controlling access to housing, extorting money and goods, and intimidating students and professors who do not toe the ruling party line. A student organization once devoted to holding government more accountable to youth has become a zealous pro-government force. Those who have tried to form an alternative student organization have been attacked and even killed.

Thus, many youths in Ivory Coast have maneuvered through a complex political environment to establish leadership positions and sources of income for themselves in an arrangement that suits the needs and desires of the ruling political class. Others have abandoned the state structure entirely through rebellion. The country has a long history of student activism, but whereas student leaders used to graduate and move on to senior posts in government or the private sector, students more recently have constructed entirely new spaces to occupy—quite literally, in the case of the *Forces Nouvelles*.

While the ruling party and its youth enforcers are unquestionably linked, it is no longer plain that the power of the youth militias depends on patronage from the state. Political elites may be just as much hostage to the desires of the militia leaders as the other way around. Youth violence features in the case of Ivory Coast primarily as a tool married to youth leaders' own political and economic agendas. The latest peace agreement, under which Soro will serve as prime minister, offers hope of reuniting the country. But until now the country has been in a stalemate in part because the impasse benefits old and young elites in both sectors of the country, despite the fact that Ivory Coast as a whole is growing poorer.

Appeals to a Higher Power

Elsewhere in Africa, increasingly influential transnational religious movements, both Christian and Muslim, are largely fueled by African youth's enthusiastic response to alternative paths to empowerment. Faith can provide surrogate social structures and supports for those who have been through traumatic experiences and have lost other moorings. In some cases, it can also provide a form of education, which may not be available from any other source. Religious movements offer prescriptions for how to improve one's life and transform society, and in Africa today, these prescriptions have explicit political significance.

Many of Africa's youth are caught in a Peter Pan scenario gone terribly wrong. Try as they might, they cannot seem to become adults.

Revivalist Christian movements are thriving in much of Africa. From Malawi to Ghana, Pentecostal churches are encouraging youths to reject the "old ways" that led to poverty and despair and to embrace a faith that promises social networking opportunities, promotes links to fellow worshippers around the world, uses mass media to impressive effect, and embraces the quest for prosperity. The renewal inherent in being "born again" also speaks to the desire for an alternative to the status quo. Prominent figures within these churches can be very young themselves, exemplifying how African youth can attain respect and prominence despite the limited opportunities they may be confronted with. Moreover, unlike university-based movements, religious youth movements are accessible to non-elites.

These religious networks are not divorced from politics. A recent survey by the Pew Forum on Religion and Public Life found that 83 percent of renewalists in Kenya and 75 percent in Nigeria believe that religious groups should express views on social and political questions. And they have put this belief into action—for example, when Christians organized to help defeat a referendum on a new constitution in Kenya in 2005.

At the same time, Muslim youths may find in an Islamic revival movement a vehicle for their rejection of the status quo and desire for an alternative. In a 2005 article in the *Journal of the Royal Anthropological Institute,* Adeline Masquelier described how unemployed young men in Niger embrace a Muslim movement that condemns extravagant customs surrounding marriage (a helpful point that brings the prospect of marriage closer to their modest reach). Foreign Muslim clerics, often from Pakistan or the Middle East, have established a notable presence in the Sahel, drawing in young people to be educated in an ideology that advocates enforcing Islamic law and abandoning the secular state.

Longstanding local movements may move in new directions as young members try to effect radical change, sometimes taking cues from abroad, as with the Al Sunna Wal Jamma group of students in Nigeria that staged attacks in several northern towns in 2004. They claimed to be inspired by Afghanistan's Taliban, and apparently wished to create an Islamic state. In countries where both Christian and Muslim movements are operating, tension is inevitable. It comes as no surprise, for example, that youth have been primary players in the religiously charged communal conflicts that have plagued Nigeria in recent years.

What Next?

People interested in Africa's future ought to concern themselves not just with potential conflict, but also potential political change. Youth populations are at the heart of these possibilities. There is a strong temptation to write off a "lost generation" in the most battle-scarred, traumatized countries, but there is no avoiding the fact that those currently holding power will not be able to wield it forever. Even those who aim to cope with vast, dissatisfied youth populations by pressing young people into the service of the ruling elite may find that, in time, their youthful foot soldiers cease to answer to their elders. Today's young people will, sooner or later, play a dominant role in society.

For policy makers, job creation clearly must be an urgent priority. A focus on educating and socializing children so that they are prepared to play a positive civic role should be another priority, particularly since so many African countries are still at an early phase of their demographic transition. In addition, by understanding youth as political actors rather than simply drivers of conflict, policy makers can aim to manage the challenge to existing orders posed by youth rather than, unrealistically, try to avoid it entirely. A viable way forward involves a thorough understanding of the various youth dynamics on the ground, and also involves a serious effort to give youth the tools, opportunities, and political space in which to pursue their interests and aspirations.

More needs to be done to shed light on how specific variables affect the capacity of youth movements to engage, reshape, and even strengthen the state. What can be done to give Africa's young people reason to believe in governing institutions or to trust that peaceful civic action can effectively address their grievances? How might a closing of the digital divide empower African youth to form new networks for change? The answers will undoubtedly vary from country to country, but the significance of the questions, and the importance of youth political engagement, will remain constant for quite some time to come.

MICHELLE GAVIN is an international affairs fellow at the Council on Foreign Relations.

Still Hungry

One Eighth of the World's People Do Not Have Enough to Eat

PER PINSTRUP-ANDERSON AND FUZHI CHENG

During the 30 minutes it will take you to read this article, 360 preschool children will die of hunger and malnutrition. Twelve a minute, around the clock; more than six million a year. But that is only the tip of the proverbial and ugly iceberg. One in four preschoolers in developing countries suffers from hunger and nutritional deficiencies. These children do not grow to their full potential, they have little resistance to disease, they learn less in school and they earn less as adults. Because of low birth weight, they are handicapped from the moment they enter the world.

More than 800 million people—two and a half times the population of the U.S.—live every day with hunger, or "food insecurity," as it is often called, as their constant companion. Many more have micronutrient deficiencies: they do not get essential vitamins or minerals in their diets. Insufficient iron, and the anemia that comes with it, is the most widespread of these maladies.

The problem does not stem, as some might think, from insufficient production. The world is awash in food, and more and more people are overeating. The so-called nutrition transition, in which diets change from basic grains and tubers to meat, dairy products and processed foods high in sugar and fat, is in full force in developing countries, bringing with it a dual nutritional problem of deficiencies and hunger in some households and obesity and related diseases in others. Technological advances in agriculture mean more food is grown at lower cost than ever before. Globalization, improved communication and efficient transport have facilitated the movement of food over long distances at reasonable rates. In fact, enough food is now being produced to meet the energy and protein needs of every person on the planet. Knowledge about nutrition is widely available, and the large humanitarian and economic costs of hunger and malnutrition are well documented—as are the benefits of eliminating these afflictions.

The main reason hunger and nutritional deficiencies persist is poverty; many millions of households simply cannot afford to buy nutritious food or the farming supplies they need to grow enough of their own. And this poverty is sustained by poor access to family planning and reproductive health care and by diseases that spread because of poor sanitation and dirty drinking water, among other factors.

Effective action to reduce hunger must be based on a thorough understanding of who the hungry are, where they are, and exactly why they are malnourished. In the pages that follow, we lay out the best current knowledge on these questions and on the steps that need to be taken to feed the world.

Who Are the Hungry?

Hunger may be long-term, or it may be transitory. Long-term hunger is pervasive among people caught in the trap of poverty. Although not all poor people are hungry, almost all hungry people are poor. The great majority—75 percent—of the chronically underfed live in rural areas of developing countries. They are landless, frequently unemployed or employed at very low wages. Or they are farmers with small land holdings and limited access to other assets, credit and agricultural necessities such as fertilizers and crop protection. They live in households headed by women with little wage-earning capacity or in households in which the adults suffer from illnesses such as HIV/AIDS. They are orphans and other individuals without families. They are usually invisible to decision makers in the societies where they reside, and the term "silent hunger" describes their condition poignantly.

Transitory hunger caused by natural or human-made disasters such as droughts, floods, earthquakes, conflicts or bad policies tends not to be silent. Most of us have seen haunting images of the starvation that occurs during such famines. And the world has demonstrated its generosity in helping the victims of transitory hunger, although they represent only a small part—roughly 10 percent—of the world's hungry. Like the chronically hungry, they are usually found in rural areas, primarily in Africa and Asia. These rural populations depend almost exclusively on agriculture; they have very few alternative sources of income, and they are therefore very vulnerable to shocks of nature. Although natural disasters continue to undermine people's food security in various regions of the world, hunger hot spots in recent years have switched to areas affected by human-induced devastation. Between 1992 and 2003, armed conflicts and economic problems accounted for more than 35 percent of food emergencies, compared with around 15 percent between 1986 and 1991.

Hunger and malnutrition affect two groups of people dispro-portionately. The first is preschool children: some 146 million are underweight because of chronic or acute hunger. This means that 18 percent of all hungry people are children younger than five years. Child hunger is frequently passed on from mothers who themselves are malnourished; about 20 million children are born underweight annually. Undernourished youngsters are less motivated to play and study, and many fail to get even the most rudimentary education. Millions leave school prema-turely. Chronic hunger also delays or stops physical and mental growth. Most tragically, infectious diseases such as measles or whooping cough can kill undernourished children more readily than well-fed ones.

Hunger, Unbalanced energy intake and vitamin and mineral deficiency account for more than half the world's disease burden.

—Food and Agriculture Organization (FAO)
of the United Nations

Women and girls are also more likely to be victims of hunger: more than 60 percent of the world's hungry are female. Although women are by and large the main producers of food through-out the world, social structures and traditions often mean that they get less to eat than men do. For example, whereas around 25 percent of men in developing countries have anemia caused by a lack of iron, 45 percent of women in the same regions are affected. Every day 300 women die during childbirth because of iron deficiency.

Where Are They?

The Food and Agriculture Organization (FAO) of the United Nations estimates that an annual average of 854 million people were undernourished over the period from 2001 through 2003: 820 million in developing countries, 25 million in transition countries (such as the former members of the Soviet Union) and nine million in industrial countries. A disproportionate share of the poorest and most food-insecure people live in Africa, although the Asia-Pacific region has the largest absolute number of chronically undernourished residents. The develop-ing countries as a group did see declines between the periods of 1990–1992 and 2001–2003, but the numbers rose by eight million in South Asia (which includes India) and by 37 million in sub-Saharan Africa.

Recent statistics show that in developing countries, 27 percent of children younger than five are underweight and 31 percent are stunted. In several large South Asian countries (India and Bangladesh among them), both underweight and stunting rates are well above those in the region as a whole and much higher than those in Africa. Undernutrition in children is the worst in Asia in terms of absolute numbers, but because the Asian region is doing well at an aggregate level, chances are that these high

undernutrition rates will escape the attention of governments and relief organizations unless special efforts are made to high-light this issue.

Why Are They Hungry?

Hunger can have many causes. As noted, insufficient food pro-duction on the global scale is not one of them. The world as a whole produces more than enough food to feed all the hungry; it is the unequal distribution of food among and within countries that has led to the world hunger problem.

Unequal distribution has its deep root in poverty: in times of food shortages, the poor country simply cannot buy enough food in the world markets, and even when food is available inside the country, the poorest of its citizens are often unable to pay for it. Poverty also limits the production of food in impoverished areas, because the destitute lack the resources to invest in agriculture.

The natural disasters such as floods, storms and drought that are the primary causes of transitory or acute hunger have increased over the past decade, and the consequences for poor countries have been severe. Drought is now the leading cause of famine throughout the world. Episodes of drought in 2004 led to heavy losses of livestock and crops in parts of Kenya, Uganda, Somalia, Eritrea and Ethiopia. In many countries, deforestation, salinization, and poor farming practices such as overcropping and overgrazing are exacerbating the natural disasters.

Food crises that can be attributed to human-induced causes have also increased in recent years. Armed conflicts in Asia, Africa and Latin America uproot millions of people and pre-cipitate some of the world's most serious hunger emergencies. Escalating conflict in the Darfur region of Sudan in 2004 drove a million people from their homes and led to a major food crisis, despite the fact that the area had enjoyed relatively good grow-ing conditions. In the 1990s, as fighting swept through Central Africa, the prevalence of hungry people rose from 36 to 56 per-cent, whereas the termination of armed conflict in Mozambique brought rapid economic growth and reduced poverty. More peaceful parts of Africa, such as Ghana, have seen decreasing levels of malnutrition.

HIV/AIDS exacerbates the plague of hunger. At the house-hold level, the disease has caused food insecurity by leaving millions of children without providers, depleting assets, increas-ing medical expenses, and diverting resources from sustainable investments. At the national level, it has reduced the ability of countries to prevent and mitigate food emergencies by taking the lives of crucial producers and professionals in different sectors of the economy. The negative effects of the pandemic are reinforced by other crises—poverty, fighting, misuse of resources, and climate stress, which together create a vicious cycle of malnutrition and disease.

What Can Be Done?

The nations of the world have not ignored hunger, but despite nice rhetoric and promises, their efforts have fallen short. At the 1996 World Food Summit political leaders from virtually

Where Are the Underweight Children?

Total (in millions)	146
India	57
Bangladesh	8
Pakistan	8
China	7
Nigeria	6
Ethiopia	6
Indonesia	6
Rest of world	48

Where Are the Low-Birth-Weight Babies Born?

Total (in millions)	20.3
South Asia	11.4
Sub-Saharan Africa	4.0
Asia	2.0
West Asia/North Africa	1.4
Latin America/Caribbean	1.1
Eastern Europe/former U.S.S.R.	0.4

The Perils of Childhood Malnutrition

- Malnutrition plays a role in more than half the annual 12 million deaths of children younger than five.
- Every year up to 500,000 children become partially or totally blind because of vitamin A deficiency.
- Iodine deficiency is the single most important cause of preventable brain damage in children.

—FAO

every country agreed to reduce the number of hungry people by half, from roughly 800 million to about 400 million, over the 25-year period from 1990 to 2015. The same countries met five years later to take stock of progress. Although some, such as China, had made strides toward achieving the target, over half the countries, mainly in sub-Saharan Africa, had *more* hungry people, and at the global level the total number had not changed significantly. The leaders renewed their promise to halve the number of hungry people, but developments since then indicate that they have taken very little new action.

A different group, the Millennium Summit, reaffirmed the target in 2000, albeit as the easier goal of halving the *proportion,* rather than the absolute number, of people who are hungry. Although East and Southeast Asia and Latin America are likely to reach this goal, it will not be attained globally. Between 800 million and 900 million of the world's citizens will still be hungry in 2015.

Implementing rapid economic growth for poor people is the backbone of any strategy to eliminate hunger and malnutrition. The specific policies that will be most fruitful will vary according to local and national circumstances. But, as we will demonstrate below, they definitely include programs supporting rural development, with an emphasis on agriculture, as well as basic education and health services, and good governance.

Because 75 percent of the world's poor live in rural areas, the most crucial component may well be agricultural and rural development. According to the FAO, in all the countries on track to reach the Millennium Development Goal, increases in income in the agricultural sector are significantly better than average. Yet many developing countries ignore this observation and continue to give priority to urban development. The bias against agriculture deters investment in infrastructure such as roads, warehouses and irrigation that would benefit farmers.

The promise of agricultural development was demonstrated many years ago in South Korea, Taiwan, India and several other Asian countries during the so-called green revolution. In the 1960s and 1970s innovations put in place by the Consultative Group on International Agricultural Research and collaborating national institutions culminated in dramatic increases in rice and wheat yields, decreased costs of production, lower food prices, higher incomes for small farmers and, ultimately, avoidance of an impending hunger catastrophe.

Among the policies directed at agriculture that are needed to pull the farmers of developing countries out of poverty are ones ensuring secure access to land and to technologies such as fertilizers, improved seed and better protection of plants against pests. Investments in rural infrastructure—roads, electrification, storage facilities and irrigation—are also essential. So are the availability of credit and savings institutions. Because well-functioning markets for selling produce and buying consumer goods will be crucial, governments must ensure that markets are not biased against small farmers, less favored areas (those with irregular rainfall and fragile soils, for example) and poor consumers. Brazil's efforts under President Luiz Inácio Lula da Silva to give land to poor rural people is an illustration of a successful, albeit limited program. In China, promotion of small-scale rural enterprises providing goods and services for farm families, as well as rural-based agro-industries (such as food processing), which create employment and add value to agricultural produce, have played a major role in reducing poverty and hunger.

Many antipoverty policies—particularly those promoting health and education—will benefit both the urban as well as the rural poor, which is important because urban destitution is on the rise. Past experience indicates that the most successful measures focus on fighting widespread micronutrient deficiencies, reducing food contamination and food-borne illnesses, and providing universal primary education for girls and boys.

What's Working in Bangladesh Fighting Hunger on Several Fronts

Once oppressed by famine and dependent on food imports, Bangladesh now not only produces almost all its own rice but also exports agricultural products, and its gross domestic product is growing. As Gordon West, formerly of the United States Agency for International Development, has pointed out, this turnaround resulted from several smart interventions.

The ability to grow rice during the dry season drove much of this transition. At one time, most rice production in the nation depended on monsoon rains. Then public research institutions developed and released rice varieties that grow abundantly in cooler weather and that require fewer daily hours of sunlight. By 2002, about half of the country's rice crop was being produced in the dry months.

Another important prod to change was government institution of a more flexible import policy. As a result, private traders began bringing food in at times when the nation did not produce enough for itself. The government also gave more attention to targeting food distribution to the impoverished. For example, a food-for-education program was begun that gives food to poor families when their children attend school instead of working. In addition to improving nutrition, this program has allowed youngsters to reach higher levels in school.

Foreign development agencies helped as well: they financed the construction and repair of roads, creating jobs and improving year-round access not only to markets but to basic services. Other agencies—notably CARE and World Vision—gave jobs to men and women in the most food-insecure areas of the country. In addition to building environmentally sound, all-season roads, participants plant trees to prevent soil erosion, and poor women find further employment in caring for the trees. In a similar vein, the United Nation's World Food Program paid people with food when they worked to restore important community resources such as roads, ponds supporting fish, and embankments that provided protection from floods.

Although the changes that occurred in Bangladesh are impressive, huge challenges remain. Rates of malnutrition continue to be among the highest in the world. Because the diets of many Bangladeshis are deficient in essential fats, minerals and vitamins, an important next step for the country will be making products such as wheat, fruit, milk, legumes and meat more widely available.

—The Editors

What's Working in Mexico Paying People to Attend Schools and Clinics

Two decades ago rising poverty in Mexico meant that almost one out of three people did not have enough to eat. Poor nutrition leads to bad health, which slows down learning capacity, which breeds poverty, which leads back to poor nutrition. So, in an example of a program that has worked well, the government introduced an innovative plan. Instead of subsidizing tortillas—which it had been doing and which provided only temporary relief from hunger—the government began paying women directly if they took certain actions.

Called PROGRESA (renamed Oportunidades), the program gives monthly cash payments—of up to about U.S. $61—for each child in grades three through nine who attends school, and awards higher amounts for those in higher grades and for girls. Each family also receives monthly food transfers worth roughly $14 if family members, especially mothers and children, make a specified number of clinic visits annually.

Perhaps the most unusual feature of the program is its channeling of funds to women. This economic power could give women a larger voice in decision making within households, which could potentially focus more of the family's resources on nutrition and education.

The plan's achievements already reflect improvements in both these areas. Participating families saw a 16 percent increase in the annual growth rate of children one to three years old and an almost 25 percent reduction in illness among children younger than five. Secondary school enrollment rose from 67 to 75 percent for girls and from 73 to 78 percent for boys, forecasting hope for even greater improvements as a better educated generation starts its own families.

—The Editors

health care in forms compatible with local cultures are also key pieces of the solution. Examples of successful programs include PROGRESA, which has improved access to education, health care, clean water, safe sanitation and child care in Mexico, and the Food for Education Program, which has increased school attendance and reduced hunger among children in Bangladesh [*see boxes above*].

Technological developments in the biological sciences, energy and communications offer new opportunities that could benefit poor people and thus ease hunger. For instance, in China and India, government approval of the genetically modified cottonseed Bt cotton, whose plants are resistant to the attack of certain insects such as the cotton bollworm, has resulted in major economic gains for millions of small farmers. Public investment in research and technology is needed to develop other innovations, and farmers and consumers should participate in setting priorities for this research.

Policies and behavioral changes that encourage gender equality in decision making and in sharing resources are extremely valuable because women are a critical link in the well-being of households. Family-planning counseling and reproductive

Good governance, including the rule of law, transparency, absence of corruption, conflict prevention and resolution, sound public administration, and respect and protection for human rights, is of critical importance to assure sustainable food security. Zimbabwe, which over a short period moved from being a food-secure country to one with widespread hunger, demonstrates what can happen in the absence of good governance. Although national governments bear the primary responsibility, civil society, as represented by local community-based groups and NGOs (nongovernmental organizations), can also assist low-income people.

Internationally, policies and institutions need to do more to guide globalization for the benefit of the poor. Industrial countries should accelerate opening their markets, and the World Trade Organization should work closely with civil society and national governments to remove barriers that hinder the movement of laborers across borders, distort prices, impose unfair intellectual-property rights, and choke competition. The U.S., the European Union and Japan have erected trade barriers against imports of food and agricultural commodities produced by poor farmers in developing countries. At the same time, they pressure developing countries to open up their markets for the products of industrial nations, including highly subsidized agricultural commodities. These practices are worse than hypocritical; they actively hinder efforts to reduce hunger.

Development assistance should be increased from the current 0.3 percent of national incomes of donor countries to the 0.7 percent the rich countries have repeatedly pledged to give since first adopting this commitment in a U.N. resolution in 1970. Ongoing negotiations for debt relief for low-income developing countries should be accelerated.

Winning the fight against hunger would not only benefit those who are hungry. We would all gain. Hungry people make poor trading partners, and they contribute to instability across nations. Even in a hypothetical world governed by purely selfish people who have plenty to eat, eradicating hunger would be a good idea. The world has the resources and the knowledge to win the fight. We have not yet shown that we have the will.

For Further Information

Consultative Group on International Agricultural Research, an alliance of agricultural centers and other organizations that mobilize science to help the poor: www.cgiar.org

Food and Agriculture Organization of the United Nations: www.fao.org

International Food Policy Research Institute: www.ifpri.org

PER PINSTRUP-ANDERSEN is H. E. Babcock Professor of Food, Nutrition, and Public Policy and J. Thomas Clark Professor of Entrepreneurship at Cornell University; professor of agricultural economics at the University of Copenhagen; and World Food Prize Laureate 2001. **FUZHI CHENG** is a postdoctoral fellow at Cornell University.

Pandemic Pandemonium

Josh N. Ruxin

Pandemic. The word can spread fear to billions overnight. One of the few public-health terms that gives Hollywood nightmare plotlines. Literally meaning "all people," a pandemic is an extraordinary global health event in which an epidemic of infectious disease spreads across regions and, potentially, the entire planet. Ebola, avian flu, SARS—each had the potential to spread rapidly and each received extraordinary attention during the past several years. Though they did not result in mass casualties, all wrought worldwide fear.

Throughout the course of human history, pandemics have wreaked havoc. The 1918 flu pandemic may have killed over 20 million people. Even then, 50 percent of the mortality difference among countries can be attributed to a single factor: per capita income. Thus, the poorest country hit, India, suffered the most, while Denmark suffered the least. That differential, however, has not yet made for compelling public policy. After all, science made landmark breakthroughs in the twentieth century, often applying scientific insights from previous centuries in innovative ways to control and, in the case of smallpox, eradicate disease. But in the days of porous borders and unprecedented global travel, viruses and other pathogens may once again have the upper hand. One key question on the table is: will the next pandemic be worse than the ones we currently face?

Viewed from where I live in Rwanda, it's clear that the sheer neglect of health of poor people has set an ideal foundation for pandemics to spread for years under the radar, evade surveillance and, as has been the case with HIV/AIDS, enter our airspace and bodies at a startling rate. The history of global health demonstrates that wealthy nations respond best to dramatic, fast-moving outbreaks like Ebola or avian flu. Unfortunately, today wealthy and poor nations alike face pandemics that move slowly and don't necessarily show symptoms during the first few years of infection.

Today's pandemics have evolved to prey on our greatest weakness: our inability to wage sustained fights against pressing health issues. This creates a doubly challenging situation in a world where disease is often socioeconomically stratified. Rich people don't generally get sick from malaria or tuberculosis (TB), so those diseases—which kill millions each year—have until very recently received far-less attention than they deserve. But now the line between rich and poor countries, and rich and poor people within countries, is murky. Dangerous infections such as drug-resistant tuberculosis can cross the globe by air in a matter of hours. These are the new, rapidly moving vectors of disease, and they provide a direct line of transmission between the most-vulnerable and least-healthy people on the planet and the wealthiest and healthiest. It augurs for the worst that health systems for the poor have failed miserably to generate the quality and accountability needed to address even the most-basic health needs.

What happens when a poor country loses 30 percent of its adult population to AIDS or to a flu epidemic? There are plenty of military models that assess decision making when a country is attacked by an enemy, but few models to assess the chaos that cuts across all segments of society when it's a disease that acts as antagonist. Plans have also not fully taken into account the impact of rapidly changing demographics on disease spread. The poorest, precisely those most at risk, are reproducing the fastest, so the chance of pandemic is growing faster than the numbers may superficially reveal. And of course, the prevalence of megacities means more poor people are living in close proximity to each other—and with greater opportunity for disease transmission.

Leaders of poor countries appear to be completely unaware of the global connections between the health of their populations and the security and stability required to ensure that they do not fall prey to unforeseen health catastrophes. The dearth of strong and transparent leadership among the world's poorest nations augurs poorly for the health of those nations, and of the world.

Meanwhile, the rich countries also continue to think about pandemics in a very linear and scientific way, which fails to account for the comprehensive economic and political chaos that would accompany a major pandemic. The World Health Organization (WHO), Centers for Disease Control, and, for that matter, the Gates Foundation and other donors, are concentrating their efforts on vaccines and, in the case of the WHO, antiviral stockpiles for a possible outbreak of avian flu. Plans are also being developed for isolation and quarantine, running through scenarios for stopping air traffic and the like. Unfortunately, it's unlikely that the pathogens will be as responsive to our efforts as we hope they will be, leading to widespread chaos, morbidity and mortality.

At a time when oil shocks have the ability to globally increase food insecurity, it may be worthwhile to consider how a pandemic could push people living on the edge into poverty and starvation. With food production suffering greatly, the urban centers that are dependent on daily imports of food could rapidly fall victim. If this sounds a bit like Jared Diamond's arguments in *Collapse,* it's intentional. The world is interconnected, but poor countries are hanging by a thread, and it's a thread that could quickly break if a pandemic hits hard enough.

Poor countries are hanging by a thread, and it's a thread that could quickly break if a pandemic hits hard enough.

Adding to the threat, it may well be that the worst pandemics on the planet are not emerging, but have simply been with us so long that we've grown accustomed to their presence and therefore have done little to address them. Women across sub-Saharan Africa continue to stand a 1 percent chance of dying in childbirth—is that a pandemic? Five hundred thousand kids die from measles every year. Africans suffer from an astonishing estimated 300 million episodes of malaria annually, with a death toll of one million. And now throughout the developing world silent killers like heart disease and diabetes are taking hold.

In the best of cases, pursuing a business-as-usual approach, the wealthy countries may get lucky: the spread of contagion may be stopped at borders and when it crosses, advanced, expensive treatment may be available. But no matter what, the economic and potential political destabilization that would result would cross these borders and be felt in everyone's bank accounts. The moral implications of continuing to adopt a merely defensive stance will guarantee that developing countries will suffer millions dead and may also cultivate the pathogens for future pandemics that will evade the best weapons the richer countries can throw at them.

Some might see the call for health improvement in poor nations in order to save our own skins as either a Machiavellian ploy to help poor people or a sad and ironic commentary on the state of humankind. Whatever the case, rich nations must begin taking health systems for the poor seriously because: new bugs and the resurgence of old ones are likely to emerge where people are sickest or treatment is inconsistent; when pandemics strike, they'll do the most harm to those without health services; and when sicknesses like a new strain of influenza inevitably come, the health personnel in these settings will be much-better equipped to identify and contain them.

If they don't, Hollywood fantasies may well come true; America and Western Europe will panic as they hear of outbreaks far away (and which may well reach inside their borders); Asia, a likely epicenter of a new flu outbreak or other zoonotically spread disease, will see its services strained and its globalizing economies wrecked; and Africa will see its people die in higher rates than everywhere else while its nascent economic connections to the rest of the world stumble. This scenario is, sadly, hardly far-fetched. The SARS epidemic alone cost Asian countries more than $16 billion and spread panic worldwide while claiming fewer than one thousand lives. That experience suggests that estimating the toll of an actual pandemic is virtually incalculable.

The Threats
AIDS

For the past decade, AIDS has garnered attention not only because of its clinical impact, but also because of its downstream effects. South African businesspeople report that they have to hire one additional worker for every manager hired because they expect so much of their workforce to die of AIDS. Social services and even traditional societal mechanisms for handling orphans are disintegrating in despair as the wave of millions of orphans builds.

More than a decade after numerous news media outlets optimistically queried whether we had reached the end of AIDS, there are troubling signs that this pandemic may yet prove to be the world's top infectious killer. The World Bank has estimated that for every six new infections, only one person is put on life-saving anti-retrovirals (ARVs). This means the disease continues to spread virtually unchecked. With 40 million infected, in all likelihood we'll continue to see 3 to 5 million people dying annually for years to come. Undeniably, AIDS has hit hardest in sub-Saharan Africa, where nearly 23 million are infected. At current rates of drug rollout, all but a couple million of them will die during the next ten years. The ramifications for each of those deaths are hidden by the numbers: for each death, roughly another six people are immediately affected emotionally and economically. Seen through this lens, nearly one-third of sub-Saharan Africa is already likely to be impacted by the current pandemic.

AIDS presents a perfect case for why all health must be global. It is not simply a philanthropic service to ensure that basic health needs are met worldwide: it's a biological necessity. AIDS may well have been around for the better part of the last century, but it went largely undetected because it was prevalent among populations with minimal access to health care. By the time it reached people with health care, it had spread across the planet, causing an estimated 25 million deaths to date.

The numbers will get worse. In the developing world there may be little data on resistance, but with more treated people, coupled with inconsistent treatments and fewer treatment options, it is likely that drug resistance will emerge as a major problem. The solutions do remain well within the grasp of our current abilities. Good surveillance and improved monitoring for patients on ARVs in developing countries will lessen the possibility of treatment failure and corresponding resistance. Expanded treatment programs that include better monitoring and access to more than first-line therapy ensure that when treatment does fail, patients have other options. This will ensure that they do not become vessels for advanced strains of the disease. But without action, strains of HIV which can tolerate even the most-sophisticated and most-expensive drug regimens available may well emerge and move around the world just as the first strains did. Thus, AIDS in the West could prove to be the definitive killer that it once was, yet again.

Malaria

Malaria, though hardly as expensive as AIDS to address, has joined the ranks of diseases being tackled on a grand scale. The Global Fund has committed $3.1 billion to the malaria fight, and the United States has launched a bold new malaria initiative. Through the use of insecticide-treated bed nets and new drug therapy, several countries have realized steep declines in malaria morbidity and mortality, one among them Rwanda. In 2000, Rwanda saw an estimated one million cases of malaria. Today, thanks in large part to bed nets, that figure has fallen by more than 60 percent. In 2000, an astonishing 10 percent of all children under five succumbed to malaria; today, those deaths have virtually disappeared. For the first time in decades, serious debate and action is emerging to eradicate or diminish the disease. Bill and Melinda Gates have set the world's sights on complete malaria eradication, a feat that will require massive breakthroughs in technology.

However, this is one fight that must be taken to the far reaches of the earth and be resolutely committed to a sustained effort. Today it is widely hypothesized that the extraordinary illness seen from malaria resulted from the failure to continue pushing the disease back with DDT in the 1960s. Instead, after some notable successes, efforts evaporated, individuals and populations lost their natural immunity, and the disease came back with a vengeance. Anything less than persistent, wholesale control and elimination efforts risks exacerbation of the disease. In the worst-case scenario, malaria could be eliminated from much of the African continent, be maintained at low levels in a few places, develop resistance to the best drugs available, and then see efforts to contain it wane. What would follow would be devastating for the continent. Malaria would return to populations lacking any natural immunity, drugs could prove ineffective, and millions of lives would potentially be lost—every year—particularly among very young children.

Tuberculosis

Tuberculosis has plagued humankind since the fourth millennia BCE. While the disease only recently ceased to be a significant public-health threat in the developed world, TB still claims five thousand lives globally every day, more than SARS, Marburg and avian flu ever have. Nine million people develop active TB each year. Although curative treatment has been around for the last several decades, it has been unevenly applied: in many cases health facilities have not ensured that patients receive a full course of treatment, and, overall, those most in need of treatment have not received it at all. Poor treatment has resulted in fiercer, more-resistant strains of TB. Three percent of all newly diagnosed patients have multi-drug-resistant TB (MDR-TB), making their treatment complicated, expensive and uncertain. In September 2006, the WHO announced a further worsening of the MDR-TB pandemic with multiple reports in all regions of the world of the emergence of extensively resistant strains of TB (XDR-TB) immune to virtually all drugs.

It should not shock Americans that this disease is making its way across the globe when every location is just a plane ride away. Yet the growth of XDR-TB, considered virtually untreatable, has gone largely unnoticed in the United States, where there have been only seventeen cases since 2000. In sub-Saharan Africa, where roughly 23 million people are HIV positive, nearly half will develop TB. If treatment is not well administered, these cases will lead to new strains of resistant TB. There is a direct connection between the AIDS pandemic, TB, and the failure of health systems to appropriately diagnose and treat these diseases. However, unlike AIDS, whose transmission relies on behavior (unsafe sex, intravenous-drug usage), TB is airborne. While the immuno-compromised and malnourished are at greater risk for developing active TB, the main risk factor for contracting it is shared by all: breathing. Those in the developed world have every reason to fear for their immunity.

Influenza

The flu may be the world's greatest risk. Recent models based on the 1918 Spanish flu have estimated that the next outbreak will cause between 51 and 157 million excess deaths, with 95 percent of those occurring in developing countries. Critics have suggested that it's overly optimistic to conclude the carnage will be so low in developed nations. Other estimates conclude that total excess deaths could exceed 300 million with 27 million occurring in rich nations and the large remainder in poor. Without sufficient health-care facilities in developing countries—in both urban and rural locations—the higher death estimates will undoubtedly be realized, as a virulent flu spreads easily and rapidly through the air. Whatever the case, a particularly vicious strain of the flu would undoubtedly be the greatest public-health catastrophe of our time.

So what precisely is at the root of the massive inequities that provide the petri dish for global pandemics? Is it simply disease burden? Transmission routes? Poverty? Corruption and poor governance? Selfishness on a grand scale? All of the above?

At the turn of the twenty-first century, the blame for the burden was placed squarely on wealthy countries. The failure to roll out simple solutions required exponential increases in funding and new initiatives—ironically fueled by one of the most-complex diseases ever faced, AIDS. Drugs and big pharmaceuticals were the scapegoats of the last several years; today, experts cite the lack of nurses and human resources. There is a predictable oscillation in the blame game, but one fact is clear: health worldwide has deteriorated.

This is perhaps most troubling in the context of pandemics because just as environmental catastrophes can spur epidemics, and potentially pandemics, pandemics can quickly take down economies and, potentially, countries. In the wake of avian flu, Southeast Asian economies experienced an enormous economic downturn; tourists have been writing me and asking whether it's safe to go to Brazil in light of the dengue epidemic; the economic, social and political cost of AIDS in sub-Saharan Africa remains to be calculated. Thus, there is a vicious cycle: pandemics can encourage chaos and breakdowns of basic systems, particularly in the poorest and poorly governed nations, and these breakdowns can in turn create better conditions for more disease to emerge. Case in point: during the chaos in Kenya at the turn of this year, 60 percent of patients on antiretroviral therapy and 35 percent of patients on TB drugs were lost to follow-up. It is likely that all those patients stopped their treatment midcourse and are now potentially cultivating resistant strains of both infections.

Policy makers are looking at the direct health consequences of pandemics (Who is sick? How do we treat them?) rather than the indirect health consequences (What other services will fail? What will happen to the food supply?). Had SARS hit anywhere in sub-Saharan Africa, where ventilators and surgical masks are a rare commodity, death rates would have been higher than in Asia. Today the response systems being put in place are to protect the wealthy with vaccines and antivirals, but do not treat those most likely to suffer. Thus, we are preparing for the next pandemic rather than doing everything in our power to prevent it.

Foundations and governments can't seem to get their heads around the fact that no disease can be treated in a vacuum: all efforts must be part of an integrated response, otherwise dollars are sure to be poorly spent. The worst-hit area on the planet for health-systems failure remains sub-Saharan Africa, where governments spend paltry amounts on health, the poor are frequently required to pay for services and there's an uncanny history of serious illnesses evolving. HIV is widely recognized today as having its roots in central Africa; resistant malaria parasites are commonplace; and bizarre outbreaks such as Ebola appear from time to time. When sexually transmitted infections go untreated and open sores ensue, the possibility for transmission increases exponentially, and that transmission doesn't stop at borders.

While epidemics get the press—the recent dengue outbreak in Brazil for example—pandemics tend to quietly work their way through populations, doing enormous harm never garnering the resources or the media attention. That's not to say that rich nations shouldn't be concerned about these epidemics, but there is an uncomfortably consistent trend in global public health to place attention on those subjects and diseases that may not pose the greatest threat to human welfare.

In the next couple of decades, with expanded funding for public health, it will be possible to radically alter the course of the future of human health, particularly in poor countries. However, sticking to traditional approaches will fail to provide macro results and may exacerbate health challenges. The uneven delivery of AIDS medications, tuberculosis drugs and antimalarials, for example, could give rise to resistant parasites, bacteria and viruses capable of beating current technology. Further, the singular focus on just a few diseases and the subspecialization that accompanies it may rob us of the expert diagnosticians who can quickly spot an unusual illness before it gets out of control.

The solution to the frightening scenario of national breakdowns and despair is to beef up efforts to build capacity in the poorest nations to handle their current problems, with an eye to avoiding such chaos. Health systems require serious strengthening. Farmers need improved agricultural techniques to push them away from the brink and toward something resembling stability. Basic infrastructure must be massively expanded and improved. The list is a long one but most everywhere you look, we have scarcely begun. It's time to shake up the public-health establishment and place investments in basic health services for the neglected and poor worldwide.

We need to step up efforts and get it right. The world's health and stability depend on it.

JOSH N. RUXIN is an assistant clinical professor of public health at Columbia University's Mailman School of Public Health. He resides in Rwanda where he directs the Access Project and the Millennium Villages Project Rwanda, and advises Rwanda Community Works.

UNIT 3

The Global Environment and Natural Resources Utilization

Unit Selections

10. **Deflating the World's Bubble Economy,** Lester R. Brown
11. **The Great Leap Backward?,** Elizabeth C. Economy
12. **Water of Life in Peril,** Sharon Palmer
13. **Ocean 'Dead Zones' Spreading Worldwide,** Randolph E. Schmid
14. **Cry of the Wild,** Sharon Begley

Key Points to Consider

- What are the basic environmental challenges that confront both governments and individual consumers?

- Has the international community adequately responded to problems of pollution and threats to our common natural heritage? Why or why not?

- What trends and issues are there in terms of the availability of clean water?

- What is the natural resource picture going to look like 30 years from now?

- How is society, in general, likely to respond to the conflicts between lifestyle and resource conservation?

- The rapid industrialization of China and India has significant impacts beyond their borders. What are some of the environmental impacts?

- Can a sustainable economy be organized, and what changes in behavior and values are necessary to accomplish this?

Student Web Site

www.mhcls.com

Internet References

National Geographic Society
http://www.nationalgeographic.com
National Oceanic and Atmospheric Administration (NOAA)
http://www.noaa.gov
SocioSite: Sociological Subject Areas
http://www.pscw.uva.nl/sociosite/TOPICS/
United Nations Environment Programme (UNEP)
http://www.unep.ch

Beginning in the eighteenth century, the modern nation-state began to emerge, and over many generations, it evolved to the point where it is now difficult to imagine a world without national governments. These legal entities have been viewed as separate, self-contained units that independently pursue their "national interests." Scholars often described the world as a political community of independent units that interact with each other (a concept that has been described as a billiard ball model).

This perspective of the international community as composed of self-contained and self-directed units has undergone major rethinking in the past 35 years. One of the reasons for this is the international consequence of the growing demands being placed on natural resources The Middle East, for example, contains a large majority of the world's known oil reserves. The United States, Western Europe, China, and Japan are very dependent on this vital source of energy. This unbalanced supply and demand equation has created an unprecedented lack of self-sufficiency for the world's major economic powers.

The increased interdependence of countries is further illustrated by the fact that air and water pollution do not respect political boundaries. One country's smoke is often another country's acid rain. The concept that independent political units control their own destiny makes less sense than it may have 100 years ago. In order to better understand why this is so, one must first look at how Earth's natural resources are being utilized and how this may be affecting the global environment.

The initial article in the unit examines the broad dimensions of the uses and abuses of natural resources. The central theme in this article is the unsustainable use of natural resources in essential economic activities such as agriculture. In many regions, an alarming decline in the quality of the natural resource base is taking place.

An important conclusion resulting from this analysis is that contemporary methods of resource utilization often create problems that transcend national boundaries. Global climate changes, for example, will affect everyone, and if these changes are to be successfully addressed, international collaboration will be required. The consequences of basic human activities such as growing and cooking food are profound when multiplied billions of times. A single country or even a few countries working together cannot have a significant impact on redressing these problems. Solutions will have to be conceived that are truly global in scope. Just as there are shortages of natural resources, there are also shortages of new ideas for solving many of these problems.

Unit 3 continues by examining specific case studies that explore in greater detail the issues raised in the first article. Implicit in these discussions is the challenge of moving from

© Dr. Parvinder Sethi

the perspective of the environment as primarily an economic resource to be consumed to a perspective that has been defined as "sustainable development." This change is easily called for, but in fact, it goes to the core of social values and basic economic activities. Developing sustainable practices, therefore, is a challenge of unprecedented magnitude.

Nature is not some object "out there" to be visited at a national park. It is the food we eat and the energy we consume. Human beings are joined in the most intimate of relationships with the natural world in order to survive from one day to the next. It is ironic how little time is spent thinking about this relationship. This lack of attention, however, is not likely to continue, for rapidly growing numbers of people and the increased use of energy-consuming technologies are placing unprecedented pressures on Earth's carrying capacity.

Deflating the World's Bubble Economy

Unless the damaging trends that have been set in motion are reversed quickly, we could see vast numbers of environmental refugees abandoning areas scarred by depleted aquifers and exhausted soils. . . .

LESTER R. BROWN

Throughout history, humans have lived on the Earth's sustainable yield—the interest from its natural endowment. Now, however, we are consuming the endowment itself. In ecology, as in economics, we can consume principal along with interest in the short run, but, for the long term, that practice leads to bankruptcy. By satisfying our excessive demands through overconsumption of the Earth's natural assets, we are in effect creating a global bubble economy. Bubble economies are not new. American investors got an up-close view of this when the bubble in high-tech stocks burst in 2000, and the Nasdaq, an indicator of the value of these stocks, declined by some 75%. Japan had a similar experience in 1989 when its real estate bubble collapsed, depreciating assets by 60%. The Japanese economy has been reeling ever since.

These two events primarily affected those living in the U.S. and Japan, but the global bubble economy that is based on the overconsumption of the Earth's natural capital will affect the entire planet. The trouble is, since Sept. 11, 2001, political leaders, diplomats, and the media have been preoccupied with terrorism and, more recently, the conflict in Iraq. These certainly are matters of concern, but if they divert us from addressing the environmental trends that are undermining our future, Osama bin Laden and his followers will have achieved their goal of disrupting our way of life in a way they could not have imagined.

Of all the sectors affected by the bubble economy, food may be the most vulnerable. Today's farmers are dealing with major new challenges: their crops must endure the highest temperatures in 11,000 years as well as widespread aquifer depletion and the resulting loss of irrigation water unknown to previous generations. The average global temperature has risen in each of the last three decades. The 16 warmest years since record-keeping began in 1880 have occurred since 1980. With the three warmest years on record—1998, 2001, and 2002—coming in the last five years, crops are facing unprecedented heat stress. Higher temperatures reduce yields through their effect on photosynthesis, moisture balance, and fertilization. As the temperature rises above 34° Celsius (94° Fahrenheit), evaporation increases and photosynthesis and fertilization are impeded. Scientists at the International Rice Research Institute in the Philippines and at the U.S. Department of Agriculture together have developed a rule of thumb that each 1° Celsius rise in temperature above the optimum during the growing season reduces grain yields by 10%.

Findings indicate that if the temperature reaches the lower end of the range projected by the Intergovernmental Panel on Climate Change, grain harvests in tropical regions could be reduced by an average of five percent by 2020 and 11% by 2050. At the upper end of the range, yields could drop 11% by 2020 and 46% by 2050. Avoiding these declines will be difficult unless scientists can develop crop strains that are not vulnerable to thermal stress.

The second challenge facing farmers—falling water tables—also is a recent phenomenon. Using traditional animal- or human-powered waterlifting devices, it was virtually impossible to exhaust aquifers. With the spread of powerful diesel and electric pumps during the last half-century, however, overuse has become commonplace. As the world demand for water has climbed, water tables have fallen in scores of countries, including China, India, and the U.S., which together produce nearly half of the world's grain. Many other nations are straining their water reserves, too, setting the stage for dramatic cutbacks in water resources. The more populous among these are Pakistan, Iran, and Mexico. Overpumping creates an illusion of food security, enabling farmers to support a growing population with a practice that virtually ensures an eventual decline in food production and skyrocketing prices.

Food is fast becoming a national security issue as growth in the world harvest slows and falling water tables and rising temperatures hint at upcoming shortages. More than 100 countries import wheat. Some 40 import rice. While a handful of nations are only marginally dependent on imports, many could not survive without them. Iran and Egypt, for example, rely on imports for 40% of their grain supply. Algeria, Japan, South Korea, and Taiwan each import 70% or more. For Israel and Yemen, over 90%. Six countries—the U.S., Canada, France, Australia, Argentina, and Thailand—supply 90% of grain exports. The U.S. alone controls close to half the planet's grain exports, a larger share than Saudi Arabia does of oil.

Thus far, the countries that import heavily are small and mid-sized. China, however, the most populous nation, soon is likely to turn to international markets in a major way. When the former Soviet Union unexpectedly moved in that direction in 1972 for roughly one-tenth of its grain supply following a weather-reduced harvest, wheat prices climbed from $1.90 to $4.89 a bushel. Bread prices soon rose, too. A politics of food scarcity emerged. Pressure from within grain-exporting countries to restrict exports in order to check the rise in domestic food prices was common.

If China depletes its wheat reserves and looks elsewhere to cover the shortfall, now 40,000,000 tons per year, the situation could destabilize overnight, because it would mean petitioning the U.S., thus presenting a potentially delicate geopolitical situation in which 1,300,000,000 Chinese consumers boasting a $100,000,000,000 trade surplus with the U.S. will be competing with U.S. consumers for American grain. If that leads to rising food prices in this country, how will the government respond? In times past, it could have restricted exports, even imposing a trade embargo, as it did with soybeans to Japan in 1974. Today, though, the U.S. has a huge stake in a politically stable China. Growing at seven to eight percent a year, China is the engine that is powering not only the Asian economy but, to some degree, the global economy as well.

For the world's poor—the millions living in cities on one dollar per day or less and already spending 70% of their income on food—escalating grain prices would be life-threatening. A doubling of prices could impoverish vast numbers in a shorter period of time than any event in history. With desperate individuals holding their governments responsible, such a price spike also could destabilize governments of low-income, grain-importing nations.

Historically, there were two food reserves: the global carryover stocks of grain and the cropland idled under the U.S. farm policy to limit production. The latter could be cultivated within a year. Since the U.S. land set-aside initiative ended in 1996, however, there have been only carryover stocks as a reserve.

Food security has changed in other ways. Traditionally, it was largely an agricultural matter. Now, though, it is something that our entire society is responsible for. National population and energy policies may have a greater impact on food security than agricultural policies do. With most of the 3,000,000,000 additional individuals forecasted by 2050 being born in countries already facing water shortages, population control may have a larger influence on food security than crop planting proposals. Achieving an acceptable balance between food and consumers depends on family planners and farmers working together.

Climate change is the wild card in the food security deck. It is perhaps a measure of the complexity of our time that decisions reached in the Ministry of Energy may have more to do with future food security than those in the Ministry of Agriculture. The effects of population and energy policies on food security differ in one important respect: population stability can be achieved by a country acting unilaterally; climate stability cannot.

While the food sector may be the first to reveal the true size of the bubble economy, other wake-up calls, including more destructive storms, deadly heat waves, and collapsing fisheries, also could signal the extent to which we have overshot our ecological limitations. Unless the damaging trends that have been set in motion are reversed quickly, we could see vast numbers of environmental refugees abandoning areas scarred by depleted aquifers and exhausted soils, as well as fleeing advancing deserts and rising seas. In a world where civilization is being squeezed between expanding deserts from the interior continents and rising seas on the periphery, refugees are likely to number not in the millions, but in the tens of millions.

Preventing the bubble from bursting will require an unprecedented degree of international cooperation. Indeed, in both scale and urgency, the effort required is comparable to the U.S. mobilization during World War II. Rapid systemic change— alteration based on market signals that tell the ecological truth—is needed. This means lowering income taxes while raising tariffs on environmentally destructive activities, such as fossil fuel burning, to incorporate the ecological costs. Unless the market can be made to send signals that reflect reality, we will continue making faulty decisions as consumers, corporate planners, and government policymakers.

Stabilizing world population at around 7,500,000,000 is central to avoiding economic breakdowns in countries with large projected population increases that are already overconsuming their natural capital assets. No less than 36 nations, all in Europe (except Japan), essentially have done so. The challenge is to create the economic and social conditions—and to adopt the priorities—that will lead to population stability in the remaining lands. The keys here are offering primary education to every child, providing vaccinations along with basic and reproductive health care, and offering family planning services.

Shifting from a carbon- to a hydrogen-based economy to stabilize climate is quite feasible. Advances in wind turbine design and solar cell manufacturing, the availability of hydrogen generators, and the evolution of fuel cells provide the technologies necessary to build a climate-benign hydrogen economy. Moving quickly to renewable energy sources and improving efficiency depend on incorporating the indirect costs of burning fossil fuels into the market price.

On the energy front, Iceland is the first nation to adopt a national plan to convert its carbon-based energy economy to one of hydrogen. It is starting with the conversion of the Reykjavik bus fleet to fuel cell engines, then will proceed with converting automobiles, and, eventually, the fishing fleet. Iceland's first hydrogen service station opened in April.

Denmark and Germany, meanwhile, are leading proponents of wind power. Denmark, the pioneer, gets 18% of its electricity from turbines and plans to upgrade to 40% by 2030. Germany has developed some 12,000 megawatts of wind-generating capacity. Its northernmost state of Schleswig-Holstein receives 28% of its electricity in that fashion. Spain also is on the fast track in this area.

Japan has emerged as the number-one manufacturer and consumer of solar cells. With its commercialization of a solar roofing material, it now leads the world in electricity generated from solar cells and is well positioned to assist in the electrification of villages in developing areas.

Preventing the bubble from bursting will require an unprecedented degree of international cooperation. Indeed, in both scale and urgency, the effort required is comparable to the U.S. mobilization during World War II.

The Netherlands leads the industrial world in utilizing the bicycle as an alternative to the automobile. In Amsterdam's pedal-friendly environment, up to 40% of all trips are taken by that mode of transportation. This reflects the priority given to bikes in the design and operation of the country's urban transport systems. At many traffic signals, for example, cyclists are allowed to go first when the light changes.

The Canadian province of Ontario is one of the leaders in phasing out coal. It plans to replace its five coal-fired power plants with gas-fired plants, wind farms, and efficiency gains. This initiative calls for the first plant to close in 2005 and the last one by 2015. The resulting reduction in carbon emissions will be the equivalent of taking 4,000,000 cars off the road. This approach is a model for local and national governments everywhere.

Meanwhile, in pioneering drip irrigation technology, Israel has become the world leader in the efficient use of agricultural water. This unusually labor-intensive irrigation practice is ideally suited where water is scarce and labor is abundant. Water pricing also can be effective in encouraging efficiency. In South Africa, for example, households receive a fixed amount of water for basic needs at a low price, but when water use exceeds this level, the price escalates. This helps ensure that basic needs are met while discouraging waste. Doesn't it make sense to reduce urban and industrial water demand by managing waste without discharging it into the local environment, thereby allowing water to be recycled indefinitely?

In stabilizing soils, South Korea stands out, as its once denuded mountainsides and hills are now covered with trees. The nation's level of flood control, water storage, and hydrological stability is an example for other countries. Although the two Koreas are separated by just a narrow, demilitarized zone, the contrast between them is stark. In North Korea, where little permanent vegetation remains, droughts and floods alternate and hunger is chronic.

The U.S. record in soil conservation is an impressive one. Beginning in the late 1980s, American farmers systematically retired roughly 10% of the most erodible cropland, planting grass on the bulk of it. In addition, they've adopted various soil-conserving initiatives, including minimum- and no-till practices. Consequently, the U.S. has reduced soil erosion by almost 40% in less than two decades.

There is a growing sense among the more thoughtful political and opinion leaders worldwide that business as usual no longer is a viable option. Unless we respond to the social and environmental issues that are undermining our future, we may not be able to avoid economic decline and social disintegration. The prospect of weakened states is growing as the HIV epidemic, water shortages, and land hunger threaten to overwhelm countries on the lower rungs of the global economic ladder. Failed states are a matter of concern not only because of the social costs to their people, but because they serve as ideal bases for international terrorist organizations.

It is easy to spend hundreds of billions in response to terrorist threats, but the reality is that the resources needed to disrupt a modern economy are small, and a Department of Homeland Security, however heavily funded, provides only minimum protection from suicidal extremists. The challenge is not just to provide a high-tech military response to terrorism, but to build a global society that is environmentally sustainable, socially equitable, and democratically based—where there is hope for everyone. Such an effort would more effectively undermine the spread of terrorism than a doubling of military expenditures.

We can construct an economy that does not destroy its natural support systems, a community where the basic needs of all the Earth's people are satisfied, and a world that will allow us to think of ourselves as civilized. The choice is ours—yours and mine. We can stay with the status quo and preside over a global bubble economy that will keep expanding until it finally bursts, or we can be the generation that stabilizes population, eradicates poverty, and alleviates climate change. Historians will record the choice, but it is ours to make.

LESTER R. BROWN is president of the Earth Policy Institute, Washington, D.C., and author of *Plan B: Rescuing a Planet Under Stress and a Civilization in Trouble.*

The Great Leap Backward?

ELIZABETH C. ECONOMY

China's environmental problems are mounting. Water pollution and water scarcity are burdening the economy, rising levels of air pollution are endangering the health of millions of Chinese, and much of the country's land is rapidly turning into desert. China has become a world leader in air and water pollution and land degradation and a top contributor to some of the world's most vexing global environmental problems, such as the illegal timber trade, marine pollution, and climate change. As China's pollution woes increase, so, too, do the risks to its economy, public health, social stability, and international reputation. As Pan Yue, a vice minister of China's State Environmental Protection Administration (SEPA), warned in 2005, "The [economic] miracle will end soon because the environment can no longer keep pace."

With the 2008 Olympics around the corner, China's leaders have ratcheted up their rhetoric, setting ambitious environmental targets, announcing greater levels of environmental investment, and exhorting business leaders and local officials to clean up their backyards. The rest of the world seems to accept that Beijing has charted a new course: as China declares itself open for environmentally friendly business, officials in the United States, the European Union, and Japan are asking not whether to invest but how much.

Unfortunately, much of this enthusiasm stems from the widespread but misguided belief that what Beijing says goes. The central government sets the country's agenda, but it does not control all aspects of its implementation. In fact, local officials rarely heed Beijing's environmental mandates, preferring to concentrate their energies and resources on further advancing economic growth. The truth is that turning the environmental situation in China around will require something far more difficult than setting targets and spending money; it will require revolutionary bottom-up political and economic reforms.

For one thing, China's leaders need to make it easy for local officials and factory owners to do the right thing when it comes to the environment by giving them the right incentives. At the same time, they must loosen the political restrictions they have placed on the courts, nongovernmental organizations (NGOs), and the media in order to enable these groups to become independent enforcers of environmental protection. The international community, for its part, must focus more on assisting reform and less on transferring cutting-edge technologies and developing demonstration projects. Doing so will mean diving into the trenches to work with local Chinese officials, factory owners, and environmental NGOs; enlisting international NGOs to help with education and enforcement policies; and persuading multinational corporations (MNCs) to use their economic leverage to ensure that their Chinese partners adopt the best environmental practices.

Without such a clear-eyed understanding not only of what China wants but also of what it needs, China will continue to have one of the world's worst environmental records, and the Chinese people and the rest of the world will pay the price.

Sins of Emission

China's rapid development, often touted as an economic miracle, has become an environmental disaster. Record growth necessarily requires the gargantuan consumption of resources, but in China energy use has been especially unclean and inefficient, with dire consequences for the country's air, land, and water.

The coal that has powered China's economic growth, for example, is also choking its people. Coal provides about 70 percent of China's energy needs: the country consumed some 2.4 billion tons in 2006—more than the United States, Japan, and the United Kingdom combined. In 2000, China anticipated doubling its coal consumption by 2020; it is now expected to have done so by the end of this year. Consumption in China is huge partly because it is inefficient: as one Chinese official told *Der Spiegel* in early 2006, "To produce goods worth $10,000 we need seven times the resources used by Japan, almost six times the resources used by the U.S. and—a particular source of embarrassment—almost three times the resources used by India."

Meanwhile, this reliance on coal is devastating China's environment. The country is home to 16 of the world's 20 most polluted cities, and four of the worst off among them are in the coal-rich province of Shanxi, in northeastern China. As much as 90 percent of China's sulfur dioxide emissions and 50 percent of its particulate emissions are the result of coal use. Particulates are responsible for respiratory problems among the population, and acid rain, which is caused by sulfur dioxide emissions, falls on one-quarter of China's territory and on one-third of its agricultural land, diminishing agricultural output and eroding buildings.

Yet coal use may soon be the least of China's air-quality problems. The transportation boom poses a growing challenge to China's air quality. Chinese developers are laying more than 52,700 miles of new highways throughout the country. Some 14,000 new cars hit China's roads each day. By 2020, China is expected to have 130 million cars, and by 2050—or perhaps as early as 2040—it is expected to have even more cars than the United States. Beijing already pays a high price for this boom. In a 2006 survey, Chinese respondents rated Beijing the 15th most livable city in China, down from the 4th in 2005, with the drop due largely to increased traffic and pollution. Levels of airborne particulates are now six times higher in Beijing than in New York City.

China's grand-scale urbanization plans will aggravate matters. China's leaders plan to relocate 400 million people—equivalent to well over the entire population of the United States—to newly developed urban centers between 2000 and 2030. In the process, they will erect half of all the buildings expected to be constructed in the world during that period. This is a troubling prospect considering that Chinese buildings are not energy efficient—in fact, they are roughly two and a half times less so than those in Germany. Furthermore, newly urbanized Chinese, who use air conditioners, televisions, and refrigerators, consume about three and a half times more energy than do their rural counterparts. And although China is one of the world's largest producer of solar cells, compact fluorescent lights, and energy-efficient windows, these are produced mostly for export. Unless more of these energy-saving goods stay at home, the building boom will result in skyrocketing energy consumption and pollution.

China's land has also suffered from unfettered development and environmental neglect. Centuries of deforestation, along with the overgrazing of grasslands and overcultivation of cropland, have left much of China's north and northwest seriously degraded. In the past half century, moreover, forests and farmland have had to make way for industry and sprawling cities, resulting in diminishing crop yields, a loss in biodiversity, and local climatic change. The Gobi Desert, which now engulfs much of western and northern China, is spreading by about 1,900 square miles annually; some reports say that despite Beijing's aggressive reforestation efforts, one-quarter of the entire country is now desert. China's State Forestry Administration estimates that desertification has hurt some 400 million Chinese, turning tens of millions of them into environmental refugees, in search of new homes and jobs. Meanwhile, much of China's arable soil is contaminated, raising concerns about food safety. As much as ten percent of China's farmland is believed to be polluted, and every year 12 million tons of grain are contaminated with heavy metals absorbed from the soil.

Water Hazard

And then there is the problem of access to clean water. Although China holds the fourth-largest freshwater resources in the world (after Brazil, Russia, and Canada), skyrocketing demand, overuse, inefficiencies, pollution, and unequal distribution have produced a situation in which two-thirds of China's approximately 660 cities have less water than they need and 110 of them suffer severe shortages. According to Ma Jun, a leading Chinese water expert, several cities near Beijing and Tianjin, in the northeastern region of the country, could run out of water in five to seven years.

Growing demand is part of the problem, of course, but so is enormous waste. The agricultural sector lays claim to 66 percent of the water China consumes, mostly for irrigation, and manages to waste more than half of that. Chinese industries are highly inefficient: they generally use 10–20 percent more water than do their counterparts in developed countries. Urban China is an especially huge squanderer: it loses up to 20 percent of the water it consumes through leaky pipes—a problem that China's Ministry of Construction has pledged to address in the next two to three years. As urbanization proceeds and incomes rise, the Chinese, much like people in Europe and the United States, have become larger consumers of water: they take lengthy showers, use washing machines and dishwashers, and purchase second homes with lawns that need to be watered. Water consumption in Chinese cities jumped by 6.6 percent during 2004–5. China's plundering of its ground-water reserves, which has created massive underground tunnels, is causing a corollary problem: some of China's wealthiest cities are sinking—in the case of Shanghai and Tianjin, by more than six feet during the past decade and a half. In Beijing, subsidence has destroyed factories, buildings, and underground pipelines and is threatening the city's main international airport.

Pollution is also endangering China's water supplies. China's ground water, which provides 70 percent of the country's total drinking water, is under threat from a variety of sources, such as polluted surface water, hazardous waste sites, and pesticides and fertilizers. According to one report by the government-run Xinhua News Agency, the aquifers in 90 percent of Chinese cities are polluted. More than 75 percent of the river water flowing through China's urban areas is considered unsuitable for drinking or fishing, and the Chinese government deems about 30 percent of the river water throughout the country to be unfit for use in agriculture or industry. As a result, nearly 700 million people drink water contaminated with animal and human waste. The World Bank has found that the failure to provide fully two-thirds of the rural population with piped water is a leading cause of death among children under the age of five and is responsible for as much as 11 percent of the cases of gastrointestinal cancer in China.

One of the problems is that although China has plenty of laws and regulations designed to ensure clean water, factory owners and local officials do not enforce them. A 2005 survey of 509 cities revealed that only 23 percent of factories properly treated sewage before disposing of it. According to another report, today one-third of all industrial wastewater in China and two-thirds of household sewage are released untreated. Recent Chinese studies of two of the country's most important sources of water—the Yangtze and Yellow rivers—illustrate the growing challenge. The Yangtze River, which stretches all the way from the Tibetan Plateau to Shanghai, receives 40 percent of the country's sewage, 80 percent of it untreated. In 2007, the Chinese government announced that it was delaying, in part because of pollution, the development of a $60 billion plan to divert the river in order to supply the water-starved cities of Beijing and Tianjin. The Yellow River supplies water to more than 150 million people and 15 percent of China's agricultural land, but two-thirds of its water is considered unsafe to drink and 10 percent of its water is classified as sewage. In early 2007, Chinese officials announced that over one-third of the fish species native to the Yellow River had become extinct due to damming or pollution.

China's leaders are also increasingly concerned about how climate change may exacerbate their domestic environmental situation. In the spring of 2007, Beijing released its first national assessment report on climate change, predicting a 30 percent drop in precipitation in three of China's seven major river regions—around the Huai, Liao, and Hai rivers—and a 37 percent decline in the country's wheat, rice, and corn yields in the second half of the century. It also predicted that the Yangtze and Yellow rivers, which derive much of their water from glaciers in Tibet, would overflow as the glaciers melted and then dry up. And both Chinese and international scientists now warn that due to rising sea levels, Shanghai could be submerged by 2050.

Collateral Damage

China's environmental problems are already affecting the rest of the world. Japan and South Korea have long suffered from the acid rain produced by China's coal-fired power plants and from the eastbound dust storms that sweep across the Gobi Desert in the spring and dump toxic yellow dust on their land. Researchers in the United States are tracking dust, sulfur, soot, and trace metals as these travel across the Pacific from China. The U.S. Environmental Protection Agency estimates that on some days, 25 percent of the particulates in the atmosphere in Los Angeles originated in China.[1] Scientists have also traced rising levels of mercury deposits on U.S. soil back to coal-fired power plants and cement factories in China. (When ingested in significant quantities, mercury can cause birth defects and developmental problems.) Reportedly, 25–40 percent of all mercury emissions in the world come from China.

What China dumps into its waters is also polluting the rest of the world. According to the international NGO the World Wildlife Fund, China is now the largest polluter of the Pacific Ocean. As Liu Quangfeng, an adviser to the National People's Congress, put it, "Almost no river that flows into the Bo Hai [a sea along China's northern coast] is clean." China releases about 2.8 billion tons of contaminated water into the Bo Hai annually, and the content of heavy metal in the mud at the bottom of it is now 2,000 times as high as China's own official safety standard. The prawn catch has dropped by 90 percent over the past 15 years. In 2006, in the heavily industrialized southeastern provinces of Guangdong and Fujian, almost 8.3 billion tons of sewage were discharged into the ocean without treatment, a 60 percent increase from 2001. More than 80 percent of the East China Sea, one of the world's largest fisheries, is now rated unsuitable for fishing, up from 53 percent in 2000.

Furthermore, China is already attracting international attention for its rapidly growing contribution to climate change. According to a 2007 report from the Netherlands Environmental Assessment Agency, it has already surpassed the United States as the world's largest contributor of carbon dioxide, a leading greenhouse gas, to the atmosphere. Unless China rethinks its use of various sources of energy and adopts cutting-edge environmentally friendly technologies, warned Fatih Birol, the chief economist of the International Energy Agency, last April, in 25 years China will emit twice as much carbon dioxide as all the countries of the Organization for Economic Cooperation and Development combined.

China's close economic partners in the developing world face additional environmental burdens from China's economic activities. Chinese multinationals, which are exploiting natural resources in Africa, Latin America, and Southeast Asia in order to fuel China's continued economic rise, are devastating these regions' habitats in the process. China's hunger for timber has exploded over the past decade and a half, and particularly since 1998, when devastating floods led Beijing to crack down on domestic logging. China's timber imports more than tripled between 1993 and 2005. According to the World Wildlife Fund, China's demand for timber, paper, and pulp will likely increase by 33 percent between 2005 and 2010.

China is already the largest importer of illegally logged timber in the world: an estimated 50 percent of its timber imports are reportedly illegal. Illegal logging is especially damaging to the environment because it often targets rare old-growth forests, endangers biodiversity, and ignores sustainable forestry practices. In 2006, the government of Cambodia, for example, ignored its own laws and awarded China's Wuzhishan LS Group a 99-year concession that was 20 times as large as the size permitted by Cambodian law. The company's practices, including the spraying of large amounts of herbicides, have prompted repeated protests by local Cambodians. According to the international NGO Global Witness, Chinese companies have destroyed large parts of the forests along the Chinese-Myanmar border and are now moving deeper into Myanmar's forests in their search for timber. In many instances, illicit logging activity takes place with the active support of corrupt local officials. Central government officials in Myanmar and Indonesia, countries where China's loggers are active, have protested such arrangements to Beijing, but relief has been limited. These activities, along with those of Chinese mining and energy companies, raise serious environmental concerns for many local populations in the developing world.

Spoiling the Party

In the view of China's leaders, however, damage to the environment itself is a secondary problem. Of greater concern to them are its indirect effects: the threat it poses to the continuation of the Chinese economic miracle and to public health, social stability, and the country's international reputation. Taken together, these challenges could undermine the authority of the Communist Party.

China's leaders are worried about the environment's impact on the economy. Several studies conducted both inside and outside China estimate that environmental degradation and pollution cost the Chinese economy between 8 percent and 12 percent of GDP annually. The Chinese media frequently publish the results of studies on the impact of pollution on agriculture, industrial output, or public health: water pollution costs of $35.8 billion one year, air pollution costs of $27.5 billion another, and on and on with weather disasters ($26.5 billion), acid rain ($13.3 billion), desertification ($6 billion), or crop damage from soil pollution ($2.5 billion). The city of Chongqing, which sits on the banks of the Yangtze River, estimates that dealing with the effects of water pollution on its agriculture and public health costs as much as 4.3 percent of the city's annual gross product. Shanxi Province has watched its coal resources fuel the rest of the country while it pays the price in withered trees, contaminated air and water, and land subsidence. Local authorities there estimate the costs of environmental degradation and pollution at 10.9 percent of the province's annual gross product and have called on Beijing to compensate the province for its "contribution and sacrifice."

China's Ministry of Public Health is also sounding the alarm with increasing urgency. In a survey of 30 cities and 78 counties released in the spring, the ministry blamed worsening air and water pollution for dramatic increases in the incidence of cancer throughout the country: a 19 percent rise in urban areas and a 23 percent rise in rural areas since 2005. One research institute affiliated with SEPA has put the total number of premature deaths in China caused by respiratory diseases related to air pollution at 400,000 a year. But this may be a conservative estimate: according to a joint research project by the World Bank and the Chinese government released this year, the total number of such deaths is 750,000 a year. (Beijing is said not to have wanted to release the latter figure for fear of inciting social unrest.) Less well documented but potentially even more devastating is the health impact of China's polluted water. Today, fully 190 million Chinese are sick from drinking contaminated water. All along China's major rivers, villages report skyrocketing rates of diarrheal diseases, cancer, tumors, leukemia, and stunted growth.

Social unrest over these issues is rising. In the spring of 2006, China's top environmental official, Zhou Shengxian, announced that there had been 51,000 pollution-related protests in 2005, which amounts to almost 1,000 protests each week. Citizen complaints about the environment, expressed on official hotlines and in letters to local officials, are increasing at a rate of 30 percent a year; they will likely top 450,000 in 2007. But few of them are resolved satisfactorily, and so people throughout the country are increasingly taking to the streets. For several months in 2006, for example, the residents of six neighboring villages in Gansu Province held repeated protests against zinc and iron smelters that they believed were poisoning them. Fully half of the 4,000–5,000 villagers exhibited lead-related illnesses, ranging from vitamin D deficiency to neurological problems.

Many pollution-related marches are relatively small and peaceful. But when such demonstrations fail, the protesters sometimes resort to violence. After trying for two years to get redress by petitioning local, provincial, and even central government officials for spoiled crops and poisoned air, in the spring of 2005, 30,000–40,000 villagers from Zhejiang Province swarmed 13 chemical plants, broke windows and overturned buses, attacked government officials, and torched police cars. The government sent in 10,000 members of the People's Armed Police in response. The plants were ordered to close down, and several environmental activists who attempted to monitor the plants' compliance with these orders were later arrested. China's leaders have generally managed to prevent—if sometimes violently—discontent over environmental issues from spreading across provincial boundaries or morphing into calls for broader political reform.

In the face of such problems, China's leaders have recently injected a new urgency into their rhetoric concerning the need to protect the country's environment. On paper, this has translated into an aggressive strategy to increase investment in environmental protection, set ambitious targets for the reduction of pollution and energy intensity (the amount of energy used to produce a unit of GDP), and introduce new environmentally friendly technologies. In 2005, Beijing set out a number of impressive targets for its next five-year plan: by 2010, it wants 10 percent of the nation's power to come from renewable energy sources, energy intensity to have been reduced by 20 percent and key pollutants such as sulfur dioxide by 10 percent, water consumption to have decreased by 30 percent, and investment in environmental protection to have increased from 1.3 percent to 1.6 percent of GDP. Premier Wen Jiabao has issued a stern warning to local officials to shut down some of the plants in the most energy-intensive industries—power generation and aluminum, copper, steel, coke and coal, and cement production—and to slow the growth of other industries by denying them tax breaks and other production incentives.

These goals are laudable—even breathtaking in some respects—but history suggests that only limited optimism is warranted; achieving such targets has proved elusive in the past. In 2001, the Chinese government pledged to cut sulfur dioxide emissions by 10 percent between 2002 and 2005. Instead, emissions rose by 27 percent. Beijing is already encountering difficulties reaching its latest goals: for instance, it has failed to meet its first target for reducing energy intensity and pollution. Despite warnings from Premier Wen, the six industries that were slated to slow down posted a 20.6 percent increase in output during the first quarter of 2007—a 6.6 percent jump from the same period last year. According to one senior executive with the Indian wind-power firm Suzlon Energy, only 37 percent of the wind-power projects the Chinese government approved in 2004 have been built. Perhaps worried that yet another target would fall by the wayside, in early 2007, Beijing revised its announced goal of reducing the country's water consumption by 30 percent by 2010 to just 20 percent.

Even the Olympics are proving to be a challenge. Since Beijing promised in 2001 to hold a "green Olympics" in 2008, the International Olympic Committee has pulled out all the stops. Beijing is now ringed with rows of newly planted trees, hybrid taxis and buses are roaming its streets (some of which are soon to be lined with solar-powered lamps), the most heavily polluting factories have been pushed outside the city limits, and the Olympic dormitories are models of energy efficiency. Yet in key respects, Beijing has failed to deliver. City officials are backtracking from their pledge to provide safe tap water to all of Beijing for the Olympics; they now say that they will provide it only for residents of the Olympic Village. They have announced drastic stopgap measures for the duration of the games, such as banning one million of the city's three million cars from the city's streets and halting production at factories in and around Beijing (some of them are resisting). Whatever progress city authorities have managed over the past six years—such as increasing the number of days per year that the city's air is deemed to be clean—is not enough to ensure that the air will be clean for the Olympic Games. Preparing for the Olympics has come to symbolize the intractability of China's environmental challenges and the limits of Beijing's approach to addressing them.

Problems with the Locals

Clearly, something has got to give. The costs of inaction to China's economy, public health, and international reputation are growing. And perhaps more important, social discontent is rising. The Chinese people have clearly run out of patience with the government's inability or unwillingness to turn the environmental situation around. And the government is well aware of the increasing potential for environmental protest to ignite broader social unrest.

One event this spring particularly alarmed China's leaders. For several days in May in the coastal city of Xiamen, after months of mounting opposition to the planned construction of a $1.4 billion petrochemical plant nearby, students and professors at Xiamen University, among others, are said to have sent out a million mobile-phone text messages calling on their fellow citizens to take to the streets on June 1. That day, and the following, protesters reportedly numbering between 7,000 and 20,000 marched peacefully through the city, some defying threats of expulsion from school or from the Communist Party. The protest was captured on video and uploaded to YouTube. One video featured a haunting voice-over that linked the Xiamen demonstration to an ongoing environmental crisis near Tai Hu, a lake some 400 miles away (a large bloom of blue-green algae caused by industrial wastewater and sewage dumped in the lake had contaminated the water supply of the city of Wuxi). It also referred to the Tiananmen Square protest of 1989. The Xiamen march, the narrator said, was perhaps "the first genuine parade since Tiananmen."

In response, city authorities did stay the construction of the plant, but they also launched an all-out campaign to discredit the protesters and their videos. Still, more comments about the protest and calls not to forget Tiananmen appeared on various Web sites. Such messages, posted openly and accessible to all Chinese, represent the Chinese leadership's greatest fear, namely, that its failure to protect the environment may someday serve as the catalyst for broad-based demands for political change.

Such public demonstrations are also evidence that China's environmental challenges cannot be met with only impressive targets and more investment. They must be tackled with a fundamental reform of how the country does business and protects the environment. So far, Beijing has structured its environmental protection efforts in much the same way that it has pursued economic growth: by granting local authorities and factory owners wide decision-making power and by actively courting the international community and Chinese NGOs for their expertise while carefully monitoring their activities.

Consider, for example, China's most important environmental authority, SEPA, in Beijing. SEPA has become a wellspring of China's most innovative environmental policies: it has promoted an environmental impact assessment law; a law requiring local officials to release information about environmental disasters, pollution statistics, and the names of known polluters to the public; an experiment to calculate the costs of environ-

mental degradation and pollution to the country's GDP; and an all-out effort to halt over 100 large-scale infrastructure projects that had proceeded without proper environmental impact assessments. But SEPA operates with barely 300 full-time professional staff in the capital and only a few hundred employees spread throughout the country. (The U.S. Environmental Protection Agency has a staff of almost 9,000 in Washington, D.C., alone.) And authority for enforcing SEPA's mandates rests overwhelmingly with local officials and the local environmental protection officials they oversee. In some cases, this has allowed for exciting experimentation. In the eastern province of Jiangsu, for instance, the World Bank and the Natural Resources Defense Council have launched the Greenwatch program, which grades 12,000 factories according to their compliance with standards for industrial wastewater treatment and discloses both the ratings and the reasons for them. More often, however, China's highly decentralized system has meant limited progress: only seven to ten percent of China's more than 660 cities meet the standards required to receive the designation of National Model Environmental City from SEPA. According to Wang Canfa, one of China's top environmental lawyers, barely ten percent of China's environmental laws and regulations are actually enforced.

One of the problems is that local officials have few incentives to place a priority on environmental protection. Even as Beijing touts the need to protect the environment, Premier Wen has called for quadrupling the Chinese economy by 2020. The price of water is rising in some cities, such as Beijing, but in many others it remains as low as 20 percent of the replacement cost. That ensures that factories and municipalities have little reason to invest in wastewater treatment or other water-conservation efforts. Fines for polluting are so low that factory managers often prefer to pay them rather than adopt costlier pollution-control technologies. One manager of a coal-fired power plant explained to a Chinese reporter in 2005 that he was ignoring a recent edict mandating that all new power plants use desulfurization equipment because the technology cost as much as would 15 years' worth of fines.

Local governments also turn a blind eye to serious pollution problems out of self-interest. Officials sometimes have a direct financial stake in factories or personal relationships with their owners. And the local environmental protection bureaus tasked with guarding against such corruption must report to the local governments, making them easy targets for political pressure. In recent years, the Chinese media have uncovered cases in which local officials have put pressure on the courts, the press, or even hospitals to prevent the wrongdoings of factories from coming to light. (Just this year, in the province of Zhejiang, officials reportedly promised factories with an output of $1.2 million or more that they would not be subjected to government inspections without the factories' prior approval.)

Moreover, local officials frequently divert environmental protection funds and spend them on unrelated or ancillary endeavors. The Chinese Academy for Environmental Planning, which reports to SEPA, disclosed this year that only half of the 1.3 percent of the country's annual GDP dedicated to environmental protection between 2001 and 2005 had found its way to legitimate projects. According to the study, about 60 percent of the environmental protection funds spent in urban areas during that period went into the creation of, among other things, parks, factory production lines, gas stations, and sewage-treatment plants rather than into waste- or wastewater-treatment facilities.

Many local officials also thwart efforts to hold them accountable for their failure to protect the environment. In 2005, SEPA launched the "Green GDP" campaign, a project designed to calculate the costs of environmental degradation and pollution to local economies and provide a basis for evaluating the performance of local officials both according to their economic stewardship and according to how well they protect the environment. Several provinces balked, however, worried that the numbers would reveal the extent of the damage suffered by the environment. SEPA's partner in the campaign, the National Bureau of Statistics of China, also undermined the effort by announcing that it did not possess the tools to do Green GDP accounting accurately and that in any case it did not believe officials should be evaluated on such a basis. After releasing a partial report in September 2006, the NBS has refused to release this year's findings to the public.

Another problem is that many Chinese companies see little direct value in ratcheting up their environmental protection efforts. The computer manufacturer Lenovo and the appliance manufacturer Haier have received high marks for taking creative environmental measures, and the solar energy company Suntech has become a leading exporter of solar cells. But a recent poll found that only 18 percent of Chinese companies believed that they could thrive economically while doing the right thing environmentally. Another poll of business executives found that an overwhelming proportion of them do not understand the benefits of responsible corporate behavior, such as environmental protection, or consider the requirements too burdensome.

Not Good Enough

The limitations of the formal authorities tasked with environmental protection in China have led the country's leaders to seek assistance from others outside the bureaucracy. Over the past 15 years or so, China's NGOs, the Chinese media, and the international community have become central actors in the country's bid to rescue its environment. But the Chinese government remains wary of them.

China's homegrown environmental activists and their allies in the media have become the most potent—and potentially explosive—force for environmental change in China. From four or five NGOs devoted primarily to environmental education and biodiversity protection in the mid-1990s, the Chinese environmental movement has grown to include thousands of NGOs, run primarily by dynamic Chinese in their 30s and 40s. These groups now routinely expose polluting factories to the central government, sue for the rights of villagers poisoned by contaminated water or air, give seed money to small newer NGOs throughout the country, and go undercover to expose multinationals that ignore international environmental standards. They often protest via letters to the government, campaigns on the Internet, and editorials in Chinese newspapers. The media are an important ally in this fight: they shame polluters, uncover environmental abuse, and highlight environmental protection successes.

Beijing has come to tolerate NGOs and media outlets that play environmental watchdog at the local level, but it remains vigilant in making sure that certain limits are not crossed, and especially that the central government is not directly criticized. The penalties for misjudging these boundaries can be severe. Wu Lihong worked for 16 years to address the pollution in Tai Hu (which recently spawned blue-green algae), gathering evidence that has forced almost 200 factories to close. Although in 2005 Beijing honored Wu as one of the country's top environmentalists, he was beaten by local thugs several times during the course of his investigations, and in 2006 the government of the town of Yixing arrested him on dubious charges of blackmail. And Yu Xiaogang, the 2006 winner of the prestigious Goldman Environmental Prize, honoring grass-roots environmentalists, was forbidden to travel abroad in retaliation for educating villagers about the potential downsides of a proposed dam relocation in Yunnan Province.

The Chinese government's openness to environmental cooperation with the international community is also fraught. Beijing has welcomed bilateral agreements for technology development or financial assistance for demonstration projects, but it is concerned about other endeavors. On the one hand, it lauds international environmental NGOs for their contributions to China's environmental protection efforts. On the other hand, it fears that some of them will become advocates for democratization.

The government also subjects MNCs to an uncertain operating environment. Many corporations have responded to the government's calls that they assume a leading role in the country's environmental protection efforts by deploying top-of-the-line environmental technologies, financing environmental education in Chinese schools, undertaking community-based efforts, and raising operating standards in their industries. Coca-Cola, for example, recently pledged to become a net-zero consumer of water, and Wal-Mart is set to launch a nationwide education and sales initiative to promote the use of energy-efficient compact fluorescent bulbs. Sometimes, MNCs have been rewarded with awards or significant publicity. But in the past two years, Chinese officials (as well as local NGOs) have adopted a much tougher stance toward them, arguing at times that MNCs have turned China into the pollution capital of the world. On issues such as electronic waste, the detractors have a point. But China's attacks, with Internet postings accusing MNCs of practicing "eco-colonialism," have become unjustifiably broad. Such antiforeign sentiment spiked in late 2006, after the release of a pollution map listing more than 3,000 factories that were violating water pollution standards. The 33 among them that supplied MNCs were immediately targeted in the media, while the other few thousand Chinese factories cited somehow escaped the frenzy. A few Chinese officials and activists privately acknowledge that domestic Chinese companies pollute far more than foreign companies, but it seems unlikely that the spotlight will move off MNCs in the near future. For now, it is simply more expedient to let international corporations bear the bulk of the blame.

From Red to Green

Why is China unable to get its environmental house in order? Its top officials want what the United States, Europe, and Japan have: thriving economies with manageable environmental problems. But they are unwilling to pay the political and economic price to get there. Beijing's message to local officials continues to be that economic growth cannot be sacrificed to environmental protection—that the two objectives must go hand in hand.

This, however, only works sometimes. Greater energy efficiency can bring economic benefits, and investments to reduce pollution, such as in building wastewater-treatment plants, are expenses that can be balanced against the costs of losing crops to contaminated soil and having a sickly work force. Yet much of the time, charting a new environmental course comes with serious economic costs up front. Growth slows down in some industries or some regions. Some businesses are forced to close down. Developing pollution-treatment and pollution-prevention technologies requires serious investment. In fact, it is because they recognize these costs that local officials in China pursue their short-term economic interests first and for the most part ignore Beijing's directives to change their ways.

This is not an unusual problem. All countries suffer internal tugs of war over how to balance the short-term costs of improving environmental protection with the long-term costs of failing to do so. But China faces an additional burden. Its environmental problems stem as much from China's corrupt and undemocratic political system as from Beijing's continued focus on economic growth. Local officials and business leaders routinely—and with impunity—ignore environmental laws and regulations, abscond with environmental protection funds, and silence those who challenge them. Thus, improving the environment in China is not simply a matter of mandating pollution-control technologies; it is also a matter of reforming the country's political culture. Effective environmental protection requires transparent information, official accountability, and an independent legal system. But these features are the building blocks of a political system fundamentally different from that of China today, and so far there is little indication that China's leaders will risk the authority of the Communist Party on charting a new environmental course. Until the party is willing to open the door to such reform, it will not have the wherewithal to meet its ambitious environmental targets and lead a growing economy with manageable environmental problems.

Given this reality, the United States—and the rest of the world—will have to get much smarter about how to cooperate with China in order to assist its environmental protection efforts. Above all, the United States must devise a limited and coherent set of priorities. China's needs are vast, but its capacity is poor; therefore, launching one or two significant initiatives over the next five to ten years would do more good than a vast array of uncoordinated projects. These endeavors could focus on discrete issues, such as climate change or the illegal timber trade; institutional changes, such as strengthening the legal system in regard to China's environmental protection efforts; or broad reforms, such as promoting energy efficiency throughout the Chinese economy. Another key to an effective U.S.-Chinese partnership is U.S. leadership. Although U.S. NGOs and U.S.-based MNCs are often at the forefront of environmental policy and technological innovation, the U.S. government itself is not a world leader on key environmental concerns. Unless the United States improves its own policies and practices on, for example, climate change, the illegal timber trade, and energy efficiency, it will have little credibility or leverage to push China.

China, for its part, will undoubtedly continue to place a priority on gaining easy access to financial and technological assistance. Granting this, however, would be the wrong way to go. Joint efforts between the United States and China, such as the recently announced project to capture methane from 15 Chinese coal mines, are important, of course. But the systemic changes needed to set China on a new environmental trajectory necessitate a bottom-up overhaul. One way to start would be to promote energy efficiency in Chinese factories and buildings. Simply bringing these up to world standards would bring vast gains. International and Chinese NGOs, Chinese environmental protection bureaus, and MNCs could audit and rate Chinese factories based on how well their manufacturing processes and building standards met a set of energy-efficiency targets. Their scores (and the factors that determined them) could then be disclosed to the public via the Internet and the print media, and factories with subpar performances could be given the means to improve their practices.

A pilot program in Guangdong Province, which is run under the auspices of the U.S. consulate in Hong Kong, provides just such a mechanism. Factories that apply for energy audits can take out loans from participating banks to pay for efficiency upgrades, with the expectation that they will pay the loans back over time out of the savings they will realize from using fewer materials or conserving energy. Such programs should be encouraged and could be reinforced by requiring, for example, that the U.S.-based MNCs that worked with the participating factories rewarded those that met or exceeded the standards and penalized those that did not (the MNCs could either expand or reduce their orders, for example). NGOs and the media in China could also publicize the names of the factories that refused to cooperate. These initiatives would have the advantages of operating within the realities of China's environmental protection system, providing both incentives and disincentives to encourage factories to comply; strengthening the role of key actors such as NGOs, the media, and local environmental protection bureaus; and engaging new actors such as Chinese banks. It is likely that as with the Greenwatch program, factory owners and local officials not used to transparency would oppose such efforts, but if they were persuaded that full participation would bring more sales to MNCs and grow local economies, many of them would be more open to public disclosure.

Of course, much of the burden and the opportunity for China to revolutionize the way it reconciles environmental protection and economic development rests with the Chinese government itself. No amount of international assistance can transform China's domestic environment or its contribution to global environmental challenges. Real change will arise only from strong central leadership and the development of a system of incentives that make it easier for local officials and the Chinese people to embrace environmental protection. This will sometimes mean making tough economic choices.

Improvements to energy efficiency, of the type promoted by the program in Guangdong, are reforms of the low-hanging-fruit variety: they promise both economic gains and benefits to the environment. It will be more difficult to implement reforms that are economically costly (such as reforms that raise the costs of manufacturing in order to encourage conservation and recycling and those that impose higher fines against polluters), are likely to be unpopular (such as reforms that hike the price of water), or could undermine the Communist Party's authority (such as reforms that open up the media or give freer rein to civil society). But such measures are also necessary. And their high up-front costs must be weighed against the long-term costs to economic growth, public health, and social stability in which the Chinese government's continued inaction would result. The government must ensure greater accountability among local officials by promoting greater grass-roots oversight, greater transparency via the media or other outlets, and greater independence in the legal system.

China's leaders have shown themselves capable of bold reform in the past. Two and half decades ago, Deng Xiaoping and his supporters launched a set of ambitious reforms despite stiff political resistance and set the current economic miracle in motion. In order to continue on its extraordinary trajectory, China needs leaders with the vision to introduce a new set of economic and political initiatives that will transform the way the country does business. Without such measures, China will not return to global preeminence in the twenty-first century. Instead, it will suffer stagnation or regression—and all because leaders who recognized the challenge before them were unwilling to do what was necessary to surmount it.

Note

1. The original Associated Press story that was the source for the statement was mistaken and has been corrected. In fact, the EPA, citing a model saying that Asia contributes about 30 percent of the background sulfate particulate matter in the western United States, estimates that Asia contributes about one percent of all particulate matter in Los Angeles.

ELIZABETH C. ECONOMY is C. V. Starr Senior Fellow and Director for Asia Studies at the Council on Foreign Relations and the author of *The River Runs Black: The Environmental Challenges to China's Future.*

Water of Life in Peril

SHARON PALMER, RD

Water, water, everywhere, nor any drop to drink.
—from *The Rime of the Ancient Mariner*
by Samuel Taylor Coleridge

It's a thirsty planet. For its 6.6 billion inhabitants—a number that continues to swell—the faucet is beginning to run dry. As the world's population tripled in the 20th century, the demand for water resources multiplied sixfold. And as our population continues to grow, becoming more urbanized and industrialized, so does its greed for water.

But the supply is dwindling due to pollution and contamination. Billions of people lack basic water services, and millions die each year from water-related diseases. In 1999, the United Nations Environment Programme (UNEP) reported that 200 scientists in 50 countries had identified water shortage as one of the two most troublesome problems for the new millennium, the other being global warming.

Even though water covers roughly two thirds of the Earth's surface, most of it is not suitable for human use. Only 0.08% of the world's total water supply is available for consumption because a mere 2.5% of it is not salty, and two thirds of that amount is tucked away in icecaps and glaciers. Of the remaining supply, much is in remote areas and comes in monsoons and floods, which is difficult to capture. To make matters worse, pollution is making more of the Earth's available water unfit for use. Just look to Central Asia's Aral Sea environmental crisis as an illustration of how pollution can poison water runoff to rivers and soil.

"Pollution of water due to industrial urbanization performed in an unplanned way, making clean freshwater less accessible, is the most pressing water global issue right now," reported Shaikh Halim, executive director of the Village Education Resource Center in Bangladesh, at this year's World Water Week.

When there's not enough water coming from rainwater and surface water, governments turn to subterranean supplies of groundwater. In turn, rivers, wetlands, and lakes that depend on groundwater can dry out and be replaced with saline seawater. According to the UNEP, water tables are falling by roughly 3 meters per year across much of the developing world. Some of the world's biggest cities, such as Bangkok, Cairo, Kolkata, London, Mexico City, and Jakarta, are dependent on groundwater. While the impact of using up rivers and lakes is obvious, the overuse of groundwater is virtually invisible to the public.

Adding to the problem is the fact that people in some parts of the world literally fight over water. More than 260 river basins are shared by two or more countries, and without strong agreements, transboundary tensions arise over water use. For example, the dispute over water resources has been a feature of the Arab-Israeli conflict since its beginning. Experts call for more international attention to develop groundwater agreements among the nations of such regions.

And lastly, it's not just humans who suffer from a water shortage. The reduction of available water can have repercussions on aquatic ecosystems and countless species that are dependent on them.

Draining the Water Supply

According to the World Water Vision Report published in 2000 by the World Water Council, "There is a water crisis today. But the crisis is not about having too little water to satisfy our needs. It is a crisis of managing water so badly that billions of people—and the environment—suffer badly."

You may think that the sheer volume of humans drinking, cooking, and washing with water is what's putting a drain on the supply, but this utilization of water is just a drop in the bucket compared with how water is used in other endeavors. The biggest abuser of water by far is irrigation, which wastes an enormous amount in inefficiency and evaporation. An estimated 60% of the total water pumped for irrigation is wasted before it even reaches the crop. Water withdrawals for irrigation comprise 66% of the total withdrawals, with up to 90% in arid areas. In Asia, it makes up 86% of total annual water used compared with 49% in North and Central America and 38% in Europe.

Agriculture is a thirsty business. It takes approximately 1,000 liters of water to produce 1 kilogram (kg) of wheat; 1,400 liters to produce 1 kg of rice; and 13,000 liters to produce 1 kg of beef. By 2020, a projected 17% more water will be needed to feed the world than is currently available. Even "eco-friendly" biofuel is a water-gulping industry. Last year in Nebraska, the nation's third-leading ethanol producer, it took 2 billion gallons of water at 15 ethanol plants to create 676 million gallons of the alternative fuel.

"Rivers and lakes are virtually emptied for part of the year as a result of heavy withdrawals for irrigation. Groundwater tables are significantly lowered as a result of this development. While we drink a few liters of water per day, we literally eat one or a few tons of water each day. Water provision to agriculture for food, biofuels, and commercial products are therefore a water problem at another order of magnitude," says Professor Jan Lundqvist, a food and nutrition expert at Stockholm International Water Institute. Domestic households, industry, and evaporation from reservoirs contribute to the water supply drain in a smaller way.

Americans rank highest among the world's water consumers. According to the Pacific Institute for Studies in Development, Environment, and Security in Oakland, Calif., America is sixth in the world behind New Zealand, Armenia, Barbados, Cuba, and the United Arab Emirates for per capita water withdrawals. Europeans use significantly less water per person for domestic purposes than Americans due to more efficient systems like low-flush toilets, as well as abundant rainfall throughout the year, which reduces the need to water gardens in the summer.

The World Water Council reports that part of the problem with valuing water as a resource is that it is underpriced. Subsidies for agricultural use are common in developed and developing countries, but by removing such subsidies and allowing water prices to rise, pushes for conservation and more efficient technology can flourish.

Deep Impact of Climate Change

It is widely accepted that climate change will have a major impact on water resources. At World Water Week, distinguished speakers from around the world discussed the link between water and climate, human societies, and ecosystems, emphasizing an immediate need for adaptation measures. The United Nations Development Programme's Human Development Report 2007 (http://hdr.undp.org) points out that massive human development costs will result from climate change unless we dramatically reduce carbon emissions within the next decade. A shift in attitudes among governments to take climate and water issues more seriously with commitments to decrease carbon emissions is critical.

"Climate risks are wavering heavily on the lives of the poor, and those living in poverty are not able to withstand the shocks," said Claes Johansson, a report coauthor, at World Water Week.

Future predictions for global climate change recently released by the UN Intergovernmental Panel on Climate Change are estimating that between 250 million and 980 million people, mostly in Africa, could find themselves without fresh water by 2050.

Water for the World's Poor

Perhaps it's difficult to grasp the meaning of a water crisis when a simple twist of the faucet handle unleashes an endless gush of clean, safe water. But this isn't the case in many of the poorest countries in the world. Nearly one third of the world's population lives in countries that are stressed for water. In Asia, per capita availability declined by 40% to 60% between 1955 and 1990, with projections that most Asian countries will have severe water problems by the year 2025. Most of Africa has always been short of water.

The daily per capita use of water in residential areas is 350 liters in North America and Japan, 200 liters in Europe, and 10 to 20 liters in sub-Saharan Africa. The UN developed the Millennium Development Goals targeted at reducing poverty and ensuring sustainable development, with goal No. 7, target 10 reading, "Halve, by 2015, the proportion of people without sustainable access to safe water and basic sanitation."

Malawi's story is a vivid example of the chain of water insecurity. Stacia Nordin, RD, and her husband, who is a social worker, began HIV/AIDS prevention work through the U.S. Peace Corps in Malawi, Africa, in 1997. Noticing that food and water security were critical in the region, they began working to promote permaculture, a philosophy that observes how nature replenishes its soil, conserves its water resources, and adapts to an area's specific

Global Water Resources

Tap into these resources to learn more about the global water crisis.

Co-operative Programme on Water and Climate:
www.waterandclimate.org

National Wildlife Federation:
www.nwf.org

Stockholm International Water Institute:
www.siwi.org

The UN Millennium Development Goals:
www.un.org/millenniumgoals

United Nations Environment Programme:
www.unep.org

World Business Council for Sustainable Development:
www.wbcsd.ch

World Water Council:
www.worldwatercouncil.org

World Water Week:
www.worldwaterweek.org

climate. "Water is a more serious problem than food security in some cases. Unclean water is often the root cause of illness for children suffering from malnutrition. For health, sanitation, and agricultural reasons, water is going to be a crisis if not addressed in an integrated manner," says Nordin.

The problems in the Malawi water supply stem from people treating the Earth carelessly by failing to manage the water, the Nordins say. In a healthy system, rainwater should be filtered through the earth's layers, but when people destroy the earth, the rain runs across the surface, collecting manures, bacteria, and harmful chemicals with it, depositing it directly into rivers, wells, and lakes. This causes water to become infected and able to transmit a variety of diseases such as typhoid, cholera, and other diarrheal diseases, as well as causing the water sources to diminish.

In Malawi, rainwater is not captured from rooftops; it is pushed into man-made water drains without being used. Water in rivers and lakes is abused by using synthetic chemicals that cause eutrophication, an explosive growth of plant matter in water that suffocates the animal life; overfishing, which removes the balance in the water source, causing areas of stagnation; and erosion, which deposits top soil and organic and nonorganic materials into water sources. The rivers and lakes must be dredged to remove the materials so the hydroelectric power plant can work properly. Flooding wipes out infrastructure such as homes, roads, and bridges and takes the lives of humans and other animals.

Right to Water, Right to Life

The moral and ethical right to water and sanitation has been planted in cultural and religious traditions around the world. The UN proclaimed that the right to water is "indispensable for leading a life in human dignity" and "a prerequisite for the realization of other human rights."

With access to safe water, child mortality between the ages of 0 to 4 could be reduced, far more children could go to school between the ages of 5 and 14, more productivity could occur among people aged 15 and 59, and people could expect to live longer after the age of 60.

The American Dietetic Association's position on the issue is as follows: "The public has the right to a safe food and water supply. The association supports collaboration among dietetics professionals, academics, representatives of the agricultural and food industries, and appropriate government agencies to ensure the safety of the food and water supply by providing education to the public and industry, promoting technologic innovation and applications and supporting further research."

Safe Water and Sanitation for the Masses

It's not just a matter of sufficient water; it's a matter of safe water for many countries in the world. Safe drinking water and sanitation is critical to preserve human health, especially in children. Water-related diseases are the most common cause of illness and death in developing countries. According to the World Health Organization, 1.6 million children die each year because of unsafe water, poor sanitation, and a lack of hygiene. But the efforts to combat preventable diseases, create better hygiene conditions, and provide more access to safe water continue to face challenges. For instance, the use of fresh water supplies can be extended by reusing water for agriculture, but there are risks that the soil and products from the field may be contaminated.

With the upcoming International Year of Sanitation in 2008, global attention will focus on the need for improved health and hygiene. Helmut Lehn, PhD, of the Institute for Technology Assessment and Systems Analysis in Germany, said at World Water Week that the most pressing water global issue now is "sustainable sanitation for all. We need to ensure better governance and make advanced technology options available to more people."

The UN Millennium Project Task Force on Water and Sanitation identified key recommendations to end the global water and sanitation crisis (http://mirror.undp.org/unmillenniumproject/facts/tf7_e.htm), which emphasize that governments must commit to moving the sanitation crisis to the top of their agendas with an increase in investments for sustainable water and sanitation.

A Watery Solution

How do we tackle the vast problem of preserving our precious water resources? The UN calls for governments to take immediate action to reverse the decline of water resources. Across the globe, more can be done for water conservation through better planning, management, and technology. "We have to be smart. We have to use conservation . . . recycling, reduction of demand, and land management. If we do that, we should be alright for the next 50 years," said Peter Rogers, PhD, of Harvard University at World Water Week.

Some countries are putting these challenges into action. Singapore has been placed on a pedestal for being a model of water efficiency. PUB Singapore, the creator of NEWater, was awarded the 2007 Stockholm Industry Award for transforming the urban nation into a vision of sustainable water management practice by focusing on sound policy, technology investment, close partnerships with business and community, and cost-effective policy implementation. PUB provided 100% of Singapore's water using four national taps: imported, desalinized, rain-captured, and recycled water.

Changes in the public's behavior are also key to preserving water. The World Water Institute encourages people to consider lifestyle choices in water consumption, such as food selections. After all, it takes 130 times more water to produce a kilogram of beef than it does to produce a kilogram of potatoes.

"Given the fact that water for our daily bread is the most significant part of society's water budget, it is important to look at our food habits," says Lundqvist, who notes that a recent study for the Swedish Environmental Advisory Council included information on how much water was used to produce food (www.sou.gov.se/mvb/pdf/WEBB-%20PDF.pdf), illustrating the "water footprint" in the food supply.

Lundqvist also points out that wastage and losses in the food chain are substantial, from the field where food is produced to actual food intake. All the food that is lost and wasted consumed water in connection with its production. "It is very important that individuals acquire a better knowledge of these connections. In urban centers, where people are far away from where food is produced and where the main water challenges are, this is a huge educational issue," says Lundqvist.

In the end, human ingenuity may be our greatest asset when it comes to plugging the leak. Better irrigation systems that drip water directly onto plants, as well as a shift to less water-intensive crops, can make a difference. Improved capture and storage of flood run-off can increase water supply. Though desalination is energy intensive and produces large quantities of waste products, it may pose answers in the future. Uganda's Water Minister Maria Mutagamba emphasizes the benefits of rainwater harvesting through local, low-cost rainwater harvesting tanks. More investments need to occur in water technology projects to stimulate innovative thinking. Getting beyond the basic levels of corporate social responsibility is one of the main goals of the World Council for Sustainable Development. For instance, water supplies destined for mining operations may be tapped along the way to give communities water.

Nordin suggests that food and nutrition professionals educate themselves on solutions to the water challenge, adding, "They should support programs that work toward sustainable water management and implement personal practices that save water."

Björn Guterstam of Global Water Partnership in Sweden said at World Water Week, "Change is necessary for individual survival and global survival. If we do not change our lifestyle, nothing will happen. We have to internalize it, especially in the Western world."

SHARON PALMER, RD, is a contributing editor at *Today's Dietitian* and a freelance food and nutrition writer in southern California.

From *Today's Dietitian*, October 2007, pp. 55–58. Copyright © 2007 by Great Valley Publishing Co., Inc. Reprinted by permission.

Ocean 'Dead Zones' Spreading Worldwide

Scientists: More than 400 areas lack sufficient oxygen to support life.

RANDOLPH E. SCHMID

Like a chronic disease spreading through the body, "dead zones" with too little oxygen for life are expanding in the world's oceans.

"We have to realize that hypoxia is not a local problem," said Robert Diaz of the Virginia Institute of Marine Science. "It is a global problem and it has severe consequences for ecosystems."

"It's getting to be a problem of such a magnitude that it is starting to affect the resources that we pull out of the sea to feed ourselves," he added.

Diaz and co-author Rutger Rosenberg report in today's edition of the journal Science that there are now more than 400 dead zones around the world, double what the United Nations reported just two years ago. They range from massive ones in the Baltic Sea and the Gulf of Mexico to small ones that episodically appear in river estuaries.

The amount of "biomass" missing because of low oxygen levels in the Chesapeake Bay would be enough to feed half the commercial crab harvest for a year, Diaz estimated.

"If we screw up the energy flow within our systems we could end up with no crabs, no shrimp, no fish. That is where these dead zones are heading unless we stop their growth," Diaz said in a telephone interview.

The newest dead areas are being found in the Southern Hemisphere—South America, Africa, parts of Asia—Diaz said. Some of the increase is due to the discovery of low-oxygen areas that may have existed for years and are just being found, he said, but others are actually newly developed.

Hypoxia is a significant measure of the downstream effect of chemical fertilizers used in agriculture. Air pollution is another factor. The nitrogen from the fertilizer or pollution feeds the

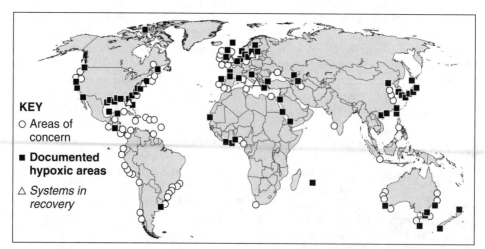

KEY
○ Areas of concern
■ **Documented hypoxic areas**
△ *Systems in recovery*

Robert Dorrell rdorrell@sacbee.com

Oxygen-depleted sites. The number of known areas of the oceans and coastal waters where life has been snuffed out due to oxygen depletion has doubled in the last two years, researchers report today in *Science* magazine. Many of the new zones being found are in the Southern Hemisphere.

Source: World Resources Institute.

growth of algae in coastal waters, particularly during summer. The algae eventually dies and sinks to the bottom, where the organic matter decays in a process that robs the bottom waters of oxygen.

Diaz and Rosenberg, of the University of Gothenburg in Sweden, conclude that it would be unrealistic to try to go back to preindustrial levels of runoff.

"Farmers aren't doing this on purpose," Diaz said. "The farmers would certainly prefer to have their (fertilizer) on the land rather than floating down the river."

He said he hopes that as fertilizers become more and more expensive farmers will begin seriously looking at ways to retain them on the land.

New low-oxygen areas have been reported in Washington's Samish Bay in the Puget Sound, Oregon's Yaquina Bay in Oregon, prawn culture ponds in Taiwan, the San Martin River in northern Spain and some fjords in Norway, Diaz said.

A portion of Big Glory Bay in New Zealand became hypoxic after salmon farming cages were set up, but began recovering when the cages were moved, he said.

A dead zone has been newly reported off the mouth of the Yangtze River in China, Diaz said, but the area has probably been hypoxic since the 1950s. "We just didn't know about it," he said.

Some of the reports are being published for the first time in journals accessible to Western scientists, he said.

Nancy Rabalais, executive director of the Louisiana Universities Marine Consortium, said she was not surprised at the increase in dead zones.

"There have been many more reported, but there truly are many more," said Rabalais, who was not a part of Diaz's research team. "What has happened in the industrialized nations with agribusiness as well that led to increased flux of nutrients from the land to the estuaries and the seas is now happening in developing countries."

Rabalais said she was told during a 1989 visit to South America that rivers there were too large to have the same problems as the Mississippi River. "Now many of their estuaries and coastal seas are suffering the same malady."

"The increase is a troubling sign for estuarine and coastal waters, which are among some of the most productive waters on the globe."

The *Washington Post* contributed to this report.

Cry of the Wild

Last week four gorillas were slaughtered in Congo. With hunting on the rise, our most majestic animals are facing a new extinction crisis.

SHARON BEGLEY

On the lush plains of Congo's Virunga National Park last week, the convoy of porters rounded the final hill and trooped into camp. They gently set down the wooden frame they had carried for miles, and with it the very symbol of the African jungle: a 600-pound silverback mountain gorilla. A leader of a troop often visited by tourists, his arms and legs were lashed to the wood, his head hanging low and spots of blood speckling his fur. The barefoot porters, shirts torn and pants caked with dust from their trek, lay him beside three smaller gorillas, all females, who had also been killed, then silently formed a semicircle around the bodies. As the stench of death wafted across the camp in the waning afternoon light, a park warden stepped forward. "What man would do this?" he thundered. He answered himself: "Not even a beast would do this."

Park rangers don't know who killed the four mountain gorillas found shot to death in Virunga, but it was the seventh killing of the critically endangered primates in two months. Authorities doubt the killers are poachers, since the gorillas' bodies were left behind and an infant—who could bring thousands of dollars from a collector—was found clinging to its dead mother in one of the earlier murders. The brutality and senselessness of the crime had conservation experts concerned that the most dangerous animal in the world had found yet another excuse to slaughter the creatures with whom we share the planet. "This area must be immediately secured," said Deo Kujirakwinja of the Wildlife Conservation Society's Congo Program, "or we stand to lose an entire population of these endangered animals."

Back when the Amazon was aflame and the forests of Southeast Asia were being systematically clear-cut, biologists were clear about what posed the greatest threat to the world's wildlife, and it wasn't men with guns. For decades, the chief threat was habitat destruction. Whether it was from impoverished locals burning a forest to raise cattle or a multinational denuding a tree-covered Malaysian hillside, wildlife was dying because species were being driven from their homes. Yes, poachers killed tigers and other trophy animals—as they had since before Theodore Roosevelt—and subsistence hunters took monkeys for bushmeat to put on their tables, but they were not a primary danger.

That has changed. "Hunting, especially in Central and West Africa, is much more serious than we imagined," says Russell Mittermeier, president of Conservation International. "It's huge," with the result that hunting now constitutes the pre-eminent threat to some species. That threat has been escalating over the past decade largely because the opening of forests to logging and mining means that roads connect once impenetrable places to towns. "It's easier to get to where the wildlife is and then to have access to markets," says conservation biologist Elizabeth Bennett of the Wildlife Conservation Society. Economic forces are also at play. Thanks to globalization, meat, fur, skins and other animal parts "are sold on an increasingly massive scale across the world," she says. Smoked monkey carcasses travel from Ghana to New York and London, while gourmets in Hanoi and Guangzhou feast on turtles and pangolins (scaly anteaters) from Indonesia. There is a thriving market for bushmeat among immigrants in Paris, New York, Montreal, Chicago and other points in the African diaspora, with an estimated 13,000 pounds of bushmeat—much of it primates—arriving every month in seven European and North American cities alone. "Hunting and trade have already resulted in widespread local extinctions in Asia and West Africa," says Bennett. "The world's wild places are falling silent."

When a company wins a logging or mining concession, it immediately builds roads wide enough for massive trucks where the principal access routes had been dirt paths no wider than a jaguar. "Almost no tropical forests remain across Africa and Asia which are not penetrated by logging or other roads," says Bennett. Hunters and weapons follow, she notes, "and wildlife flows cheaply and rapidly down to distant towns where it is either sold directly or links in to global markets." How quickly can opening a forest ravage the resident wildlife? Three weeks after a logging company opened up one Congo forest, the density of animals fell more than 25 percent; a year after a logging road went into forest areas in Sarawak, Malaysia, in 2001, not a single large mammal remained.

A big reason why hunting used to pale next to habitat destruction is that as recently as the 1990s animals were killed mostly for subsistence, with locals taking only what they needed to live. Governments and conservation groups helped reduce even that through innovative programs giving locals an economic stake in the preservation of forests and the survival of wildlife. In the mountains of Rwanda, for instance, tourists pay $500 to spend an hour with the majestic mountain gorillas, bolstering the economy of the surrounding region. But recent years have brought a more dangerous kind of hunter, and not only because they use AK-47s and even land mines to hunt.

The problem now is that hunting, even of supposedly protected animals, is a global, multimillion-dollar business. Eating bushmeat "is now a status symbol," says Thomas Brooks of Conservation International. "It's not a subsistence issue. It's not a poverty issue. It's considered supersexy to eat bushmeat." Exact figures are hard to come by, but what conservation groups know about is sobering. Every year a single province in Laos exports $3.6 million worth of wildlife, including pangolins, cats, bears and primates. In Sumatra, about 51 tigers were killed each year between 1998 and 2002; there are currently an estimated 350 tigers left on the island (down from 1,000 or so in the 1980s) and fewer than 5,000 in the world.

If a wild population is large enough, it can withstand hunting. But for many species that "if" has not existed for decades. As a result, hunting in Kilum-Ijim, Cameroon, has pushed local elephants, buffalo, bushbuck, chimpanzees, leopards and lions to the brink of extinction. The common hippopotamus, which in 1996 was classified as of "least concern" because its numbers seemed to be healthy, is now "vulnerable": over the past 10 years its numbers have fallen as much as 20 percent, largely because the hippos are illegally hunted for meat and ivory. Pygmy hippos, classified as "vulnerable" in 2000, by last year had become endangered, at risk of going extinct. Logging has allowed bushmeat hunters to reach the West African forests where the hippos live; fewer than 3,000 remain.

Setting aside parks and other conservation areas is only as good as local enforcement. "Half of the major protected areas in Southeast Asia have lost at least one species of large mammal due to hunting, and most have lost many more," says Bennett. In Thailand's Doi Inthanon and Doi Suthep National Parks, for instance, elephants, tigers and wild cattle have been hunted into oblivion, as has been every primate and hornbill in Sarawak's Kubah National Park. The world-famous Project Tiger site in India's Sariska National Park has no tigers, biologists announced in 2005. Governments cannot afford to pay as many rangers as are needed to patrol huge regions, and corruption is rife. The result is "empty-forest syndrome": majestic landscapes where flora and small fauna thrive, but where larger wildlife has been hunted out.

Which is not to say the situation is hopeless. With governments and conservationists recognizing the extinction threat posed by logging and mining, they are taking steps to ensure that animals do not come out along with the wood and minerals. In one collaboration, the government of Congo and the WCS work with a Swiss company, Congolaise Industrielle des Bois—which has a logging concession near Nouabalé-Ndoki National Park—to ensure that employees and their families hunt only for their own food needs; the company also makes sure that bushmeat does not get stowed away on logging trucks as illegal hunters try to take their haul to market. Despite the logging, gorillas, chimps, forest elephants and bongos are thriving in the park.

Anyone who thrills at the sight of man's distant cousins staring silently through the bush can only hope that the executions of Virunga's gorillas is an aberration. At the end of the week, UNESCO announced that it was sending a team to investigate the slaughter.

UNIT 4
Political Economy

Unit Selections

15. **Globalization and Its Contents,** Peter Marber
16. **It's a Flat World, After All,** Thomas L. Friedman
17. **Why the World Isn't Flat,** Pankaj Ghemawat
18. **The Case against the West: America and Europe in the Asian Century,** Kishore Mahbubani
19. **A Bigger World,** *The Economist*
20. **The Lost Continent,** Moisés Naím
21. **Promises and Poverty,** Tom Knudson
22. **Drugs,** Ethan Nadelmann
23. **Ensuring Energy Security,** Daniel Yergin
24. **The Power and the Glory,** Geoffrey Carr
25. **Nuclear Now!: How Clean, Green Atomic Energy Can Stop Global Warming,** Peter Schwartz and Spencer Reiss
26. **Life After Peak Oil,** Gregory Clark

Key Points to Consider

- Are those who argue that globalization is inevitable overly optimistic? Why or why not?

- What are some of the impediments to a truly global political economy?

- How has globalization accelerated the growth of criminal behavior?

- What transformations will societies that are heavy users of fossil fuels have to undergo in order to meet future energy needs?

- How are the political economies of traditional societies different from those of the consumer-oriented societies?

- What are some of the barriers that make it difficult for nonindustrial countries to develop?

- How are China and other emerging countries trying to alter their ways of doing business in order to meet the challenges of globalization? Are they likely to succeed?

- What economic challenges do countries like Japan and the United States face in the years to come?

Student Web Site
www.mhcls.com

Internet References

Belfer Center for Science and International Affairs (BCSIA)
http://ksgwww.harvard.edu/csia/
U.S. Agency for International Development
http://www.usaid.gov
The World Bank Group
http://www.worldbank.org

A defining characteristic of the twentieth century was the intense struggle between proponents of two economic ideologies. At the heart of the conflict was the question of what role the government should play in the management of a country's economy. For some, the dominant, capitalist economic system appeared to be organized primarily for the benefit of a few wealthy people. From their perspective, the masses were trapped in poverty, supplying cheap labor to further enrich the privileged elite. These critics argued that the capitalist system could be changed only by gaining control of the political system and radically changing the ownership of the means of production. In striking contrast to this perspective, others argued that the best way to create wealth and eliminate poverty was through the profit motive, which encouraged entrepreneurs to create new products and businesses. An open and competitive marketplace, from this point of view, minimized government interference and was the best system for making decisions about production, wages, and the distribution of goods and services.

Violent conflict at times characterized the contest between capitalism and socialism/communism. The Russian and Chinese revolutions overthrew the old social order and created radical changes in the political and economic systems in these two important countries. The political structures that were created to support new systems of agricultural and industrial production (along with the centralized planning of virtually all aspects of economic activity) eliminated most private ownership of property. These two revolutions were, in short, unparalleled experiments in social engineering.

The economic collapse of the Soviet Union and the dramatic market reforms in China have recast the debate about how to best structure contemporary economic systems. Some believe that with the end of communism and the resulting participation of hundreds of millions of new consumers in the global market, an unprecedented new era has begun. Many have noted that this process of "globalization" is being accelerated by a revolution in communication and computer technologies. Proponents of this view argue that a new global economy is emerging that will ultimately eliminate national economic systems.

Others are less optimistic about the prospects of globalization. They argue that the creation of a single economic system where there are no boundaries to impede the flow of both capital and goods and services does not mean a closing of the gap between the world's rich and poor. Rather, they argue that the giant corporations will have fewer legal constraints on their behavior, and this will lead to greater exploitation of workers and the accelerated destruction of the environment. Further, these critics point out that the unintended globalization of drug trafficking and other criminal behaviors is developing more rapidly than appropriate remedies can be developed.

© The McGraw-Hill Companies/Barry Barker, photographer

The use of the term "political economy" for the title of this unit recognizes that economic and political systems are not separate. All economic systems have some type of marketplace where goods and services are bought and sold. The government (either national or international) regulates these transactions to some degree; that is, the government sets the rules that regulate the marketplace.

One of the most important concepts in assessing the contemporary political economy is "development." For the purposes of this unit, the term "development" is defined as an improvement in the basic aspects of life: lower infant mortality rates, longer life expectancy, lower disease rates, higher rates of literacy, healthier diets, and improved sanitation. Judged by these standards, some countries are more "developed" than others. A fundamental question that a thoughtful reader must consider is whether globalization is resulting in increased development not only for a few people but also for all of those participating in the global political economy.

The unit is organized into three sections. The first is a general discussion of the concept of globalization. How is it defined, and what are some of the differing perspectives on this process? For example, is the idea of a global economy merely wishful thinking by those who sit on top of the power hierarchy, self-deluded into believing that globalization is an inexorable force that will evolve in its own way, following its own rules? Or will there continue to be the traditional tensions of nation-state power politics that transcend global economic processes, that is, conflict between the powerful and those who are either ascending or descending in power?

Following the first section are two sets of case studies. The first focuses on specific countries and/or economic sectors. The second set of case studies examines the global energy sector. All of the case studies have been selected to challenge the reader to develop his or her own conclusions about the positive and negative consequences of the globalization process. Does the contemporary global political economy result in increasing the gap between economic winners and losers, or can everyone positively benefit from its system of wealth creation and distribution?

was not unknown for US troops to summarily shoot Nazi guards at concentration camps. The US had all relevant Germans fill out a questionnaire detailing their involvement with the Nazi system.

All of this was background noise for what was to become the Nuremberg trials.

How did Germans respond?

OMGUS(Office of the Military Gov't of the US) surveys in the US zone provide some useful insight. The percentages cited are from the US zone.

Globalization and Its Contents

Peter Marber

Ask ten different people to define the term "globalization" and you are likely to receive ten different answers. For many, the meaning of globalization has been shaped largely by media coverage of an angry opposition: from right-wing nationalist xenophobes and left-wing labor leaders who fear rampant economic competition from low-wage countries to social activists who see a conspiracy on the part of multinational corporations to seek profits no matter what the cost to local cultures and economic equality to environmentalists who believe the earth is being systematically ravaged by capitalism run amok. "Globalization"—as if it were a machine that could be turned off—has been presented as fundamentally flawed and dangerous. But "globalization" is a term that encompasses all cross-border interactions, whether economic, political, or cultural. And behind the negative headlines lies a story of human progress and promise that should make even the most pessimistic analysts view globalization in an entirely different light.

Two decades ago, globalization was hardly discussed. At the time, less than 15 percent of the world's population participated in true global trade. Pessimism colored discussions of the Third World, of "lesser developed" or "backward" countries. Pawns in the Cold War's global chess game, these countries conjured images of famine, overpopulation, military dictatorship, and general chaos. At the time, the prospect of the Soviet Union or Communist China integrating economically with the West, or of strongman regimes in Latin America or Asia abandoning central planning, seemed farfetched. The possibility of these countries making meaningful socioeconomic progress and attaining Western standards of living appeared utterly unrealistic. Yet the forces of globalization were already at work.

On average, people are living twice as long as they did a century ago. Moreover, the world's aggregate material infrastructure and productive capabilities are hundreds—if not thousands—of times greater than they were a hundred years ago.[1] Much of this acceleration has occurred since 1950, with a powerful upsurge in the last 25 years. No matter how one measures wealth—whether by means of economic, bio-social, or financial indicators—there have been gains in virtually every meaningful aspect of life in the last two generations, and the trend should continue upward at least through the middle of the twenty-first century.

Most people are living longer, healthier, fuller lives. This is most evident in poor parts of the world. For example, since 1950, life expectancy in emerging markets (countries with less than one-third the per capita income of the United States, or nearly 85 percent of the world's population) has increased by more than 50 percent, reaching levels the West enjoyed only two generations ago. These longevity gains are linked to lower infant mortality, better nutrition (including an 85 percent increase in daily caloric intake), improved sanitation, immunizations, and other public health advances.

Literacy rates in developing countries have also risen dramatically in the last 50 years. In 1950, only a third of the people in Eastern Europe and in parts of Latin [America] living in these countries (roughly 800 million) could read or write; today nearly two-thirds—more than 3.2 billion people—are literate. And while it took the United States and Great Britain more than 120 years to increase average formal education from 2 years in the early nineteenth century to 12 years by the mid-twentieth century, some fast-growing developing countries, like South Korea, have accomplished this feat in fewer than 40 years.

The world now has a far more educated population with greater intellectual capacity than at any other time in history. This is particularly clear in much of Asia, where mass public education has allowed billions of people to increase their productivity and integrate in the global economy as workers and consumers. Similar trends can be seen in Eastern Europe and in parts of Latin America. This increase in human capital has led to historic highs in economic output and financial assets per capita (see chart).

During the twentieth century, economic output in the United States and other West European countries often doubled in less than 30 years, and Japan's postwar economy doubled in less than 16 years. In recent decades, developing country economies have surged so quickly that some—like South Korea in the 1960s and 1970s, or China in recent years—have often doubled productive output in just 7 to 10 years.

We often forget that poverty was the human living standard for most of recorded history. Until approximately two hundred years ago, virtually everyone lived at a subsistence level. As the economist John Maynard Keynes wrote in 1931 in *Essays in Persuasion*: "From the earliest times of which we have record—back, say, to two thousand years before Christ—down to the beginning of the eighteenth century, there was no very great change in the standard life of the average man living in civilized centers of the earth. Ups and downs certainly. Visitation

	1950	2000	2050
Global Output, Per Capita ($)	586	6,666	15,155
Global Financial Market Capitalization, Per Capita ($)	158	13,333	75,000
Percent of Global GDP			
Emerging Markets	5	50	55
Industrial Countries	95	75	45
Life Expectancy (years)			
Emerging Markets	41	64	76
Industrial Countries	65	77	82
Daily Caloric Intake			
Emerging Markets	1200	2600	3000
Industrial Countries	2200	3100	3200
Infant Mortality (per 1000)			
Emerging Markets	140	65	10
Industrial Countries	30	8	4
Literacy Rate (per 100)			
Emerging Markets	33	64	90
Industrial Countries	95	98	99

Sources: Bloomberg, World Bank, United Nations, and author's estimates.
Output and financial market capitalization figures are inflation-adjusted.

Figure 1 Measured Global Progress, 1950–2050E.

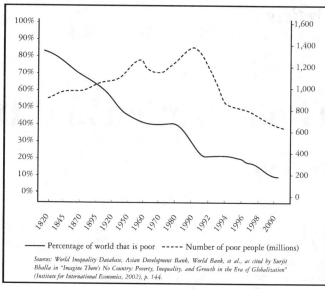

— Percentage of world that is poor   - - - - Number of poor people (millions)

Sources: World Inequality Database, Asian Development Bank, World Bank, et al., as cited by Surjit Bhalla in "Imagine There's No Country: Poverty, Inequality, and Growth in the Era of Globalization" (Institute for International Economics, 2002), p. 144.

Figure 2 Historic World Poverty Levels, 1820–2000.

of plague, famine, and war. Golden intervals. But no progressive violent change. This slow rate of progress was due to two reasons—to the remarkable absence of technical improvements and the failure of capital to accumulate." Beginning in the early nineteenth century, this picture began to change. The proportion of the world's population living in poverty declined from over 80 percent in 1820 to under 15 percent in 2000; moreover, the actual number of people living in poverty over that period declined, even as the world's population exploded from something over 1 billion to more than 6 billion.

The application of mass production technology, together with excess capital (or "profit") and a free market technologies—is at the root of our modern prosperity. Upon further examination, one can see the virtuous cycle that connects human progress, technology, and globalization. Let's take two countries, one being richer than the other. The richer country has a more educated workforce, with nearly 99 percent literacy, while the poor one has only 50 percent literacy. Due to its less educated workforce and lack of infrastructure, the poor country might only be able to participate in global trade through exporting commodities—let's say fruits and vegetables. The rich country grows fruits and vegetables as well, but it also produces clothing and light manufactured goods such as radios. In the classic Ricardo/Smith models of comparative advantage and free trade, the wealthy country should utilize its skilled workforce to produce more clothing and radios for domestic consumption and export, and it should import more fruits and vegetables from the poorer country. This would, in turn, provide the poorer country with capital to improve education and infrastructure.

As this trade pattern creates profits for both countries, human capital can be mutually developed. Eventually, the poorer country (by boosting literacy and education) should develop its own ability to produce clothes and radios. Over time, the wealthier country—having reinvested profits in higher education, research and development, etc.—will begin to produce higher-tech goods rather than clothes and radios, perhaps televisions and cars. At this stage, the wealthy country would export its cars and televisions, and import clothes and radios. In turn, the poorer country begins to import agricultural products from an even poorer third country while exporting clothing and radios to both countries. As participating countries make progress through crossborder trade and the continuous upgrading of their workforces, it follows naturally that patterns of labor and employment will evolve over time.

It is sometimes argued that free trade harms economic growth and the poor by causing job losses, particularly in wealthier countries. But trade liberalization works by encouraging a shift of labor and capital from import-competitive sectors to more dynamic export industries where comparative advantages lie. Therefore, the unemployment caused by open trade can be expected to be temporary, being offset by job creation in other export sectors (which often requires some transition time). Output losses due to this transitional unemployment should also be small relative to long-term gains in national income (and lower prices) due to production increases elsewhere. In other words, these short-term labor adjustments should be seen as lesser evils when compared to the costs of continued economic stagnation and isolation that occur without open trade.

The shifting U.S. labor pattern from low-wage agricultural labor to manufacturing to higher-paid office and service employment during the nineteenth and twentieth centuries resulted largely from trade. Similar shifts are now seen all over the globe. In the 1950 and 1960s, the United States imported electronics from Japan, and exported cars and other heavy goods. In the 1970s, we began importing small cars from Japan. In the last 30-odd years, Japan has seen its dominance in electronics and economy cars wither amid competition from China and South

Korea. But Japan has made a successful push upmarket into larger, pricier luxury cars and sport utility vehicles. While these markets were shifting over the last three decades, jobs were lost, gained, and relocated in the United States and abroad. But living standards in America, Japan, South Korea, and China have all improved dramatically over that same time.

Working Less, Producing More

There is a growing consensus that international trade has a positive effect on per capita income. A 1999 World Bank study estimates that increasing the ratio of trade to national output by one percentage point raises per capita income by between 0.5 and 2 percent.[2] But the most dramatic illustration of how greater prosperity is spread through globalization is by our increased purchasing power. Ultimately, what determines wealth is the ability to work less and consume more. The time needed for an average American worker to earn the purchase price of various goods and services decreased dramatically during the twentieth century.

In 1919, it took an American worker 30 minutes of labor to earn enough to buy a pound of ground beef. This number dropped to 23 minutes in 1950, 11 minutes in 1975, and 6 minutes in 1997.[3] But this downward trend is even more impressive with respect to manufactured goods and services. For example, in 1895 the list price for an American-made bicycle in the Montgomery Ward catalog was $65. Today an American can buy a Chinese-manufactured 21-speed bike at any mass retailer for the same amount. But an average American needed to work some 260 hours in 1895 to earn the purchase price of the old bicycle, whereas it would take the average worker less than 5 hours to earn enough to buy today's bicycle.[4] In our own lifetimes, the costs of goods and services, everything from televisions to household appliances to telephone calls, computers, and airplane travel have plummeted relative to income—and not just in the United States.

Around the world, both basic commodities and items once considered luxury items now fill store shelves and pantries as increasing output and income have lifted most people above the subsistence level. The 50 most populous countries average more than 95 televisions per 100 households. In the 25 wealthiest countries, there are approximately 450 automobiles per 1,000 people, and China is now among the fastest-growing markets for cars, clothes, computers, cellular phones, and hundreds of household items.

This deflationary effect has also led to a radically improved quality of life. In 1870, the average American worker labored 3,069 hours per year—or six 10-hour days a week. By 1950, the average hours worked had fallen to 2,075.[5] Today, that number is closer to 1,730.[6] This pattern has been repeated around the world. In 1960, the average Japanese worker toiled 2,432 hours a year over a six-day work week; by 1988, this figure had dropped to 2,111 hours a year, and by 2000 it was down to 1,878 hours. There were even more dramatic reductions in European countries like France, Germany, and Sweden.[7] The Nobel Prize–winning economist Robert William Fogel estimates that the average American's lifetime working hours will have declined from 182,100 in 1880 to a projected 75,900 by 2040, with similar trends in other wealthy industrial countries. Fogel notes that while work took up 60 percent of an American's life in 1870, by 1990 it only took up about 30 percent. Between 1880 and 1990, the average American's cumulative lifetime leisure time swelled from 48,300 hours to a remarkable 246,000 hours, or 22 years.[8] This is a pattern of improvement in the human condition that we first saw in the industrialized West and then in Japan, and which is now spreading to dozens of developing countries that are integrating into the global economy.

A Thriving Middle Class

The recent surge in progress is certainly tied to technological advances, but it is also due to the adoption of free-market practices. Cross-border trade has ballooned by a factor of 20 over the past 50 years and now accounts for more than 20 percent of global output, according to the World Bank. Indeed, trade—which grew twice as fast as global output in the 1990s—will continue to drive economic specialization and growth. The global economy is becoming more sophisticated, segmented, and diversified.

The adoption of free-market practices has gone hand-in-hand with greater political freedoms. At the beginning of the twentieth century, less than 10 percent of the world's population had the right to vote, according to Freedom House. By 1950, approximately 35 percent of the global population in less than a quarter of the world's countries enjoyed this right. By 2000, more than two-thirds of the world's countries had implemented universal suffrage.

These symbiotic developments have helped completely recompose the world's "middle class"—those with a per capita income of roughly $10–40 per day, adjusted for inflation and purchasing power parity (PPP). According to the United Nations, in 1960 two-thirds of the world's middle-class citizens lived in the industrialized world—that is, in the United States, Canada, Western Europe, Japan, and Australia. By 1980, over 60 percent of the global middle class lived in developing countries, and by 2000 this number had reached a remarkable 83 percent. It is anticipated that India and China combined could easily produce middle classes of 400–800 million people over the next two generations—roughly the size of the current middle-class populations of the United States, Western Europe, and Japan combined.

A thriving middle class is an important component of economic, political, and social stability that comes with globalization. According to the World Bank, a higher share of income for the middle class is associated with increased national income and growth, improved health, better infrastructure, sounder economic policies, less instability and civil war, and more social modernization and democracy. There are numerous studies that also suggest that increasing wealth promotes gender equality, greater voter participation, income equality, greater concern for the environment, and more transparency in the business and political arenas, all of the quality-of-life issues that concern globalization skeptics.[9]

Measuring Inequality

Even if they concede that the world is wealthier overall, many critics of globalization cite the dangers of growing income inequality. Although the science of analyzing such long-term trends is far from perfect, there are indicators that point toward measurable progress even on this front.[10] The preoccupation with income or gross national product (GNP) as the sole measure of progress is unfortunate. Income is one measure of wealth, but not the only one. And income comparisons do not always reflect informal or unreported economic activity, which tends to be more prevalent in poor countries.

Many social scientists use Gini coefficients (a measure of income dispersion between and within countries) to bolster their arguments about inequality. The lower the Gini figure (between one and zero), the more equal income distribution tends to be. Unfortunately, the Gini index does not take into consideration purchasing power parity, the age dispersion of a population, and other variables that affect the overall picture. When adjusted for PPP, the Gini index for world income distribution decreased from 0.59 to 0.52 between 1965 and 1997, an improvement of nearly 12 percent.[11] Poverty rate trends are also cited by condemners of globalization, but this approach is problematic as well. The impoverished are often defined as those who earn 50 percent less than the median income in a country. But because 50 percent of median American income is very different than 50 percent of median income in Bangladesh, poverty rates may not tell us as much about human progress as we might think.

We can better gauge human progress by examining broader trends in bio-social development than income-centered analyses. A yardstick like the United Nations Development Program's human development index (HDI), for example, which looks at not only income but also life expectancy and education (including literacy and school enrollment), with the higher numbers denoting greater development, provides a clearer picture of global well-being:

	1960	1993	2002
OECD Countries	.80	.91	.91
Developing Countries	.26	.56	.70
Least Developed Countries	.16	.33	.44

What these numbers show is not only that human development has improved overall but that differentials between rich and poor countries are closing. While the HDI figure for wealthy OECD countries in 1960 was five times greater than that for the least developed countries (and three times higher than that for developing countries), those gaps were nearly halved by 1993. And in the most intense period of recent globalization, from 1993 to 2002, these gaps closed even further.

This by no means negates the reality of poverty in many parts of the world. There are still an estimated 1 billion people living in "abject" poverty today, but the World Bank estimates that this number should decline by 50 percent by 2015, if current growth trends hold.

Potholes on the Road to Globalization

The great gains and momentum of the last 25 years should not be seen as sufficient or irreversible. There are still formidable impediments to continued progress, the four most serious being protectionism, armed conflict, environmental stress, and demographic imbalances.

- *Protectionism*. One of the responses to globalization has been the attempt to pull inward, to save traditional industries and cultures, and to expel foreigners and foreign ideas. In India, consumers have protested against McDonald's restaurants for violating Hindu dietary laws. In France, angry farmers have uprooted genetically engineered crops, saying they threatened domestic control over food production.

    Possibly the most harmful protectionism today relates to global agricultural policy. Farming subsidies in wealthy countries now total approximately $350 billion a year, or seven times the $50 billion that such countries provide annually in foreign aid to the developing world.[12] Global trade policies may exclude developing countries from $700 billion in commerce annually, denying them not only needed foreign currency but also the commercial and social interaction necessary to bio-social progress.[13]

    Protectionism in the form of tariffs, rigid labor and immigration laws, capital controls, and regressive tax structures also should be resisted. Wealthy countries should not cling to old industries like apparel or agriculture; it is far more profitable, economically and socially, to look forward and outward, to focus on growing higher-skill industries—like aviation, pharmaceuticals, and entertainment—and to embrace new markets. In turn, poorer countries have generally grown richer through economic interaction with foreign countries, by refocusing nationalistic energies and policies toward future-oriented, internationally engaged commercial activity. The late-twentieth-century march away from closed economies has improved the lives of billions of people. To bow to nationalistic calls for protectionist policies could slow and even reverse this momentum.

- *Armed Conflict*. Countries cannot compete economically, cultivate human capital, or develop financial markets in the midst of armed conflict. According to the Stockholm International Peace Research Institute, there were 57 major armed conflicts in 45 different locations between 1990 and 2001; all but 3 of these were civil wars, which inflict deep economic damage and stunt development. In addition to ongoing civil wars, there are a number of potential cross-border powder kegs (beyond the recent U.S. invasions of Afghanistan and Iraq): Kashmir, over which nuclearized India and Pakistan have been at odds for decades; Taiwan, over which China claims sovereignty; Israel and its Arab neighbors; and the Korean peninsula. The economic, political, and cultural uncertainty surrounding these areas of potential conflict restricts the flow of capital, and paralyzes businesses, investors, and consumers.

To the extent that defense budgets continue to grow in tandem with global tensions and economic resources are used for military purposes, there will be fewer resources devoted to the development of human capital and economic competitiveness.

- *Environmental Stress.* There is no getting around the fact that the success of globalization is underscored by dramatic increases in consumption. With increased consumption comes environmental degradation. Damage to the environment, current or projected, can impede economic progress in many ways. Climatic changes attributed to greenhouse gas emissions and pressure on natural resources are serious problems. Resource scarcity is only one issue we will have to confront as 2–3 billion more people consume like middle-class Americans over the next 50 years. In the face of these environmental dangers, a host of new regulations may be enacted locally or globally. Increased environmental awareness among wealthier populations may lead to domestic policies that will raise costs to businesses and consumers, which in turn could curb economic expansion.

One step in the right direction would be increased public spending on alternative and renewable energy sources in the wealthier countries. The world is clearly underpowered, and the need for diversified energy grows as we speak. The benefits of a burgeoning alternative energy sector could be multiplicative. First, it might spur new economic growth areas for employment in rich countries, supplying them with potential technologies for export while reducing their reliance on foreign oil. Second, it might encourage developing countries that are over-reliant on oil exports to develop and modernize their economies and societies. Third, it would allow developing countries to build their infrastructures with a more diversified, sustainable energy approach than the first wave of industrializing countries.

- *Demographic Imbalances.* There are sharply contrasting population trends around the globe: developing nations are experiencing a youth bulge while industrialized countries are aging rapidly. This divergence may present a variety of challenges to globalization. In poorer developing countries, the youth bulge equals economic opportunity but is also potentially disruptive. In more than 50 of these countries, 50 percent of the population is under the age of 25. In some cases, half the population is under 20, and in extreme cases, even younger. These developing nations are also among the poorest, the fastest urbanizing, and the least politically or institutionally developed, making them susceptible to violence and instability. The large number of unemployed, disenfranchised young men in these countries may explain the growth of Islamic fundamentalism and the existence of pillaging bands of armed warriors in sub-Saharan Africa. Large young

populations may also lead to unregulated, unlawful migration that can create long-lasting instability.[14]

While the youth bulge can cause problems that derail global progress, the richest countries may fall victim to their past success. Prosperity, while providing more lifestyle choices and wellness, also results in lower birth rates and increasing longevity which could dampen long-term economic demand. The aging of wealthier populations also stresses public pension schemes that were conceived under different demographic circumstances—eras of robust population and consumption growth. In economies where populations are stagnant or shrinking, the specter of lengthy "aging recessions"—characterized by vicious cycles of falling demand for consumer goods (and deflation), collapsing asset values (including real estate), shrinking corporate profits, deteriorating household and financial institution balance sheets, weakening currencies, and soaring budget pressures—looms large.

Preparing for the Best, Not the Worst

Globalization and its major engines—burgeoning human capital, freer markets, increasing cross-border interaction—have created a new world order that has incited passionate debate, pro and con. However, both sides have more in common than one might imagine.

First, if human capital is a key component of improved living standards, it is arguable that increased spending on education should become a priority in rich and poor countries alike. Wealthier nations continually need to boost productivity and comparative advantage, while poorer countries need to develop skills to compete in the global economy. By adding to the numbers of the educated, there will be a wider base of workers and consumers to contribute to the virtuous cycle of prosperity we have witnessed in the last 50 years.

Second, boosting human capital in poor countries through increased financial and technical aid should also help broaden the marketplace in terms of workers and consumers. Appropriating an extra $100 billion in aid each year—a drop in the bucket for the 20 richest countries—could help some 2 billion people overcome their daily struggles with malnutrition, HIV/AIDS, malaria, and dirty drinking water, thereby increasing the number of healthy, productive workers and consumers.

Third, reorienting wealthy country subsidies away from low-tech areas like agriculture and mining toward higher-tech industries (including alternative energy development) would accelerate comparative advantage and stimulate greater trade. With wealthy countries focusing on higher-value-added industries for domestic consumption and export, poorer countries could pick up the slack in lower-skilled sectors where they can begin to engage the global economy. Over time, the poorer countries would become larger markets for goods and services. This, along with the two attitudinal and policy shifts mentioned above, could have a positive effect on the well-being of the world's population.

Even with its positive trends, globalization is not a perfect process. It is not a panacea for every problem for every person at every moment in time. It is a messy, complicated web of interdependent relationships, some long-term, some fleeting. But globalization is too often cited as creating a variety of human miseries such as sweatshop labor, civil war, and corruption—as if such ills never existed before 1980. Poverty is more at the root of such miseries. That is why the wholesale rejection of globalization—without acknowledging its tremendously positive record in alleviating poverty—is shortsighted. Indeed, one could see how simply embracing globalization as inevitable—rather than debating its definition and purported shortcomings—could potentially foster more cross-border coordination on a variety of issues such as drug trafficking, ethnic cleansing, illegal immigration, famine, epidemic disease, environmental stress, and terrorism.

Emotion and confusion have unfortunately tainted the globalization debate both in the United States and abroad, and the focus is often on anecdotal successes or failures. Anxieties and economies may ebb and flow in the short run, but the responsibility to manage these progressive evolutions and revolutions—with worldwide human prosperity as the goal—should be our consistent aim in both government and the marketplace.

Notes

Many of the issues and arguments presented here in abbreviated form are examined at greater length in my book, *Money Changes Everything: How Global Prosperity Is Reshaping Our Needs, Values, and Lifestyles* (Upper Saddle River, NJ: FT Prentice Hall, 2003).

1. See Angus Maddison, *Monitoring the World Economy: 1820–1992* (Paris: OECD, 1995).

2. Jeffrey A. Frankel and David Romer, "Does Trade Growth Cause Growth?" *American Economic Review,* vol. 89 (June 1999), pp. 379–99.

3. W. Michael Cox and Richard Alm, *Time Well Spent: The Declining Real Cost of Living in America*, annual report (Dallas: Federal Reserve Bank, 1997), p. 4.

4. Based on average U.S. industrial wages of approximately $15 per hour in 2000.

5. W. Michael Cox and Richard Alm, *These Are the Good Old Days: A Report on US Living Standards*, annual report (Dallas: Federal Reserve Bank, 1994), p. 7.

6. Robert William Fogel, *The Fourth Great Awakening and the Future of Egalitarianism* (Chicago: University of Chicago Press, 2000), p. 185.

7. Ibid., p. 186.

8. Ibid., pp. 184–90.

9. See Marber, *Money Changes Everything*. For more on specific shifts in attitudes and values relative to economic development, the University of Michigan's Ron Inglehart's seminal Human Values Surveys are an invaluable resource.

10. For a balanced study of this subject, see Arne Mechoir, Kjetil Telle, and Henrik Wiig, *Globalisation and Inequality: World Income and Living Standards, 1960–1998*, Norwegian Ministry of Foreign Affairs, Report 6B:2000, October 2000, available at http://odin.dep.no/archive/udvedlegg/01/01/rev_016.pdf.

11. Ibid., p. 14.

12. James Wolfensohn, "How Rich Countries Keep the Rest of the World in Poverty," *Irish Independent*, September 30, 2002.

13. Ibid.

14. See Michael Teitelbaum, "Are North/South Population Growth Differentials a Prelude to Conflict?" at http://www.csis.org/gai/Graying/speeches/teitelbaum.html.

PETER MARBER is an author, professional money manager, and faculty member at the School of International and Public Affairs at Columbia University.

It's a Flat World, After All

THOMAS L. FRIEDMAN

In 1492 Christopher Columbus set sail for India, going west. He had the Nina, the Pinta and the Santa Maria. He never did find India, but he called the people he met "Indians" and came home and reported to his king and queen: "The world is round." I set off for India 512 years later. I knew just which direction I was going. I went east. I had Lufthansa business class, and I came home and reported only to my wife and only in a whisper: "The world is flat."

And therein lies a tale of technology and geoeconomics that is fundamentally reshaping our lives—much, much more quickly than many people realize. It all happened while we were sleeping, or rather while we were focused on 9/11, the dot-com bust and Enron—which even prompted some to wonder whether globalization was over. Actually, just the opposite was true, which is why it's time to wake up and prepare ourselves for this flat world, because others already are, and there is no time to waste.

I wish I could say I saw it all coming. Alas, I encountered the flattening of the world quite by accident. It was in late February [2004], and I was visiting the Indian high-tech capital, Bangalore, working on a documentary for the Discovery Times channel about outsourcing. In short order, I interviewed Indian entrepreneurs who wanted to prepare my taxes from Bangalore, read my X-rays from Bangalore, trace my lost luggage from Bangalore and write my new software from Bangalore. The longer I was there, the more upset I became—upset at the realization that while I had been off covering the 9/11 wars, globalization had entered a whole new phase, and I had missed it. I guess the eureka moment came on a visit to the campus of Infosys Technologies, one of the crown jewels of the Indian outsourcing and software industry. Nandan Nilekani, the Infosys C.E.O., was showing me his global video-conference room, pointing with pride to a wall-size flat-screen TV, which he said was the biggest in Asia. Infosys, he explained, could hold a virtual meeting of the key players from its entire global supply chain for any project at any time on that supersize screen. So its American designers could be on the screen speaking with their Indian software writers and their Asian manufacturers all at once. That's what globalization is all about today, Nilekani said. Above the screen there were eight clocks that pretty well summed up the Infosys workday: 24/7/365. The clocks were labeled U.S. West, U.S. East, G.M.T., India, Singapore, Hong Kong, Japan, Australia.

"Outsourcing is just one dimension of a much more fundamental thing happening today in the world," Nilekani explained. "What happened over the last years is that there was a massive investment in technology, especially in the bubble era, when hundreds of millions of dollars were invested in putting broadband connectivity around the world, undersea cables, all those things." At the same time, he added, computers became cheaper and dispersed all over the world, and there was an explosion of e-mail software, search engines like Google and proprietary software that can chop up any piece of work and send one part to Boston, one part to Bangalore and one part to Beijing, making it easy for anyone to do remote development. When all of these things suddenly came together around 2000, Nilekani said, they "created a platform where intellectual work, intellectual capital, could be delivered from anywhere. It could be disaggregated, delivered, distributed, produced and put back together again—and this gave a whole new degree of freedom to the way we do work, especially work of an intellectual nature. And what you are seeing in Bangalore today is really the culmination of all these things coming together."

At one point, summing up the implications of all this, Nilekani uttered a phrase that rang in my ear. He said to me, "Tom, the playing field is being leveled." He meant that countries like India were now able to compete equally for global knowledge work as never before—and that America had better get ready for this. As I left the Infosys campus that evening and bounced along the potholed road back to Bangalore, I kept chewing on that phrase: "The playing field is being leveled."

"What Nandan is saying," I thought, "is that the playing field is being flattened. Flattened? Flattened? My God, he's telling me the world is flat!"

Here I was in Bangalore—more than 500 years after Columbus sailed over the horizon, looking for a shorter route to India using the rudimentary navigational technologies of his day, and returned safely to prove definitively that the world was round—and one of India's smartest engineers, trained at his country's top technical institute and backed by the most modern technologies of his day, was telling me that the world was flat, as flat as that screen on which he can host a meeting of his whole global supply chain. Even more interesting, he was citing this development as a new milestone in human progress and a great opportunity for India and the world—the fact that we had made our world flat!

This has been building for a long time. Globalization 1.0 (1492 to 1800) shrank the world from a size large to a size medium, and the dynamic force in that era was countries globalizing for resources and imperial conquest. Globalization 2.0 (1800 to 2000) shrank the world from a size medium to a size small, and it was spearheaded by companies globalizing for markets and labor. Globalization 3.0 (which started around 2000) is shrinking the world from a size small to a size tiny and flattening the playing field at the same time. And while the dynamic force in Globalization 1.0 was countries globalizing and the dynamic force in Globalization 2.0 was companies globalizing, the dynamic force in Globalization 3.0—the thing that gives it its unique character—is individuals and small groups globalizing. Individuals must, and can, now ask: where do I fit into the global competition and opportunities of the day, and how can I, on my own, collaborate with others globally? But Globalization 3.0 not only differs from the previous eras in how it is shrinking and flattening the world and in how it is empowering individuals. It is also different in that Globalization 1.0 and 2.0 were driven primarily by European and American companies and countries. But going forward, this will be less and less true. Globalization 3.0 is not only going to be driven more by individuals but also by a much more diverse—non-Western, nonwhite—group of individuals. In Globalization 3.0, you are going to see every color of the human rainbow take part.

"Today, the most profound thing to me is the fact that a 14-year-old in Romania or Bangalore or the Soviet Union or Vietnam has all the information, all the tools, all the software easily available to apply knowledge however they want," said Marc Andreessen, a co-founder of Netscape and creator of the first commercial Internet browser. "That is why I am sure the next Napster is going to come out of left field. As bioscience becomes more computational and less about wet labs and as all the genomic data becomes easily available on the Internet, at some point you will be able to design vaccines on your laptop."

Andreessen is touching on the most exciting part of Globalization 3.0 and the flattening of the world: the fact that we are now in the process of connecting all the knowledge pools in the world together. We've tasted some of the downsides of that in the way that Osama bin Laden has connected terrorist knowledge pools together through his Qaeda network, not to mention the work of teenage hackers spinning off more and more lethal computer viruses that affect us all. But the upside is that by connecting all these knowledge pools we are on the cusp of an incredible new era of innovation, an era that will be driven from left field and right field, from West and East and from North and South. Only 30 years ago, if you had a choice of being born a B student in Boston or a genius in Bangalore or Beijing, you probably would have chosen Boston, because a genius in Beijing or Bangalore could not really take advantage of his or her talent. They could not plug and play globally. Not anymore. Not when the world is flat, and anyone with smarts, access to Google and a cheap wireless laptop can join the innovation fray.

When the world is flat, you can innovate without having to emigrate. This is going to get interesting. We are about to see creative destruction on steroids.

How did the world get flattened, and how did it happen so fast?

It was a result of 10 events and forces that all came together during the 1990's and converged right around the year 2000. Let me go through them briefly. The first event was 11/9. That's right—not 9/11, but 11/9. Nov. 9, 1989, is the day the Berlin Wall came down, which was critically important because it allowed us to think of the world as a single space. "The Berlin Wall was not only a symbol of keeping people inside Germany; it was a way of preventing a kind of global view of our future," the Nobel Prize-winning economist Amartya Sen said. And the wall went down just as the windows went up—the breakthrough Microsoft Windows 3.0 operating system, which helped to flatten the playing field even more by creating a global computer interface, shipped six months after the wall fell.

The second key date was 8/9. Aug. 9, 1995, is the day Netscape went public, which did two important things. First, it brought the Internet alive by giving us the browser to display images and data stored on Web sites. Second, the Netscape stock offering triggered the dot-com boom, which triggered the dot-com bubble, which triggered the massive overinvestment of billions of dollars in fiber-optic telecommunications cable. That overinvestment, by companies like Global Crossing, resulted in the willy-nilly creation of a global undersea-underground fiber network, which in turn drove down the cost of transmitting voices, data and images to practically zero, which in turn accidentally made Boston, Bangalore and Beijing next-door neighbors overnight. In sum, what the Netscape revolution did was bring people-to-people connectivity to a whole new level. Suddenly more people could connect with more other people from more different places in more different ways than ever before.

No country accidentally benefited more from the Netscape moment than India. "India had no resources and no infrastructure," said Dinakar Singh, one of the most respected hedge-fund managers on Wall Street, whose parents earned doctoral degrees in biochemistry from the University of Delhi before emigrating to America. "It produced people with quality and by quantity. But many of them rotted on the docks of India like vegetables. Only a relative few could get on ships and get out. Not anymore, because we built this ocean crosser, called fiber-optic cable. For decades you had to leave India to be a professional. Now you can plug into the world from India. You don't have to go to Yale and go to work for Goldman Sachs." India could never have afforded to pay for the bandwidth to connect brainy India with high-tech America, so American shareholders paid for it. Yes, crazy overinvestment can be good. The overinvestment in railroads turned out to be a great boon for the American economy. "But the railroad overinvestment was confined to your own country and so, too, were the benefits," Singh said. In the case of the digital railroads, "it was the foreigners who benefited." India got a free ride.

The first time this became apparent was when thousands of Indian engineers were enlisted to fix the Y2K—the year 2000—computer bugs for companies from all over the world. (Y2K should be a national holiday in India. Call it "Indian Interdependence Day," says Michael Mandelbaum, a foreign-policy analyst at Johns Hopkins.) The fact that the Y2K work could be outsourced to Indians was made possible by the first two flatteners, along with a third, which I call "workflow." Workflow is shorthand for all the software applications, standards and electronic transmission pipes, like middleware, that connected all those computers and fiber-optic cable. To put it another way, if the Netscape moment connected people to people like never before, what the workflow revolution did was connect applications to applications so that people all over the world could work together in manipulating and shaping words, data and images on computers like never before.

Indeed, this breakthrough in people-to-people and application-to-application connectivity produced, in short order, six more flatteners—six new ways in which individuals and companies could collaborate on work and share knowledge. One was "outsourcing." When my software applications could connect seamlessly with all of your applications, it meant that all kinds of work—from accounting to software-writing—could be digitized, disaggregated and shifted to any place in the world where it could be done better and cheaper. The second was "offshoring." I send my whole factory from Canton, Ohio, to Canton, China. The third was "open-sourcing." I write the next operating system, Linux, using engineers collaborating together online and working for free. The fourth was "insourcing." I let a company like UPS come inside my company and take over my whole logistics operation—everything from filling my orders online to delivering my goods to repairing them for customers when they break. (People have no idea what UPS really does today. You'd be amazed!). The fifth was "supply-chaining." This is Wal-Mart's specialty. I create a global supply chain down to the last atom of efficiency so that if I sell an item in Arkansas, another is immediately made in China. (If Wal-Mart were a country, it would be China's eighth-largest trading partner.) The last new form of collaboration I call "informing"—this is Google, Yahoo and MSN Search, which now allow anyone to collaborate with, and mine, unlimited data all by themselves.

So the first three flatteners created the new platform for collaboration, and the next six are the new forms of collaboration that flattened the world even more. The 10th flattener I call "the steroids," and these are wireless access and voice over Internet protocol (VoIP). What the steroids do is turbocharge all these new forms of collaboration, so you can now do any one of them, from anywhere, with any device.

The world got flat when all 10 of these flatteners converged around the year 2000. This created a global, Web-enabled playing field that allows for multiple forms of collaboration on research and work in real time, without regard to geography, distance or, in the near future, even language. "It is the creation of this platform, with these unique attributes, that is the truly important sustainable breakthrough that made what you call the flattening of the world possible," said Craig Mundie, the chief technical officer of Microsoft.

No, not everyone has access yet to this platform, but it is open now to more people in more places on more days in more ways than anything like it in history. Wherever you look today—whether it is the world of journalism, with bloggers bringing down Dan Rather; the world of software, with the Linux code writers working in online forums for free to challenge Microsoft; or the world of business, where Indian and Chinese innovators are competing against and working with some of the most advanced Western multinationals—hierarchies are being flattened and value is being created less and less within vertical silos and more and more through horizontal collaboration within companies, between companies and among individuals.

Do you recall "the IT revolution" that the business press has been pushing for the last 20 years? Sorry to tell you this, but that was just the prologue. The last 20 years were about forging, sharpening and distributing all the new tools to collaborate and connect. Now the real information revolution is about to begin as all the complementarities among these collaborative tools start to converge. One of those who first called this moment by its real name was Carly Fiorina, the former Hewlett-Packard C.E.O., who in 2004 began to declare in her public speeches that the dot-com boom and bust were just "the end of the beginning." The last 25 years in technology, Fiorina said, have just been "the warm-up act." Now we are going into the main event, she said, "and by the main event, I mean an era in which technology will truly transform every aspect of business, of government, of society, of life."

As if this flattening wasn't enough, another convergence coincidentally occurred during the 1990's that was equally important. Some three billion people who were out of the game walked, and often ran, onto the playing field. I am talking about the people of China, India, Russia, Eastern Europe, Latin America and Central Asia. Their economies and political systems all opened up during the course of the 1990s so that their people were increasingly free to join the free market. And when did these three billion people converge with the new playing field and the new business processes? Right when it was being flattened, right when millions of them could compete and collaborate more equally, more horizontally and with cheaper and more readily available tools. Indeed, thanks to the flattening of the world, many of these new entrants didn't even have to leave home to participate. Thanks to the 10 flatteners, the playing field came to them!

It is this convergence—of new players, on a new playing field, developing new processes for horizontal collaboration—that I believe is the most important force shaping global economics and politics in the early 21st century. Sure, not all three billion can collaborate and compete. In fact, for most people the world is not yet flat at all. But even if we're talking about only 10 percent, that's 300 million people—about twice the size of the American work force. And be advised: the Indians and Chinese are not racing us to the bottom. They are racing us to the top. What China's leaders really want is that the next generation of underwear and airplane wings not just be "made in China" but also be "designed in China." And that is where things are heading. So in 30 years we will have gone from "sold in China" to "made in China" to "designed in China" to "dreamed up in China"—or from China as collaborator with the worldwide manufacturers on nothing to China as a low-cost, high-quality, hyperefficient collaborator with worldwide manufacturers on everything. Ditto India. Said

Craig Barrett, the C.E.O. of Intel, "You don't bring three billion people into the world economy overnight without huge consequences, especially from three societies"—like India, China and Russia—"with rich educational heritages."

That is why there is nothing that guarantees that Americans or Western Europeans will continue leading the way. These new players are stepping onto the playing field legacy free, meaning that many of them were so far behind that they can leap right into the new technologies without having to worry about all the sunken costs of old systems. It means that they can move very fast to adopt new, state-of-the-art technologies, which is why there are already more cellphones in use in China today than there are people in America.

If you want to appreciate the sort of challenge we are facing, let me share with you two conversations. One was with some of the Microsoft officials who were involved in setting up Microsoft's research center in Beijing, Microsoft Research Asia, which opened in 1998—after Microsoft sent teams to Chinese universities to administer I.Q. tests in order to recruit the best brains from China's 1.3 billion people. Out of the 2,000 top Chinese engineering and science students tested, Microsoft hired 20. They have a saying at Microsoft about their Asia center, which captures the intensity of competition it takes to win a job there and explains why it is already the most productive research team at Microsoft: "Remember, in China, when you are one in a million, there are 1,300 other people just like you."

The other is a conversation I had with Rajesh Rao, a young Indian entrepreneur who started an electronic-game company from Bangalore, which today owns the rights to Charlie Chaplin's image for mobile computer games. "We can't relax," Rao said. "I think in the case of the United States that is what happened a bit. Please look at me: I am from India. We have been at a very different level before in terms of technology and business. But once we saw we had an infrastructure that made the world a small place, we promptly tried to make the best use of it. We saw there were so many things we could do. We went ahead, and today what we are seeing is a result of that. There is no time to rest. That is gone. There are dozens of people who are doing the same thing you are doing, and they are trying to do it better. It is like water in a tray: you shake it, and it will find the path of least resistance. That is what is going to happen to so many jobs—they will go to that corner of the world where there is the least resistance and the most opportunity. If there is a skilled person in Timbuktu, he will get work if he knows how to access the rest of the world, which is quite easy today. You can make a Web site and have an e-mail address and you are up and running. And if you are able to demonstrate your work, using the same infrastructure, and if people are comfortable giving work to you and if you are diligent and clean in your transactions, then you are in business."

Instead of complaining about outsourcing, Rao said, Americans and Western Europeans would "be better off thinking about how you can raise your bar and raise yourselves into doing something better. Americans have consistently led in innovation over the last century. Americans whining—we have never seen that before."

Rao is right. And it is time we got focused. As a person who grew up during the cold war, I'll always remember driving down the highway and listening to the radio, when suddenly the music would stop and a grim-voiced announcer would come on the air and say: "This is a test. This station is conducting a test of the Emergency Broadcast System." And then there would be a 20-second high-pitched siren sound. Fortunately, we never had to live through a moment in the cold war when the announcer came on and said, "This is a not a test."

That, however, is exactly what I want to say here: "This is not a test."

The long-term opportunities and challenges that the flattening of the world puts before the United States are profound. Therefore, our ability to get by doing things the way we've been doing them—which is to say not always enriching our secret sauce—will not suffice any more. "For a country as wealthy as we are, it is amazing how little we are doing to enhance our natural competitiveness," says Dinakar Singh, the Indian-American hedge-fund manager. "We are in a world that has a system that now allows convergence among many billions of people, and we had better step back and figure out what it means. It would be a nice coincidence if all the things that were true before were still true now, but there are quite a few things you actually need to do differently. You need to have a much more thoughtful national discussion."

If this moment has any parallel in recent American history, it is the height of the cold war, around 1957, when the Soviet Union leapt ahead of America in the space race by putting up the Sputnik satellite. The main challenge then came from those who wanted to put up walls; the main challenge to America today comes from the fact that all the walls are being taken down and many other people can now compete and collaborate with us much more directly. The main challenge in that world was from those practicing extreme Communism, namely Russia, China and North Korea. The main challenge to America today is from those practicing extreme capitalism, namely China, India and South Korea. The main objective in that era was building a strong state, and the main objective in this era is building strong individuals.

Meeting the challenges of flatism requires as comprehensive, energetic and focused a response as did meeting the challenge of Communism. It requires a president who can summon the nation to work harder, get smarter, attract more young women and men to science and engineering and build the broadband infrastructure, portable pensions and health care that will help every American become more employable in an age in which no one can guarantee you lifetime employment.

We have been slow to rise to the challenge of flatism, in contrast to Communism, maybe because flatism doesn't involve ICBM missiles aimed at our cities. Indeed, the hot line, which used to connect the Kremlin with the White House, has been replaced by the help line, which connects everyone in America to call centers in Bangalore. While the other end of the hot line might have had Leonid Brezhnev threatening nuclear war, the other end of the help line just has a soft voice eager to help you sort out your AOL bill or collaborate with you on a new piece of software. No, that voice has none of the menace of Nikita Khrushchev pounding a shoe on the table at the United Nations, and it has none of the sinister snarl of the bad guys in "From Russia with Love." No, that voice on the help line just has a friendly Indian lilt that masks any sense of threat or challenge. It simply says: "Hello, my name is Rajiv. Can I help you?"

No, Rajiv, actually you can't. When it comes to responding to the challenges of the flat world, there is no help line we can call. We have to dig into ourselves. We in America have all the basic economic and educational tools to do that. But we have not been improving those tools as much as we should. That is why we are in what Shirley Ann Jackson, the 2004 president of the American Association for the Advancement of Science and president of Rensselaer Polytechnic Institute, calls a "quiet crisis"—one that is slowly eating away at America's scientific and engineering base.

"If left unchecked," said Jackson, the first African-American woman to earn a Ph.D. in physics from M.I.T., "this could challenge our pre-eminence and capacity to innovate." And it is our ability to constantly innovate new products, services and companies that has been the source of America's horn of plenty and steadily widening middle class for the last two centuries. This quiet crisis is a product of three gaps now plaguing American society. The first is an "ambition gap." Compared with the young, energetic Indians and Chinese, too many Americans have gotten too lazy. As David Rothkopf, a former official in the Clinton Commerce Department, puts it, "The real entitlement we need to get rid of is our sense of entitlement." Second, we have a serious numbers gap building. We are not producing enough engineers and scientists. We used to make up for that by importing them from India and China, but in a flat world, where people can now stay home and compete with us, and in a post-9/11 world, where we are insanely keeping out many of the first-round intellectual draft choices in the world for exaggerated security reasons, we can no longer cover the gap. That's a key reason companies are looking abroad. The numbers are not here. And finally we are developing an education gap. Here is the dirty little secret that no C.E.O. wants to tell you: they are not just outsourcing to save on

salary. They are doing it because they can often get better-skilled and more productive people than their American workers.

These are some of the reasons that Bill Gates, the Microsoft chairman, warned the governors' conference in a Feb. 26 speech that American high-school education is "obsolete." As Gates put it: "When I compare our high schools to what I see when I'm traveling abroad, I am terrified for our work force of tomorrow. In math and science, our fourth graders are among the top students in the world. By eighth grade, they're in the middle of the pack. By 12th grade, U.S. students are scoring near the bottom of all industrialized nations. . . . The percentage of a population with a college degree is important, but so are sheer numbers. In 2001, India graduated almost a million more students from college than the United States did. China graduates twice as many students with bachelor's degrees as the U.S., and they have six times as many graduates majoring in engineering. In the international competition to have the biggest and best supply of knowledge workers, America is falling behind."

We need to get going immediately. It takes 15 years to train a good engineer, because, ladies and gentlemen, this really is rocket science. So parents, throw away the Game Boy, turn off the television and get your kids to work. There is no sugar-coating this: in a flat world, every individual is going to have to run a little faster if he or she wants to advance his or her standard of living. When I was growing up, my parents used to say to me, "Tom, finish your dinner—people in China are starving." But after sailing to the edges of the flat world for a year, I am now telling my own daughters, "Girls, finish your homework—people in China and India are starving for your jobs."

I repeat, this is not a test. This is the beginning of a crisis that won't remain quiet for long. And as the Stanford economist Paul Romer so rightly says, "A crisis is a terrible thing to waste."

Thomas L. Friedman is the author of "*The World Is Flat: A Brief History of the Twenty-First Century*," to be published this week by Farrar, Straus & Giroux and from which this article is adapted. His column appears on the Op-Ed page of *The Times,* and his television documentary "Does Europe Hate Us?" was shown on the Discovery Channel on April 7, 2005.

Why the World Isn't Flat

Globalization has bound people, countries, and markets closer than ever, rendering national borders relics of a bygone era—or so we're told. But a close look at the data reveals a world that's just a fraction as integrated as the one we thought we knew. In fact, more than 90 percent of all phone calls, Web traffic, and investment is local. What's more, even this small level of globalization could still slip away.

Pankaj Ghemawat

Ideas will spread faster, leaping borders. Poor countries will have immediate access to information that was once restricted to the industrial world and traveled only slowly, if at all, beyond it. Entire electorates will learn things that once only a few bureaucrats knew. Small companies will offer services that previously only giants could provide. In all these ways, the communications revolution is profoundly democratic and liberating, leveling the imbalance between large and small, rich and poor. The global vision that Frances Cairncross predicted in her *Death of Distance* appears to be upon us. We seem to live in a world that is no longer a collection of isolated, "local" nations, effectively separated by high tariff walls, poor communications networks, and mutual suspicion. It's a world that, if you believe the most prominent proponents of globalization, is increasingly wired, informed, and, well, "flat."

It's an attractive idea. And if publishing trends are any indication, globalization is more than just a powerful economic and political transformation; it's a booming cottage industry. According to the U.S. Library of Congress's catalog, in the 1990s, about 500 books were published on globalization. Between 2000 and 2004, there were more than 4,000. In fact, between the mid-1990s and 2003, the rate of increase in globalization-related titles more than doubled every 18 months.

Amid all this clutter, several books on the subject have managed to attract significant attention. During a recent TV interview, the first question I was asked—quite earnestly—was why I still thought the world was round. The interviewer was referring of course to the thesis of *New York Times* columnist Thomas L. Friedman's bestselling book *The World Is Flat*. Friedman asserts that 10 forces—most of which enable connectivity and collaboration at a distance—are "flattening" the Earth and leveling a playing field of global competitiveness, the likes of which the world has never before seen.

It sounds compelling enough. But Friedman's assertions are simply the latest in a series of exaggerated visions that also include the "end of history" and the "convergence of tastes." Some writers in this vein view globalization as a good thing—an escape from the ancient tribal rifts that have divided humans, or an opportunity to sell the same thing to everyone on Earth. Others lament its cancerous spread, a process at the end of which everyone will be eating the same fast food. Their arguments are mostly characterized by emotional rather than cerebral appeals, a reliance on prophecy, semiotic arousal (that is, treating everything as a sign), a focus on technology as the driver of change, an emphasis on education that creates "new" people, and perhaps above all, a clamor for attention. But they all have one thing in common: They're wrong.

In truth, the world is not nearly as connected as these writers would have us believe. Despite talk of a new, wired world where information, ideas, money, and people can move around the planet faster than ever before, just a fraction of what we consider globalization actually exists. The portrait that emerges from a hard look at the way companies, people, and states interact is a world that's only beginning to realize the potential of true global integration. And what these trend's backers won't tell you is that globalization's future is more fragile than you know.

The 10 Percent Presumption

The few cities that dominate international financial activity—Frankfurt, Hong Kong, London, New York—are at the height of modern global integration; which is to say, they are all relatively well connected with one another. But when you examine the numbers, the picture is one of extreme connectivity at the local level, not a flat world. What do such statistics reveal? Most types of economic activity that could be conducted either within or across borders turn out to still be quite domestically concentrated.

One favorite mantra from globalization champions is how "investment knows no boundaries." But how much of all the capital being invested around the world is conducted by companies outside of their home countries? The fact is, the total amount of the world's capital formation that is generated from foreign direct investment (FDI) has been less than 10 percent for the last three years for which data are available (2003–05). In other words, more than 90 percent of the fixed investment around the world is still domestic. And though merger waves can push the ratio higher, it has never reached 20 percent. In a thoroughly globalized environment, one would expect this number to be much higher—about 90 percent, by my calculation. And FDI isn't an odd or unrepresentative example.

The levels of internationalization associated with cross-border migration, telephone calls, management research and education, private charitable giving, patenting, stock investment, and trade, as a fraction of gross domestic product (GDP), all stand much closer to 10 percent than 100 percent. The biggest exception in absolute terms—the trade-to-GDP—recedes most of the way back down toward 20 percent if you adjust for certain kinds of double-counting. So if someone asked me to guess the internationalization level of some activity about which I had no particular information, I would guess it to be much closer to 10 percent—than to 100 percent. I call this the "10 Percent Presumption."

More broadly, these and other data on cross-border integration suggest a semiglobalized world, in which neither the bridges nor the barriers between countries can be ignored. From this perspective, the most astonishing aspect of various writings on globalization is the extent of exaggeration involved. In short, the levels of internationalization in the world today are roughly an order of magnitude lower than those implied by globalization proponents.

A Strong National Defense

If you buy into the more extreme views of the globalization triumphalists, you would expect to see a world where national borders are irrelevant, and where citizens increasingly view themselves as members of ever broader political entities. True, communications technologies have improved dramatically during the past 100 years. The cost of a three-minute telephone call from New York to London fell from $350 in 1930 to about 40 cents in 1999, and it is now approaching zero for voice-over-Internet telephony. And the Internet itself is just one of many newer forms of connectivity that have progressed several times faster than plain old telephone service. This pace of improvement has inspired excited proclamations about the pace of global integration. But it's a huge leap to go from predicting such changes to asserting that declining communication costs will obliterate the effects of distance. Although the barriers at borders have declined significantly, they haven't disappeared.

To see why, consider the Indian software industry—a favorite of Friedman and others. Friedman cites Nandan Nilekani, the CEO of the second-largest such firm, Infosys, as his muse for the notion of a flat world. But what Nilekani has pointed out privately is that while Indian software programmers can now serve the United States from India, access is assured, in part, by U.S. capital being invested—quite literally—in that outcome. In other words, the success of the Indian IT industry is not exempt

from political and geographic constraints. The country of origin matters—even for capital, which is often considered stateless.

Or consider the largest Indian software firm, Tata Consultancy Services (TCS). Friedman has written at least two columns in the *New York Times* on TCS's Latin American operations: "[I]n today's world, having an Indian company led by a Hungarian-Uruguayan servicing American banks with Montevidean engineers managed by Indian technologists who have learned to eat Uruguayan veggie is just the new normal," Friedman writes. Perhaps. But the real question is why the company established those operations in the first place. Having worked as a strategy advisor to TCS since 2000, I can testify that reasons related to the tyranny of time zones, languages, and the need for proximity to clients' local operations loomed large in that decision. This is a far cry from globalization proponents' oft-cited world in which geography, language, and distance don't matter.

Trade flows certainly bear that theory out. Consider Canadian-U.S. trade, the largest bilateral relationship of its kind in the world. In 1988, before the North American Free Trade Agreement (NAFTA) took effect, merchandise trade levels between Canadian provinces—that is, within the country—were estimated to be 20 times as large as their trade with similarly sized and similarly distant U.S. states. In other words, there was a built-in "home bias." Although NAFTA helped reduce this ratio of domestic to international trade—the home bias—to 10 to 1 by the mid-1990s, it still exceeds 5 to 1 today. And these ratios are just for merchandise; for services, the ratio is still several times larger. Clearly, the borders in our seemingly "borderless world" still matter to most people.

Geographical boundaries are so pervasive, they even extend to cyberspace. If there were one realm in which borders should be rendered meaningless and the globalization proponents should be correct in their overly optimistic models, it should be the Internet. Yet Web traffic within countries and regions has increased far faster than traffic between them. Just as in the real world, Internet links decay with distance. People across the world may be getting more connected, but they aren't connecting with each other. The average South Korean Web user may be spending several hours a day online—connected to the rest of the world in theory—but he is probably chatting with friends across town and e-mailing family across the country rather than meeting a fellow surfer in Los Angeles. We're more wired, but no more "global."

Just look at Google, which boasts of supporting more than 100 languages and, partly as a result, has recently been rated the most globalized Web site. But Google's operation in Russia (cofounder Sergey Brin's native country) reaches only 28 percent of the market there, versus 64 percent for the Russian market leader in search services, Yandex, and 53 percent for Rambler.

Indeed, these two local competitors account for 91 percent of the Russian market for online ads linked to Web searches. What has stymied Google's expansion into the Russian market? The biggest reason is the difficulty of designing a search engine to handle the linguistic complexities of the Russian language. In addition, these local competitors are more in tune with the Russian market, for example, developing payment methods through traditional banks to compensate for the dearth of credit cards. And, though Google has doubled its reach since 2003, it's had to set up a Moscow office in Russia and hire Russian software engineers, underlining the continued importance of physical location. Even now, borders between countries define—and constrain—our movements more than globalization breaks them down.

Turning Back the Clock

If globalization is an inadequate term for the current state of integration, there's an obvious rejoinder: Even if the world isn't quite flat today, it will be tomorrow. To respond, we have to look at trends, rather than levels of integration at one point in time. The results are telling. Along a few dimensions, integration reached its all-time high many years ago. For example, rough calculations suggest that the number of long-term international migrants amounted to 3 percent of the world's population in 1900—the high-water mark of an earlier era of migration—versus 2.9 percent in 2005.

Along other dimensions, it's true that new records are being set. But this growth has happened only relatively recently, and only after long periods of stagnation and reversal. For example, FDI stocks divided by GDP peaked before World War I and didn't return to that level until the 1990s. Several economists have argued that the most remarkable development over the long term was the declining level of internationalization between the two World Wars. And despite the records being set, the current level of trade intensity falls far short of completeness, as the Canadian-U.S. trade data suggest. In fact, when trade economists look at these figures, they are amazed not at how much trade there is, but how little.

It's also useful to examine the considerable momentum that globalization proponents attribute to the constellation of policy changes that led many countries—particularly China, India, and the former Soviet Union—to engage more extensively with the international economy. One of the better-researched descriptions of these policy changes and their implications is provided by economists Jeffrey Sachs and Andrew Warner:

"The years between 1970 and 1995, and especially the last decade, have witnessed the most remarkable institutional harmonization and economic integration among nations in world history. While economic integration was increasing throughout the 1970s and 1980s, the extent of integration has come sharply into focus only since the collapse of communism in 1989. In 1995, one dominant global economic system is emerging."

Yes, such policy openings are important. But to paint them as a sea change is inaccurate at best. Remember the 10 Percent Presumption, and that integration is only beginning. The policies that we fickle humans enact are surprisingly reversible. Thus, Francis Fukuyama's *The End of History,* in which liberal democracy and technologically driven capitalism were supposed to have triumphed over other ideologies, seems quite quaint today. In the wake of Sept. 11, 2001, Samuel Huntington's *Clash of Civilizations* looks at least a bit more prescient. But even if you stay on the economic plane, as Sachs and Warner mostly do, you quickly see counterevidence to the supposed decisiveness of policy openings. The so-called Washington Consensus around market-friendly policies ran up against the 1997 Asian currency crisis and has since frayed substantially—for example, in the swing toward neopopulism across much of Latin America. In terms of economic outcomes, the number of countries—in Latin America, coastal Africa, and the former Soviet Union—that have dropped out of the "convergence club" (defined in terms of narrowing productivity and structural gaps vis-à-vis the advanced industrialized countries) is at least as impressive as the number of countries that have joined the club. At a multilateral level, the suspension of the Doha round of trade talks in the summer of 2006—prompting *The Economist* to run a cover titled "The Future of Globalization" and depicting a beached wreck—is no promising omen. In addition, the recent wave of cross-border mergers and acquisitions seems to be encountering more protectionism, in a broader range of countries, than did the previous wave in the late 1990s.

Of course, given that sentiments in these respects have shifted in the past 10 years or so, there is a fair chance that they may shift yet again in the next decade. The point is, it's not only possible to turn back the clock on globalization-friendly policies, it's relatively easy to imagine it happening. Specifically, we have to entertain the possibility that deep international economic integration may be inherently incompatible with national sovereignty—especially given the tendency of voters in many countries, including advanced ones, to support more protectionism, rather than less. As Jeff Immelt, CEO of GE, put it in late 2006, "If you put globalization to a popular vote in the U.S., it would lose." And even if cross-border integration continues on its upward path, the road from here to there is unlikely to be either smooth or straight. There will be shocks and cycles, in all likelihood, and maybe even another period of stagnation or reversal that will endure for decades. It wouldn't be unprecedented.

The champions of globalization are describing a world that doesn't exist. It's a fine strategy to sell books and even describe a potential environment that may someday exist. Because such episodes of mass delusion tend to be relatively short-lived even when they do achieve broad currency, one might simply be tempted to wait this one out as well. But the stakes are far too high for that. Governments that buy into the flat world are likely to pay too much attention to the "golden straitjacket" that Friedman emphasized in his earlier book, *The Lexus and the Olive Tree,* which is supposed to ensure that economics matters more and more and politics less and less. Buying into this version of an integrated world—or worse, using it as a basis for policymaking—is not only unproductive. It is dangerous.

PANKAJ GHEMAWAT is the Anselmo Rubiralta professor of global strategy at IESE Business School and the Jaime and Josefina Chua Tiampo professor of business administration at Harvard Business School. His new book is *Redefining Global Strategy* (Boston: Harvard Business School Press, September 2007).

The Case against the West
America and Europe in the Asian Century

KISHORE MAHBUBANI

There is a fundamental flaw in the West's strategic thinking. In all its analyses of global challenges, the West assumes that it is the source of the solutions to the world's key problems. In fact, however, the West is also a major source of these problems. Unless key Western policymakers learn to understand and deal with this reality, the world is headed for an even more troubled phase.

The West is understandably reluctant to accept that the era of its domination is ending and that the Asian century has come. No civilization cedes power easily, and the West's resistance to giving up control of key global institutions and processes is natural. Yet the West is engaging in an extraordinary act of self-deception by believing that it is open to change. In fact, the West has become the most powerful force preventing the emergence of a new wave of history, clinging to its privileged position in key global forums, such as the UN Security Council, the International Monetary Fund, the World Bank, and the G-8 (the group of highly industrialized states), and refusing to contemplate how the West will have to adjust to the Asian century.

Partly as a result of its growing insecurity, the West has also become increasingly incompetent in its handling of key global problems. Many Western commentators can readily identify specific failures, such as the Bush administration's botched invasion and occupation of Iraq. But few can see that this reflects a deeper structural problem: the West's inability to see that the world has entered a new era.

Apart from representing a specific failure of policy execution, the war in Iraq has also highlighted the gap between the reality and what the West had expected would happen after the invasion. Arguably, the United States and the United Kingdom intended only to free the Iraqi people from a despotic ruler and to rid the world of a dangerous man, Saddam Hussein. Even if George W. Bush and Tony Blair had no malevolent intentions, however, their approaches were trapped in the Western mindset of believing that their interventions could lead only to good, not harm or disaster. This led them to believe that the invading U.S. troops would be welcomed with roses thrown at their feet by happy Iraqis. But the twentieth century showed that no country welcomes foreign invaders. The notion that any Islamic nation would approve of Western military boots on its soil was ridiculous. Even in the early twentieth century, the British

invasion and occupation of Iraq was met with armed resistance. In 1920, Winston Churchill, then British secretary for war and air, quelled the rebellion of Kurds and Arabs in British-occupied Iraq by authorizing his troops to use chemical weapons. "I am strongly in favor of using poisoned gas against uncivilized tribes," Churchill said. The world has moved on from this era, but many Western officials have not abandoned the old assumption that an army of Christian soldiers can successfully invade, occupy, and transform an Islamic society.

Many Western leaders often begin their speeches by remarking on how perilous the world is becoming. Speaking after the August 2006 discovery of a plot to blow up transatlantic flights originating from London, President Bush said, "The American people need to know we live in a dangerous world." But even as Western leaders speak of such threats, they seem incapable of conceding that the West itself could be the fundamental source of these dangers. After all, the West includes the best-managed states in the world, the most economically developed, those with the strongest democratic institutions. But one cannot assume that a government that rules competently at home will be equally good at addressing challenges abroad. In fact, the converse is more likely to be true. Although the Western mind is obsessed with the Islamist terrorist threat, the West is mishandling the two immediate and pressing challenges of Afghanistan and Iraq. And despite the grave threat of nuclear terrorism, the Western custodians of the nonproliferation regime have allowed that regime to weaken significantly. The challenge posed by Iran's efforts to enrich uranium has been aggravated by the incompetence of the United States and the European Union. On the economic front, for the first time since World War II, the demise of a round of global trade negotiations, the Doha Round, seems imminent. Finally, the danger of global warming, too, is being mismanaged.

Yet Westerners seldom look inward to understand the deeper reasons these global problems are being mismanaged. Are there domestic structural reasons that explain this? Have Western democracies been hijacked by competitive populism and structural short-termism, preventing them from addressing long-term challenges from a broader global perspective?

Fortunately, some Asian states may now be capable of taking on more responsibilities, as they have been strengthened by implementing Western principles. In September 2005, Robert

Zoellick, then U.S. deputy secretary of state, called on China to become a "responsible stakeholder" in the international system. China has responded positively, as have other Asian states. In recent decades, Asians have been among the greatest beneficiaries of the open multilateral order created by the United States and the other victors of World War II, and few today want to destabilize it. The number of Asians seeking a comfortable middle-class existence has never been higher. For centuries, the Chinese and the Indians could only dream of such an accomplishment; now it is within the reach of around half a billion people in China and India. Their ideal is to achieve what the United States and Europe did. They want to replicate, not dominate, the West. The universalization of the Western dream represents a moment of triumph for the West. And so the West should welcome the fact that the Asian states are becoming competent at handling regional and global challenges.

The Middle East Mess

Western Policies have been most harmful in the Middle East. The Middle East is also the most dangerous region in the world. Trouble there affects not just seven million Israelis, around four million Palestinians, and 200 million Arabs; it also affects more than a billion Muslims worldwide. Every time there is a major flare-up in the Middle East, such as the U.S. invasion of Iraq or the Israeli bombing of Lebanon, Islamic communities around the world become concerned, distressed, and angered. And few of them doubt the problems origin: the West.

The invasion and occupation of Iraq, for example, was a multidimensional error. The theory and practice of international law legitimizes the use of force only when it is an act of self-defense or is authorized by the UN Security Council. The U.S.-led invasion of Iraq could not be justified on either count. The United States and the United Kingdom sought the Security Council's authorization to invade Iraq, but the council denied it. It was therefore clear to the international community that the subsequent war was illegal and that it would do huge damage to international law.

This has created an enormous problem, partly because until this point both the United States and the United Kingdom had been among the primary custodians of international law. American and British minds, such as James Brierly, Philip Jessup, Hersch Lauterpacht, and Hans Morgenthau, developed the conceptual infrastructure underlying international law, and American and British leaders provided the political will to have it accepted in practice. But neither the United States nor the United Kingdom will admit that the invasion and the occupation of Iraq were illegal or give up their historical roles as the chief caretakers of international law. Since 2003, both nations have frequently called for Iran and North Korea to implement UN Security Council resolutions. But how can the violators of UN principles also be their enforcers?

One rare benefit of the Iraq war may be that it has awakened a new fear of Iran among the Sunni Arab states. Egypt, Jordan, and Saudi Arabia, among others, do not want to deal with two adversaries and so are inclined to make peace with Israel. Saudi Arabia's King Abdullah used the opportunity of the special Arab League summit meeting in March 2007 to relaunch his long-standing proposal for a two-state solution to the Israeli-Palestinian conflict. Unfortunately, the Bush administration did not seize the opportunity—or revive the Taba accords that President Bill Clinton had worked out in January 2001, even though they could provide a basis for a lasting settlement and the Saudis were prepared to back them. In its early days, the Bush administration appeared ready to support a two-state solution. It was the first U.S. administration to vote in favor of a UN Security Council resolution calling for the creation of a Palestinian state, and it announced in March 2002 that it would try to achieve such a result by 2005. But here it is 2008, and little progress has been made.

The United States has made the already complicated Israeli-Palestinian conflict even more of a mess. Many extremist voices in Tel Aviv and Washington believe that time will always be on Israel's side. The pro-Israel lobby's stranglehold on the U.S. Congress, the political cowardice of U.S. politicians when it comes to creating a Palestinian state, and the sustained track record of U.S. aid to Israel support this view. But no great power forever sacrifices its larger national interests in favor of the interests of a small state. If Israel fails to accept the Taba accords, it will inevitably come to grief. If and when it does, Western incompetence will be seen as a major cause.

Never Say Never

Nuclear nonproliferation is another area in which the West, especially the United States, has made matters worse. The West has long been obsessed with the danger of the proliferation of weapons of mass destruction, particularly nuclear weapons. It pushed successfully for the near-universal ratification of the Biological and Toxin Weapons Convention, the Chemical Weapons Convention, and the Nuclear Nonproliferation Treaty (NPT).

But the West has squandered many of those gains. Today, the NPT is legally alive but spiritually dead. The NPT was inherently problematic since it divided the world into nuclear haves (the states that had tested a nuclear device by 1967) and nuclear have-nots (those that had not). But for two decades it was reasonably effective in preventing horizontal proliferation (the spread of nuclear weapons to other states). Unfortunately, the NPT has done nothing to prevent vertical proliferation, namely, the increase in the numbers and sophistication of nuclear weapons among the existing nuclear weapons states. During the Cold War, the United States and the Soviet Union agreed to work together to limit proliferation. The governments of several countries that could have developed nuclear weapons, such as Argentina, Brazil, Germany, Japan, and South Korea, restrained themselves because they believed the NPT reflected a fair bargain between China, France, the Soviet Union, the United Kingdom, and the United States (the five official nuclear weapons states and five permanent members of the UN Security Council) and the rest of the world. Both sides agreed that the world would be safer if the five nuclear states took steps to reduce their arsenals and worked toward the eventual goal of universal disarmament and the other states refrained from acquiring nuclear weapons at all.

So what went wrong? The first problem was that the NPT's principal progenitor, the United States, decided to walk away from the postwar rule-based order it had created, thus eroding the infrastructure on which the NPT's enforcement depends. During the time I was Singapore's ambassador to the UN, between 1984 and 1989, Jeane Kirkpatrick, the U.S. ambassador to the UN, treated the organization with contempt. She infamously said, "What takes place in the Security Council more closely resembles a mugging than either a political debate or an effort at problem-solving." She saw the postwar order as a set of constraints, not as a set of rules that the world should follow and the United States should help preserve. This undermined the NPT, because with no teeth of its own, no self-regulating or sanctioning mechanisms, and a clause allowing signatories to ignore obligations in the name of "supreme national interest," the treaty could only really be enforced by the UN Security Council. And once the United States began tearing holes in the fabric of the overall system, it created openings for violations of the NPT and its principles. Finally, by going to war with Iraq without UN authorization, the United States lost its moral authority to ask, for example, Iran to abide by Security Council resolutions.

Another problem has been the United States'—and other nuclear weapons states'—direct assault on the treaty. The NPT is fundamentally a social contract between the five nuclear weapons states and the rest of the world, based partly on the understanding that the nuclear powers will eventually give up their weapons. Instead, during the Cold War, the United States and the Soviet Union increased both the quantity and the sophistication of their nuclear weapons: the United States' nuclear stockpile peaked in 1966 at 31,700 warheads, and the Soviet Union's peaked in 1986 at 40,723. In fact, the United States and the Soviet Union developed their nuclear stockpiles so much that they actually ran out of militarily or economically significant targets. The numbers have declined dramatically since then, but even the current number of nuclear weapons held by the United States and Russia can wreak enormous damage on human civilization.

The nuclear states' decision to ignore Israel's nuclear weapons program was especially damaging to their authority. No nuclear weapons state has ever publicly acknowledged Israel's possession of nuclear weapons. Their silence has created a loophole in the NPT and delegitimized it in the eyes of Muslim nations. The consequences have been profound. When the West sermonizes that the world will become a more dangerous place when Iran acquires nuclear weapons, the Muslim world now shrugs.

India and Pakistan were already shrugging by 1998, when they tested their first nuclear weapons. When the international community responded by condemning the tests and applying sanctions on India, virtually all Indians saw through the hypocrisy and double standards of their critics. By not respecting their own obligations under the NPT, the five nuclear states had robbed their condemnations of any moral legitimacy; criticisms from Australia and Canada, which have also remained silent about Israel's bomb, similarly had no moral authority. The near-unanimous rejection of the NPT by the Indian establishment, which is otherwise very conscious of international opinion, showed how dead the treaty already was.

The world has lost its trust in the five nuclear weapons states and now sees them as the NPT's primary violators.

From time to time, common sense has entered discussions on nuclear weapons. President Ronald Reagan said more categorically than any U.S. president that the world would be better off without nuclear weapons. Last year, with the NPT in its death throes and the growing threat of loose nuclear weapons falling into the hands of terrorists forefront in everyone's mind, former Secretary of State George Shultz, former Defense Secretary William Perry, former Secretary of State Henry Kissinger, and former Senator Sam Nunn warned in *The Wall Street Journal* that the world was "now on the precipice of a new and dangerous nuclear era." They argued, "Unless urgent new actions are taken, the U.S. soon will be compelled to enter a new nuclear era that will be more precarious, psychologically disorienting, and economically even more costly than was Cold War deterrence." But these calls may have come too late. The world has lost its trust in the five nuclear weapons states and now sees them as the NPT's primary violators rather than its custodians. Those states' private cynicism about their obligations to the NPT has become public knowledge.

Contrary to what the West wants the rest of the world to believe, the nuclear weapons states, especially the United States and Russia, which continue to maintain thousands of nuclear weapons, are the biggest source of nuclear proliferation. Mohamed ElBaradei, the director general of the International Atomic Energy Agency, warned in *The Economist* in 2003, "The very existence of nuclear weapons gives rise to the pursuit of them. They are seen as a source of global influence, and are valued for their perceived deterrent effect. And as long as some countries possess them (or are protected by them in alliances) and others do not, this asymmetry breeds chronic global insecurity." Despite the Cold War, the second half of the twentieth century seemed to be moving the world toward a more civilized order. As the twenty-first century unfurls, the world seems to be sliding backward.

Irresponsible Stakeholders

After leading the world toward a period of spectacular economic growth in the second half of the twentieth century by promoting global free trade, the West has recently been faltering in its global economic leadership. Believing that low trade barriers and increasing trade interdependence would result in higher standards of living for all, European and U.S. economists and policymakers pushed for global economic liberalization. As a result, global trade grew from seven percent of the world's GDP in 1940 to 30 percent in 2005.

But a seismic shift has taken place in Western attitudes since the end of the Cold War. Suddenly, the United States and Europe no longer have a vested interest in the success of the East Asian economies, which they see less as allies and more as competitors. That change in Western interests was reflected in the fact that the West provided little real help to East Asia during the Asian financial crisis of 1997–98. The entry of China into the global marketplace, especially after its admission to the World Trade Organization, has made a huge difference in both economic and psychological terms. Many Europeans have lost confidence in their ability to compete with the Asians. And many Americans have lost confidence in the virtues of competition.

There are some knotty issues that need to be resolved in the current global trade talks, but fundamentally the negotiations are stalled because the conviction of the Western "champions" of free trade that free trade is good has begun to waver. When Americans and Europeans start to perceive themselves as losers in international trade, they also lose their drive to push for further trade liberalization. Unfortunately, on this front at least, neither China nor India (nor Brazil nor South Africa nor any other major developing country) is ready to take over the West's mantle. China, for example, is afraid that any effort to seek leadership in this area will stoke U.S. fears that it is striving for global hegemony. Hence, China is lying low. So, too, are the United States and Europe. Hence, the trade talks are stalled. The end of the West's promotion of global trade liberalization could well mean the end of the most spectacular economic growth the world has ever seen. Few in the West seem to be reflecting on the consequences of walking away from one of the West's most successful policies, which is what it will be doing if it allows the Doha Round to fail.

At the same time that the Western governments are relinquishing their stewardship of the global economy, they are also failing to take the lead on battling global warming. The awarding of the Nobel Peace Prize to former U.S. Vice President Al Gore, a longtime environmentalist, and the UN's Intergovernmental Panel on Climate Change confirms there is international consensus that global warning is a real threat. The most assertive advocates for tackling this problem come from the U.S. and European scientific communities, but the greatest resistance to any effective action is coming from the U.S. government. This has left the rest of the world confused and puzzled. Most people believe that the greenhouse effect is caused mostly by the flow of current emissions. Current emissions do aggravate the problem, but the fundamental cause is the stock of emissions that has accumulated since the Industrial Revolution. Finding a just and equitable solution to the problem of greenhouse gas emissions must begin with assigning responsibility both for the current flow and for the stock of greenhouse gases already accumulated. And on both counts the Western nations should bear a greater burden.

The West has to learn to share power and responsibility for the management of global issues with the rest of the world.

When it comes to addressing any problem pertaining to the global commons, such as the environment, it seems only fair that the wealthier members of the international community should shoulder more responsibility. This is a natural principle of justice. It is also fair in this particular case given the developed countries' primary role in releasing harmful gases into the atmosphere. R. K. Pachauri, chair of the Intergovernmental Panel on Climate Change, argued last year, "China and India are certainly increasing their share, but they are not increasing their per capita emissions anywhere close to the levels that you have in the developed world." Since 1850, China has contributed less than 8 percent of the world's total emissions of carbon dioxide, whereas the United States is responsible for 29 percent and western Europe is responsible for 27 percent. Today, India's per capita greenhouse gas emissions are equivalent to only 4 percent of those of the United States and 12 percent of those of the European Union. Still, the Western governments are not clearly acknowledging their responsibilities and are allowing many of their citizens to believe that China and India are the fundamental obstacles to any solution to global warming.

Washington might become more responsible on this front if a Democratic president replaces Bush in 2009. But people in the West will have to make some real concessions if they are to reduce significantly their per capita share of global emissions. A cap-and-trade program may do the trick. Western countries will probably have to make economic sacrifices. One option might be, as the journalist Thomas Friedman has suggested, to impose a dollar-per-gallon tax on Americans' gasoline consumption. Gore has proposed a carbon tax. So far, however, few U.S. politicians have dared to make such suggestions publicly.

Temptations of the East

The Middle East, nuclear proliferation, stalled trade liberalization, and global warming are all challenges that the West is essentially failing to address. And this failure suggests that a systemic problem is emerging in the West's stewardship of the international order—one that Western minds are reluctant to analyze or confront openly. After having enjoyed centuries of global domination, the West has to learn to share power and responsibility for the management of global issues with the rest of the world. It has to forgo outdated organizations, such as the Organization for Economic Cooperation and Development, and outdated processes, such as the G-8, and deal with organizations and processes with a broader scope and broader representation. It was always unnatural for the 12 percent of the world population that lived in the West to enjoy so much global power. Understandably, the other 88 percent of the world population increasingly wants also to drive the bus of world history.

First and foremost, the West needs to acknowledge that sharing the power it has accumulated in global forums would serve its interests. Restructuring international institutions to reflect the current world order will be complicated by the absence of natural leaders to do the job. The West has become part of the problem, and the Asian countries are not yet ready to step in. On the other hand, the world does not need to invent any new principles to improve global governance; the concepts of domestic good governance can and should be applied to the international community. The Western principles of democracy, the rule of law, and social justice are among the world's best bets. The ancient virtues of partnership and pragmatism can complement them.

Democracy, the foundation of government in the West, is based on the premise that each human being in a society is an equal stakeholder in the domestic order. Thus, governments are selected on the basis of "one person, one vote." This has produced long-term stability and order in Western societies. In order to produce long-term stability and order worldwide, democracy should be the cornerstone of global society, and the planet's 6.6 billion inhabitants should become equal stakeholders. To inject the spirit of democracy into global governance and global decision-making, one must turn to institutions with universal representation, especially the UN. UN institutions such as the World Health Organization and the World Meteorological Organization enjoy widespread legitimacy because of their universal membership, which means their decisions are generally accepted by all the countries of the world.

The problem today is that although many Western actors are willing to work with specialized UN agencies, they are reluctant to strengthen the UN's core institution, the UN General Assembly, from which all these specialized agencies come. The UN General Assembly is the most representative body on the planet, and yet many Western countries are deeply skeptical of it. They are right to point out its imperfections. But they overlook the fact that this imperfect assembly enjoys legitimacy in the eyes of the people of this imperfect world. Moreover, the General Assembly has at times shown more common sense and prudence than some of the most sophisticated Western democracies. Of course, it takes time to persuade all of the UN's members to march in the same direction, but consensus building is precisely what gives legitimacy to the result. Most countries in the world respect and abide by most UN decisions because they believe in the authority of the UN. Used well, the body can be a powerful vehicle for making critical decisions on global governance.

The world today is run not through the General Assembly but through the Security Council, which is effectively run by the five permanent member states. If this model were adopted in the United States, the U.S. Congress would be replaced by a selective council comprised of only the representatives from the country's five most powerful states. Would the populations of the other 45 states not deem any such proposal absurd? The West must cease its efforts to prolong its undemocratic management of the global order and find ways to effectively engage the majority of the world's population in global decision-making.

Another fundamental principle that should underpin the global order is the rule of law. This hallowed Western principle insists that no person, regardless of his or her status, is above the law. Ironically, while being exemplary in implementing the rule of law at home, the United States is a leading international outlaw in its refusal to recognize the constraints of international law. Many Americans live comfortably with this contradiction while expecting other countries to abide by widely accepted treaties. Americans react with horror when Iran tries to walk away from the NPT. Yet they are surprised that the world is equally shocked when Washington abandons a universally accepted treaty such as the Comprehensive Test Ban Treaty.

The Bush administration's decision to exempt the United States from the provisions of international law on human rights is even more damaging. For over half a century, since Eleanor Roosevelt led the fight for the adoption of the Universal Declaration of Human Rights, the United States was the global champion of human rights. This was the result of a strong ideological conviction that it was the United States' God-given duty to create a more civilized world. It also made for a good ideological weapon during the Cold War: the free United States was fighting the unfree Soviet Union. But the Bush administration has stunned the world by walking away from universally accepted human rights conventions, especially those on torture. And much as the U.S. electorate could not be expected to tolerate an attorney general who broke his own laws from time to time, how can the global body politic be expected to respect a custodian of international law that violates these very rules?

Finally, on social justice, Westerns nations have slackened. Social justice is the cornerstone of order and stability in modern Western societies and the rest of the world. People accept inequality as long as some kind of social safety net exists to help the dispossessed. Most western European governments took this principle to heart after World War II and introduced welfare provisions as a way to ward off Marxist revolutions seeking to create socialist societies. Today, many Westerners believe that they are spreading social justice globally with their massive foreign aid to the developing world. Indeed, each year, the members of the Organization for Economic Cooperation and Development, according to the organization's own estimates, give approximately $104 billion to the developing world. But the story of Western aid to the developing world is essentially a myth. Western countries have put significant amounts of money into their overseas development assistance budgets, but these funds' primary purpose is to serve the immediate and short-term security and national interests of the donors rather than the long-term interests of the recipients.

Some Asian countries are now ready to join the West in becoming responsible custodians of the global order.

The experience of Asia shows that where Western aid has failed to do the job, domestic good governance can succeed. This is likely to be Asia's greatest contribution to world history. The success of Asia will inspire other societies on different continents to emulate it. In addition, Asia's march to modernity can help produce a more stable world order. Some Asian countries are now ready to join the West in becoming responsible custodians of the global order; as the biggest beneficiaries of the current system, they have powerful incentives to do so. The West is not welcoming Asia's progress, and its short-term interests in preserving its privileged position in various global institutions are trumping its long-term interests in creating a more just and stable world order. Unfortunately, the West has gone from being the world's primary problem solver to being its single biggest liability.

KISHORE MAHBUBANI is Dean of the Lee Kuan Yew School of Public Policy at the National University of Singapore. This essay is adapted from his latest book, *The New Asian Hemisphere: The Irresistible Shift of Global Power to the East* (Public Affairs, 2008).

A Bigger World

Globalisation is entering a new phase, with emerging-market companies now competing furiously against rich-country ones. Matthew Bishop asks what that will mean for capitalism.

Globalisation used to mean, by and large, that business expanded from developed to emerging economies. Now it flows in both directions, and increasingly also from one developing economy to another. Business these days is all about "competing with everyone from everywhere for everything", write the authors of "Globality", a new book on this latest phase of globalisation by the Boston Consulting Group (BCG).

One sign of the times is the growing number of companies from emerging markets that appear in the *Fortune* 500 rankings of the world's biggest firms. It now stands at 62, mostly from the so-called BRIC economies of Brazil, Russia, India and China, up from 31 in 2003 (see Figure 1), and is set to rise rapidly. On current trends, emerging-market companies will account for one-third of the *Fortune* list within ten years, predicts Mark Spelman, head of a global think-tank run by Accenture, a consultancy.

There has been a sharp increase in the number of emerging-market companies acquiring established rich-world businesses and brands (see Table 2, next page), starkly demonstrating that "globalisation" is no longer just another word for "Americanisation". Within the past year, Budweiser, America's favourite beer, has been bought by a Belgian-Brazilian conglomerate. And several of America's leading financial institutions avoided bankruptcy only by going cap in hand to the sovereign-wealth funds (state-owned investment funds) of various Arab kingdoms and the Chinese government.

One example of this seismic shift in global business is Lenovo, a Chinese computer-maker. It became a global brand in 2005, when it paid around $1.75 billion for the personal-computer business of one of America's best-known companies, IBM—including the ThinkPad laptop range beloved of many businessmen. Lenovo had the right to use the IBM brand for five years, but dropped it two years ahead of schedule, such was its confidence in its own brand. It has only just squeezed into 499th place in the *Fortune* 500, with worldwide revenues of $16.8 billion last year. But "this is just the start. We have big plans to grow," says Yang Yuanqing, Lenovo's chairman.

One reason why his company could afford to buy a piece of Big Blue was its leading position in a domestic market buoyed by GDP growth rates that dwarf those in developed countries.

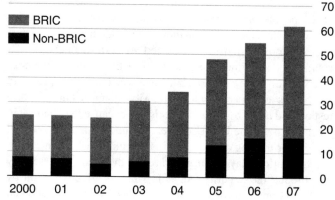

Figure 1   Sixty-two, and counting. Emerging-market companies in the *Fortune* Global 500.

Source: *Fortune*

These are lifting the incomes of millions of people to a level where they start to splash out on everything from new homes to cars to computers. "It took 25 years for the PC to get to the first billion consumers; the next billion should take seven years," says Bill Amelio, Lenovo's chief executive.

The sheer size of the consumer markets now opening up in emerging economies, especially in India and China, and their rapid growth rates, will shift the balance of business activity far more than the earlier rise of less populous economies such as Japan and South Korea and their handful of "new champions" that seemed to threaten the old order at the time.

This special report will argue that the age of "globality" is creating huge opportunities—as well as threats—for developed-world multinationals and new champions alike. The macroeconomic turbulence that the world is now going through after almost a decade of smooth growth will probably not alter the picture fundamentally, but it will complicate it. Despite all the talk of "decoupling", emerging economies have recently been growing more slowly because of their exposure to increasingly cautious American consumers.

Moreover, high oil and food prices are creating inflationary pressures in many emerging countries that had enjoyed years of stable, low prices along with extraordinary economic growth.

Table 1 Lean and Hungry

Top five emerging-market M&As.

Year	Target	Buyer	Deal Value $bn
2006	Inco *Canada*	Companhia Vale do Rio Doce, *Brazil*	18.7
2006	Rinker Group *Australia*	Cemex SA de CV *Mexico*	16.7
2008	Rio Tinto (12%) *Britain*	Alcoa; Aluminum Corp of China *US; China*	14.3
2006	Corus Group *Britain*	Tata Group *India*	13.0
2007	GE Plastics *US*	Saudi Basic Industries Corp, *Saudi Arabia*	11.6

Source: Dealogic.

Table 2 The New Giants

Ten biggest *Fortune* Global 500 emerging-market companies, 2008.

Company	Country	Global 500 Rank	Revenue $bn
Sinopec	China	16	159.3
State Grid	China	24	132.9
China National Petroleum	China	25	129.8
Pemex	Mexico	42	104.0
Gazprom	Russia	47	98.6
Petrobras	Brazil	63	87.7
Lukoil	Russia	90	67.2
Petronas	Malaysia	95	66.2
Indian Oil	India	116	57.4
Industrial & Commercial Bank of China	China	133	51.5

Source: *Fortune*.

The side-effects of rapid development, such as pollution and water shortages, also need to be tackled. "After a long period in which globalisation has been all about labour productivity, the business challenge everywhere, and especially in emerging markets, will increasingly be to raise resource productivity—using fuel, raw materials and water more efficiently," says Bob Hormats of Goldman Sachs, an investment bank.

A Cheaper Mousetrap

Assuming that the upbeat growth forecasts for emerging markets remain broadly on track and the developed economies get back on their feet, what will be the main competitive battlegrounds of global business? One is those new consumers, who often demand products at far lower prices and often in more basic forms or smaller sizes than their developed-country counterparts. Emerging-market firms with experience of serving these consumers think they are better placed to devise such products than their developed-world competitors. Lenovo, for example, is going after the developing world's rural markets with a cheap, customised PC that enables farmers to become networked.

Some of these innovations have global potential. Lenovo's Chinese R&D labs developed a button that recovers a computer system within 60 seconds of a crash, essential in countries with an unreliable power supply. Known as "Express Repair", this is now being incorporated into its computers everywhere.

The same logic may apply to innovations in business models that allow goods and services to be delivered in fundamentally different ways and at much lower cost. Lenovo, for example, has developed a highly effective formula for selling to Chinese consumers that it has since taken to India and America.

Yet the rise of the new champions has brought a vigorous response from some of the old ones. IBM may have felt that it was no longer worth its while to compete in PCs, but Lenovo is facing fierce competition from American companies such as Hewlett-Packard and Dell everywhere, including in China. Nor was IBM's

decision to sell its (low-margin) PC business due to a lack of commitment to emerging markets: it now employs 73,000 people in India, against 2,000 at the start of the decade, and hopes to increase the share of its global revenues coming from emerging markets from 18% now to 30% within five years.

Although multinational companies in developed countries must grapple with legacy costs of various kinds—financial (pensions, health-care liabilities), organisational (headquarters far away from new markets) and cultural (old ways of thinking)—they have advantages too. The greatest of these may be a deep well of managerial experience, which emerging-market firms often lack. Yet Lenovo has shown how to overcome this management deficit by hiring a group of seasoned international executives, including Mr Amelio, an American who cut his managerial teeth at IBM and Dell.

But Lenovo went further than hiring international managers. "We are proud of our Chinese roots," says Mr Yang, but "we no longer want to be positioned as a Chinese company. We want to be a truly global company." So the firm has no headquarters; the meetings of its senior managers rotate among its bases around the world. Its development teams are made up of people in several centres around the world, often working together virtually. The firm's global marketing department is in Bangalore.

A huge effort has been made to integrate the different cultures within the firm. "In all situations: assume good intentions; be intentional about understanding others and being understood; respect cultural differences," reads one of many tip sheets issued by the firm to promote "effective teamwork across cultures". Mr Yang even moved his family to live in North Carolina to allow him to learn more about American culture and to improve his already respectable command of English, the language of global business.

In short, Lenovo is well on its way to becoming a role model for a successful multinational company in the age of globality: a good reason to be optimistic about the future of capitalism, even capitalism with a Chinese face. Perhaps Lenovo and other new champions will become the first of a new breed of truly global companies, rooted in neither rich nor developed countries but aiding wealth creation by making the most of opportunities the world over.

Good and Bad Capitalism

But is such optimism justified? Indeed, would Lenovo even have been allowed to buy IBM's PC business today? Congress nearly blocked the deal at the time because it feared that valuable intellectual property might fall into the hands of the Chinese government. Since then, China-bashing has increased, there has been some Arab-bashing too, deals have been blocked and the rhetoric in Washington, DC, has become ever more protectionist.

One fear is that American jobs will disappear overseas. This is despite plenty of academic evidence that open economies generally do better than closed ones, that in America in particular many more and generally better jobs have been created in recent years than have been destroyed, and that the number of jobs lost to outsourcing is tiny compared with those wiped out by technological innovation. Mr Yang explains that "people thought we would manufacture all our products in China, but in fact we have opened new plants in Greensboro and also Poland, as we need to be close to our customers."

Lately a new fear has been adding to the protectionist sentiment, turning even some usually enthusiastic global capitalists into protectionists. Could the rise of the new champions reflect the advance of bad forms of capitalism at the expense of good forms?

In their 2007 book, "Good Capitalism, Bad Capitalism and the Economics of Prosperity and Growth", William Baumol, Robert Litan and Carl Schramm identify four main models of capitalism around the world: entrepreneurial, big-firm, oligarchic (dominated by a small group of individuals) and state-led. Most economies are a mixture of at least two of these. The best economies, say the authors, blend big-firm and entrepreneurial capitalism. The worst combination may be of oligarchic and state-led capitalism, both of which are prevalent in many emerging markets.

The worriers point out that, through corporate acquisitions and the investments of sovereign-wealth funds, the role of the state (often an undemocratic one) in the global economy is rapidly expanding. Given the lamentable history of state intervention in business, they say, this does not bode well.

Such fears are not easily dismissed, if only because what is happening is so new that there is not much evidence either way. Sovereign-wealth funds insist that they are interested only in getting a good return on their money and will not meddle in politics. Perhaps they will turn out to be sources of good corporate governance and patient capital, in admirable contrast to the growing number of short-termist institutional investors in developed countries. But perhaps they will not.

Again, Lenovo offers an encouraging example. Even though its largest shareholder is in effect the government of China, its acquisition of IBM's PC business does not seem to have had any troubling consequences. But maybe the Chinese government was restrained by its co-investors, two of America's leading private-equity firms. Besides, the new champions may be typified not by Lenovo but by, say, Gazprom, through which the Russian state can make mischief abroad. As Mr Yang points out, of the 29 Chinese firms in the *Fortune* 500, Lenovo is the "only one that is truly market-driven". Most of the rest enjoy monopoly power or operate in the natural-resources industries, where there is far more scope for politics and corruption than in consumer electronics.

At the very least, the growing role of states that often lack democratic credentials creates a sense that the competition from emerging-economy champions and investors is unfair, and that rich-country firms may lose out to less well-run competitors which enjoy subsidised capital, help from political cronies or privileged access to resource supplies.

So there is a real risk that bad capitalism will spread in the coming decades. Yet at the same time this latest, multidirectional phase of globalisation offers enormous potential for business to raise living standards around the world.

The Lost Continent

For decades, Latin America's weight in the world has been shrinking. It is not an economic powerhouse, a security threat, or a population bomb. Even its tragedies pale in comparison to Africa's. The region will not rise until it ends its search for magic formulas. It may not make for a good sound bite, but patience is Latin America's biggest deficit of all.

MOISÉS NAÍM

Latin America has grown used to living in the backyard of the United States. For decades, it has been a region where the U.S. government meddled in local politics, fought communists, and promoted its business interests. Even if the rest of the world wasn't paying attention to Latin America, the United States occasionally was. Then came September 11, and even the United States seemed to tune out. Naturally, the world's attention centered almost exclusively on terrorism, the wars in Afghanistan, Iraq, and Lebanon, and on the nuclear ambitions of North Korea and Iran. Latin America became Atlantis—the lost continent. Almost overnight, it disappeared from the maps of investors, generals, diplomats, and journalists.

Indeed, as one commentator recently quipped, Latin America can't compete on the world stage in any aspect, even as a threat. Unlike anti-Americans elsewhere, Latin Americans are not willing to die for the sake of their geopolitical hatreds. Latin America is a nuclear-weapons free zone. Its only weapon of mass destruction is cocaine. In contrast to emerging markets like India and China, Latin America is a minor economic player whose global significance is declining. Sure, a few countries export oil and gas, but only Venezuela is in the top league of the world's energy market.

Not even Latin America's disasters seem to elicit global concern anymore. Argentina experienced a massive financial stroke in 2001, and no one abroad seemed to care. Unlike prior crashes, no government or international financial institution rushed to bail it out. Latin America doesn't have Africa's famines, genocides, an HIV/AIDS pandemic, wholesale state failures, or rock stars who routinely adopt its tragedies. Bono, Bill Gates, and Angelina Jolie worry about Botswana, not Brazil.

But just as the five-year-old war on terror pronounced the necessity of confronting threats where they linger, it also underscored the dangers of neglect. Like Afghanistan, Latin America shows how quickly and easy it is for the United States to lose its influence when Washington is distracted by other priorities.

In both places, Washington's disinterest produced a vacuum that was filled by political groups and leaders hostile to the United States.

No, Latin America is not churning out Islamic terrorists as Afghanistan was during the days of the Taliban. In Latin America, the power gap is being filled by a group of disparate leaders often lumped together under the banner of populism. On the rare occasions that Latin American countries do make international news, it's the election of a so-called populist, an apparently anti-American, anti-market leader, that raises hackles. However, Latin America's populists aren't a monolith. Some are worse for international stability than is usually reported. But some have the potential to chart a new, positive course for the region. Underlying the ascent of these new leaders are several real, stubborn threads running through Latin Americans' frustration with the status quo in their countries. Unfortunately, the United States'—and the rest of the world's—lack of interest in that region means that the forces that are shaping disparate political movements in Latin America are often glossed over, misinterpreted, or ignored. Ultimately, though, what matters most is not what the northern giant thinks or does as much as what half a billion Latin Americans think and do. And in the last couple of decades, the wild swings in their political behavior have created a highly unstable terrain where building the institutions indispensable for progress or for fighting poverty has become increasingly difficult. There is a way out. But it's not the quick fix that too many of Latin America's leaders have promised and that an impatient population demands.

The Left Turn That Wasn't

In the 1990s, politicians throughout Latin America won elections by promising economic reforms inspired by the "Washington Consensus" and closer ties to the United States. The Free Trade Area of the Americas offered hope for a better economic future for all. The United States could count on its neighbors to the south as reliable international allies. In Argentina, for example, the country's political and military links with the United States were so strong that in 1998, it was invited to become part of a select group of "major non-NATO allies." Today, however, President Néstor Kirchner nurtures a 70-percent approval rating by lobbing derision and invective against the "empire" up north. His main ally abroad is Venezuelan President Hugo Chávez, not George W. Bush. Nowadays, running for political office in Latin America openly advocating privatization, free trade, or claiming the support of the U.S. government is political suicide. Denouncing the corruption and inequality spurred by the "savage capitalism" of the 1990s, promising to help the poor and battle the rich, and disparaging the abusive international behavior of the American superpower and what is seen as its "globalization" ruse is a political platform that has acquired renewed potency throughout the region. In nearly every country, these ideas have helped new political leaders gain a national following and in Argentina, Bolivia, and Venezuela, even to win the presidency. In most other countries, notably in Mexico, Peru, Ecuador, and Nicaragua, proponents of these views enjoy wide popular support and are a fundamental factor in their countries' politics.

Latin America can't compete on the world stage in any way, not even as a threat.

So what happened? The first alarm bells sounded with the election in rapid succession of Chávez in Venezuela in 1998, Luiz Inácio "Lula" da Silva in Brazil in 2002, Kirchner in Argentina in 2003, and Tabaré Vázquez in Uruguay in 2004. All of them represented left-of-center coalitions and all promised to undo the "neoliberal excesses" of their predecessors. All of them also stressed the need to reassert their nations' independence from the United States and limit the superpower's influence.

Yet, none of these new presidents really delivered on their more extreme campaign promises, especially their plans to roll back the economic reforms of the 1990s. Brazil's Lula has followed an orthodox economic policy, anchored in painfully high interest rates and the active promotion of foreign investments. In Argentina, the only significant departure from the economic orthodoxy of the 1990s has been the adoption of widespread price controls and a disdainful attitude toward foreign investors.

In Venezuela, the rhetoric (and sometimes the deeds) are more in line with rabid anti-American, anti-free trade, and anti-market postures. Chávez routinely denounces free-trade agreements with the United States: He has been known to say that "[c]apitalism will lead to the destruction of humanity," and that the United States is the "devil that represents capitalism." Chávez's anti-trade posture conveniently glosses over the reality that Venezuela enjoys a de facto free trade agreement with the United States. In fact, America is the top market for Venezuela's oil. During Chávez's tenure, Venezuela has become one of the world's fastest-growing markets for manufactured American

products. And even the capitalist devils that are the objects of Chávez's wrath aren't suffering as much as might be expected. As the *Financial Times* reported in August, "Bankers traditionally face firing squads in times of revolution. But in Venezuela, they are having a party." Local bankers close to the regime are reaping huge profits. Foreign bankers who cater to the wealthy return from trips to Caracas with long lists of newly acquired clients in need of discreet "asset management" abroad.

Although some of these populist leaders have so far failed to live up to the radical economic changes they promised on the campaign trail, the gaps between incendiary rhetoric and actual practice have been far narrower in the region's foreign policies—especially in Venezuela and its relations with the United States. President Chávez, easily the world's most vocal anti-American leader, has called President George W. Bush, among other things, a "donkey," "a drunkard," and "an assassin." Not even Osama bin Laden has spouted such vitriol. Chávez has embraced Cuban leader Fidel Castro as his mentor and comrade-in-arms, and in so doing, he has become the region's most visible leader since Che Guevara. Like Che, Chávez often seems hellbent on sparking an armed confrontation to further his revolution; he calls Saddam Hussein a "brother," and is arming new local militias with 100,000 AK-47s to repel the "imminent" U.S. invasion. His international activism now routinely takes him around the world. In Damascus this summer, Chávez and Syrian President Bashar Assad issued a joint declaration stating that they were "firmly united against imperialist aggression and the hegemonic intentions of the U.S. Empire."

The main concern is not just that Chávez is developing close ties with prominent U.S. foes worldwide, but rather his efforts to refashion the domestic politics of his neighboring countries. His persona and his message are certainly attractive to large blocs of voters in other countries. Politicians elsewhere in Latin America who emulate him and his platforms are gaining popularity, and it's hard to imagine that Chávez is refraining from using his enormous oil wealth to support their political ascendancy. The international concern about trends in Latin America peaked in late 2005, as 12 presidential elections were scheduled for the ensuing months. In several countries—Bolivia, Costa Rica, Ecuador, Mexico, Nicaragua, and Peru—leftist candidates with Chávez-sounding platforms stood a good chance of winning.

Yet that expectation did not come to pass. So far, the only election where a Chávez ally has won is Bolivia. There, Evo Morales, the leader of the coca growers, announced that he would become "the United States' worst nightmare," and quickly proceeded to enter into a close alliance with Venezuela and Cuba. But the election of Chávez-backed candidates turned out to be more the exception than the rule. Surprisingly, running for office with too close an identification with Chávez or his policies has become an electoral kiss of death. Not even his promises of supplying cheap oil and financial aid if his candidate won were enough to compensate for the strong voter backlash against a foreign president openly trying to influence the outcome of national elections.

But the electoral defeat of candidates running on platforms perceived to be too extreme or too close to Chávez does not mean that the ideas they represent are unappealing. Latin

American voters are aggrieved, impatient, and eager to vote for new candidates who offer a break with the past and who promise a way out of the dire present.

If Not Left, Then Where?

Since the late 1990s, Latin American political systems have been rocked by a wide variety of frustrations. Therefore lumping the different types of discontent under generic "leftist" or "populist" monikers is misleading. Indeed, in today's Latin America, some of the grievances are clearly anti-market, while others are rooted in dissatisfactions caused not by overreliance on the market but by governmental overreach. Curbing corruption, for example, is a strong political demand that is unlikely to be satisfied by increasing the economic activities controlled by an already overwhelmed and corrupt public sector. Other grievances unite the far left and the far right. Economic nationalists who resent the market-opening reforms that allow foreign products to displace locally made ones include both right-wing business groups who profited handsomely from the protectionism, as well as leftist labor leaders who have seen their ranks shrink as local factories went out of business, unable to compete with foreign imports.

The responses to these political demands have also been varied. Some leaders, like Chávez and Kirchner, are behaving in a traditional, populist fashion, relying on massive and often wasteful public spending, on prices kept artificially low through governmental controls, or the scapegoating of the private sector to cement their popularity. Many others, however, like Lula in Brazil, Vicente Fox in Mexico, Alvaro Uribe in Colombia, or Ricardo Lagos in Chile have been models of more responsible economic governance and have shown a willingness to absorb the costs of unpopular but necessary economic policies.

What unites almost all Latin American countries, however, are two long-standing trends that multiply and deepen the variety of the grievances that are sprouting throughout the region: Prolonged mediocre economic performance, and the decay of traditional forms of political organization, and political parties in particular.

Latin America has suffered from slow economic growth for more than a quarter-century. Episodes of rapid growth have been short lived and often ended in painful financial crashes with devastating effects on the poor and the middle class. Economic growth in Latin America has been slower than it was in the 1960s and 70s, worse relative to all other emerging markets in the world, and unremittingly less than what the region itself needs to lift the poor standard of living of most of the population. This economic disappointment has become increasingly unacceptable to voters who have been promised much and gotten little and who have become better informed than ever about the standards of living of others at home and abroad. Latin Americans are fed up. Naturally, the frustrations produced by the wide gap between expectations and reality and between the living standards of the few who have so much and the many who have almost nothing create fertile ground for the fractious politics that make governing so difficult. Inevitably, political parties,

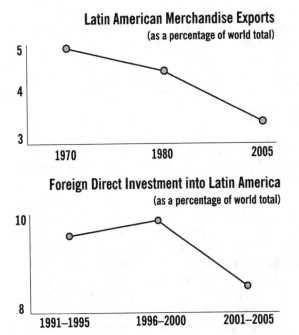

Latin American Merchandise Exports
(as a percentage of world total)

Foreign Direct Investment into Latin America
(as a percentage of world total)

Figure 1 Shrinking Share. Latin America's economic clout continues to slide.

and especially those in power, have suffered tremendous losses in loyalty, credibility, and legitimacy. Some of this disrepute is well deserved and often self-inflicted, as most political parties have failed to modernize their thinking or replace their ineffectual leaders. Corruption, patronage, and the use of politics as the fastest route for personal wealth are also rampant.

But it is also true that governing in a region where the political attitudes of large swaths of the population are imbued with rage, revenge, and impatience, and where the machinery of the public sector is often broken, is bound to end in failure. Because the region is resource-rich, the most common explanation for poverty amid so much imagined wealth is corruption. End the corruption and the standard of living of the poor will more or less automatically improve, goes the thinking. This assumption of course ignores the fact that a nation's prosperity depends more on being rich in competent public institutions, rule of law, and a well-educated population than in exportable raw materials.

Moreover, while the widespread presence and ravaging effects of corruption are indisputable, the reality is that poverty in Latin America owes as much, if not more, to the region's inability to find ways to compete more effectively in a globalized economy than to the pervasive thievery of those in power. It is hard to argue that China or India or the fast-growing economies of East Asia are substantially less corrupt than Latin America. Yet their growth rates and their ability to lift their populations out of poverty have been better than those of Latin America. Why? The fact is that the region's democracy and activist politics make its wages too high to compete with the low-wage Asian economies. Latin America's poor educational systems and low level of technological development make it unable to compete effectively in most international markets where success is driven by know-how and innovation. With its high wages and low technology, Latin America is having a hard time fitting into the hypercompetitive global economy. That fact gets far less attention than others that are more urgent, visible, or politically popular. Yet many of these problems—unemployment, poverty, slow economic growth—are manifestations of national economies that are ill-suited to prosper under the conditions prevalent in today's world.

The Waiting Game

Like all fundamental development problems, Latin America's global competitive shortcomings cannot be reduced simply or quickly. The specific reasons behind a country's disadvantageous position in the global economy vary. Alleviating them requires simultaneous efforts on many fronts by different actors over a long period. And herein lies a central difficulty besetting all attempts to create positive, sustained change in Latin America: They all take more time than voters, politicians, investors, social activists, and journalists are willing to wait before moving on to another idea or another leader.

Latin America's most important deficit is patience. Unless the patience of all influential actors is raised, efforts will continue to fail before they are fully tested or executed. Investors will continue to ignore good projects that cannot offer quick returns, governments will only pick policies that can generate rapid, visible results even if they are unsustainable or mostly cosmetic, and voters will continue to shed leaders that don't deliver soon enough.

Reducing the patience deficit is impossible without alleviating Latin America's most immediate and urgent needs. But it is a mistake to assume that sustainable improvements will only occur as a result of radical, emergency measures. Large-scale social progress will require years of sustained efforts that are not prematurely terminated and replaced by a new, "big-bang" solution. Continuous progress demands the stability created by agreement on a set of basic shared goals and ideas among major political players. In the past, this patience was either ruthlessly forced on the population by military governments or induced by the adoption of a similar ideology shared by influential social groups. Both approaches are highly problematic and not viable in the long run.

Therefore, rather than seeking ideological consensus or forcing ideological hegemony, Latin Americans should build from what exists and seems to be working, rather than dismiss what already exists just because its champions are political competitors. Only those individuals and organizations who are able to bridge ideological divides and bring together different approaches will fix Latin America's long-standing problems. And give them time.

It's not as though there's no precedent for this kind of progressive governance. Former Presidents Fernando Henrique Cardoso in Brazil and Lagos in Chile integrated different ideological perspectives and developed pragmatic approaches to balance conflicting demands. Both came from socialist backgrounds and while in office made enormous and often successful efforts to fight poverty and improve social conditions. But they were also quite sensitive about the need to maintain economic stability—which often meant painful cuts in public spending—and to foster an attractive business environment for investors. Although neither Cardoso nor Lagos was able to drastically overhaul his nation's poor social conditions, both easily rank among the most effective and successful presidents of the last decade—anywhere. They made far more progress in alleviating poverty in their countries than any of the more strident Latin American revolutionaries whose radical efforts on behalf of the poor so often ended up creating only more poverty and inequality.

With its high wages and low technology, Latin America is having a hard time fitting into the global economy.

It is natural for Latin American citizens and politicians to be captivated by promises that seem too good to be true. People who find themselves in dire straits naturally want extreme, quick solutions. Latin Americans have been experimenting with brutal, heavy-handed swings in their political economies since the 1970s. Yet, this search for silver-bullet solutions, though understandable given the grave problems of the region, is mistaken. Latin Americans must learn that, precisely because their illnesses are so acute, the solutions must be, paradoxically, more tempered. It might seem counterintuitive to reject the promises of the men and women offering radical change for a region so used to failure and neglect. But it may be the only way to lift millions out of poverty. And in the process, get Latin America back on the map.

MOISÉS NAÍM is editor in chief of *Foreign Policy*.

Promises and Poverty

Starbucks calls its coffee worker-friendly— but in Ethiopia, a day's pay is a dollar.

TOM KNUDSON

Gemadro, Ethiopia—Tucked inside a fancy black box, the $26-a-pound Starbucks Black Apron Exclusives coffee promised to be more than just another bag of beans.

Not only was the premium coffee from a remote plantation in Ethiopia "rare, exotic, cherished," according to Starbucks advertising, it was grown in ways that were good for the environment—and for local people, too.

Companies routinely boast about what they're doing for the planet, in part because guilt-ridden consumers expect as much—and are willing to pay extra for it. But, in this case, Starbucks' eco-friendly sales pitch does not begin to reflect the complex story of coffee in East Africa.

Inside the front flap of Starbucks' box are African arabica beans grown on a plantation in a threatened mountain rain forest. Behind the lofty phrases on the back label are coffee workers who make less than a dollar a day and a dispute between plantation officials and neighboring tribal people, who accuse the plantation of using their ancestral land and jeopardizing their way of life.

"We used to hunt and fish in there, and also we used to have honeybee hives in trees," one tribal member, Mikael Yatola, said through a translator. "But now we can't do that. . . . When we were told to remove our beehives from there, we felt deep sorrow, deep sadness."

25 New U.S. Stores per Week

Few companies have so dramatically conquered the American retail landscape as Starbucks. Last year, the $7.8 billion company opened an average of 25 new stores a week in the United States alone. Nowhere is Starbucks a more common sight than in environmentally conscious California, which has 2,350 outlets, more than New York, Massachusetts, Florida, Oregon and Washington—Starbucks' home state—combined.

No coffee company claims to do more for the environment and Third World farmers than Starbucks either. In full-page ads in *The New York Times,* in brochures and on its Web page, Starbucks says that it pays premium prices for premium beans, protects tropical forests and enhances the lives of farmers by building schools, clinics and other projects.

In places, Starbucks delivers on those promises, certainly more so than other multinational coffee companies. In parts of Latin America, for instance, its work has helped improve water quality, educate children and protect biodiversity.

Inside many Starbucks outlets across America, the African décor is hard to miss. There are photographs and watercolors of quaint coffee-growing scenes from Ethiopia to Tanzania to Zimbabwe. Yet such images clash with the reality of African life.

They don't show the industrial arm of coffee—the large farms and estates that encroach on wild forest regions. They don't reveal that even in the best of times in Ethiopia, the birthplace of wild coffee and the source of some of Starbucks' priciest offerings, there is barely enough for the peasant coffee farmers who still grow most of the nation's beans.

Even where Starbucks has built its bricks-and-mortar projects in Ethiopia, poverty remains a cornerstone of life, visible in the soot-stained cooking pots, spindly legs and ragged T-shirts, in the mad scramble of children for a visitor's cookie or empty water bottle.

"We plant coffee, harvest coffee but we never get anything out of it," said Muel Alema, a rail-thin coffee farmer who lives near a Starbucks-funded footbridge spanning a narrow chasm in Ethiopia's famous Sidamo coffee-growing region.

Alema's tattered shirt looked years old. So did his mud-splattered thongs. The red coffee berries he sold to a local buyer last fall were mixed with mountains of others, stripped of their pulp and sold as beans to distant companies—like other farmers, he did not know which ones—that made millions selling Sidamo coffee. Only $220 dribbled back to him.

This February, after Alema paid workers to pick the beans and bought grain for his family, just $110 remained—not enough, he said, to feed his wife and three children, to buy them clothes until the crop ripens again.

'A Marketing Genius'

Starbucks conveys a different image on the white foil bags of Ethiopia Sidamo whole bean coffee it sells for $10.45 a pound. "Good coffee, doing good," says lettering on the side.

"We believe there's a connection between the farmers who grow our coffees, us and you. That's why we work together with coffee-growing communities—paying prices that help farmers support their families . . . and funding projects like building a bridge in Ethiopia's Sidamo region to help farmers get to market safely. . . . By drinking this coffee, you're helping to make a difference."

And while the Sidamo footbridge does make travel safer, it is but a simple yellow-brown concrete slab, 10 paces long.

Dean Cycon, founder of Dean's Beans, an organic coffee company in Massachusetts, calls Starbucks "a marketing genius."

"They put out cleverly crafted material that makes the consumer feel they are doing everything possible," Cycon said. "But there is no institutional commitment. They do it to capture a market and shut up the activists."

Starbucks officials insist such critics have it wrong. As proof, they point to Latin America, the source of the bulk of the company's beans.

"You go to Nariño, Colombia. We built 1,800 (coffee) washing stations and sanitation facilities and homes," said Dub Hay, Starbucks senior vice president for global coffee procurement. "It's literally changed the face of that whole area."

"The same is true throughout Latin America," Hay added. "They call it the Starbucks effect."

Starbucks' dealings in Latin America have drawn some fire. Near the El Triunfo Biosphere Reserve in Chiapas, Mexico, for instance, farmers cut off relations about three years ago over a dispute about selling to an exporter instead of directly to Starbucks. The new arrangement, farmers said, would drain profits from peasant growers.

Starbucks, the farmers charged in a memo to coffee buyers, was supporting "a pseudo-fair trade system, adapted to their own neo-liberal interests, to dismantle structures and advances that we have made."

In an e-mailed response to The Bee, Starbucks vice president for global communications, Frank Kern, wrote that the Chiapas farmers were ultimately "given the opportunity to ship directly to us as they requested, but they were unable to manage it."

Sharper Focus on Africa

In Ethiopia, Starbucks says, it spent $25,000 on three footbridges in 2004. The company estimates the structures are used by 70,000 farmers and family members—about 1 percent of those who depend upon coffee for income. Some Ethiopian coffee leaders say there is a better way to help.

"If we are paid a (coffee) price which is decent, the people can make the bridge on their own," said Tadesse Meskela, general manager of the Oromia Coffee Farmers' Cooperative Union of 100,000 farmers, which has sold to Starbucks. "We don't have to be always beggars."

Starbucks won't disclose what it pays for Ethiopian coffee. Instead, it lumps its purchases together into a global average, which last year was $1.42 a pound, 16 cents more than the Fair Trade minimum. Much of that money, though, never makes it into the pockets of farmers but instead is siphoned off by buyers, processors and other middlemen.

Starbucks executives say they want to shrink that supply chain. "You end up at least five levels removed from the farmer and that's where the money goes," said Hay. "And that's a shame." Hay said that as the company buys more coffee from Africa—it plans to double its purchases there to 36 million pounds by 2009—the commerce will spur more progress.

"That's our goal," Hay said. "Africa is 6 percent of our purchases. . . . Seventy percent is from Latin America. So that's where our money has gone."

Making an impact in Ethiopia is undeniably a challenge. Good roads, electricity, potable water don't exist in many places. The climate is often hostile. There are ethnic conflicts, border disputes and rebel movements, and a sea of young faces that gather every time a car stops.

Since 1990, Ethiopia's population has jumped from 52 million to about 80 million: two new Los Angeleses. The more people, the less there is to go around. Ethiopia's per capita annual income is only $180, one of the lowest on Earth.

The environment is hurting, too, as coffee and tea plantations—as well as peasant farmers—spread into once wild areas, raising concern about the demise of one of the country's natural treasures: its biologically rich southwestern rain forest.

However, Samuel Assefa, the Ethiopian ambassador to the United States, said human suffering must be taken into consideration, too.

"We have a population of more than 80 million people, many of them living in rural and impoverished circumstances," he wrote in an e-mail. "Returning all cleared land to rain forest might be a victory for some extreme environmentalists, but it would condemn millions of my fellow citizens to starvation."

Atonement in a Cup

Starbucks has bought coffee from Africa for years. But now it is expanding rapidly there because it wants more of the continent's high-quality arabica beans. In Ethiopia alone, Starbucks purchases jumped 400 percent between 2002 and 2006.

While Starbucks is rapidly cloning retail outlets globally, 79 percent of its revenue last year was made in one caffeine-crazed country: the United States. With just 5 percent of the world's people, the United States drinks one-fifth of its coffee, more than any other nation.

Thanks largely to Starbucks, coffee is no longer just coffee. Now it is a vanilla soy latte, a java chip Frappuccino, a grande zebra mocha or—if you're feeling guilty—a Fair Trade-certified, bird-friendly, shade-grown caramel macchiato.

Starbucks did not pioneer the push for more equitable, conservation-based coffee. But it has woven the theme into everything from the earthy feel of its stores to its own certification program—called Coffee and Farmer Equity practices, or C.A.F.E.—that rewards farmers for meeting social and environmental goals.

"Social justice is becoming increasingly important to consumers," said industry analyst Judith Ganes-Chase as she flashed slides across a screen at a Long Beach coffee conference. One slide read: "Fair Trade is absolution in a cup."

Atonement, though, is not as simple as it may seem.

"It's very comfortable to believe Starbucks is doing the right thing—and to some degree, they are," said Eric Perkunder, a Seattle resident who worked as a Starbucks environmental manager in the 1980s and '90s. "They lull us into complacency. The stores are comfortable. You see pictures of people from origin countries. You believe

certain things they are telling you. But there's more to the story."

Dirt Road, Stick Huts

Part of that story lies in the southwestern corner of Ethiopia, in a swath of mountains not far from the Sudan border. There, a dirt road snakes through one of the country's largest coffee plantations—the Ethiopia Gemadro Estate—and comes to a halt in a dense mat of reeds and grasses.

A narrow path winds through the thicket and spills out into a clearing of stick huts. This is the home of an African Sheka tribe that for generations has lived off the land—catching fish, gathering wild honey and trapping animals in the forest. They call themselves the Shabuyye.

"The land over there used to belong to our forefathers," said Yatola, the tribal member in his 20s, as he nodded toward the plantation.

Conflict with local people and tribes is growing across southwest Ethiopia as coffee and tea plantations spread into the region under the government's effort to sow more development. At Gemadro, 2,496 acres of coffee were planted from 1998 to 2001 on land the company obtained from the government in a countylike jurisdiction called the Sheka Zone.

"One of Ethiopia's last remaining forests, Sheka Forest, is under huge pressure. . . . The rate of deforestation is now increasing and threatens the forest biodiversity . . . and the very livelihood" of forest-dwelling tribes, says the 2006 annual report of Melca Mahiber, an environmental group in the nation's capital, Addis Ababa.

However, Haile Michael Shiferaw, the plantation's manager—who attended the Long Beach coffee conference—said the Gemadro Estate had not displaced any tribe members.

"Before our farm was started," he said, "very few people were living in Gemadro."

Last year, Starbucks bought about 75,000 pounds of coffee from the Gemadro plantation and sold it as one of its "Black Apron Exclusives." At the time, the purchase was the 12th in the series of vintage offerings, six of which originated in Africa.

Starbucks packaged the beans in the fancy black box and inserted a flier touting the plantation's environmental and social track record. It also donated $15,000 to the Gemadro Estate for a school and health clinic.

"With its pure water supply, near pristine growing environment and dedication to conservation-based farming methods, this 2,300-hectare (5,700-acre) farm . . . is setting new standards for progressive, sustainable coffee farming," the flier said. "Gemadro workers and their families enjoy access to clean water, health care, housing and schools, all in keeping with the estate's commitment to maintain the highest standards of social and environmental stewardship."

Family's Income: 66 Cents a Day

Hailu is one of those workers. He stood outside his one-room, dirt-floor home, folded his arms across his chest and said that while he was happy to have a job, he was struggling to support his wife and family on just 6 Ethiopian birr per day—66 cents.

"Life is expensive," he said. "We have to go all the way to the town of Tepi (about 35 miles) for supplies." The round-trip bus ticket costs him four days' pay.

Plantation manager Shiferaw said Gemadro Estate wages are higher than the 55 cents a day workers earn at a government plantation near Tepi. Gemadro workers—most of whom are classified as temporary—also subsequently received a raise to between 77 cents and $1.10 a day, he said, adding, "We pay more than the minimum wage of the country."

That's still not a livable wage, according to the U.S. State Department. In a 2006 report on human rights in Ethiopia, the agency said that "there is no national minimum wage" and that public employees earn about $23 a month; private workers, $27. Those wages, it said, do "not provide a decent standard of living."

The Gemadro Estate is owned by Ethiopian-born Saudi Sheik Mohammed Al Amoudi, ranked by Forbes magazine as one of the world's 100 wealthiest individuals, with a net worth of $8 billion.

Al Amoudi owns many businesses in Ethiopia, from the posh Sheraton Hotel in Addis Ababa where rooms start at $270 a night—about a year's wages on the coffee plantation—to Ethio Agri-CEFT Plc, the farm management company that oversees the plantation.

Asked about the contrast between the sheik's wealth and the plantation wages, Assefa Tekle, Ethio Agri-CEFT's commercial manager, said, "There is no additional income that has been given from Sheik Al Amoudi. So what can you do? You have to be profitable to exist."

Ethiopian Ecology Suffers

Plantation wages are only one issue for workers and neighbors, however. The health care partially supported by Starbucks is another.

"When the estate came, they said they were going to give us adequate health service," said Geremew Gelito, an elder in the tiny village of Gemadro, where many estate workers live. He called the clinic bureaucratic and ineffective.

"As far as the promise of adequate health service, we have not received it," Gelito said. Shiferaw—the farm manager—said there are plans to improve the care. "It is not a very big clinic," he said, "but now we are increasing."

In his office above a furniture store in Addis Ababa, 2½ days' drive to the northeast, the agricultural manager for Ethio Agri-CEFT, Biru Abebe, said he was unaware of any complaints.

"Everybody goes and gets treatment," he said.

That even includes the native tribe, said Tekle, the commercial manager, a claim that exceeds that of Starbucks. "They are people of the environment so the farm has to give assistance."

But tribal member Yatola said the Shabuyye who live just downstream cannot get health care. "The company just gives medical attention to people who work for the company," he charged. Sitting in a stick hut, Yatola looked pensive. "We were isolated before. We didn't interact with anyone," he said as women outside pounded grain into mash with heavy wooden sticks. "But since the company has come, the road has acquainted us with the outside world."

Outsiders show up along the river, catching fish that feed the tribe, Yatola said. "There are less fish—and more people fishing," he said. "When we hear that the company, the way they have operated, they have created a nice relationship with the community, we know it's not true."

What's unfolding in the Gemadro region is not unique. An article in the April 2007 Journal of Agrarian Change points out that as coffee growing expands in southwest Ethiopia, the ecology can suffer.

"Environmental degradation is a serious concern with rates of deforestation estimated at 10,000 hectares per year (25,000 acres) in the coffee growing areas," the article said. "High levels of river pollution are also a major problem near coffee pulping and washing stations."

During the fall harvest, Yatola said, coffee processing pulp appears in the river from somewhere upstream. "The river becomes black, almost like oil," he said. "It smells like a dead horse."

Abebe, Ethio Agri-CEFT's agricultural manager, said the plantation has a lagoon to control pollution, that no waste flows from the Gemadro Estate. "The river is clean throughout the year. There is no pollution from our farm," he said. "Zero."

However, plantation manager Shiferaw said that not long ago valuable coffee beans did show up in the estate's wastewater lagoon, where a handful of workers and area farmers had dumped them in a failed theft attempt. "They are in prison now," he said.

In late February, four months after the bustling coffee harvest season, the Gemadro River looked clean. But in one of the ankle-deep side streams flowing into it, a white truck used to haul coffee was parked in the silvery water, being scrubbed of dirt and grease—a different but obvious pollution source.

"Sometimes it happens," acknowledged Tekle, the commercial manager.

"We don't have any control over that," Abebe said. "That road, though we made it, is a public road, so any truck can go and come."

Deforestation Takes a Toll

Although public, the road into the Gemadro Estate felt private. Armed guards checked vehicles entering or leaving to prevent coffee smuggling.

A row of rusty metal shacks looked like tool sheds, but were in fact worker housing. Even Shiferaw, the plantation manager, acknowledged they were not adequate.

"Yes, some is not. OK?" he said. "But we have a program to improve. When you see the standards of the country, it is better than most."

Along the bumpy dirt road, waxy green rows of coffee trees sprouted in rows, shaded by clumps of taller trees that not long ago were part of a denser, more diverse forest.

To Tadesse Gole—an ecologist in Addis Ababa and a native Ethiopian whose doctoral thesis at the University of Bonn, Germany, focused on preservation of wild arabica coffee—that manicured landscape is a biological calamity.

"This is an Afromontane rain forest—an area of high plant diversity, of unique epiphytic plants that grow on the branches of trees," Gole said. "We lose those plant species. And we lose many of the animals, birds and insects dependent on them."

Gole is the author of a recent study about the environmental and cultural impacts of coffee and tea plantations in Ethiopia, including the Gemadro Estate. The estate has spawned a wave of imitators, Gole said: smaller coffee and tea farms that are toppling more trees.

The estate itself is growing, too.

Last year, the Ethiopian Herald cited the plantation's project manager, Asenake Nigatu, telling the Ethiopian News Agency that Gemadro had "developed coffee on 1,000 hectares (about 2,470 acres) of land" it had obtained from the state investment bureau and had begun "activities to develop additional coffee on 1,500 hectares (about 3,700 acres) of land."

Gole tapped the touchpad on his laptop. An image based on satellite photography popped up showing land use changes in the Gemadro region from 1973 to 1987. A small puddle of red blotches appeared, indicating deforested areas. Gole tapped again, bringing up an image

through 2001—three years after the plantation started. The red blotches had spread across the map, like measles. His eyes widened.

"This is quite big," he said.

In his study, prepared for a future book, Gole analyzed coffee planting and forest change across two woredas—local districts—in the Sheka Zone. "The area under forest cover has dropped significantly in all parts," he wrote in the study. One area in particular stood out.

"The highest deforestation rate was observed in Gemadro, with (an) annual deforestation rate of 12.2 percent," he wrote.

But Abebe, the Ethio-Agri CEFT agricultural manager, said Gole's statements are misleading because the region was partially settled and cleared before the plantation came.

Ambassador Assefa agreed. "As I understand it, the land was largely cleared before Gemadro acquired the property," he said.

In addition, Abebe said, Gemadro is helping the land recover by incorporating conservation principles into its practices. To bolster his point, he pointed to an award the estate recently received from the Southern Nations, Nationalities and Peoples' Regional State for, he said, "being a model coffee farm."

Those model practices include planting grasses and reeds to slow erosion, planting shade trees for coffee and leaving 3,200 acres untouched for wildlife, Abebe said, adding that they "have even planted indigenous trees in the appropriate areas."

Gole, however, said such practices come up short. Many trees are non-native, he said, changing the composition of the forests. The plantation's Web site says cover crops planted there include some from South America, Mexico and India.

Struggle over Trademarks

The Ethiopian government's advocacy for its coffee industry—as well as for tea and other rural developments—has drawn international concern about the fate of its highland rain forests. A 2007 article by two German scientists blamed a lack of consistent forest policies.

"Ethiopia's montane rain forests are declining at an alarming rate," scientists Carmen Richerzhagen and Detlef Virchow wrote in the International Journal of Biotechnology. "The absence of a land use policy in Ethiopia creates spontaneous decisions on land allocations in a disorganized manner—therefore the forest is always the one to suffer."

But Ethiopia's push to grow more coffee drew plenty of encouragement at a conference in Addis Ababa in

February attended by representatives of the world's leading coffee companies, including Starbucks.

At the time, Starbucks and Ethiopia were locked in a struggle over the government's effort to trademark its famous coffee names—including Muel Alema's Sidamo—to create a distinctive brand that could funnel more profits back to the countryside.

Starbucks fought the effort, saying geographical certification programs, such as those in place for Colombian coffees, keep prices higher by guaranteeing that coffee from Colombia really is from Colombia.

"A trademark does not do that," said Hay, the Starbucks vice president, in a February interview in Addis Ababa. "It could be Sidamo and toilet paper. It doesn't mean anything about the region or the quality."

At times, the dispute turned bitter.

"What I don't understand is why Starbucks is resisting this," said Getachew Mengistie, director general of Ethiopia's Intellectual Property Office. "They are for improving the lives of the farmers. We are for improving the lives of the farmers. Where is the problem?"

In May, the issue was resolved in the government's favor, a positive step, said the ambassador.

"Starbucks is an important supporter of Ethiopia's efforts to control our specialty coffee brands, and it is critical that our relationship isn't about charity but about sound business," Ambassador Assefa said. "While the company only buys a small fraction of Ethiopia's coffee, our agreement will encourage market forces to allow Ethiopian farmers to capture a greater share of retail prices. This broad effort already has benefited thousands of poor farmers and could potentially benefit millions more."

Who Checked the Plantation?

Improving the lives of farmers and the environment is the goal of many coffee certification systems, such as Fair Trade, Rain Forest Alliance and Smithsonian Bird-Friendly. The Gemadro Estate has been approved by the European-based Utz Certified, an organization started by a Dutch coffee roaster and Guatemalan growers.

"It's good," said Yehasab Aschale, Utz's field representative in Ethiopia who said he toured the Gemadro plantation last year. "They are environmentally friendly. They are planting shade trees of the indigenous types. And they are improving the working conditions of the workers."

Starbucks also gave the estate's beans its own C.A.F.E. practices approval last year, signifying that the plantation

protected the environment, paid workers fairly and provided them with decent housing.

Yet no one from Starbucks ever inspected the Gemadro plantation for C.A.F.E. certification. Dub Hay—the Starbucks global purchasing executive—said he knew little about the plantation because he hadn't been there. Starbucks bought the coffee after tasting it in Europe, Hay said, adding that a coffee buyer from Switzerland visited at some point.

No one from the company Starbucks pays to oversee C.A.F.E. verification, Scientific Certification Systems of Emeryville, inspected Gemadro either. Instead, the plantation hired and paid an Africa-based company to do the job—a common industry practice.

Then, something out of the ordinary happened: The African company's inspector was fired for doing a poor job, a fact that emerged only after The Bee asked about the verification process.

"Clearly, the inspector didn't do as good, or as thorough, a job as is to be expected in C.A.F.E. practices," said Ted Howes, vice president of corporate social responsibility for Scientific Certification Systems.

Howes declined to release a copy of the inspection report, but he said his company would visit the plantation this year. "There are issues we want to look at more closely," he said.

Dennis Macray, Starbucks' director of corporate responsibility, added that such problems "can happen in any kind of a system. . . . You can have something go wrong."

If the C.A.F.E. certification process was flawed, why did Starbucks certify the beans?

"I can't tell you," Macray said at the Long Beach conference. With that, the trail went cold. Macray did not return follow-up calls. Starbucks spokeswoman Stacey Krum said details are confidential.

Krum, however, defended C.A.F.E. practices in general.

"There isn't a standard code for the coffee industry; this is something we are learning as we go along," she said. "And we are proud of it and confident it is achieving results."

Bee reporter **TOM KNUDSON** spent three weeks in Ethiopia during his four months of reporting this story, including journeys to the Gemadro Estate, the Sidamo and Yirgacheffe regions, and an international coffee conference in Addis Ababa. He interviewed coffee farmers, plantation workers, tribal people, scientists and coffee industry leaders in Africa and the United States. And he reviewed dozens of studies, reports, books and scientific journal articles about coffee growing and marketing. Travel and research were underwritten by a grant from the Alicia Patterson Foundation in Washington, D.C.

Drugs

Prohibition has failed—again. Instead of treating the demand for illegal drugs as a market, and addicts as patients, policymakers the world over have boosted the profits of drug lords and fostered narcostates that would frighten Al Capone. Finally, a smarter drug control regime that values reality over rhetoric is rising to replace the "war" on drugs.

Ethan Nadelmann

"The Global War on Drugs Can Be Won"

No, it can't. A "drug-free world," which the United Nations describes as a realistic goal, is no more attainable than an "alcohol-free world"—and no one has talked about that with a straight face since the repeal of Prohibition in the United States in 1933. Yet futile rhetoric about winning a "war on drugs" persists, despite mountains of evidence documenting its moral and ideological bankruptcy. When the U.N. General Assembly Special Session on drugs convened in 1998, it committed to "eliminating or significantly reducing the illicit cultivation of the coca bush, the cannabis plant and the opium poppy by the year 2008" and to "achieving significant and measurable results in the field of demand reduction." But today, global production and consumption of those drugs are roughly the same as they were a decade ago; meanwhile, many producers have become more efficient, and cocaine and heroin have become purer and cheaper.

It's always dangerous when rhetoric drives policy—and especially so when "war on drugs" rhetoric leads the public to accept collateral casualties that would never be permissible in civilian law enforcement, much less public health. Politicians still talk of eliminating drugs from the Earth as though their use is a plague on humanity. But drug control is not like disease control, for the simple reason that there's no popular demand for smallpox or polio. Cannabis and opium have been grown throughout much of the world for millennia. The same is true for coca in Latin America. Methamphetamine and other synthetic drugs can be produced anywhere. Demand for particular illicit drugs waxes and wanes, depending not just on availability but also fads, fashion, culture, and competition from alternative means of stimulation and distraction. The relative harshness of drug laws and the intensity of enforcement matter surprisingly little, except in totalitarian states. After all, rates of illegal drug use in the United States are the same as, or higher than, Europe, despite America's much more punitive policies.

"We Can Reduce the Demand for Drugs"

Good luck. Reducing the demand for illegal drugs seems to make sense. But the desire to alter one's state of consciousness, and to use psychoactive drugs to do so, is nearly universal—and mostly not a problem. There's virtually never been a drug-free society, and more drugs are discovered and devised every year. Demand-reduction efforts that rely on honest education and positive alternatives to drug use are helpful, but not when they devolve into unrealistic, "zero tolerance" policies.

As with sex, abstinence from drugs is the best way to avoid trouble, but one always needs a fallback strategy for those who can't or won't refrain. "Zero tolerance" policies deter some people, but they also dramatically increase the harms and costs for those who don't resist. Drugs become more potent, drug use becomes more hazardous, and people who use drugs are marginalized in ways that serve no one.

The better approach is not demand reduction but "harm reduction." Reducing drug use is fine, but it's not nearly as important as reducing the death, disease, crime, and suffering associated with both drug misuse and failed prohibitionist policies. With respect to legal drugs, such as alcohol and cigarettes, harm reduction means promoting responsible drinking and designated drivers, or persuading people to switch to nicotine patches, chewing gums, and smokeless tobacco. With respect to illegal drugs, it means reducing the transmission of infectious disease through syringe-exchange programs, reducing overdose fatalities by making antidotes readily available, and allowing people addicted to heroin and other illegal opiates to obtain methadone from doctors and even pharmaceutical heroin from clinics. Britain, Canada, Germany, the Netherlands, and Switzerland have already embraced this last option. There's no longer any question that these strategies decrease drug-related harms without increasing drug use. What blocks expansion of such programs is not cost; they typically save taxpayers' money that would otherwise go to criminal justice and healthcare. No, the roadblocks are abstinence-only ideologues and a cruel indifference to the lives and well-being of people who use drugs.

"Reducing the Supply of Drugs Is the Answer"

Not if history is any guide. Reducing supply makes as much sense as reducing demand; after all, if no one were planting cannabis, coca, and opium, there wouldn't be any heroin, cocaine, or marijuana to sell or consume. But the carrot and stick of crop eradication and substitution have been tried and failed, with rare exceptions, for half a century. These methods may succeed in targeted locales, but they usually simply shift production from one region to another: Opium production moves from Pakistan to Afghanistan; coca from Peru to Colombia; and cannabis from Mexico to the United States, while overall global production remains relatively constant or even increases.

The carrot, in the form of economic development and assistance in switching to legal crops, is typically both late and inadequate. The stick, often in the form of forced eradication, including aerial spraying, wipes out illegal and legal crops alike and can be hazardous to both people and local environments. The best thing to be said for emphasizing supply reduction is that it provides a rationale for wealthier nations to spend a little money on economic development in poorer countries. But, for the most part, crop eradication and substitution wreak havoc among impoverished farmers without diminishing overall global supply.

The global markets in cannabis, coca, and opium products operate essentially the same way that other global commodity markets do: If one source is compromised due to bad weather, rising production costs, or political difficulties, another emerges. If international drug control circles wanted to think strategically, the key question would no longer be how to reduce global supply, but rather: Where does illicit production cause the fewest problems (and the greatest benefits)? Think of it as a global vice control challenge. No one expects to eradicate vice, but it must be effectively zoned and regulated—even if it's illegal.

"U.S. Drug Policy Is the World's Drug Policy"

Sad, but true. Looking to the United States as a role model for drug control is like looking to apartheid-era South Africa for how to deal with race. The United States ranks first in the world in per capita incarceration—with less than 5 percent of the world's population, but almost 25 percent of the world's prisoners. The number of people locked up for U.S. drug-law violations has increased from roughly 50,000 in 1980 to almost 500,000 today; that's more than the number of people Western

Europe locks up for everything. Even more deadly is U.S. resistance to syringe-exchange programs to reduce HIV/AIDS both at home and abroad. Who knows how many people might not have contracted HIV if the United States had implemented at home, and supported abroad, the sorts of syringe-exchange and other harm-reduction programs that have kept HIV/AIDS rates so low in Australia, Britain, the Netherlands, and elsewhere. Perhaps millions.

And yet, despite this dismal record, the United States has succeeded in constructing an international drug prohibition regime modeled after its own highly punitive and moralistic approach. It has dominated the drug control agencies of the United Nations and other international organizations, and its federal drug enforcement agency was the first national police organization to go global. Rarely has one nation so successfully promoted its own failed policies to the rest of the world.

But now, for the first time, U.S. hegemony in drug control is being challenged. The European Union is demanding rigorous assessment of drug control strategies. Exhausted by decades of service to the U.S.-led war on drugs, Latin Americans are far less inclined to collaborate closely with U.S. drug enforcement efforts. Finally waking up to the deadly threat of HIV/AIDS, China, Indonesia, Vietnam, and even Malaysia and Iran are increasingly accepting of syringe-exchange and other harm-reduction programs. In 2005, the ayatollah in charge of Iran's Ministry of Justice issued a *fatwa* declaring methadone maintenance and syringe-exchange programs compatible with *sharia* (Islamic) law. One only wishes his American counterpart were comparably enlightened.

"Afghan Opium Production Must Be Curbed"

Be careful what you wish for. It's easy to believe that eliminating record-high opium production in Afghanistan—which today accounts for roughly 90 percent of global supply, up from 50 percent 10 years ago—would solve everything from heroin abuse in Europe and Asia to the resurgence of the Taliban.

But assume for a moment that the United States, NATO, and Hamid Karzai's government were somehow able to cut opium production in Afghanistan. Who would benefit? Only the Taliban, warlords, and other black-market entrepreneurs whose stockpiles of opium would skyrocket in value. Hundreds of thousands of Afghan peasants would flock to cities, ill-prepared to find work. And many Afghans would return to their farms the following year to plant another illegal harvest, utilizing guerrilla farming methods to escape intensified eradication efforts. Except now, they'd soon be competing with poor farmers elsewhere in Central Asia, Latin America, or even Africa. This is, after all, a global commodities market.

And outside Afghanistan? Higher heroin prices typically translate into higher crime rates by addicts. They also invite cheaper but more dangerous means of consumption, such as switching from smoking to injecting heroin, which results in higher HIV and hepatitis C rates. All things considered, wiping out opium in Afghanistan would yield far fewer benefits than is commonly assumed.

So what's the solution? Some recommend buying up all the opium in Afghanistan, which would cost a lot less than is now being spent trying to eradicate it. But, given that farmers somewhere will produce opium so long as the demand for heroin persists, maybe the world is better off, all things considered, with 90 percent of it coming from just one country. And if that heresy becomes the new gospel, it opens up all sorts of possibilities for pursuing a new policy in Afghanistan that reconciles the interests of the United States, NATO, and millions of Afghan citizens.

"Legalization Is the Best Approach"

It might be. Global drug prohibition is clearly a costly disaster. The United Nations has estimated the value of the global market in illicit drugs at $400 billion, or 6 percent of global trade. The extraordinary profits available to those willing to assume the risks enrich criminals, terrorists, violent political insurgents, and corrupt politicians and governments. Many cities, states, and even countries in Latin America, the Caribbean, and Asia are reminiscent of Chicago under Al Capone—times 50. By bringing the market for drugs out into the open, legalization would radically change all that for the better.

More importantly, legalization would strip addiction down to what it really is: a health issue. Most people who use drugs are like the responsible alcohol consumer, causing no harm to themselves or anyone else. They would no longer be the state's business. But legalization would also benefit those who struggle with drugs by reducing the risks of overdose and disease associated with unregulated products, eliminating the need to obtain drugs from dangerous criminal markets, and allowing addiction problems to be treated as medical rather than criminal problems.

No one knows how much governments spend collectively on failing drug war policies, but it's probably at least $100 billion a year, with federal, state, and local governments in the United States accounting for almost half the total. Add to that the tens of billions of dollars to be gained annually in tax revenues from the sale of legalized drugs. Now imagine if just a third of that total were committed to reducing drug-related disease and addiction. Virtually everyone, except those who profit or gain politically from the current system, would benefit.

Some say legalization is immoral. That's nonsense, unless one believes there is some principled basis for discriminating against people based solely on what they put into their bodies, absent harm to others. Others say legalization would open the floodgates to huge increases in drug abuse. They forget that we already live in a world in which psychoactive drugs of all sorts are readily available—and in which people too poor to buy drugs resort to sniffing gasoline, glue, and other industrial products, which can be more harmful than any drug. No, the greatest downside to legalization may well be the fact that the legal markets would fall into the hands of the powerful alcohol, tobacco, and pharmaceutical companies. Still, legalization is a far more pragmatic option than living with the corruption, violence, and organized crime of the current system.

"Legalization Will Never Happen"

Never say never. Wholesale legalization may be a long way off—but partial legalization is not. If any drug stands a chance of being legalized, it's cannabis. Hundreds of millions of people have used it, the vast majority without suffering any harm or going on to use "harder" drugs. In Switzerland, for example, cannabis legalization was twice approved by one chamber of its parliament, but narrowly rejected by the other.

Elsewhere in Europe, support for the criminalization of cannabis is waning. In the United States, where roughly 40 percent of the country's 1.8 million annual drug arrests are for cannabis possession, typically of tiny amounts, 40 percent of Americans say that the drug should be taxed, controlled, and regulated like alcohol. Encouraged by Bolivian President Evo Morales, support is also growing in Latin America and Europe for removing coca from international antidrug conventions, given the absence of any credible health reason for keeping it there. Traditional growers would benefit economically, and there's some possibility that such products might compete favorably with more problematic substances, including alcohol.

The global war on drugs persists in part because so many people fail to distinguish between the harms of drug abuse and the harms of prohibition. Legalization forces that distinction to the forefront. The opium problem in Afghanistan is primarily a prohibition problem, not a drug problem. The same is true of the narcoviolence and corruption that has afflicted Latin America and the Caribbean for almost three decades—and that now threatens Africa. Governments can arrest and kill drug lord after drug lord, but the ultimate solution is a structural one, not a prosecutorial one. Few people doubt any longer that the war on drugs is lost, but courage and vision are needed to transcend the ignorance, fear, and vested interests that sustain it.

ETHAN NADELMANN is founder and executive director of the Drug Policy Alliance.

From *Foreign Policy*, September/October 2007, pp. 24–26, 28–29. Copyright © 2007 by the Carnegie Endowment for International Peace. Reprinted with permission. www.foreignpolicy.com

Ensuring Energy Security

DANIEL YERGIN

Old Questions, New Answers

On the eve of World War I, First Lord of the Admiralty Winston Churchill made a historic decision: to shift the power source of the British navy's ships from coal to oil. He intended to make the fleet faster than its German counterpart. But the switch also meant that the Royal Navy would rely not on coal from Wales but on insecure oil supplies from what was then Persia. Energy security thus became a question of national strategy. Churchill's answer? "Safety and certainty in oil," he said, "lie in variety and variety alone."

Since Churchill's decision, energy security has repeatedly emerged as an issue of great importance, and it is so once again today. But the subject now needs to be rethought, for what has been the paradigm of energy security for the past three decades is too limited and must be expanded to include many new factors. Moreover, it must be recognized that energy security does not stand by itself but is lodged in the larger relations among nations and how they interact with one another.

Energy security will be the number one topic on the agenda when the group of eight highly industrialized countries (G-8) meets in St. Petersburg in July. The renewed focus on energy security is driven in part by an exceedingly tight oil market and by high oil prices, which have doubled over the past three years. But it is also fueled by the threat of terrorism, instability in some exporting nations, a nationalist backlash, fears of a scramble for supplies, geopolitical rivalries, and countries' fundamental need for energy to power their economic growth. In the background—but not too far back—is renewed anxiety over whether there will be sufficient resources to meet the world's energy requirements in the decades ahead.

Concerns over energy security are not limited to oil. Power blackouts on both the East and West Coasts of the United States, in Europe, and in Russia, as well as chronic shortages of electric power in China, India, and other developing countries, have raised worries about the reliability of electricity supply systems. When it comes to natural gas, rising demand and constrained supplies mean that North America can no longer be self-reliant, and so the United States is joining the new global market in natural gas that will link countries, continents, and prices together in an unprecedented way.

At the same time, a new range of vulnerabilities has become more evident. Al Qaeda has threatened to attack what Osama bin Laden calls the "hinges" of the world's economy, that is, its critical infrastructure—of which energy is among the most crucial elements. The world will increasingly depend on new sources of supply from places where security systems are still being developed, such as the oil and natural gas fields offshore of West Africa and in the Caspian Sea. And the vulnerabilities are not limited to threats of terrorism, political turmoil, armed conflict, and piracy. In August and September 2005, Hurricanes Katrina and Rita delivered the world's first integrated energy shock, simultaneously disrupting flows of oil, natural gas, and electric power.

Events since the beginning of this year have underlined the significance of the issue. The Russian-Ukrainian natural gas dispute temporarily cut supplies to Europe. Rising tensions over Tehran's nuclear program brought threats from Iran, the second-largest OPEC producer, to "unleash an oil crisis." And scattered attacks on some oil facilities reduced exports from Nigeria, which is a major supplier to the United States.

Since Churchill's day, the key to energy security has been diversification. This remains true, but a wider approach is now required that takes into account the rapid evolution of the global energy trade, supply-chain vulnerabilities, terrorism, and the integration of major new economies into the world market.

Although in the developed world the usual definition of energy security is simply the availability of sufficient supplies at affordable prices, different countries interpret what the concept means for them differently. Energy-exporting countries focus on maintaining the "security of demand" for their exports, which after all generate the overwhelming share of their government revenues. For Russia, the aim is to reassert state control over "strategic resources" and gain primacy over the main pipelines and market channels through which it ships its hydrocarbons to international markets. The concern for developing countries is how changes in energy prices affect their balance of payments. For China and India, energy security now lies in their ability to rapidly adjust to their new dependence on global markets, which represents a major shift away from their former commitments to self-sufficiency. For Japan, it means offsetting its stark scarcity of domestic resources through diversification, trade, and investment. In Europe, the major debate centers on how to manage dependence on imported natural gas—and in most countries, aside from France and Finland, whether to build new nuclear power plants and perhaps to return to (clean) coal. And the United States must face the uncomfortable fact that its goal of "energy independence"—a phrase that has become a mantra since it was first articulated by Richard Nixon four weeks after the 1973 embargo was put in place—is increasingly at odds with reality.

Shocks to Supply and Demand

After the Persian Gulf War, concerns over energy security seemed to recede. Saddam Hussein's bid to dominate the Persian Gulf had been foiled, and it appeared that the world oil market would remain a market (rather than becoming Saddam's instrument of political manipulation) and that supplies would be abundant at prices that would not impede the global economy. But 15 years later, prices are high, and fears of shortages dominate energy markets. What happened? The answer is to be found in both markets and politics.

The last decade has witnessed a substantial increase in the world's demand for oil, primarily because of the dramatic economic growth in developing countries, in particular China and India. As late as 1993, China was self-sufficient in oil. Since then, its GDP has almost tripled and its demand for oil has more than doubled. Today, China imports 3 million barrels of oil per day, which accounts for almost half of its total consumption. China's share of the world oil market is about 8 percent, but its share of total growth in demand since 2000 has been 30 percent. World oil demand has grown by 7 million barrels per day since 2000; of this growth, 2 million barrels each day have gone to China. India's oil consumption is currently less than 40 percent of China's, but because India has now embarked on what the economist Vijay Kelkar calls the "growth turnpike," its demand for oil will accelerate. (Ironically, India's current high growth rates were partly triggered by the spike in oil prices during the 1990–91 Persian Gulf crisis. The resulting balance-of-payments shock left India with almost no foreign currency reserves, opening the door to the reforms initiated by then Finance Minister Manmohan Singh, now India's prime minister.)

The impact of growth in China, India, and elsewhere on the global demand for energy has been far-reaching. In the 1970s, North America consumed twice as much oil as Asia. Last year, for the first time ever, Asia's oil consumption exceeded North America's. The trend will continue: half of the total growth in oil consumption in the next 15 years will come from Asia, according to projections by Cambridge Energy Research Associates (CERA). However, Asia's growing impact became widely apparent only in 2004, when the best global economic performance in a generation translated into a "demand shock"—that is, unexpected worldwide growth in petroleum consumption that represented a rate of growth that was more than double the annual average growth rates of the preceding decade. China's demand in 2004 rose by an extraordinary 16 percent compared to 2003, driven partly by electricity bottlenecks that led to a surge in oil use for improvised electric generation. U.S. consumption also grew strongly in 2004, as did that of other countries. The result was the tightest oil market in three decades (except for the first couple of months after Saddam's invasion of Kuwait in 1990). Hardly any wells were available to produce

additional oil. That remains the case today, and there is a further catch. What additional oil might be produced cannot be easily sold because it would not be of sufficiently good quality to be used in the world's available oil refineries.

Refining capacity is a major constraint on supply, because there is a significant mismatch between the product requirements of the world's consumers and refineries' capabilities. Although often presented solely as a U.S. problem, inadequate refining capacity is in fact a global phenomenon. The biggest growth in demand worldwide has been for what are called "middle distillates": diesel, jet fuel, and heating oil. Diesel is a favorite fuel of European motorists, half of whom now buy diesel cars, and it is increasingly used to power economic growth in Asia, where it is utilized not just for transportation but also to generate electricity. But the global refining system does not have enough so-called deep conversion capacity to turn heavier crudes into middle distillates. This shortfall in capacity has created additional demand for the lighter grades of crude, such as the benchmark WTI (West Texas Intermediate), further boosting prices.

Last year, for the first time ever, Asia's oil consumption exceeded North America's.

Other factors, including problems in several major energy-exporting countries, have also contributed to high prices. Indeed, the current era of high oil prices really began in late 2002 and early 2003, just before the start of the Iraq war, when President Hugo Chavez's drive to consolidate his control over Venezuela's political system, state-owned oil company, and oil revenues sparked strikes and protests. This shut down oil production in Venezuela, which had been among the most reliable of oil exporters since World War II. The loss of oil to the world market from the strikes was significant, greater than the impact of the war in Iraq on supplies. Venezuela's output has never fully recovered, and it is currently running about 500,000 barrels per day below the prestrike level.

Saddam's failing regime in Iraq did not torch oil facilities during the 2003 war, as many had feared, but the large postwar surge in Iraqi output that some had expected has certainly not occurred. The tens of billions of dollars required to bring the industry's output back up to its 1978 peak of 3.5 million barrels per day have not been invested both because of the continuing attacks on the country's infrastructure and work force and because of uncertainty about Iraq's political and legal structures and the contractual framework for investment. As a result, Iraqi oil exports are 30 to 40 percent below prewar levels.

Over the past five years, by contrast, Russia's oil fields have been central to the growth of worldwide supply, providing almost 40 percent of the world's total production increase since 2000. But the growth of Russia's output slowed substantially last year because of political risks, insufficient investment, uncertainties over government policy, regulatory obstacles, and, in some regions, geological challenges. Meanwhile, despite such problems in some major supplier countries, other sources that get less attention, such as Brazil's and Angola's offshore fields, were increasing their output—until Hurricanes Katrina and Rita shut down 27 percent of U.S. oil production (as well as 21 percent of U.S. refining capacity). As late as January 2006, U.S. facilities that before the hurricanes had produced 400,000 barrels of oil a day were still out of operation. Altogether, the experience of the last couple of years confirms the maxim that a tight market is a market vulnerable to events.

All of these problems have provoked a new round of fears that the world is running out of oil. Such bouts of anxiety have recurred since as far back as the 1880s. But global output has actually increased by 60 percent since the 1970s, the last time the world was supposedly running out of oil. (The demand shock of 2004 attracted more notice than the cooling off of the growth in demand that occurred in 2005, when Chinese consumption did not grow at all and world demand returned to the average growth rates of 1994–2003.) Although talk about an imminent peak in oil output followed by a rapid decline has become common in some circles, CERA's field-by-field analysis of projects and development plans indicates that net productive capacity could increase by as much as 20 to 25 percent over the next decade. Despite the current pessimism, higher oil prices will do what higher prices usually do: fuel growth in new supplies by significantly increasing investment and by turning marginal opportunities into commercial prospects (as well as, of course, moderating demand and stimulating the development of alternatives).

A good part of this capacity growth is already in the works. A substantial part of it will come from the exploitation of nontraditional supplies, ranging from Canadian oil sands (also known as tar sands) to deposits in ultradeep water to a very high-quality diesel-like fuel derived from natural gas—all made possible by continuing advances in technology. But conventional supplies will grow as well: Saudi Arabia is on track to increase its capacity by about 15 percent, to over 12 million barrels per day, by 2009, and other projects are under way elsewhere, such as in the Caspian Sea and even in the United States' offshore fields. Although energy companies will be prospecting in more difficult environments, the major obstacle to the development of new supplies is not geology but what happens above ground: namely, international affairs, politics, decision-making by governments, and energy investment and new technological development. It should be noted, however, that current projections do show that after 2010 the major growth in supplies will come from fewer countries than it comes from today, which could accentuate security concerns.

A New Framework

The current energy security system was created in response to the 1973 Arab oil embargo to ensure coordination among the industrialized countries in the event of a disruption in supply, encourage collaboration on energy policies, avoid bruising scrambles for supplies, and deter any future use of an "oil weapon" by exporters. Its key elements are the Paris-based International Energy Agency (IEA), whose members are the industrialized countries; strategic stockpiles of oil, including the U.S. Strategic Petroleum Reserve; continued monitoring and analysis of energy markets and policies; and energy conservation and coordinated emergency sharing of supplies in the event of a disruption. The emergency system was set up to offset major disruptions that threatened the global economy and stability, not to manage prices and the commodity cycle. Since the system's inception in the 1970s, a coordinated emergency drawdown of strategic stockpiles has occurred only twice: on the eve of the Gulf War in 1991 and in the autumn of 2005 after Hurricane Katrina. (The system was also readied in anticipation of possible use before January 1, 2000, because of concerns over the potential problems arising from the Y2K computer bug, during the shutdown of production in Venezuela in 2002–3, and in the spring of 2003, before the invasion of Iraq.)

Experience has shown that to maintain energy security countries must abide by several principles. The first and most familiar is what Churchill urged more than 90 years ago: diversification of supply. Multiplying one's supply sources reduces the impact of a disruption in supply from one source by providing alternatives, serving the interests of both consumers and producers, for whom stable markets are a prime concern. But diversification is not enough. A second principle is resilience, a "security margin" in the energy supply system that provides a buffer against shocks and facilitates recovery after disruptions. Resilience can come from many factors, including sufficient spare production capacity, strategic reserves, backup supplies of equipment, adequate storage capacity along the supply chain, and the stockpiling of critical parts for electric power production and distribution, as well as carefully conceived plans for responding to disruptions that may affect large regions. Hence the third principle: recognizing the reality of integration. There is only one oil market, a complex and worldwide system that moves and consumes about 86 million barrels of oil every day. For all consumers, security resides in the stability of this market. Secession is not an option.

A fourth principle is the importance of information. High-quality information underpins well-functioning markets. On an international level, the IEA has led the way in improving the flow of information about world markets and energy prospects. That work is being complemented by the new International Energy Forum, which will seek to integrate information from producers and consumers. Information is no less crucial in a crisis, when consumer panics can be instigated by a mixture of actual disruptions, rumors, and fear. Reality can be obscured by accusations, acrimony, outrage, and a fevered hunt for conspiracies, transforming a difficult situation into something much worse. In such situations, governments and the private sector should collaborate to counter panics with high-quality, timely information. The U.S. government can promote flexibility and market adjustments by expediting its communication with companies and permitting the exchange of information among them, with appropriate antitrust safeguards, when necessary.

As important as these principles are, the past several years have highlighted the need to expand the concept of energy security in two critical dimensions: the recognition of the globalization of the energy security system, which can be achieved especially by engaging China and India, and the acknowledgment of the fact that the entire energy supply chain needs to be protected.

China's thirst for energy has become a decisive plot element in suspense novels and films. Even in the real world there is no shortage of suspicion: some in the United States see a Chinese grand strategy to preempt the United States and the West when it comes to new oil and gas supplies, and some strategists in Beijing fear that the United States may someday try to interdict China's foreign energy supplies. But the actual situation is less dramatic. Despite all the attention being paid to China's efforts to secure international petroleum reserves, for example, the entire amount that China currently produces per day outside of its own borders is equivalent to just 10 percent of the daily production of one of the supermajor oil companies. If there were a serious controversy between the United States and China involving oil or gas, it would likely arise not because of a competition for the resources themselves, but rather because they had become part of larger foreign policy issues (such as a clash over a specific regime or over how to respond to Iran's nuclear program). Indeed, from the viewpoint of consumers in North America, Europe, and Japan, Chinese and Indian investment in the development of new energy supplies around the world is not a threat but something to be desired, because it means there will be more energy available for everyone in the years ahead as India's and China's demand grows.

It would be wiser—and indeed it is urgent—to engage these two giants in the global network of trade and investment rather than see them tilt toward a mercantilist, state-to-state approach. Engaging India and China will require understanding what energy security means for them. Both countries are rapidly moving from self-sufficiency to integration into the world economy, which means they will grow increasingly dependent on global markets even as they are under tremendous pressure to deliver economic growth for their huge populations, which cope with energy shortages and blackouts on a daily basis. Thus, the primary concern for both China and India is to ensure that they have sufficient energy to support economic growth and prevent debilitating energy shortfalls that could trigger social and political turbulence. For India, where the balance-of-payments crisis of 1990 is still on policymakers' minds, international production is also a way to hedge against high oil prices. And so India and China, and other key countries such as Brazil, should be brought into coordination with the existing IEA energy security system to assure them that their interests will be protected in the event of turbulence and to ensure that the system works more effectively.

Security and Flexibility

The current model of energy security, which was born of the 1973 crisis, focuses primarily on how to handle any disruption of oil supplies from producing countries. Today, the concept of energy security needs to be expanded to include the protection of the entire energy supply chain and infrastructure—an awesome task. In the United States alone, there are more than 150 refineries, 4,000 offshore platforms, 160,000 miles of oil pipelines, facilities to handle 15 million barrels of oil a day of imports and exports, 10,400 power plants, 160,000 miles of high-voltage electric power transmission lines and millions of miles of electric power distribution wires, 410 underground gas storage fields, and 1.4 million miles of natural gas pipelines. None of the world's complex, integrated supply chains were built with security, defined in this broad way, in mind. Hurricanes Katrina and Rita brought a new perspective to the security question by demonstrating how fundamental the electric grid is to everything else. After the storms, the Gulf Coast refineries and the big U.S. pipelines were unable to operate—not because they were damaged, but because they could not get power.

Energy interdependence and the growing scale of energy trade require continuing collaboration among both producers and consumers to ensure the security of the entire supply chain. Long-distance, cross-border pipelines are becoming an ever-larger fixture in the global energy trade. There are also many chokepoints along the transportation routes of seaborne oil and, in many cases, liquefied natural gas (LNG) that create particular vulnerabilities: the Strait of Hormuz, which lies at the entrance to the Persian Gulf; the Suez Canal, which connects the Red Sea and the Mediterranean; the Bab el Mandeb strait, which provides entrance to the Red Sea; the Bosporus strait, which is a major export channel for Russian and Caspian oil; and the Strait of Malacca, through which passes 80 percent of Japan's and South Korea's oil and about half of China's. Ships commandeered and scuttled in these strategic waterways could disrupt supply lines for extended periods. Securing pipelines and chokepoints will require augmented monitoring as well as the development of multilateral rapid-response capabilities.

The challenge of energy security will grow more urgent in the years ahead, because the scale of the global trade in energy will grow substantially as world markets become more integrated. Currently, every day some 40 million barrels of oil cross oceans on tankers; by 2020, that number could jump to 67 million. By then, the United States could be importing 70 percent of its oil (compared to 58 percent today and 33 percent in 1973), and so could China. The amount of natural gas crossing oceans as LNG will triple to 460 million tons by 2020. The United States will be an important part of that market: although LNG meets only about 3 percent of U.S. demand today, its share could reach more than 25 percent by 2020. Assuring the security of global energy markets will require coordination on both an international and a national basis among companies and governments, including energy, environmental, military, law enforcement, and intelligence agencies.

But in the United States, as in other countries, the lines of responsibility—and the sources of funding—for protecting critical infrastructures, such as energy, are far from clear. The private sector, the federal government, and state and local agencies need to take steps to better coordinate their activities. Maintaining the commitment to do so during periods of low or moderate prices will require discipline as well as vigilance. As Stephen Flynn, a homeland security expert at the Council on Foreign Relations, observes, "Security is not free." Both the public and private sectors need to invest in building a higher degree of security into the energy system—meaning that energy security will be part of both the price of energy and the cost of homeland security.

Markets need to be recognized as a source of security in themselves. The energy security system was created when energy prices were regulated in the United States, energy trading was only just beginning, and futures markets were several years away. Today, large, flexible, and well-functioning energy markets provide security by absorbing shocks and allowing supply and demand to respond more quickly and with greater ingenuity than a controlled system could. Such markets will guarantee security for the growing LNG market and thereby boost the confidence of the countries that import it. Thus, governments must resist the temptation to bow to political pressure and micromanage markets. Intervention and controls, however well meaning, can backfire, slowing and even preventing the movement of supplies to respond to disruptions. At least in the United States, any price spike or disruption evokes the memory of the infamous gas lines of the 1970s—even for those who were only toddlers then (and perhaps even for those not yet born at the time). Yet those lines were to a considerable degree self-inflicted—the consequence of price controls and a heavy-handed allocation system that sent gasoline where it was not needed and denied its being sent where it was.

Contrast that to what happened immediately after Hurricane Katrina. A major disruption to the U.S. oil supply was compounded by reports of price gouging and of stations running out of gasoline, which together could have created new gas lines along the East Coast. Yet the markets were back in balance sooner and prices came down more quickly than almost anyone had expected. Emergency supplies from the U.S. Strategic Petroleum Reserve and other IEA reserves were released, sending a "do not panic" message to the market. At the same time, two critical regulatory restrictions were eased. One was the Jones Act (which bars non-U.S.-flagged ships from carrying cargo between U.S. ports), which was waived to allow non-U.S. tankers to ship supplies bottlenecked on the Gulf Coast around Florida to the East Coast, where they were needed. The other was the set of "boutique gasoline" regulations that require different qualities of gasoline for different cities, which were temporarily lifted to permit supplies from other parts of the country to move into the Southeast. The experience highlights the need to incorporate regulatory and environmental flexibility—and a clear understanding of the impediments to adjustment—into the energy security machinery in order to cope as effectively as possible with disruptions and emergencies.

The U.S. government and the private sector should also make a renewed commitment to energy efficiency and conservation. Although often underrated, the impact of conservation on the economy has been enormous over the past several decades. Over the past 30 years, U.S. GDP has grown by 150 percent, while U.S.

energy consumption has grown by only 25 percent. In the 1970s and 1980s, many considered that kind of decoupling impossible, or at least certain to be economically ruinous. True, many of the gains in energy efficiency have come because the U.S. economy is "lighter," as former Federal Reserve Chair Alan Greenspan has put it, than it was three decades ago—that is, GDP today is composed of less manufacturing and more services (especially information technology) than could have been imagined in the 1970s. But the basic point remains: conservation has worked. Current and future advances in technology could permit very large additional gains, which would be highly beneficial not only for advanced economies such as that of the United States, but also for the economies of countries such as India and China (in fact, China has recently made conservation a priority).

Finally, the investment climate itself must become a key concern in energy security. There needs to be a continual flow of investment and technology in order for new resources to be developed. The IEA recently estimated that as much as $17 trillion will be required for new energy development over the next 25 years. These capital flows will not materialize without reasonable and stable investment frameworks, timely decision-making by governments, and open markets. How to facilitate energy investment will be one of the critical questions on the G-8's energy security agenda in 2006.

Future Shocks

Inevitably, there will be shocks to energy markets in the future. Some of the possible causes may be roughly foreseeable, such as coordinated attacks by terrorists, disruptions in the Middle East and Africa, or turmoil in Latin America that affects output in Venezuela, the third-largest OPEC producer. Other possible causes, however, may come as a surprise. The offshore oil industry has long built facilities to withstand a "hundred-year storm"—but nobody anticipated that two such devastating storms would strike the energy complex in the Gulf of Mexico within a matter of weeks. And the creators of the IEA emergency sharing system in the 1970s never for a moment considered that it might have to be activated to blunt the effects of a disruption in the United States.

Diversification will remain the fundamental starting principle of energy security for both oil and gas. Today, however, it will likely also require developing a new generation of nuclear power and "clean coal" technologies and encouraging a growing role for a variety of renewable energy sources as they become more competitive. It will also require investing in new technologies, ranging from near-term ones, such as the conversion of natural gas into a liquid fuel, to ones that are still in the lab, such as the biological engineering of energy supplies. Investment in technology all along the energy spectrum is surging today, and this will have a positive effect not only on the future energy picture but also on the environment.

Yet energy security also exists in a larger context. In a world of increasing interdependence, energy security will depend much on how countries manage their relations with one another, whether bilaterally or within multilateral frameworks. That is why energy security will be one of the main challenges for U.S. foreign policy in the years ahead. Part of that challenge will be anticipating and assessing the "what ifs." And that requires looking not only around the corner, but also beyond the ups and downs of cycles to both the reality of an ever more complex and integrated global energy system and the relations among the countries that participate in it.

DANIEL YERGIN is Chair of Cambridge Energy Research Associates and the author of *The Prize: The Epic Quest for Oil, Money, and Power*. He is currently writing a new book on oil and geopolitics.

The Power and the Glory

The next technology boom may well be based on alternative energy, says Geoffrey Carr. But which sort to back?

GEOFFREY CARR

Everyone loves a booming market, and most booms happen on the back of technological change. The world's venture capitalists, having fed on the computing boom of the 1980s, the internet boom of the 1990s and the biotech and nanotech boomlets of the early 2000s, are now looking around for the next one. They think they have found it: energy.

Many past booms have been energy-fed: coal-fired steam power, oil-fired internal-combustion engines, the rise of electricity, even the mass tourism of the jet era. But the past few decades have been quiet on that front. Coal has been cheap. Natural gas has been cheap. The 1970s aside, oil has been cheap. The one real novelty, nuclear power, went spectacularly off the rails. The pressure to innovate has been minimal.

In the space of a couple of years, all that has changed. Oil is no longer cheap; indeed, it has never been more expensive. Moreover, there is growing concern that the supply of oil may soon peak as consumption continues to grow, known supplies run out and new reserves become harder to find.

The idea of growing what you put in the tank of your car, rather than sucking it out of a hole in the ground, no longer looks like economic madness. Nor does the idea of throwing away the tank and plugging your car into an electric socket instead. Much of the world's oil is in the hands of governments who have little sympathy with the rich West. When a former head of America's Central Intelligence Agency allies himself with tree-hugging greens that his outfit would once have suspected of subversion, you know something is up. Yet that is one tack James Woolsey is trying in order to reduce his country's dependence on imported oil.

The price of natural gas, too, has risen in sympathy with oil. That is putting up the cost of electricity. Wind- and solar-powered alternatives no longer look so costly by comparison. It is true that coal remains cheap, and is the favoured fuel for power stations in industrialising Asia. But the rich world sees things differently.

In theory, there is a long queue of coal-fired power stations waiting to be built in America. But few have been completed in the past 15 years and many in that queue have been put on hold or withdrawn, for two reasons. First, Americans have become intolerant of large, polluting industrial plants on their doorsteps. Second, American power companies are fearful that they will soon have to pay for one particular pollutant, carbon dioxide, as is starting to happen in other parts of the rich world. Having invested heavily in gas-fired stations, only to find themselves locked into an increasingly expensive fuel, they do not want to make another mistake.

That has opened up a capacity gap and an opportunity for wind and sunlight. The future price of these resources—zero—is known. That certainty has economic value as a hedge, even if the capital cost of wind and solar power stations is, at the moment, higher than that of coal-fired ones.

The reasons for the boom, then, are tangled, and the way they are perceived may change. Global warming, a long-range phenomenon, may not be uppermost in people's minds during an economic downturn. High fuel prices may fall as new sources of supply are exploited to fill rising demand from Asia. Security of supply may improve if hostile governments are replaced by friendly ones and sources become more diversified. But none of the reasons is likely to go away entirely.

Global warming certainly will not. "Peak oil", if oil means the traditional sort that comes cheaply out of holes in the ground, probably will arrive soon. There is oil aplenty of other sorts (tar sands, liquefied coal and so on), so the stuff is unlikely to run out for a long time yet. But it will get more expensive to produce, putting a floor on the price that is way above today's. And political risk will always be there—particularly for oil, which is so often associated with bad government for the simple reason that its very presence causes bad government in states that do not have strong institutions to curb their politicians.

A Prize beyond the Dreams of Avarice

The market for energy is huge. At present, the world's population consumes about 15 terawatts of power. (A terawatt is 1,000 gigawatts, and a gigawatt is the capacity of the largest sort of coal-fired power station.) That translates into a business worth $6 trillion a year—about a tenth of the world's economic

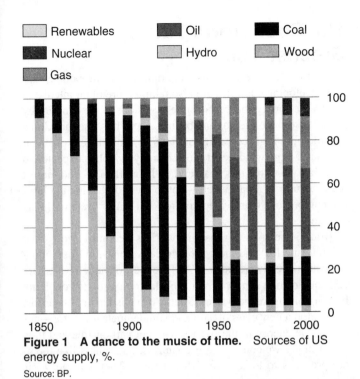

Figure 1 A dance to the music of time. Sources of US energy supply, %.

Source: BP.

World primary-energy consumption by fuel 2004, %

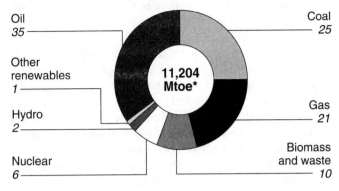

World electricity production by energy source 2004, %

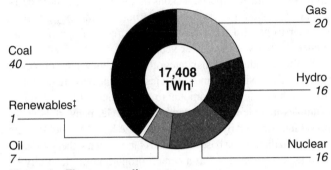

Figure 2 The way we live now.

*Megatonnes of oil equivalent.
†Terawatt-hours.
‡Biomass and waste, wind, geothermal and solar.

Source: IEA.

output—according to John Doerr, a venture capitalist who is heavily involved in the industry. And by 2050, power consumption is likely to have risen to 30 terawatts.

Scale is one of the important differences between the coming energy boom, if it materialises, and its recent predecessors—particularly those that relied on information technology, a market measured in mere hundreds of billions. Another difference is that new information technologies tend to be disruptive, forcing the replacement of existing equipment, whereas, say, building wind farms does not force the closure of coal-fired power stations.

For both of these reasons, any transition from an economy based on fossil fuels to one based on renewable, alternative, green energy—call it what you will—is likely to be slow, as similar changes have been in the past (see Figure 1). On the other hand, the scale of the market provides opportunities for alternatives to prove themselves at the margin and then move into the mainstream, as is happening with wind power at the moment. And some energy technologies do have the potential to be disruptive. Plug-in cars, for example, could be fuelled with electricity at a price equivalent to 25 cents a litre of petrol. That could shake up the oil, carmaking and electricity industries all in one go.

The innovation lull of the past few decades also provides opportunities for technological leapfrogging. Indeed, it may be that the field of energy gives the not-quite-booms in biotechnology and nanotechnology the industrial applications they need to grow really big, and that the three aspiring booms will thus merge into one.

The possibility of thus recapturing the good times of their youth has brought many well-known members of the "technorati" out of their homes in places like Woodside, California. Energy has become supercool. Elon Musk, who co-founded PayPal, has developed a battery-powered sports car. Larry Page and Sergey Brin, the founders of Google, have started an outfit called Google.org that is searching for a way to make renewable energy truly cheaper than coal (or RE<C, as they describe it to their fellow geeks).

Vinod Khosla, one of the founders of Sun Microsystems, is turning his considerable skills as a venture capitalist towards renewable energy, as are Robert Metcalfe, who invented the ethernet system used to connect computers together in local networks, and Mr Doerr, who works at Kleiner Perkins Caufield & Byers, one of Silicon Valley's best-known venture-capital firms. Sir Richard Branson, too, is getting in on the act with his Virgin Green Fund.

This renewed interest in energy is bringing forth a raft of ideas, some bright, some batty, that is indeed reminiscent of the dotcom boom. As happened in that boom, most of these ideas will come to naught. But there could just be a PayPal or a Google or a Sun among them.

More traditional companies are also taking an interest. General Electric (GE), a large American engineering firm, already has a thriving wind-turbine business and is gearing up its solar-energy business. The energy researchers at its laboratories in Schenectady, New York, enjoy much of the intellectual freedom associated with start-up firms, combined with a secure supply of money.

Meanwhile, BP and Shell, two of the world's biggest oil companies, are sponsoring both academic researchers and new, small firms with bright ideas, as is DuPont, one of the biggest chemical companies. Not everyone has joined in. Exxon Mobil, the world's largest oil company not in government hands, is conspicuously absent. But in many boardrooms renewables are no longer seen as just a way of keeping environmentalists off companies' backs.

Some people complain that many existing forms of renewable energy rely on subsidies or other forms of special treatment for their viability. On the surface, that is true. Look beneath, though, and the whole energy sector is riddled with subsidies, both explicit and hidden, and costs that are not properly accounted for. Drawing on the work of people like Boyden Gray, a former White House counsel, Mr Woolsey estimates that American oil companies receive preferential treatment from their government worth more than $250 billion a year. And the Intergovernmental Panel on Climate Change (IPCC), a United Nations-appointed group of scientific experts, reckons that fossil fuels should carry a tax of $20–50 for every tonne of carbon dioxide they generate in order to pay for the environmental effects of burning them (hence the fears of the power-generators).

So the subsidies and mandates offered to renewable sources of power such as wind turbines often just level the playing field. It is true that some subsidies amount to unwarranted market-rigging: examples include those handed by cloudy Germany to its solar-power industry and by America to its maize-based ethanol farmers when Brazilian sugar-based ethanol is far cheaper. Others, though, such as a requirement that a certain proportion of electricity be derived from non-fossil-fuel sources, make no attempt to pick particular technological winners. They merely act to stimulate innovation by guaranteeing a market to things that actually work.

If the world were rational, all of these measures would be swept away and replaced by a proper tax on carbon—as is starting to happen in Europe, where the price arrived at by the cap-and-trade system being introduced is close to the IPCC's recommendation. If that occurred, wind-based electricity would already be competitive with fossil fuels and others would be coming close. Failing that, special treatment for alternatives is probably the least bad option—though such measures need to be crafted in ways that favour neither incumbents nor particular ways of doing things, and need to be withdrawn when they are no longer necessary.

The Poor World Turns Greener Too

That, at least, is the view from the rich world. But poorer, rapidly developing countries are also taking more of an interest in renewable energy sources, despite assertions to the contrary by some Western politicians and businessmen. It is true that China is building coal-fired power stations at a blazing rate. But it also has a large wind-generation capacity, which is expected to grow by two-thirds this year, and is the world's second-largest manufacturer of solar panels—not to mention having the largest number of solar-heated rooftop hot-water systems in its buildings.

Brazil, meanwhile, has the world's second-largest (just behind America) and most economically honest biofuel industry, which already provides 40% of the fuel consumed by its cars and should soon supply 15% of its electricity, too (through the burning of sugarcane waste). South Africa is leading the effort to develop a new class of safe and simple nuclear reactor—not renewable energy in the strict sense, but carbon-free and thus increasingly welcome. These countries, and others like them, are prepared to look beyond fossil fuels. They will get their energy where they can. So if renewables and other alternatives can compete on cost, the poor and the rich world alike will adopt them.

That, however, requires innovation. Such innovation is most likely to come out of the laboratories of rich countries. At a recent debate at Columbia University, which *The Economist* helped to organise, Mr Khosla defended the proposition, "The United States will solve the climate-change problem". The Californian venture capitalist argued that if cheaper alternatives to fossil fuels are developed, simple economics will ensure their adoption throughout the world. He also insisted that the innovation which will create those alternatives will come almost entirely out of America.

As it happens, he lost. But that does not mean he is wrong. There are lots of terawatts to play for and lots of money to be made. And if the planet happens to be saved on the way, that is all to the good.

Nuclear Now!

How Clean, Green Atomic Energy Can Stop Global Warming

PETER SCHWARTZ AND SPENCER REISS

On a cool spring morning a quarter century ago, a place in Pennsylvania called Three Mile Island exploded into the headlines and stopped the US nuclear power industry in its tracks. What had been billed as the clean, cheap, limitless energy source for a shining future was suddenly too hot to handle.

In the years since, we've searched for alternatives, pouring billions of dollars into windmills, solar panels, and biofuels. We've designed fantastically efficient lightbulbs, air conditioners, and refrigerators. We've built enough gas-fired generators to bankrupt California. But mainly, each year we hack 400 million more tons of coal out of Earth's crust than we did a quarter century before, light it on fire, and shoot the proceeds into the atmosphere.

The consequences aren't pretty. Burning coal and other fossil fuels is driving climate change, which is blamed for everything from western forest fires and Florida hurricanes to melting polar ice sheets and flooded Himalayan hamlets. On top of that, coal-burning electric power plants have fouled the air with enough heavy metals and other noxious pollutants to cause 15,000 premature deaths annually in the US alone, according to a Harvard School of Public Health study. Believe it or not, a coal-fired plant releases 100 times more radioactive material than an equivalent nuclear reactor—right into the air, too, not into some carefully guarded storage site. (And, by the way, more than 5,200 Chinese coal miners perished in accidents last year.)

Burning hydrocarbons is a luxury that a planet with 6 billion energy-hungry souls can't afford. There's only one sane, practical alternative: nuclear power.

We now know that the risks of splitting atoms pale beside the dreadful toll exacted by fossil fuels. Radiation containment, waste disposal, and nuclear weapons proliferation are manageable problems in a way that global warming is not. Unlike the usual green alternatives—water, wind, solar, and biomass—nuclear energy is here, now, in industrial quantities. Sure, nuke plants are expensive to build—upward of $2 billion apiece—but they start to look cheap when you factor in the true cost to people and the planet of burning fossil fuels. And nuclear is our best hope for cleanly and efficiently generating hydrogen, which would end our other ugly hydrocarbon addiction—dependence on gasoline and diesel for transport.

Some of the world's most thoughtful greens have discovered the logic of nuclear power, including Gaia theorist James Lovelock, Greenpeace cofounder Patrick Moore, and Britain's Bishop Hugh Montefiore, a longtime board member of Friends of the Earth. Western Europe is quietly backing away from planned nuclear phaseouts. Finland has ordered a big reactor specifically to meet the terms of the Kyoto Protocol on climate change. China's new nuke plants—26 by 2025—are part of a desperate effort at smog control.

Even the shell-shocked US nuclear industry is coming out of its stupor. The 2001 report of Vice President Cheney's energy task force was only the most high profile in a series of pro-nuke developments. Nuke boosters are especially buoyed by more efficient plant designs, streamlined licensing procedures, and the prospect of federal subsidies.

In fact, new plants are on the way, however tentatively. Three groups of generating companies have entered a bureaucratic maze expected to lead to formal applications for plants by 2008. If everything breaks right, the first new reactors in decades will be online by 2014. If this seems ambitious, it's not; the industry hopes merely to hold on to nuclear's current 20 percent of the rapidly growing US electric power market.

That's not nearly enough. We should be shooting to match France, which gets 77 percent of its electricity from nukes. It's past time for a decisive leap out of the hydrocarbon era, time to send King Coal and, soon after, Big Oil shambling off to their well-deserved final resting places—maybe on a nostalgic old steam locomotive.

Besides, wouldn't it be a blast to barrel down the freeway in a hydrogen Hummer with a clean conscience as your copilot? Or not to feel like a planet killer every time you flick on the A/C? That's how the future could be, if only we would get over our fear of the nuclear bogeyman and forge ahead—for real this time—into the atomic age.

The granola crowd likes to talk about conservation and efficiency, and surely substantial gains can be made in those areas. But energy is not a luxury people can do without, like a gym membership or hair gel. The developed world built its wealth on cheap power—burning firewood, coal, petroleum, and natural gas, with carbon emissions the inevitable byproduct.

Indeed, material progress can be tracked in what gets pumped out of smokestacks. An hour of coal-generated 100-watt electric light creates 0.05 pounds of atmospheric carbon, a bucket of ice makes 0.3 pounds, an hour's car ride 5. The average American sends nearly half a ton of carbon spewing into the atmosphere every month. Europe and Japan are a little more economical, but even the most remote forest-burning peasants happily do their part.

And the worst—by far—is yet to come. An MIT study forecasts that worldwide energy demand could triple by 2050. China could build a Three Gorges Dam every year forever and still not meet its growing demand for electricity. Even the carbon reductions required by the Kyoto Protocol—which pointedly exempts developing countries like China—will be a drop in the atmospheric sewer.

What is a rapidly carbonizing world to do? The high-minded answer, of course, is renewables. But the notion that wind, water, solar, or biomass will save the day is at least as fanciful as the once-popular idea that nuclear energy would be too cheap to meter. Jesse Ausubel, director of the human environment program at New York's Rockefeller University, calls renewable energy sources "false gods"—attractive but powerless. They're capital- and land-intensive, and solar is not yet remotely cost-competitive. Despite all the hype, tax breaks, and incentives, the proportion of US electricity production from renewables has actually fallen in the past 15 years, from 11.0 percent to 9.1 percent.

The decline would be even worse without hydropower, which accounts for 92 percent of the world's renewable electricity. While dams in the US are under attack from environmentalists trying to protect wild fish populations, the Chinese are building them on an ever grander scale. But even China's autocrats can't get past Nimby. Stung by criticism of the monumental Three Gorges project—which required the forcible relocation of 1 million people—officials have suspended an even bigger project on the Nu Jiang River in the country's remote southwest. Or maybe someone in Beijing questioned the wisdom of reacting to climate change with a multibillion-dollar bet on rainfall.

Solar power doesn't look much better. Its number-one problem is cost: While the price of photovoltaic cells has been slowly dropping, solar-generated electricity is still four times more expensive than nuclear (and more than five times the cost of coal). Maybe someday we'll all live in houses with photovoltaic roof tiles, but in the real world, a run-of-the-mill 1,000-megawatt photovoltaic plant will require about 60 square miles of panes alone. In other words, the largest industrial structure ever built.

Wind is more promising, which is one reason it's the lone renewable attracting serious interest from big-time equipment manufacturers like General Electric. But even though price and performance are expected to improve, wind, like solar, is inherently fickle, hard to capture, and widely dispersed. And wind turbines take up a lot of space; Ausubel points out that the wind equivalent of a typical utility plant would require 300 square miles of turbines plus costly transmission lines from the wind-scoured fields of, say, North Dakota. Alternatively, there's California's Altamont Pass, where 5,400 windmills slice and dice some 1,300 birds of prey annually.

What about biomass? Ethanol is clean, but growing the amount of cellulose required to shift US electricity production to biomass would require farming—no wilting organics, please—an area the size of 10 Iowas.

Among fossil fuels, natural gas holds some allure; it emits a third as much carbon as coal. That's an improvement but not enough if you're serious about rolling back carbon levels. Washington's favorite solution is so-called clean coal, ballyhooed in stump speeches by both President Bush (who offered a $2 billion research program) and challenger John Kerry (who upped the ante to $10 billion). But most of the work so far has been aimed at reducing acid rain by cutting sulphur dioxide and nitrogen oxide emissions, and more recently gasifying coal to make it burn cleaner. Actual zero-emissions coal is still a lab experiment that even fans say could double or triple generating costs. It would also leave the question of what to do with 1 million tons of extracted [Sulphur] each year.

By contrast, nuclear power is thriving around the world despite decades of obituaries. Belgium derives 58 percent of its electricity from nukes, Sweden 45 percent, South Korea 40, Switzerland 37 percent, Japan 31 percent, Spain 27 percent, and the UK 23 percent. Turkey plans to build three plants over the next several years. South Korea has eight more reactors coming, Japan 13, China at least 20. France, where nukes generate more than three-quarters of the country's electricity, is privatizing a third of its state-owned nuclear energy group, Areva, to deal with the rush of new business.

The last US nuke plant to be built was ordered in 1973, yet nuclear power is growing here as well. With clever engineering and smart management, nukes have steadily increased their share of generating capacity in the US. The 103 reactors operating in the US pump out electricity at more than 90 percent of capacity, up from 60 percent when Three Mile Island made headlines. That increase is the equivalent of adding 40 new reactors, without bothering anyone's backyard or spewing any more carbon into the air.

So atomic power is less expensive than it used to be—but could it possibly be cost-effective? Even before Three Mile Island sank, the US nuclear industry was foundering on the shoals of economics. Regulatory delays and billion-dollar construction-cost overruns turned the business into a financial nightmare. But increasing experience and efficiency gains have changed all that. Current operating costs are the lowest ever—1.82 cents per kilowatt-hour versus 2.13 cents for coal-fired plants and 3.69 cents for natural gas. The ultimate vindication of nuclear economics is playing out in the stock market: Over the past five years, the stocks of leading nuclear generating companies such as Exelon and Entergy have more than doubled. Indeed, Exelon is feeling so flush that it bought New Jersey's Public Service Enterprise Group in December, adding four reactors to its former roster of 17.

This remarkable success suggests that nuclear energy realistically could replace coal in the US without a cost increase and ultimately lead the way to a clean, green future. The trick is to start building nuke plants and keep building them at a furious pace. Anything less leaves carbon in the climatic driver's seat.

A decade ago, anyone thinking about constructing nuclear plants in the US would have been dismissed as out of touch with reality. But today, for the first time since the building of Three Mile Island, new nukes in the US seem possible. Thanks to improvements in reactor design and increasing encouragement from Washington, DC, the nuclear industry is posed for unlikely revival. "All the planets seem to be coming into alignment," says David Brown, VP for congressional affairs at Exelon.

The original US nuclear plants, built during the 1950s and '60s, were descended from propulsion units in 1950s-vintage nuclear submarines, now known as generation I. During the '80s and '90s, when new construction halted in the US, the major reactor makers—GE Power Systems, British-owned Westinghouse, France's Framatome (part of Areva), and Canada's AECL—went after customers in Europe. This new round of business led to system improvements that could eventually, after some prototyping, be deployed back in the US.

By all accounts, the latest reactors, generation III+, are a big improvement. They're fuel-efficient. They employ passive safety technologies, such as gravity-fed emergency cooling rather than pumps. Thanks to standardized construction, they may even be cost-competitive to build—$1,200 per kilowatt-hour of generating capacity versus more than $1,300 for the latest low-emission (which is not to say low-carbon) coal plants. But there's no way to know for sure until someone actually builds one. And even then, the first few will almost certainly cost more.

Prodded by the Cheney report, the US Department of Energy agreed in 2002 to pick up the tab of the first hurdle—getting from engineering design to working blueprints. Three groups of utility companies and reactor makers have stepped up for the program, optimistically dubbed Nuclear Power 2010. The government's bill to taxpayers for this stage of development could top $500 million, but at least we'll get working reactors rather than "promising technologies."

But newer, better designs don't free the industry from the intense public oversight that has been nuclear power's special burden from the start. Believe it or not, Three Mile Island wasn't the ultimate nightmare; that would be Shoreham, the Long Island power plant shuttered in 1994 after a nine-year legal battle, without ever having sold a single electron. Construction was already complete when opponents challenged the plant's application for an operating license. Wall Street won't invest billions in new plants ($5.5 billion in Shoreham's case) without a clear path through the maze of judges and regulators.

Shoreham didn't die completely in vain. The 1992 Energy Policy Act aims to forestall such debacles by authorizing the Nuclear Regulatory Commission to issue combined construction and operating licenses. It also allows the NRC to pre-certify specific reactor models and the energy companies to bank preapproved sites. Utility executives fret that no one has ever road-tested the new process, which still requires public hearings and shelves of supporting documents. An idle reactor site at Browns Ferry, Alabama, could be an early test case; the Tennessee Valley Authority is exploring options to refurbish it rather than start from scratch.

Meanwhile, Congress looks ready to provide a boost to the nuclear energy industry. Pete Domenici (R-New Mexico), chair of the Senate's energy committee and the patron saint of nuclear power in Washington, has vowed to revive last year's energy bill, which died in the Senate. Earlier versions included a 1.85 cent per-kilowatt-hour production tax credit for the first half-dozen nuke plants to come online. That could add up to as much as $8 billion in federal outlays and should go a long way toward luring Wall Street back into the fray. As pork goes, the provision is easy to defend. Nuclear power's extraordinary startup costs and safety risks make it a special case for government intervention. And the amount is precisely the same bounty Washington spends annually in tax credits for wind, biomass, and other zero-emission kilowattage.

Safer plants, more sensible regulation, and even a helping hand from Congress—all are on the way. What's still missing is a place to put radioactive waste. By law, US companies that generate nuclear power pay the Feds a tenth of a cent per kilowatt-hour to dispose of their spent fuel. The fund—currently $24 billion and counting—is supposed to finance a permanent waste repository, the ill-fated Yucca Mountain in Nevada. Two decades ago when the payments started, opening day was scheduled for January 31, 1998. But the Nevada facility remains embroiled in hearings, debates, and studies, and waste is piling up at 30-odd sites around the country. Nobody will build a nuke plant until Washington offers a better answer than "keep piling."

At Yucca Mountain, perfection has been the enemy of adequacy. It's fun to discuss what the design life of an underground nuclear waste facility ought to be. One hundred years? Two hundred years? How about 100,000? A quarter of a million? Science fiction meets the US government budgeting process. In court!

But throwing waste into a black hole at Yucca Mountain isn't such a great idea anyway. For one thing, in coming decades we might devise better disposal methods, such as corrosion-proof containers that can withstand millennia of heat and moisture. For another, used nuclear fuel can be recycled as a source for the production of more energy. Either way, it's clear that the whole waste disposal problem has been misconstrued. We don't need a million-year solution. A hundred years will do just fine—long enough to let the stuff cool down and allow us to decide what to do with it.

The name for this approach is interim storage: Find a few patches of isolated real estate—we're not talking about taking it over for eternity—and pour nice big concrete pads; add floodlights, motion detectors, and razor wire; truck in nuclear waste in bombproof 20-foot-high concrete casks. Voilà: safe storage while you wait for either Yucca Mountain or plan B.

Two dozen reactor sites around the country already have their own interim facilities; a private company has applied with the NRC to open one on the Goshute Indian reservation in Skull Valley, Utah. Establishing a half- dozen federally managed sites is closer to the right idea. Domenici says he'll introduce legislation this year for a national interim storage system.

A handful of new US plants will be a fine start, but the real goal has to be dethroning King Coal and—until something better comes along—pushing nuclear power out front as the world's default energy source. Kicking carbon cold turkey won't be easy, but it can be done. Four crucial steps can help increase the momentum: Regulate carbon emissions, revamp the fuel cycle, rekindle innovation in nuclear technology, and, finally, replace gasoline with hydrogen.

- **Regulate carbon emissions.** Nuclear plants have to account for every radioactive atom of waste. Meanwhile, coal-fired plants dump tons of deadly refuse into the atmosphere at zero cost. It's time for that free ride to end, but only the government can make it happen.

The industry seems ready to pay up. Andy White, CEO of GE Energy's nuclear division, recently asked a roomful of US utility executives what they thought about the possibility of regulating carbon emissions. The idea didn't faze them. "The only question any of them had," he says, "was when and how much."

A flat-out carbon tax is almost certainly a nonstarter in Washington. But an arrangement in which all energy producers are allowed a limited number of carbon pollution credits to use or sell could pass muster; after all, this kind of cap-and-trade scheme is already a fact of life for US utilities with a variety of other pollutants. Senators John McCain and Joe Lieberman have been pushing legislation [for] such a system. This would send a clear message to utility executives that fossil energy's free pass is over.

- **Recycle nuclear fuel.** Here's a fun fact: Spent nuclear fuel—the stuff intended for permanent disposal at Yucca Mountain—retains 95 percent of its energy content. Imagine what Toyota could do for fuel efficiency if 95 percent of the average car's gasoline passed through the engine and out the tailpipe. In France, Japan, and Britain, nuclear engineers do the sensible thing: recycle. Alone among the nuclear powers, the US doesn't, for reasons that have nothing to do with nuclear power.

Recycling spent fuel—the technical word is reprocessing—is one way to make the key ingredient of a nuclear bomb, enriched uranium. In 1977, Jimmy Carter, the only nuclear engineer ever to occupy the White House, banned reprocessing in the US in favor of a so-called once-through fuel cycle. Four decades later, more than a dozen countries reprocess or enrich uranium, including North Korea and Iran. At this point, hanging onto spent fuel from US reactors does little good abroad and real mischief at home.

The Bush administration has reopened the door with modest funding to resume research into the nuclear fuel cycle. The president himself has floated a proposal to provide all comers with a guaranteed supply of reactor fuel in exchange for a promise not to reprocess spent fuel themselves. Other proposals would create a global nuclear fuel company, possibly under the auspices of the International Atomic Energy Agency. This company would collect, reprocess, and distribute fuel to every nation in the world, thus keeping potential bomb fixings out of circulation.

In the short term, reprocessing would maximize resources and minimize the problem of how to dispose of radioactive waste. In fact, it would eliminate most of the waste from nuclear power

production. Over decades, it could also ease pressure on uranium supplies. The world's existing reserves are generally reckoned sufficient to withstand 50 years of rapid nuclear expansion without a significant price increase. In a pinch, there's always the ocean, whose 4.5 billion tons of dissolved uranium can be extracted today at 5 to 10 times the cost of conventional mining.

Uranium is so cheap today that reprocessing is more about reducing waste than stretching the fuel supply. But advanced breeder reactors, which create more fuel as they generate power, could well be the economically competitive choice—and renewable as well.

- **Rekindle innovation.** Although nuclear technology has come a long way since Three Mile Island, the field is hardly a hotbed of innovation. Government-funded research—such as the DOE's Next Generation Nuclear Plant program—is aimed at designing advanced reactors, including high temperature, gas-cooled plants of the kind being built in China and South Africa and fast-breeder reactors that will use uranium 60 times more efficiently than today's reactors. Still, the nuclear industry suffers from its legacy of having been born under a mushroom cloud and raised by your local electric company. A tight leash on nuclear R&D may be good, even necessary. But there's nothing like a little competition to spur creativity. That's reason enough to want to see US companies squarely back on the nuclear power field—research is great, but more and smarter buyers ultimately drive quality up and prices down.

In fact, the possibility of a nuclear gold rush—not just a modest rebirth—depends on economics as much as technology. The generation IV pebble-bed reactors being developed in China and South Africa get attention for their meltdown-proof designs. . . . But it's their low capital cost and potential for fast, modular construction that could blow the game open, as surely as the PC did for computing. As long as investments come in $2 billion increments, purchase orders will be few and far between. At $300 million a pop for safe, clean energy, watch the floodgates open around the world.

- **Replace gasoline with hydrogen.** If a single change could truly ignite nuclear power, it's the grab bag of technologies and wishful schemes traveling under the rubric of the hydrogen economy. Leaving behind petroleum is as important to the planet's future as eliminating coal. The hitch is that it takes energy to extract hydrogen from substances like methane and water. Where will it come from?

Today, the most common energy source for producing hydrogen is natural gas, followed by oil. It's conceivable that renewables could do it in limited quantities. By the luck of physics, though, two things nuclear reactors do best—generate both electricity and very high temperatures—are exactly what it takes to produce hydrogen most efficiently. Last November, the DOE's Idaho National Engineering and Environmental Laboratory showed how a single next-gen nuke could produce the hydrogen equivalent of 400,000 gallons of gasoline every day. Nuclear energy's potential for freeing us not only from coal but also oil holds the promise of a bright green future for the US and the world at large.

The more seriously you take the idea of global warming, the more seriously you have to take nuclear power. Clean coal, solar-powered roof tiles, wind farms in North Dakota—they're all pie in the emissions-free sky. Sure, give them a shot. But zero-carbon reactors are here and now. We know we can build them. Their price tag is no mystery. They fit into the existing electric grid without a hitch. Flannel-shirted environmentalists who fight these realities run the risk of ending up with as much soot on their hands as the slickest coal-mining CEO.

America's voracious energy appetite doesn't have to be a bug—it can be a feature. Shanghai, Seoul, and São Paolo are more likely to look to Los Angeles or Houston as a model than to some solar-powered idyll. Energy technology is no different than any other; innovation can change all the rules. But if the best we can offer the developing world is bromides about energy independence, we'll deserve the carbon-choked nightmare of a planet we get.

Nuclear energy is the big bang still reverberating. It's the power to light a city in a lump the size of a soda can. Peter Huber and Mark Mills have written an iconoclastic new book on energy, *The Bottomless Well*. They see nuclear power as merely the latest in a series of technologies that will gradually eliminate our need to carve up huge swaths of the planet. "Energy isn't the problem. Energy is the solution," they write. "Energy begets more energy. The more of it we capture and put to use, the more readily we will capture still more."

The best way to avoid running out of fossil fuels is to switch to something better. The Stone Age famously did not end for lack of stones, and neither should we wait for the last chunk of anthracite to flicker out before we kiss hydrocarbons good-bye. Especially not when something cleaner, safer, more efficient, and more abundant is ready to roll. It's time to get real.

Life After Peak Oil

Following an initial period of painful adaptation, we can live happily and healthily in a world with high energy costs.

GREGORY CLARK

Oil prices have receded from their recent flirtation with $100 a barrel, but demand soars from China and India, rapidly industrializing countries with a massive energy thirst. The combination of increased demand, high prices and the prospect of an eventual peak in oil production, has caught Americans paralyzed between twin terrors: the fear that rampant consumption of oil and coal is irreversibly warming the Earth and the dread that without cheap oil our affluent lifestyles will evaporate.

Can't live with oil, can't live without it.

Study of the long economic history of the world suggests two things, however. Cheap fossil fuels actually explain little of how we got rich since the Industrial Revolution. And after an initial period of painful adaptation, we can live happily, opulently and indeed more healthily, in a world of permanent $100-a-barrel oil or even $500-a-barrel oil.

The first lesson of history is that cheap energy explains only a modest portion of our current wealth. We are now, as a result of the Industrial Revolution, 12 times richer than the average person in the pre-industrial world. Modern economic growth has been accompanied by huge declines in energy costs from exploiting coal and oil. A worker today can buy a gallon of gas with his wages from 20 minutes of work. Before the Industrial Revolution to buy the energy in a gallon of gas the English worker of the 1760s needed to work four hours.

As energy prices declined consumption rose. Currently in the United States we consume the equivalent in energy of six gallons of gas per person per day. In England in 1770 energy consumption (mainly coal) was equivalent to only 0.5 gallons of gas per day.

Many people think mistakenly that modern prosperity was founded on this fossil energy revolution, and that when the oil and coal is gone, it is back to the Stone Age. If we had no fossil energy, then we would be forced to rely on an essentially unlimited amount of solar power, available at five times current energy costs. With energy five times as expensive as at present we would take a substantial hit to incomes. Our living standard would decline by about 11 percent. But we would still be fantastically rich compared to the pre-industrial world.

That may seem like a lot of economic hurt, but put it in context. Our income would still be above the current living standards in Canada, Sweden or England. Oh, the suffering humanity! At current rates of economic growth we would gain back the income losses from having to convert to solar power in less than six years. And then onward on our march to ever greater prosperity.

The ability to sustain such high energy prices at little economic cost depends on the assumption that we can cut back from using the equivalent of six gallons of gas per person per day to 1.5 gallons. Is that really possible? The answer is that we know already it is.

The economy would withstand enormous increases in energy costs with modest damage because energy is even now so extravagantly cheap that most of it is squandered in uses of little value. Recently, I drove my 13-year-old son 230 miles round-trip from Davis to Chico, to play a 70-minute soccer game. Had every gallon of gas cost four hours of my wage, I am sure his team could have found opposition closer to home.

The median-sized U.S. home is now nearly 2,400 square feet, for an average family size of 2.6 people, almost 1,000 square feet per person. Much of that heated, air-conditioned and lighted square footage rarely gets used. Cities in the Central Valley, such as Elk Grove, that were developed in the world of cheap gas have sprawled across the landscape so that the only way to get to work or to shops is by car. Ninety-four percent of the inhabitants of Elk Grove drive to work. Sidewalks have disappeared in some locations.

Some countries in Europe, such as Denmark, which have by public policy made energy much more expensive, already use only the equivalent of about three gallons of gas per person. I have been to Copenhagen, and believe me the Danes are not suffering a lot from those the daily three gallons of gas they gave up.

> **So the future after peak oil will involve living in such dense urban settings where destinations are walkable or bikeable, just as in pre-industrial cities . . . Such a lifestyle is not only possible it will be much healthier.**

But can we get down to 1.5 gallons without huge pain? We can see even now communities where for reasons of land scarcity people have been forced to adopt a lifestyle that uses much less energy—places like Manhattan, London or Singapore. Manhattan, for example, has 67,000 people per square mile. Kensington and Chelsea in London have 37,000 people per square mile. Housing space per person is much smaller, people walk or take public transit to work and to shop, and energy usage is correspondingly much lower, despite the inhabitants being very rich.

So the future after peak oil will involve living in such dense urban settings where destinations are walkable or bikeable, just as in pre-industrial cities (the city of London in 1801 had 100,000 inhabitants in one square mile). Homes will be much smaller, but instead of caverns of off-white sheet rock, we will spend our money in making much more attractive interiors. Nights will be darker. We will not have retail outlets lit up like the glare of the midday sun in Death Valley.

Such a lifestyle is not only possible it will be much healthier. We are not biologically adapted to the suburban lifestyle of Central California—lots of cheap calories delivered right to your seat in the SUV that shuttles you from your sofa at home, to your chair at work, to the gym where you try and work on your weight problem. It will also make aging more graceful. We now live as much in fear of losing our gas-fueled mobility as we age as we are of the Grim Reaper himself.

So life after peak oil should hold no terror for us—unless, of course, you have invested in a lot of suburban real estate.

GREGORY CLARK is professor and chair of the Department of Economics at the University of California, Davis. He is the author of *A Farewell to Alms: A Brief Economic History of the World,* Princeton University Press.

UNIT 5
Conflict

Unit Selections

27. **Terrorist Rivals: Beyond the State-Centric Model,** Louise Richardson
28. **The Long March to Be a Superpower,** *The Economist*
29. **What Russia Wants,** Ivan Krastev
30. **Lifting the Veil: Understanding the Roots of Islamic Militancy,** Henry Munson
31. **A Mideast Nuclear Chain Reaction?,** Joseph Cirincione
32. **The Politics of Death in Darfur,** Gérard Prunier
33. **Banning the Bomb: A New Approach,** Ward Wilson

Key Points to Consider

- Are violent conflicts and warfare increasing or decreasing?

- What are the major hotspots in the world where conflict is taking place?

- What changes have taken place in recent years in the types of conflicts and in terms of the participants?

- How is military doctrine changing to reflect new political realities?

- How is the nature of terrorism different from conventional warfare? What new threats do terrorists pose?

- What are the motivations and attitudes of those who use terror as a political tool?

- What challenges does nuclear proliferation pose to the United States?

- How is the national security policy of the United States likely to change? What about Russia, India, and China?

Student Web Site
www.mhcls.com

Internet References

DefenseLINK
   http://www.defenselink.mil
Federation of American Scientists (FAS)
   http://www.fas.org
ISN International Relations and Security Network
   http://www.isn.ethz.ch
The NATO Integrated Data Service (NIDS)
   http://www.nato.int/structur/nids/nids.htm

Do you lock your doors at night? Do you secure your personal property to avoid theft? These are basic questions that have to do with your sense of personal security. Most individuals take steps to protect what they have, including their lives. The same is true for groups of people, including countries.

In the international arena, governments frequently pursue their national interest by entering into mutually agreeable "deals" with other governments. Social scientists call these types of arrangements "exchanges" (i.e., each side gives up something it values in order to gain something in return that it values even more). On an economic level, it functions like this: "I have the oil that you need and am willing to sell it. In return I want to buy from you the agricultural products that I lack." Whether on the governmental level or the personal level: "If you help me with my homework, then I will drive you home this weekend," exchange is the process used by most individuals and groups to obtain and protect what is of value. The exchange process, however, can break down. When threats and punishments replace mutual exchanges, conflict ensues. Neither side benefits and there are costs to both. Further, each may use threats with the expectation that the other will capitulate. But if efforts at intimidation and coercion fail, the conflict may escalate into violent confrontation.

With the end of the cold war, issues of national security and the nature of international conflict have changed. In the late 1980s, agreements between the former Soviet Union and the United States led to the elimination of superpower support for participants in low-intensity conflicts in Central America, Africa, and Southeast Asia. Fighting the cold war by proxy is now a thing of the past. In addition, cold war military alliances have either collapsed or have been significantly redefined. Despite these historic changes, there is no shortage of conflicts in the world today.

Many experts initially predicted that the collapse of the Soviet Union would decrease the arms race and diminish the threat of nuclear war. However, some analysts now believe that the threat of nuclear war has in fact increased, as control of nuclear weapons has become less centralized and the command structure less reliable. In addition, the proliferation of nuclear weapons into North Korea and South Asia (India and Pakistan) is a growing security issue. Further, there are concerns about both dictatorial governments and terrorist organizations obtaining weapons of mass destruction. What these changing circumstances mean for U.S. policy is a topic of considerable debate.

The unit focuses on two general issues. The first is the changing nature of conflict and traditional measures of power

© Department of Defense photo by Airman 1st Class Kurt Gibbons III, U.S. Air Force

and influence, including the role of nuclear weapons. The second are case studies that provide insights into the roots of terrorism and armed conflicts in the Middle East, North Africa, and Asia.

As in the case of the other global issues described in this anthology, international conflict is a dynamic problem. It is important to understand that conflicts are not random events, but follow patterns and trends. Forty-five years of cold war established discernable patterns of international conflict as the superpowers deterred each other with vast expenditures of money and technological know-how. The consequence of this stalemate was often a shift to the developing world for conflict by superpower proxy.

The changing circumstances of the post-cold war era generate a series of important new policy questions: Will there be more nuclear proliferation? Is there an increased danger of so-called "rogue" states destabilizing the international arena? Is the threat of terror a temporary or permanent feature of world affairs? Will there be a growing emphasis on low-intensity conflicts related to the interdiction of drugs, or will some other unforeseen issue determine the world's hot spots? Will the United States and its European allies lose interest in security issues that do not directly involve their economic interests and simply look the other way, for example, as age-old ethnic conflicts become brutally violent? Can the international community develop viable institutions to mediate and resolve disputes before they become violent? The answers to these and related questions will determine the patterns of conflict in the twenty-first century.

Terrorist Rivals
Beyond the State-Centric Model

LOUISE RICHARDSON

By any standard measure, the United States is currently the most powerful country in the history of the world. Its defense budget of US$440 billion in 2007 (US$560 billion if one includes the budgets for the wars in Iraq and Afghanistan) is greater than the combined military expenditure of the rest of the world. In 2003 the International Institute for Strategic Studies calculated that the US defense budget was greater than the combined budgets of the next 13 countries and more than double the combination of the remaining 158 countries. Potential challengers cannot even begin to rival this power. The European Union can compete with the United States in terms of population and GNP, but it does not have the will or the institutional ability to act in concert on foreign or security initiatives. Russia, which until relatively recently was considered the closest challenger, retains vast armies but lags dramatically in military spending and technological development. The United States even outspends China, the nation most often mentioned as a challenger, by about seven to one. China is a formidable economic powerhouse, but only spends 3.9 percent of its GDP on defense, whereas it would have to spend about 25 percent to begin to rival the United States.

Yet in spite of this extraordinary and quite unprecedented preeminence, the United States has been unable to impose its will on the impoverished state of Afghanistan, on the sectarian chaos that is Iraq, or even on an organization, Al Qaeda, which is led by a few men believed to be hiding in caves in remote parts of Afghanistan and Pakistan. What does it say about traditional conceptions of the balance of power when the most powerful country on the planet cannot effectively apply its power to achieve its objectives?

The inability of the United States to achieve its security objectives is not due to the fact that other countries have balanced or "bandwagoned" against it, as traditional conceptions of a balance of power mechanism would have claimed. On the contrary, most of our would-be rivals share the United States' desire to destroy Al Qaeda, have supported its efforts to rebuild Afghanistan, and have acquiesced, albeit reluctantly, to its operations in Iraq. Indeed the United States has failed to achieve its security objectives because it has failed to appreciate the nature of the adversaries it faces and because of its inability to transform its military might into an effective arsenal against these adversaries.

Military Strength Misapplied

On September 11, 2001, a small substate group inflicted greater casualties on US civilians than any enemy government had ever inflicted on the United States before. The Japanese attack on Pearl Harbor killed 2,403 servicemen and 68 civilians, and vastly more US citizens were killed by fellow countrymen in the course of the Civil War, but an attack from an enemy state of this scale was simply unprecedented. In the words of President George W. Bush, "September 11 changed our world." Vice President Dick Cheney was more specific, commenting on NBC News that "9/11 changed everything. It changed the way we think about threats to the United States. It changed our recognition of our vulnerabilities. It changed in terms of the kind of national security strategy we need to pursue, in terms of guaranteeing the safety and security of the American people."

The US government nevertheless responded in an entirely traditional way: it declared war. However, rather than declaring war on an enemy state, it declared war first on the tactic of terrorism and later, and even less sensibly, on the emotion of terror. As a practical matter, however, it waged a conventional war—first against Afghanistan, whose government had harbored the terrorists who committed the attacks on New York and Washington, and later against Iraq, whose government had no connection to these same attacks. Its overwhelming military force brought down both governments in short order and with little cost in terms of US lives.

More than five years after the attack, however, the leaders of Al Qaeda, Osama bin Laden and Ayman Al Zawahiri, as well as the head of the government that supported them, Mullah Mohammed Omar, remain at large. A new government was democratically elected in Afghanistan, but within six months of the US invasion more civilians had been killed than on September 11, the security situation had deteriorated significantly, and opium production had spiralled out of control. Meanwhile more US citizens have been killed in Iraq than on September 11, and tens of thousands of Iraqis have been killed in sectarian violence as the country slips into a bloody civil war. For all its preeminent power, the United States has manifestly failed to capture its greatest enemies or to impose its will, much less its democratic principles, on two infinitely weaker polities.

The fact that the Taliban were defeated while Al Qaeda remained at large should have demonstrated to the Bush administration that it was not facing a traditional state adversary. Instead, however, it insisted on attributing Al Qaeda's strength to state support and, in flagrant denial of all available evidence, insisted on fabricating a link between the government of Iraq and Al Qaeda. Indeed, the current military occupation has only succeeded in allowing for the rise of an Al Qaeda faction in Iraq. Like the drunk who searches for his car keys under the street lamp, not because he lost them there but because the light is better, the United States used its military might against two countries simply because this might is formidable, and not because military force is the most effective means to defeat terrorism. Indeed, it is not.

A New Brand of Enemy

It can certainly be argued that the threat the United States faces in the 21st century is from terrorism itself, rather than from a rising power. The Bush administration came into office convinced that China would soon become the new Soviet Union, but it has since substituted terrorism as the principal threat to the American way of life. Many of the behavior patterns seen in the Cold War are beginning to re-emerge. In that era, attitudes toward communism were the litmus test for alliance with the United States. Indeed, the US government found itself in alliance with a great many unsavory states that in no way shared its commitment to liberal democratic principles but rather its abhorrence of communism. Today, it is similarly prepared to overlook the domestic abuses of regimes that are willing to join in the war against terror.

During the Cold War, this approach severely undermined the United States' moral authority in the world by suggesting that its commitment to human and civil rights reached only as far as its borders. It also precluded the possibility of the United States allying itself with those seeking legitimate democratic change in their societies and caused it to neglect the domestic forces at play in countries for which the bipolar distribution of power was largely irrelevant. Today the pattern seems to be repeating itself. The difference, of course, is that during the Cold War the United States did have a major state rival that was prepared to play a game of deterrence and balance. However, there is now no state basis to the forces currently emerging to oppose US power: these actors have no interest in interstate rivalry and play by an entirely different set of rules.

Terrorism itself is not a threat. It is a tactic used by the weak in an effort to exact vengeance against the strong, to acquire glory for oneself and to provoke one's adversaries into overreaction. It is a tactic used in many parts of the world by many different groups seeking many different political objectives. The particular terrorists who pose a threat to the United States today are jihadis rebelling against the pervasiveness of US culture and the projection of US power throughout the world. They completely reject the notion of a balance of power, which they see as an entirely Western construct. They mobilized to attack the United States only after they had successfully defeated the Soviet Union in Afghanistan, which convinced them that having defeated one superpower, they could take on another. Their ultimate goal is to eliminate Western influence in the region entirely and to restore the empire of the caliphate, with borders stretching from Spain to Indonesia.

There is obviously no way of computing terrorists' actual military strength or financial resources, but, as they freely admit, they are infinitely weaker than their adversaries. In the words of their chief strategist, Ayman Al Zawahiri: "However far our capabilities reach, they will never be equal to one thousandth of the capabilities of the kingdom of Satan that is waging war on us." Their strength derives not from traditional military calculations but instead from the popularity of their ideology and their unwavering fanaticism, which manifests itself in a disregard for personal survival and a willingness to act outside the norms of behavior by killing as many civilians and spreading as much fear as is possible. Nevertheless, US citizens feel more vulnerable today than they did when facing 10,000 strategic and 30,000 non-strategic nuclear warheads directed at them from the Soviet Union.

The potential of militant Islam posing a greater threat to the United States than any rising power is a real one. This is not because these groups can rival US power or resources. However, given that a fifth of the world's population is Muslim, if the United States were to define itself as an enemy of Islam or to act in such a way that Muslims come to believe the small number of extremists in their midst who insist that the West wishes to wage war on them, then the United States would indeed be facing a real threat. The realist response to this security dilemma would be to form alliances with as many moderate Muslim states as possible in order to balance against Muslim extremists. But the problem with this approach is that many of these moderate Muslim leaders do not share Western values, do not represent their citizens, and do not have the popular support of their resident populations.

In a feat of astonishing naivety, the Bush administration believed that it could bring democracy to the Middle East and recreate the region in the United States' image. The belief was that democracy would bring prosperity, stability, trade, and a secure supply of oil, which would serve both US and regional interests. From the hegemonic point of view, this was an entirely reasonable way to extend one's influence and power without acquiring the formal trappings of empire. The problem, of course, is that local citizens often have their own ideas. Many citizens in the Middle East seek to counter pervasive US influence in the region. When given a choice, many have not voted for democrats, claiming instead that the groups that provide most effectively for their social needs—Hamas, Hezbollah, and the Muslim Brotherhood, for example—deserve representation, regardless of their views on democracy. Confronted with the election of those we consider enemies, US enthusiasm for democracy in the Middle East has waned significantly.

An Obsolete Framework

The successful functioning of the balance of power mechanism requires the predictable behavior of a small group of leaders who understand the rules of the game and pursue their states' interests within a set of predetermined boundaries. But today's leaders no longer have the requisite monopoly on information or on power. While the West might see globalization as a means of spreading its wealth around the world and contributing to the development of all, for others, that wealth appears to be distributed very inequitably and is acquired only with considerable cost. Indeed many see globalization as little more than a latter-day version of US imperialism. Photographs of US soldiers abusing Muslim prisoners in Iraq undermine national leaders' ability to claim that it is in their country's interest to be allied with the United States. These images also make it immeasurably more difficult for the US government to persuade the world that the United States is a power with which they should wish to be aligned.

Terrorist groups have no interest in balancing or bandwagoning against US power.

The balance of power as traditionally practiced was based on the state as the fundamental unit in the international order. The difference today is that due to technological developments, smaller and smaller groups are now able to acquire weapons of ever greater lethality. Moreover, through effective use of the Internet, these groups can coordinate actions across borders, recruit followers, plan complex attacks, and generate support from all over the world. Indeed, terrorist groups have no interest in balancing or bandwagoning against US power; they wish simply to expel the United States from the Middle East altogether.

That a country with secure borders, a formidable nuclear deterrent, and no military rivals in sight nevertheless feels vulnerable speaks to the inadequacies of the traditional formulation of the balance of power. This is not the first time in history in which military preeminence has bred hubris, as evinced by the casual deployment of 5,000 US troops to Saudi Arabia following the first Gulf War despite the action's local unpopularity. A similar miscalculation was the decision to launch a military invasion of Iraq without first taking the trouble to understand the nature of the task ahead.

Indeed, the weakness of the world's sole remaining superpower is not the result of any bandwagoning of rivals against it, but of deficiencies within its own borders. Ironically, increased military expenditures are undermining US security by contributing to federal deficits and reliance on foreign creditors, particularly China, to keep the economy afloat. Moreover, the projection of its power abroad is serving to ignite emnity against the United States. And meanwhile, confidence in US military superiority is diverting attention away from other important vulnerabilities, most crucially US dependence on foreign oil. But the vagaries of electoral politics guarantee that efforts to enhance US security through developing societal resilience to terrorism, or through questioning the appropriateness of spiraling defense expenditures, will never be successful.

Principles for the Future

The forces emerging against the United States are not being recruited, organized, or mobilized by any single state, but rather by loose networks of individuals with an appealing ideology disseminated by means of recent technological developments. With the United States' wealth, technological advantages, and attractive national ideology, it is in a unique position to confront this threat. To do so effectively, however, requires appealing not to the heads of other governments, but also to their populations and the potential recruits of terrorist adversaries.

The six principles that should guide US actions are first, the development of a defensible and achievable goal, second, a commitment to live by US principles, third, acquiring intelligence about the enemy, fourth, a separation of terrorists from their

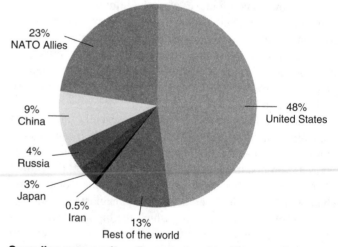

Spending on security. Percent of world military expenditures.

This pie chart shows the relative sizes of military budgets among several world powers. Total world military spending is estimated at $ 1.36 trillion USD, and the US budget for 2008 is almost half of this total, at $644 billion. Iran, despite its role in the "Axis of Evil" and as a security threat to the United States, spends a meager $6.6 billion annually on its military.

Source: International Institute for Strategic Studies, U.S. Department of Defense.

communities, fifth, a willingness to engage others in countering terrorism, and sixth, a commitment to patience and maintaining perspective. Such a strategy requires recognition of the limits of the traditional state-centric approach and an appreciation of the ever growing importance of substate and trans-state actors in international relations. If the United States continues to rely on its military and diplomacy, it will find itself quite unprepared to take on the adversary that it currently faces—an adversary that does not play by the rules and does not consider itself in any sort of balance of power arrangement.

LOUISE RICHARDSON is Executive Dean of the Radcliffe Institute for Advanced Study, Senior Lecturer in Government at Harvard University, and Lecturer on Law at Harvard Law School.

From *Harvard International Review,* Vol. 29, Issue 1, Spring 2007. Copyright © 2007 by the President of Harvard College. Reprinted by permission.

The Long March to Be a Superpower

The People's Liberation Army is investing heavily to give China the military muscle to match its economic power. But can it begin to rival America?

The sight is as odd as its surroundings are bleak. Where a flat expanse of mud flats, salt pans and fish farms reaches the Bohai Gulf, a vast ship looms through the polluted haze. It is an aircraft-carrier, the *Kiev,* once the proud possession of the Soviet Union. Now it is a tourist attraction. Chinese visitors sit on the flight deck under Pepsi umbrellas, reflecting perhaps on a great power that was and another, theirs, that is fast in the making.

Inside the *Kiev,* the hangar bay is divided into two. On one side, bored-looking visitors watch an assortment of dance routines featuring performers in ethnic-minority costumes. On the other side is a full-size model of China's new J-10, a plane unveiled with great fanfare in January as the most advanced fighter built by the Chinese themselves (except for the Ukrainian or Russian turbofan engines—but officials prefer not to advertise this). A version of this, some military analysts believe, could one day be deployed on a Chinese ship.

The Pentagon is watching China's aircraft-carrier ambitions with bemused interest. Since the 1980s, China has bought four of them (three from the former Soviet Union and an Australian one whose construction began in Britain during the second world war). Like the *Kiev,* the *Minsk* (berthed near Hong Kong) has been turned into a tourist attraction having first been studied closely by Chinese naval engineers. Australia's carrier, the *Melbourne,* has been scrapped. The biggest and most modern one, the *Varyag,* is in the northern port city of Dalian, where it is being refurbished. Its destiny is uncertain. The Pentagon says it might be put into service, used for training carrier crews, or become yet another floating theme-park.

American global supremacy is not about to be challenged by China's tinkering with aircraft-carriers. Even if China were to commission one—which analysts think unlikely before at least 2015—it would be useless in the most probable area of potential conflict between China and America, the Taiwan Strait. China could far more easily launch its jets from shore. But it would be widely seen as a potent symbol of China's rise as a military power. Some Chinese officers want to fly the flag ever farther afield as a demonstration of China's rise. As China emerges as a trading giant (one increasingly dependent on imported oil), a few of its military analysts talk about the need to protect distant sea lanes in the Malacca Strait and beyond.

This week China's People's Liberation Army (PLA), as the armed forces are known, is celebrating the 80th year since it was born as a group of ragtag rebels against China's then rulers. Today it is vying to become one of the world's most capable forces: one that could, if necessary, keep even the Americans at bay. The PLA has little urge to confront America head-on, but plenty to deter it from protecting Taiwan.

The pace of China's military upgrading is causing concern in the Pentagon. Eric McVadon, a retired rear admiral, told a congressional commission in 2005 that China had achieved a "remarkable leap" in the modernisation of forces needed to overwhelm Taiwan and deter or confront any American intervention. And the pace of this, he said, was "urgently continuing". By Pentagon standards, Admiral McVadon is doveish.

In its annual report to Congress on China's military strength, published in May, the Pentagon said China's "expanding military capabilities" were a "major factor" in altering military balances in East Asia. It said China's ability to project power over long distances remained limited. But it repeated its observation, made in 2006, that among "major and emerging powers" China had the "greatest potential to compete militarily" with America.

Since the mid-1990s China has become increasingly worried that Taiwan might cut its national ties with the mainland. To instil fear into any Taiwanese leader so inclined, it has been deploying short-range ballistic missiles (SRBMs) on the coast facing the island as fast as it can produce them—about 100 a year. The Pentagon says there are now about 900 of these DF-11s (CSS-7) and DF-15s (CSS-6). They are getting more accurate. Salvoes of them might devastate Taiwan's military infrastructure so quickly that any war would be over before America could respond.

Much has changed since 1995 and 1996, when China's weakness in the face of American power was put on stunning display. In a fit of anger over America's decision in 1995 to allow Lee Teng-hui, then Taiwan's president, to make a high-profile trip to his alma mater, Cornell University, China fired ten unarmed DF-15s into waters off Taiwan. The Americans, confident that China would quickly back off, sent two aircraft-carrier battle groups to the region as a warning. The tactic worked. Today America would have to think twice. Douglas Paal, America's unofficial ambassador to Taiwan from 2002 to 2006, says the "cost of conflict has certainly gone up."

The Chinese are now trying to make sure that American aircraft-carriers cannot get anywhere near. Admiral McVadon worries about their development of DF-21 (CSS-5) medium-range ballistic missiles. With their far higher re-entry velocities than the SRBMs, they would be much harder for Taiwan's missile defences to cope with. They could even be launched far beyond Taiwan into the Pacific to hit aircraft-carriers. This would be a big technical challenge. But Admiral McVadon says America "might have to worry" about such a possibility within a couple of years.

Once the missiles have done their job, China's armed forces could (so they hope) follow up with a panoply of advanced Russian weaponry—mostly amassed in the past decade. Last year the Pentagon said China had imported around $11 billion of weapons between 2000 and 2005, mainly from Russia.

China knows it has a lot of catching up to do. Many Americans may be unenthusiastic about America's military excursions in recent years, particularly about the war in Iraq. But Chinese military authors, in numerous books and articles, see much to be inspired by.

On paper at least, China's gains have been impressive. Even into the 1990s China had little more than a conscript army of ill-educated peasants using equipment based largely on obsolete Soviet designs of the 1950s and outdated cold-war (or even guerrilla-war) doctrine. Now the emphasis has shifted from ground troops to the navy and air force, which would spearhead any attack on Taiwan. China has bought 12 Russian Kilo-class diesel attack submarines. The newest of these are equipped with supersonic Sizzler cruise missiles that America's carriers, many analysts believe, would find hard to stop.

There are supersonic cruise missiles too aboard China's four new Sovremenny-class destroyers, made to order by the Russians and designed to attack aircraft-carriers and their escorts. And China's own shipbuilders have not been idle. In an exhibition marking the 80th anniversary, Beijing's Military Museum displays what Chinese official websites say is a model of a new nuclear-powered attack submarine, the *Shang*. These submarines would allow the navy to push deep into the Pacific, well beyond Taiwan, and, China hopes, help defeat American carriers long before they get close. Last year, much to America's embarrassment, a newly developed Chinese diesel submarine for shorter-range missions surfaced close to the American carrier *Kitty Hawk* near Okinawa without being detected beforehand.

American air superiority in the region is now challenged by more than 200 advanced Russian Su-27 and Su-30 fighters China has acquired since the 1990s. Some of these have been made under licence in China itself. The Pentagon thinks China is also interested in buying Su-33s, which would be useful for deployment on an aircraft-carrier, if China decides to build one.

During the Taiwan Strait crisis of 1995–96, America could be reasonably sure that, even if war did break out (few seriously thought it would), it could cope with any threat from China's nuclear arsenal. China's handful of strategic missiles capable of hitting mainland America were based in silos, whose positions the Americans most probably knew. Launch preparations would take so long that the Americans would have plenty of time to knock them out. China has been working hard to remedy this. It is deploying six road-mobile, solid-fuelled (which means quick to launch) intercontinental DF-31s and is believed to be developing DF-31As with a longer range that could hit anywhere in America, as well as submarine-launched (so more concealable) JL-2s that could threaten much of America too.

All Dressed Up and Ready to Fight?

But how much use is all this hardware? Not a great deal is known about the PLA's fighting capability. It is by far the most secretive of the world's big armies. One of the few titbits it has been truly open about in the build-up to the celebrations is the introduction of new uniforms to mark the occasion: more body-hugging and, to howls of criticism from some users of popular Chinese internet sites, more American-looking.

As Chinese military analysts are well aware, America's military strength is not just about technology. It also involves training, co-ordination between different branches of the military ("jointness", in the jargon), gathering and processing intelligence, experience and morale. China is struggling to catch up in these areas too. But it has had next to no combat experience since a brief and undistinguished foray into Vietnam in 1979 and a huge deployment to crush pro-democracy unrest ten years later.

China is even coyer about its war-fighting capabilities than it is about its weaponry. It has not rehearsed deep-sea drills against aircraft-carriers. It does not want to create alarm in the region, nor to rile America. There is also a problem of making all this Russian equipment work. Some analysts say the Chinese have not been entirely pleased with their Su-27 and Su-30 fighters. Keeping them maintained and supplied with spare parts (from Russia) has not been easy. A Western diplomat says China is also struggling to keep its Russian destroyers and submarines in good working order. "We have to be cautious about saying 'wow'," he suggests of the new equipment.

China is making some progress in its efforts to wean itself off dependence on the Russians. After decades of effort, some analysts believe, China is finally beginning to use its own turbofan engines, an essential technology for advanced fighters. But self-sufficiency is still a long way off. The Russians are sometimes still reluctant to hand over their most sophisticated technologies. "The only trustworthy thing [the Chinese] have is missiles," says Andrew Yang of the Chinese Council of Advanced Policy Studies in Taiwan.

The Pentagon, for all its fretting, is trying to keep channels open to the Chinese. Military exchanges have been slowly reviving since their nadir of April 2001, when a Chinese fighter jet hit an American spy plane close to China. Last year, for the first time, the two sides conducted joint exercises—search-and-rescue missions off the coasts of America and China. But these were simple manoeuvres and the Americans learned little from them. The Chinese remain reluctant to engage in anything more complex, perhaps for fear of revealing their weaknesses.

The Russians have gained deeper insights. Two years ago the PLA staged large-scale exercises with them, the first with a foreign army. Although not advertised as such, these were partly aimed at scaring the Taiwanese. The two countries practised blockades, capturing airfields and amphibious landings. The

Russians showed off some of the weaponry they hope to sell to the big-spending Chinese.

Another large joint exercise is due to be held on August 9th–17th in the Urals (a few troops from other members of the Shanghai Co-operation Organisation, a six-nation group including Central Asian states, will also take part). But David Shambaugh of George Washington University says the Russians have not been very impressed by China's skills. After the joint exercise of 2005, Russians muttered about the PLA's lack of "jointness", its poor communications and the slowness of its tanks.

China has won much praise in the West for its increasing involvement in United Nations peacekeeping operations. But this engagement has revealed little of China's combat capability. Almost all of the 1,600 Chinese peacekeepers deployed (including in Lebanon, Congo and Liberia) are engineers, transport troops or medical staff.

A series of "white papers" published by the Chinese government since 1998 on its military developments have shed little light either, particularly on how much the PLA is spending and on what. By China's opaque calculations, the PLA enjoyed an average annual budget increase of more than 15% between 1990 and 2005 (nearly 10% in real terms). This year the budget was increased by nearly 18%. But this appears not to include arms imports, spending on strategic missile forces and research and development. The International Institute for Strategic Studies in London says the real level of spending in 2004 could have been about 1.7 times higher than the officially declared budget of 220 billion yuan ($26.5 billion at then exchange rates).

This estimate would make China's spending roughly the same as that of France in 2004. But the different purchasing power of the dollar in the two countries—as well as China's double-digit spending increases since then—push the Chinese total far higher. China is struggling hard to make its army more professional—keeping servicemen for longer and attracting better-educated recruits. This is tough at a time when the civilian economy is booming and wages are climbing. The PLA is having to spend much more on pay and conditions for its 2.3m people.

Keeping the army happy is a preoccupation of China's leaders, mindful of how the PLA saved the party from probable destruction during the unrest of 1989. In the 1990s they encouraged military units to run businesses to make more money for themselves. At the end of the decade, seeing that this was fuelling corruption, they ordered the PLA to hand over its business to civilian control. Bigger budgets are now helping the PLA to make up for some of those lost earnings.

The party still sees the army as a bulwark against the kind of upheaval that has toppled communist regimes elsewhere. Chinese leaders lash out at suggestions (believed to be supported by some officers) that the PLA should be put under the state's control instead of the party's. The PLA is riddled with party spies who monitor officers' loyalty. But the party also gives the army considerable leeway to manage its own affairs. It worries about military corruption but seldom moves against it, at least openly (in a rare exception to this, a deputy chief of the navy was dismissed last year for taking bribes and "loose morals"). The PLA's culture of secrecy allowed the unmonitored spread of SARS, an often fatal respiratory ailment, in the army's medical system in 2003.

Carrier Trade

The PLA knows its weaknesses. It has few illusions that China can compete head-on with the Americans militarily. The Soviet Union's determination to do so is widely seen in China as the cause of its collapse. Instead China emphasises weaponry and doctrine that could be used to defeat a far more powerful enemy using "asymmetric capabilities".

The idea is to exploit America's perceived weak points such as its dependence on satellites and information networks. China's successful (if messy and diplomatically damaging) destruction in January of one of its own ageing satellites with a rocket was clearly intended as a demonstration of such power. Some analysts believe Chinese people with state backing have been trying to hack into Pentagon computers. Richard Lawless, a Pentagon official, recently said China had developed a "very sophisticated" ability to attack American computer and internet systems.

The Pentagon's fear is that military leaders enamoured of new technology may underestimate the diplomatic consequences of trying it out. Some Chinese see a problem here too. The anti-satellite test has revived academic discussion in China of the need for setting up an American-style national security council that would help military planners co-ordinate more effectively with foreign-policy makers.

But the Americans find it difficult to tell China bluntly to stop doing what others are doing too (including India, which has aircraft-carriers and Russian fighter planes). In May Admiral Timothy Keating, the chief of America's Pacific Command, said China's interest in aircraft-carriers was "understandable". He even said that if China chose to develop them, America would "help them to the degree that they seek and the degree that we're capable." But, he noted, "it ain't as easy as it looks."

A senior Pentagon official later suggested Admiral Keating had been misunderstood. Building a carrier for the Chinese armed forces would be going a bit far. But the two sides are now talking about setting up a military hotline. The Americans want to stay cautiously friendly as the dragon grows stronger.

What Russia Wants

From Gorbachev to Yeltsin to Putin, every new Russian president has drastically altered his country's relationship with the world. How will President Dmitry Medvedev change it again? Here are the clues that reveal what the Kremlin is thinking, and, more importantly, what it really wants.

IVAN KRASTEV

This much we know: In the two decades since the collapse of the Soviet Union, Russia has transformed itself from a one-party state into a one-pipeline state—a semiauthoritarian regime in democratic clothing. At the same time, Russia has grown increasingly independent and unpredictable on the international political scene. And now that Vladimir Putin has successfully installed his handpicked successor, Dmitry Medvedev, he is nowhere near relinquishing his grip on power. Putin's foreign policy is here to stay.

But there's so much we can't know about the direction Russia is heading. It is, at once, a regime that offers its citizens consumer rights but not political freedoms, state sovereignty but not individual autonomy, a market economy but not genuine democracy. It is both a rising global power and a weak state with corrupt and inefficient institutions. The Kremlin's regime seems both rock solid and extremely vulnerable, simultaneously authoritarian and wildly popular. Although Russia's economy has performed well in the past 10 years, it is more dependent on the production and export of natural resources today than it was during Soviet times. Its foreign policy is no less puzzling. Russia may be more democratic today, but it is less predictable and reliable as a world player than was the Soviet Union. The more capitalist and Westernized Russia becomes, the more anti-Western its policies seem. The more successful Russia's foreign policy looks, the more unclear its goals appear.

Russia's contradictory development has succeeded once again in capturing the world's political imagination. Putin's tenure has left most people confused about what role Russia now wants to play in the world. In recent years, for example, Moscow has orchestrated a noisy and confrontational return to the international scene. It decided not to cooperate with the West in taming Iran's nuclear ambitions or in settling the final status of Kosovo. Last year, the Kremlin unilaterally suspended the Treaty on Conventional Armed Forces in Europe. It blocked the work of the Organization for security and Cooperation in Europe. Gazprom, Russia's gas monopoly, aggressively tries to control the energy supply throughout the region. The country's military budget has increased sixfold since 2000. Russian planes are patrolling the Atlantic. Moscow's intelligence network is creeping into all corners of Europe. Not since the hottest days of the Cold War have so many wondered just what was going on behind the Kremlin's closed doors.

Once a Superpower . . .

Some look at Russia and see a wounded enemy readying itself for another round. They interpret Moscow's new assertiveness as a simple overreaction to the humiliation of the 1990s. These realists are quick to blame NATO expansion and Western triumphalism after the Soviet collapse for the direction of Russia's current foreign policy. What Moscow learned in its "decade of humiliation" is that the West respects strength, not shared values. On the other hand, the liberals who shaped the West's policies toward Russia in the 1990s are not in a selfcritical mood. They tend to believe that Putin's foreign policy is simply a new incarnation of Moscow's traditional imperial policies. Plus, though they may concede that the West has lost some of its ability to shape Russian politics, they insist that the West can still focus on the rule of law—if not full democracy. In their view,

Russia's gains in the international arena are temporary and the Putin miracle is a mirage. In short, even the experts are far from unanimous in divining the motives of Russia's recent turn.

It would be easy to assume Russia is simply grasping power for power's sake, or to conclude that just as "there are no ex-KGB officers," there are also no ex-imperial powers. But to understand why the Kremlin acts the way it does, one must first recognize how haunted it is by uncertainty and paranoia. How Russia thinks is closely linked to how Russia's political elites feel. Moscow's current strategy is not merely a reflection of its new economic power or a geopolitical change. It is the expression of the traumatic experience of the collapse of the Soviet Union and the omnipresent political vulnerability of the current regime.

In effect, Russian foreign policy is held hostage by the sense of fragility that marked the Russian experience of the 1990s. It explains Moscow's preference for the pre-World War II international order based on unrestricted sovereignty and sphere-of-influence politics. It explains Russia's open resistance to American hegemony and its opposition to the postmodern European order promoted by the European Union (EU). The EU, with its emphasis on human rights and openness, threatens the Kremlin's monopoly on power. The West's policy of democracy promotion awakens in Moscow the nightmare of ethnic and religious politics and the threat of the territorial disintegration of the Russian Federation. Russia feels threatened by the invasion of Western funded nongovernmental organizations, and the Kremlin is tempted to recreate the police state to prevent foreign interference in its domestic politics. The recent "color" revolutions that shook the post-Soviet space embodied the ultimate threat for Russia: popular revolt orchestrated by remote control. Moscow is in an elusive quest for absolute stability.

Putin's foreign policy—and, by extension, Medvedev's—rests on two key assumptions and one strategic calculation. It assumes the United States is facing a collapse that is not much different from the collapse of Soviet power. It also assumes that the EU—despite being, in Russia's view, a temporary phenomenon—is a threat to the Russian regime by its very existence as a postmodern empire. The calculation is that the next decade presents a strategic window of opportunity for Russia to position itself as a great power in the emerging multipolar world while also securing the legitimacy of the regime, even if that means following a more assertive and confrontational foreign policy.

Unlike China, where the consensus these days is that world order does not collapse over a weekend and that

betting on America's decline is a risky gamble, Russia demonstrates complete confidence in the end of American hegemony. Russian elites are tempted to view the crisis of America's global power as a replay of the crisis of Soviet power in the 1980s. Moscow looks at the United States' debacle in Iraq and sees its own failure in Afghanistan. It views the United States' conflicts with the EU as proof of the dismantling of the informal American empire. In this sense, when Jacques Chirac openly questioned the wisdom of American leadership in the lead-up to the war in Iraq, Russians saw echoes of Lech Walesa's defiance of the Soviet Union at Gdansk. Moscow's policies, in other words, are informed by the assumption that great powers are less stable than they look and their positions are more vulnerable than classical balance-of-power analysis suggests.

Why Russia Fights

Of course, none of these calculations is necessarily comforting to a United States that views itself as the world's preeminent political, economic, and military power, or an EU that sees strength in unity and integration. Russia's resurgence comes at a time when the global hegemony of the United States is in decline and the EU is suffering a profound crisis of self-confidence. Russia's revisionism threatens the very nature of this existing international order. The paradox is that, faced with new Russian revisionism, the West is becoming nostalgic for the old Soviet Union. Even as a longing for a familiar foe has dramatically declined among the Russian public, it is on the rise in Western capitals. In the words of one senior French diplomat, "The Soviet Union was easier to deal with than Russia is today. Sometimes the Soviets were difficult, but you knew they were being obstructive in order to achieve an objective. Now, Russia seeks to block the West systematically on every subject, apparently without purpose." In other words, Russia is not simply a revisionist power—it is something potentially more dangerous: a spoiler at large. The Kremlin's recent actions easily fit this threatening image. In reality, though, Russia is not a spoiler so much as it likes to be viewed as one. Where the West seeks to find aggressiveness and imperial tendencies, it will find uncertainty and vulnerability. Demonizing Russia won't help—pitying it won't help either.

In 10 years' time, Russia will not be a failed state. But neither will it be a mature democracy.

In 10 years' time, Russia will not be a failed state. But neither will it be a mature democracy. Russian foreign policy will remain independent—one that promotes Russia's great-power status in a multipolar world. It will be selectively confrontational. Russia will remain more integrated in the world than it has ever been in its history, and it will remain as suspicious as ever. At base, the Kremlin's strategic dilemma is how to remain integrated in the world while also making the country impervious to political influence from abroad. Russia is a rising global power but also a declining state. The key to understanding the Kremlin's foreign-policy thinking is that simple—and that complicated.

IVAN KRASTEV is editor of *Foreign Policy*'s Bulgarian edition.

Lifting the Veil

Understanding the Roots of Islamic Militancy

HENRY MUNSON

In the wake of the attacks of September 11, 2001, many intellectuals have argued that Muslim extremists like Osama bin Laden despise the United States primarily because of its foreign policy. Conversely, US President George Bush's administration and its supporters have insisted that extremists loathe the United States simply because they are religious fanatics who "hate our freedoms." These conflicting views of the roots of militant Islamic hostility toward the United States lead to very different policy prescriptions. If US policies have caused much of this hostility, it would make sense to change those policies, if possible, to dilute the rage that fuels Islamic militancy. If, on the other hand, the hostility is the result of religious fanaticism, then the use of brute force to suppress fanaticism would appear to be a sensible course of action.

Groundings for Animosity

Public opinion polls taken in the Islamic world in recent years provide considerable insight into the roots of Muslim hostility toward the United States, indicating that for the most part, this hostility has less to do with cultural or religious differences than with US policies in the Arab world. In February and March 2003, Zogby International conducted a survey on behalf of Professor Shibley Telhami of the University of Maryland involving 2,620 men and women in Egypt, Jordan, Lebanon, Morocco, and Saudi Arabia. Most of those surveyed had "unfavorable attitudes" toward the United States and said that their hostility to the United States was based primarily on US policy rather than on their values. This was true of 67 percent of the Saudis surveyed. In Egypt, however, only 46 percent said their hostility resulted from US policy, while 43 percent attributed their attitudes to their values as Arabs. This is surprising given that the prevailing religious values in Saudi Arabia are more conservative than in Egypt. Be that as it may, a plurality of people in all the countries surveyed said that their hostility toward the United States was primarily based on their opposition to US policy.

The issue that arouses the most hostility in the Middle East toward the United States is the Israeli-Palestinian conflict and what Muslims perceive as US responsibility for the suffering of the Palestinians. A similar Zogby International survey from the summer of 2001 found that more than 80 percent of

the respondents in Egypt, Kuwait, Lebanon, and Saudi Arabia ranked the Palestinian issue as one of the three issues of greatest importance to them. A survey of Muslim "opinion leaders" released by the Pew Research Center for the People and the Press in December 2001 also found that the US position on the Israeli-Palestinian conflict was the main source of hostility toward the United States.

It is true that Muslim hostility toward Israel is often expressed in terms of anti-Semitic stereotypes and conspiracy theories—think, for example, of the belief widely-held in the Islamic world that Jews were responsible for the terrorists attacks of September 11, 2001. Muslim governments and educators need to further eliminate anti-Semitic bias in the Islamic world. However, it would be a serious mistake to dismiss Muslim and Arab hostility toward Israel as simply a matter of anti-Semitism. In the context of Jewish history, Israel represents liberation. In the context of Palestinian history, it represents subjugation. There will always be a gap between how the West and how the Muslim societies perceive Israel. There will also always be some Muslims (like Osama bin Laden) who will refuse to accept any solution to the Israeli-Palestinian conflict other than the destruction of the state of Israel. That said, if the United States is serious about winning the so-called "war on terror," then resolution of the Israeli-Palestinian conflict should be among its top priorities in the Middle East.

Eradicating, or at least curbing, Palestinian terrorism entails reducing the humiliation, despair, and rage that drive many Palestinians to support militant Islamic groups like Hamas and Islamic Jihad. When soldiers at an Israeli checkpoint prevented Ahmad Qurei (Abu al Ala), one of the principal negotiators of the Oslo accords and president of the Palestinian Authority's parliament, from traveling from Gaza to his home on the West Bank, he declared, "Soon, I too will join Hamas." Qurei's words reflected his outrage at the subjugation of his people and the humiliation that Palestinians experience every day at the checkpoints that surround their homes. Defeating groups like Hamas requires diluting the rage that fuels them. Relying on force alone tends to increase rather than weaken their appeal. This is demonstrated by some of the unintended consequences of the US-led invasion and occupation of Iraq in the spring of 2003.

On June 3, 2003, the Pew Research Center for the People and the Press released a report entitled *Views of a Changing World*

June 2003. This study was primarily based on a survey of nearly 16,000 people in 21 countries (including the Palestinian Authority) from April 28 to May 15, 2003, shortly after the fall of Saddam Hussein's regime. The survey results were supplemented by data from earlier polls, especially a survey of 38,000 people in 44 countries in 2002. The study found a marked increase in Muslim hostility toward the United States from 2002 to 2003. In the summer of 2002, 61 percent of Indonesians held a favorable view of the United States. By May of 2003, only 15 percent did. During the same period of time, the decline in Turkey was from 30 percent to 15 percent, and in Jordan it was from 25 percent to one percent.

Indeed, the Bush administration's war on terror has been a major reason for the increased hostility toward the United States. The Pew Center's 2003 survey found that few Muslims support this war. Only 23 percent of Indonesians did so in May of 2003, down from 31 percent in the summer of 2002. In Turkey, support dropped from 30 percent to 22 percent. In Pakistan, support dropped from 30 percent to 16 percent, and in Jordan from 13 percent to two percent. These decreases reflect overwhelming Muslim opposition to the war in Iraq, which most Muslims saw as yet another act of imperial subjugation of Muslims by the West.

The 2003 Zogby International poll found that most Arabs believe that the United States attacked Iraq to gain control of Iraqi oil and to help Israel. Over three-fourths of all those surveyed felt that oil was a major reason for the war. More than three-fourths of the Saudis and Jordanians said that helping Israel was a major reason, as did 72 percent of the Moroccans and over 50 percent of the Egyptians and Lebanese. Most Arabs clearly do not believe that the United States overthrew Saddam Hussein out of humanitarian motives. Even in Iraq itself, where there was considerable support for the war, most people attribute the war to the US desire to gain control of Iraqi oil and help Israel.

Not only has the Bush administration failed to win much Muslim support for its war on terrorism, its conduct of the war has generated a dangerous backlash. Most Muslims see the US fight against terror as a war against the Islamic world. The 2003 Pew survey found that over 70 percent of Indonesians, Pakistanis, and Turks were either somewhat or very worried about a potential US threat to their countries, as were over half of Jordanians and Kuwaitis.

This sense of a US threat is linked to the 2003 Pew report's finding of widespread support for Osama bin Laden. The survey of April and May 2003 found that over half those surveyed in Indonesia, Jordan, and the Palestinian Authority, and almost half those surveyed in Morocco and Pakistan, listed bin Laden as one of the three world figures in whom they had the most confidence "to do the right thing." For most US citizens, this admiration for the man responsible for the attacks of September 11, 2001, is incomprehensible. But no matter how outrageous this widespread belief may be, it is vitally important to understand its origins. If one does not understand why people think the way they do, one cannot induce them to think differently. Similarly, if one does not understand why people act as they do, one cannot hope to induce them to act differently.

The Appeal of Osama bin Laden

Osama bin Laden first engaged in violence because of the occupation of a Muslim country by an "infidel" superpower. He did not fight the Russians in Afghanistan because he hated their values or their freedoms, but because they had occupied a Muslim land. He participated in and supported the Afghan resistance to the Soviet occupation from 1979 to 1989, which ended with the withdrawal of the Russians. Bin Laden saw this war as legitimate resistance to foreign occupation. At the same time, he saw it as a *jihad*, or holy war, on behalf of Muslims oppressed by infidels.

When Saddam Hussein invaded Kuwait in August 1990, bin Laden offered to lead an army to defend Saudi Arabia. The Saudis rejected this offer and instead allowed the United States to establish bases in their kingdom, leading to bin Laden's active opposition to the United States. One can only speculate what bin Laden would have done for the rest of his life if the United States had not stationed hundreds of thousands of US troops in Saudi Arabia in 1990. Conceivably, bin Laden's hostility toward the United States might have remained passive and verbal instead of active and violent. All we can say with certainty is that the presence of US troops in Saudi Arabia did trigger bin Laden's holy war against the United States. It was no accident that the bombing of two US embassies in Africa on August 7, 1998, marked the eighth anniversary of the introduction of US forces into Saudi Arabia as part of Operation Desert Storm.

Part of bin Laden's opposition to the presence of US military presence in Saudi Arabia resulted from the fact that US troops were infidels on or near holy Islamic ground. Non-Muslims are not allowed to enter Mecca and Medina, the two holiest places in Islam, and they are allowed to live in Saudi Arabia only as temporary residents. Bin Laden is a reactionary Wahhabi Muslim who undoubtedly does hate all non-Muslims. But that hatred was not in itself enough to trigger his *jihad* against the United States.

Indeed, bin Laden's opposition to the presence of US troops in Saudi Arabia had a nationalistic and anti-imperialist tone. In 1996, he declared that Saudi Arabia had become an American colony. There is nothing specifically religious or fundamentalist about this assertion. In his book *Chronique d'une Guerre d'Orient*, Gilles Kepel describes a wealthy whiskey-drinking Saudi who left part of his fortune to bin Laden because he alone "was defending the honor of the country, reduced in his eyes to a simple American protectorate."

In 1996, bin Laden issued his first major manifesto, entitled a "Declaration of Jihad against the Americans Occupying the Land of the Two Holy Places." The very title focuses on the presence of US troops in Saudi Arabia, which bin Laden calls an "occupation." But this manifesto also refers to other examples of what bin Laden sees as the oppression of Muslims by infidels. "It is no secret that the people of Islam have suffered from the oppression, injustice, and aggression of the alliance of Jews and Christians and their collaborators to the point that the blood of the Muslims became the cheapest and their wealth was loot in the hands of the enemies," he writes. "Their blood was spilled in Palestine and Iraq."

Bin Laden has referred to the suffering of the Palestinians and the Iraqis (especially with respect to the deaths caused by sanctions) in all of his public statements since at least the mid-1990s. His 1996 "Declaration of Jihad" is no exception. Nonetheless, it primarily focuses on the idea that the Saudi regime has "lost all legitimacy" because it "has permitted the enemies of the Islamic community, the Crusader American forces, to occupy our land for many years." In this 1996 text, bin Laden even contends that the members of the Saudi royal family are apostates because they helped infidels fight the Muslim Iraqis in the Persian Gulf War of 1991.

A number of neo-conservatives have advocated the overthrow of the Saudi regime because of its support for terrorism. It is true that the Saudis have funded militant Islamic movements. It is also true that Saudi textbooks and teachers often encourage hatred of infidels and allow the extremist views of bin Laden to thrive. It is also probably true that members of the Saudi royal family have financially supported terrorist groups. The fact remains, however, that bin Laden and his followers in Al Qaeda have themselves repeatedly called for the overthrow of the Saudi regime, saying that it has turned Saudi Arabia into "an American colony."

If the United States were to send troops to Saudi Arabia once again, this time to overthrow the Saudi regime itself, the main beneficiaries would be bin Laden and those who think like him. On January 27, 2002, a *New York Times* article referenced a Saudi intelligence survey conducted in October 2001 that showed that 95 percent of educated Saudis between the ages of 25 and 41 supported bin Laden. If the United States were to overthrow the Saudi regime, such people would lead a guerrilla war that US forces would inevitably find themselves fighting. This war would attract recruits from all over the Islamic world outraged by the desecration of "the land of the two holy places." Given that US forces are already fighting protracted guerrilla wars in Iraq and Afghanistan, starting a third one in Saudi Arabia would not be the most effective way of eradicating terror in the Middle East.

Those who would advocate the overthrow of the Saudi regime by US troops seem to forget why bin Laden began his holy war against the United States in the first place. They also seem to forget that no one is more committed to the overthrow of the Saudi regime than bin Laden himself. Saudi Arabia is in dire need of reform, but yet another US occupation of a Muslim country is not the way to make it happen.

In December 1998, Palestinian journalist Jamal Abd al Latif Isma'il asked bin Laden, "Who is Osama bin Laden, and what does he want?" After providing a brief history of his life, bin Laden responded to the second part of the question, "We demand that our land be liberated from the enemies, that our land be liberated from the Americans. God almighty, may He be praised, gave all living beings a natural desire to reject external intruders. Take chickens, for example. If an armed soldier enters a chicken's home wanting to attack it, it fights him even though it is just a chicken." For bin Laden and millions of other Muslims, the Afghans, the Chechens, the Iraqis, the Kashmiris, and the Palestinians are all just "chickens" defending their homes against the attacks of foreign soldiers.

In his videotaped message of October 7, 2001, after the attacks of September 11, 2001, bin Laden declared, "What America is tasting now is nothing compared to what we have been tasting for decades. For over 80 years our *umma* has been tasting this humiliation and this degradation. Its sons are killed, its blood is shed, its holy places are violated, and it is ruled by other than that which God has revealed. Yet no one hears. No one responds."

Bin Laden's defiance of the United States and his criticism of Muslim governments who ignore what most Muslims see as the oppression of the Palestinians, Iraqis, Chechens, and others, have made him a hero of Muslims who do not agree with his goal of a strictly Islamic state and society. Even young Arab girls in tight jeans praise bin Laden as an anti-imperialist hero. A young Iraqi woman and her Palestinian friends told Gilles Kepel in the fall of 2001, "He stood up to defend us. He is the only one."

Looking Ahead

Feelings of impotence, humiliation, and rage currently pervade the Islamic world, especially the Muslim Middle East. The invasion and occupation of Iraq has exacerbated Muslim concerns about the United States. In this context, bin Laden is seen as a heroic Osama Maccabeus descending from his mountain cave to fight the infidel oppressors to whom the worldly rulers of the Islamic world bow and scrape.

The violent actions of Osama bin Laden and those who share his views are not simply caused by "hatred of Western freedoms." They result, in part at least, from US policies that have enraged the Muslim world. Certainly, Islamic zealots like bin Laden do despise many aspects of Western culture. They do hate "infidels" in general, and Jews in particular. Muslims do need to seriously examine the existence and perpetuation of such hatred in their societies and cultures. But invading and occupying their countries simply exacerbates the sense of impotence, humiliation, and rage that induce them to support people like bin Laden. Defeating terror entails diluting the rage that fuels it.

HENRY MUNSON is Chair of the Department of Anthropology at the University of Maine.

A Mideast Nuclear Chain Reaction?

Joseph Cirincione

A nuclear arms race has begun in the Middle East. It is not overt—no country has declared its desire for nuclear weapons, and none is rushing to build a bomb through a "Manhattan Project." But there is a race nonetheless, one with the potential to be truly catastrophic.

In the past two years, over a dozen Middle Eastern nations have declared their interest in civilian nuclear power or research programs. While several nations in the region already have small nuclear research reactors, and Israel has used its research reactor to produce enough plutonium for 100 to 180 nuclear weapons, the only Middle East nation to build a nuclear power plant has been Iran. In all of Africa, meanwhile, there are only two nuclear power reactors, both in South Africa. But suddenly, 63 years after the dawn of the nuclear age, these dozen states in the Middle East are rushing to invest billions in nuclear plants. This is not about energy; this is about Iran.

It is not Iran's nuclear reactor that concerns its neighbors—more than 40 nations around the world have nuclear power reactors. What is ringing alarm bells around the region is Iran's drive to build facilities to enrich uranium and produce plutonium. The same centrifuges that can enrich uranium to low levels for fuel can be used to produce highly enriched uranium for bombs. The same factories that can reprocess nuclear fuel rods for waste disposal can separate out plutonium for bombs from the spent fuel.

Once Iran's plants are fully operational, the nation will be just a political decision away from a nuclear weapon. A US National Intelligence Estimate on Iran in December 2007 concluded that, while Iran had ended its dedicated nuclear weapons programs in 2003 and had not resumed them since, it would be technically capable of producing enough highly enriched uranium for a weapon some time between 2010 and 2015.

Iran denies wanting nuclear weapons, and public opinion polls show most Iranians want the right to make nuclear fuel and energy but do not want the weapons. (I confirmed these views in interviews during a visit to Iran in 2005.) Nor does it appear that an official decision has been made to acquire nuclear weapons. Most likely, there is a consensus among the ruling factions to acquire the technologies that would allow Tehran to build weapons in the future should it decide to do so—a situation similar to Japan's.

The likely factors driving Iran's considerations are those that influence most nations: the three P's of power, prestige, and politics. Nuclear weapons would offer some protection against attacks by the United States or Israel and enhance Iran's ability to project power throughout the region. Nuclear bombs are also still seen as a totem of great power status, a status that Iranians believe their history and geopolitical role warrant. Finally, President Mahmoud Ahmadinejad has skillfully used the nuclear issue to mobilize nationalist sentiment behind his otherwise unpopular government. By posing as the warrior leader defending Iran from the United States and Israel, he is able to distract attention—at least for a while—from his failed economic and reform policies.

Tit for Tat

In any case, the Sunni Arab and Turkish rivals of this Shiite Persian state have decided that they cannot allow Iran alone to gain the military, political, and diplomatic advantage that nuclear weapons confer. They are now embarked on the decades-long process of acquiring the technological and industrial capacity to match Iran. And it is all legal—all allowed under the rules of the nuclear Non-Proliferation Treaty that each of the nations has signed.

These nations claim that their purpose in developing nuclear capacity is to diversify energy sources, combat global warming, and preserve oil for export. And perhaps it is for some. But King Abdullah of Jordan, in a rare moment of candor, admitted in January 2007: "The rules have changed on the nuclear subject through the whole region. Where I think Jordan was saying, 'We'd like to have a nuclear-free zone in the area,' after this summer, everybody's going for nuclear programs."

The summer of 2006 was indeed a critical time, but not because any breakthroughs were achieved regarding the cost, safety, or waste disposal problems of nuclear reactors, nor because of regional screenings of the climate change documentary *An Inconvenient Truth*. Instead, Sunni Muslim states decided at that time to hedge their nuclear bets as US and European efforts to rein in Iran's enrichment program faltered; as the United States appeared bogged down in Iraq and Afghanistan, limiting its ability to confront Iran militarily even as its removal of two regional rivals strengthened Tehran; and as Iran demonstrated its expanded strategic reach in the 2006 Lebanon war, thwarting Israel through its ally, Hezbollah.

Egypt and Turkey, two of Iran's main rivals, have progressed the furthest in the nuclear race. Both have flirted with nuclear weapons programs in the past and both have now announced ambitious nuclear construction plans. In March 2008, Egypt signed a $1.5 billion agreement with Russia that will result in the first of several Egyptian nuclear power reactors that were proposed by President Hosni Mubarak in October 2007. Turkey plans to build three reactors, with the first slated to start construction by the end of 2008.

Not to be outdone, Saudi Arabia this year has signed nuclear energy agreements with France and the United States. The United States in May agreed to help Saudi Arabia "develop civilian nuclear energy for use in medicine, industry, and power generation." This followed France's winning a multibillion-dollar deal in January to assist in the construction of nuclear power stations. France, in fact, has been the most aggressive of the nuclear salesmen rushing to the region. In addition to working with Saudi Arabia, France in January agreed to a $3.4 billion deal to build nuclear power stations in Qatar and the United Arab Emirates. France over the past year also has inked nuclear agreements with Algeria, Jordan, Morocco, and Libya.

The Gulf Cooperation Council (representing Bahrain, Kuwait, Oman, Qatar, and the United Arab Emirates) is conducting a joint study on the use of nuclear technology for peaceful purposes. An overall umbrella for such initiatives was provided by the Arab League when, at the end of its summit meeting in March 2007, it called on the Arab states to expand the use of peaceful nuclear technology in all domains. Thus far, only Turkey has hinted that its nuclear plans could include uranium enrichment facilities. But if the nuclear programs proceed and nations in the region acquire a broad range of nuclear technology and skills, enrichment or reprocessing capabilities would be far easier to justify (as a necessary domestic source of fuel) and to develop (as foreign companies transfer nuclear skills and knowledge to national engineers and scientists).

A Recipe for Nuclear War

Thus, the true danger of Iran's developing the ability to make a nuclear weapon is not that Iran would use the weapon against its neighbors or the United States. The threat of instant and overwhelming response would deter such use. Nor is the critical danger that Iran would willingly provide a nuclear weapon to a terrorist group. No nation ever has, not China during the Cultural Revolution nor North Korea over the 20 years that it has had bomb material. The real danger is that Iran's nuclearization would help create a region in which four or five nations are nuclear-armed, instead of just one (Israel). If existing territorial, political, and religious disputes remain unresolved, this is a recipe for nuclear war.

The real danger is that Iran's nuclearization would help create a region in which four or five nations are nuclear-armed, instead of just one (Israel).

John Chipman, director of the International Institute for Strategic Studies, warns of "a regional cascade of proliferation among Iran's neighbors." He adds that "Iran's program could become a powerful regional proliferation driver, building on regional rivalry, security concerns, and one-upmanship."

A report prepared for the Senate Foreign Relations Committee in February 2008 similarly warned of a chain reaction. The authors concluded that Saudi Arabia was "the state most likely to pursue nuclear weapons in response" to Iran's actions. Egypt "would perceive a nuclear-armed Iran as especially threatening," the report found, predicting "significant pressure on Egypt to follow suit." Such pressure could push Turkey toward acquiring nuclear weapons as well.

The clock is ticking. CIA Director Michael Hayden warned in September 2008: "Our judgment is that [Iran could achieve nuclear capability] toward the middle of the next decade. It can be accelerated, it can be decelerated, based on a variety of factors."

Bad and Better Options

Although military attacks offer the illusion of a solution, strikes by the United States or Israel would damage Iran's facilities but likely result in regional war and an *acceleration* of the program, not its delay. Israel lacks the military ability to destroy many of Iran's nuclear facilities. More powerful US attacks might also fail to destroy underground, hardened plants. But both would end all debate inside Iran about the nuclear program, rally the nation around the regime, and likely spawn an all-out sprint to get a nuclear weapon by any means necessary.

This was Saddam Hussein's reaction when Israel attacked the Osirak reactor in 1981. Iraq went from a public program with several hundred workers to a secret program with several thousand, and was closer to a bomb by 1991 than anyone knew. Tehran likely would not take that long.

Iran could also strike back with a number of asymmetrical responses, none easy to counter—including mining or otherwise shutting down the Strait of Hormuz, a critical chokepoint for oil transport in the Persian Gulf; attacks on Israel, either directly or through surrogate forces, that could bring Arab publics to its side; attacks on US forces in Iraq through Shiite militias; and attacks on American commercial and military sites around the world. Other states would try to remain neutral but could be drawn in by popular pressure or be attacked if they aided one side or the other. These are some of the reasons why Chairman of the Joint Chiefs of Staff Admiral Michael Mullen has said the United States does not need a third war in the region.

The National Intelligence Estimate (NIE) offers a policy prescription based on its judgment that when Tehran halted its nuclear weapons program in 2003, it did so primarily in response to international pressure. According to the report, "Tehran's decisions are guided by a cost-benefit approach rather than a rush to a weapon irrespective of the political, economic, and military costs." The intelligence agencies responsible for the NIE conclude that a successful strategy should include "some combination of threats of intensified international scrutiny and pressures, along with opportunities for Iran to achieve its security, prestige, and goals for regional influence in other ways."

If a negotiated cessation of Iran's program is not reached soon, it may be impossible to stop the nuclear momentum developing in the region. This is just one reason why a dramatically new and more effective nuclear proliferation policy must be at the top of the next president's agenda.

The incoming administration of Barack Obama will need both to contain and to engage Iran. Following the NIE's guidance, the president should use threats of economic sanctions and promises of financial and security benefits resulting from cooperation. This will mean direct US negotiations with Iran over an extended period that will, by necessity, have to include other pressing security concerns including stabilizing Iraq and Afghanistan and relations with Israel. The ultimate goal must be a transformation of US-Iranian relations.

The effort will have to be placed, moreover, in the larger context of building a new security system for the region, one in which all states' right to exist and territorial integrity are respected, and one that takes seriously the long-standing US and Israeli goal of a Middle East free of nuclear weapons. The United States cannot do this alone, nor with just the European powers; Russia and China must also be part of this effort. It is a tall order, but that is all the more reason to get started.

Joseph Cirincione, president of the Ploughshares Fund, is author of *Bomb Scare: The History and Future of Nuclear Weapons* (Columbia University Press, paperback, 2008).

From *Current History,* December 2008, pp. 439–442. Copyright © 2008 by Current History, Inc. Reprinted by permission.

The Politics of Death in Darfur

'Genocide' is big because it carries the Nazi label, which sells well. . . . But simply killing is boring, especially in Africa.

GÉRARD PRUNIER

For the world at large Darfur has been and remains the quintessential "African crisis": distant, esoteric, extremely violent, rooted in complex ethnic and historical factors that few understand, and devoid of any identifiable practical interest for the rich countries.

Since the international media got hold of it in 2004, Darfur has become not a political or military crisis but a "humanitarian crisis"—in other words, something that many "realist" politicians see (without saying so) as just another insoluble problem. In the post–cold war world such problems have been passed on to the United Nations. But the UN has not known what to do with this one, especially since the possibility emerged that this was another genocide.

Fearing that it would have to intervene and that the developed world would encourage it to act without giving it the means to do so, the UN passed the catastrophe on to the care of the newly reborn African Union, formerly the Organization of African Unity. For a continental organization wanting a new start, this was a dangerous gift. "African solutions to African problems" had become the politically correct way of saying "We do not really care."

Thus, in many ways, the hard reality of Darfur has been kept at arm's length, while statistics, press releases, UN resolutions, and photo opportunities have taken center stage. As in all globalized world crises, this recreation of the situation resulting from media attention and UN discussion has acquired as much importance as the reality it has been applied to, if not more, because whether real or not, it has deeply affected the initial reality. The result is continued talk and hand-wringing in the face of a crisis that, even now, grows worse.

Arabs and Africans

Darfur was for several hundred years an independent Islamic sultanate, with a population of both Arabs and black African tribes. As a result of intermarriage, the "Arabs" are all quite

black, and the distinction between the two groups—since both are Muslim—has been based on their respective native tongues. Annexed to Sudan by the British in 1916 (because London feared that the sultanate might enter the war on the side of Turkey and Germany), Darfur was thereafter completely neglected by the colonial power. When Sudan became independent in 1956, the new government continued this policy of neglect.

This was far from exceptional. Sudan is both enormous and overcentralized. The core area, centered around Khartoum and inhabited by riverine Arabs, has largely ignored the country's peripheral areas, though they represent the greatest part both of the territory and the population. The south, being Negro-African in culture and Christian religiously, was the first to rebel. The Muslim areas, blinded by the illusory "common bond" of Islam, took much longer to realize that they were no better off than the Christian south.

In February 2003, the Darfuri realized that the southern Christians were about to sign a peace agreement with the Islamist government in Khartoum and that they, the Muslims, would most likely be completely excluded from the new power- and wealth-sharing arrangements. After years of marginalization, resentment, frustration, and increasing social troubles, the Darfuri revolted in their turn.

Since they made up a large chunk of the army, Khartoum could not ask Darfuri soldiers to go home and shoot their own relatives. So, because the insurgents were mostly blacks, the government tapped the Darfuri Arab tribes for militiamen, telling them that the *abid* (slaves) were about to take over. The strategy worked wonderfully. Soon the Darfuri Arab militias, known as the *janjaweed* (which can be loosely translated as "the evil horsemen"), were looting, burning, raping, and killing entire black villages.

The Killer Story

At first the Darfur crisis went almost unnoticed by the media. For a year there was hardly any reaction on the part of the international community, which had always misunderstood the Sudanese civil war, taking it to be a religious conflict and not a racial one. The logic explaining why Muslims were now killing Muslims was not part of the international community's available conceptual equipment.

The focus remained instead on peace negotiations in Naivasha, Kenya, between the Sudanese government and a rebel group in the south, the Sudan People's Liberation Army (SPLA). Even in Khartoum, Sudan's capital, a few nomads shooting up villages in distant Darfur did not draw much attention. After all, had not these people devoted themselves to fighting each other for as long as anyone could remember?

The school of explaining conflicts by "ancient tribal hatreds" is not the sole preserve of Western journalists. It has many adherents in Africa itself. An unconscious form of Sudanese cultural racism enabled the government (which in some ways believed its own propaganda) to dismiss the whole thing as "another instance of tribal conflict."

The deteriorating situation in Darfur had been known to the wider world since about 1999, but only through specialized publications such as *Africa Confidential* or the *Indian Ocean Newsletter*. In Sudan itself the national press began to give some space to the activities of the "bandits" around the middle of 2003, and the word "janjaweed" first appeared in September of that year when an attack on the small town of Kadnir in Jebel Marra was reported.

Everyone knew that a military operation was the only form of intervention that could have any drastic effect.

But the international media did not pick up on "evil horsemen" who had attacked yet another African village in a God-forsaken province at the center of the continent. It was nongovernmental organizations that began noting Darfur, first Amnesty International and then the International Crisis Group, and it is largely through them that the crisis began to emerge from the shadows.

Given their interest in Chad, the French media were among the first to give attention to the Darfur situation. The first US article on the subject appeared in *The New York Times*. It focused immediately on the "black versus Arab" side of the problem, an aspect that, even if justified, was going to obscure rather than clarify the essential elements

in the following months. By then the Voice of America had followed the BBC in covering the growing crisis, and press agencies had begun sending reporters to eastern Chad.

What actually "blew the ratings," however, was an interview given by the UN Human Rights Coordinator for Sudan, Mukesh Kapila, to the UN's own IRIN network in March 2004. Kapila declared that Darfur was "the world's greatest humanitarian crisis" and that "the only difference between Rwanda and Darfur is now the numbers involved." He cited a tentative figure of 10,000 casualties. Having worked in Rwanda at the time of the genocide there, he knew what he was talking about. And although Rwanda itself had been neglected in its hour of need 10 years before, it had by then become the baseline reference for absolute evil and the need to care.

Newspapers went wild, and *The New York Times* started to write about "genocide." The "angle" had been found: Darfur was a genocide and the Arabs were killing the blacks. The journalists did not seem unduly concerned by the fact that the Arabs were often black, or that the "genocide" was strangely timed given Khartoum's goal of reaching a peace accord in Naivasha. Few people had ever heard of Darfur before; its history was a mystery that nobody particularly wanted to plumb. But now there was a good story: the first genocide of the twenty-first century.

Suddenly it was the Naivasha talks in which interest seemed to slacken. Here was something really serious and happening *now*, not like the peace negotiations, which had been dragging on for two years. Heart-wrenching images of children, rapes, and horsemen appeared, and suddenly everyone was interested, from the quality press to the mass media by way of the intellectual publications. What is conventionally known as "world opinion" finally cared about Darfur, even if the actual mechanics of what was happening remained obscure.

Delayed Reaction

The moral outrage that was felt tended to overshadow, if not hide completely, the political nature of the problem. Some specialized articles started to disentangle the various lines of causality, but they soon were lost amid the loud humanitarian demands for action. "Action" was a big word, although no one went so far to as to demand military intervention. Iraq and its image of easy military success leading to political discomfiture were still too present on television screens.

Moral indignation and its attendant media coverage kept rolling on until the end of 2004. Darfur was *the* humanitarian crisis and horror story of the year and writing about it was now obligatory. Then came the Asian tsunami on December 26, and Darfur instantly vanished from television screens and newspaper pages. The media could handle only one emotion-laden story at a time.

Darfur had enjoyed its famous 15 minutes of Warholian celebrity. It had even remained in the limelight for over six months, which for an African horror story is a considerable amount of time. And if it was true that some sort of "peace" had been signed in Nairobi on January 9, 2005, surely the show was over.

But before we move back to reality as opposed to its media image, we have to answer one question about the Darfur coverage: Why so much so late? The lateness is probably easiest to explain. Darfur was not expected to happen when it did, and it did not fit the common patterns of thinking about Sudan. Everyone knew Sudan's north-south conflict was a religious war in which wicked Muslims killed desperately struggling Christians. There had been over a million casualties, perhaps as many as a million and a half, and we had accepted that. Peace was at last about to be achieved now that the evil Hassan al-Turabi had been replaced as Sudan's leader by the far from virtuous but acceptable Omar Hassan al-Beshir. Yet this sudden Muslim-on-Muslim violence had surged to the forefront of world attention in a way that was completely unexpected and hardly explicable.

This violation of settled understanding also helps to explain the intensity of the media coverage once it finally took off. There was a kind of delayed reaction, a substitute for disappointment. The media were preparing for a nice story: peace at last, returning refugees, selfless NGO and UN workers helping the destitute, Muslim-Christian coexistence and perhaps even reconciliation, a farewell to arms. In other words, an African success story.

Now everything, even the way of interpreting the situation, had turned topsy-turvy, which is why the "genocide" angle soon became so important. No one denied that an enormous quantity of human beings had been killed, but was it or was it not genocide? Although it made little difference to the interested parties who continued to die without recourse to international legal concepts, the word became a question of the utmost relevance in the media.

Meanwhile humanitarian action was trying, as so often before in similar circumstances, to fill the gap between the media-raised expectations of public opinion and the prudent procrastination of the political and diplomatic segments of the international community.

The Missing Cavalry

Washington was embarrassed by the Darfur crisis, not least because it did not fit well within either of the two main camps in the administration and on Capitol Hill: the "realists" and the "Garang lobby" (that is, supporters of

the SPLA leader John Garang). The "realists" were found mostly in the State Department, the CIA, and the Defense Intelligence Agency. They argued that, given the useful role that Khartoum was playing in the war on terrorism by supplying information about its erstwhile friends, it should at least be helped even if perhaps not fully supported, especially if it showed any signs of cooperation at Naivasha.

The "Garang lobby" was found mostly in Congress and at the US Agency for International Development. On June 1, 2004, members of Congress who sympathized with the SPLA sent President George W. Bush a list of 23 names of janjaweed supporters, controllers, and commanders who were either members of the Sudanese government or closely linked to it. The message was clear: do something about these people.

President Bush seemed discomfited by the implicit demand. Supporters of anti-Khartoum legislation tended to be more "on the left." Yet there was a core group of anti-Khartoum activists at the opposite end of the political spectrum from where he drew most of his electoral support. Many fundamentalist Protestant organizations had rallied to the anti-Khartoum lobby. By mid-2004, vocal Jewish groups such as the Committee for the Holocaust Memorial in Washington had also joined in the indignant chorus of protests about Darfur.

The president thus found himself under pressure from an array of public opinion elements too wide to be ignored during an election year. Yet, since the "realists" in the intelligence community kept insisting that Khartoum was too important to be harshly treated, these contradictory pressures led the White House to compromise on all fronts—supporting the Naivasha negotiations; not putting too much practical pressure on Khartoum, but nevertheless approving legislation that could be used as a sword of Damocles in case of noncompliance; becoming vocal on Darfur; putting a fair amount of money on its humanitarian aspect—but doing nothing at the military level.

This author was assured that Secretary of State Colin Powell had practically been ordered to use the term "genocide" during his high-profile September 9, 2004, testimony to the Senate Committee on Foreign Relations, but that he also had been advised to add in the same breath that this did not oblige the United States to undertake any sort of drastic action, such as a military intervention.

President Bush in short tried to be all things to all people on the Sudan/Darfur question. Never mind that the result was predictably confused. What mattered was that attractive promises could be handed around without any sort of firm commitment being made. Unsurprisingly, the interest level of US diplomacy on the Sudan question dropped sharply as soon as Bush was reelected.

Likewise, in its usual way of treating diplomatic matters, the European Union presented a spectacle of complete lack of resolve and coordination when it came to Darfur. The French only cared about protecting Idris Deby's regime in Chad from possible destabilization. The British blindly followed Washington's lead, finding this somewhat difficult since Washington was not very clear about which direction it wished to take. The Scandinavian countries and the Netherlands gave large sums of money and remained silent. Germany made anti-Sudanese government noises that it never backed up with any sort of action and gave only limited cash. And the Italians remained bewildered.

The result was a purely humanitarian approach to the crisis, with the EU and its member states giving $142 million (out of a total of $301 million; that is, more than the United States) without coming up with anything meaningful in terms of policy.

Everyone knew that a military operation was the only form of intervention that could have any drastic effect. But Brussels was quite incapable of mustering the energy to do in distant Darfur what it had failed to do without American or NATO prompting in neighboring Bosnia or Kosovo a few years earlier.

Even on the question of deciding on the nature of what was happening in Darfur, the union could not manage to speak with any clearly recognizable voice, its parliament only declaring that what was going on was "tantamount to genocide." During several Darfur "cease-fire" or "peace" talks in Abéché and Abuja, the Europeans pushed for a "no fly zone" above Darfur. But even when it was accepted, they did strictly nothing to try to enforce it.

The UN's Dilemma

The UN was in a terrible position regarding the Darfur crisis for a number of reasons. First, it was deeply involved in the Naivasha process, boosting the capacity and resolve of regional governments in what ended up being a saga of endless procrastination and obfuscation. Khartoum kept playing Darfur against Naivasha in order to win at both levels or, if a choice had to be made, at least to keep Darfur out of the military reach of the international community. Second, the UN was at the forefront of the humanitarian effort both in southern Sudan and in Darfur.

Third, UN Secretary General Kofi Annan knew that the US administration hated him (and the UN in general) and would do anything in its power to make the world body and its secretary general make a potentially fatal false move. Fourth, the Arab/black African split that was implicit in the Darfur crisis had many echoes inside the UN. And finally, the EU member states and America kept pushing the world body to act as if they were not themselves responsible for it.

Annan knew that the December 1948 genocide convention only obliged the member states to "refer" such a matter to the UN, but that once the world body had accepted the challenge, it became mandatory for it to act. Therefore, his permanent nightmare over Darfur was that member states would corner him into saying "genocide," thereby forcing him to act, and then fail to give him the necessary financial, military, and political means to do so. For the United Nations, which had been shaken by the United States' bypassing it on the Iraq question, such a debacle would have been a catastrophe.

Caught on the horns of so many dilemmas, Annan tried to act without upsetting things, to scold without being threatening, and to help without intruding too much. The result was that he appeared weak and irresolute at a time when the United Sates and some of his own staff were insisting on more "action," even if it was no more than symbolic. In June 2004, after he had been booed by demonstrators in Harvard Square, Annan declared: "Based on reports I have received, I cannot at this stage call it genocide or ethnic cleansing yet."

The Darfur tragedy will continue to unfold. And the cry of "never again" heard after the Rwandese genocide will ring hollowly as "once again."

This was the worst of both worlds: he had uttered the big taboo words, but prevaricated over their relevance. The pressure kept building on the UN to come up with some radical solution. And the more the pressure built up, the more the secretary general resisted it, because he knew only too well that those who were applying it had no real intention of doing anything.

The more the crisis developed, the less the UN seemed capable of doing anything political about it, even though at the humanitarian level it carried over 60 percent of the financial burden. In many ways, this situation came to demonstrate the UN's practical limitations in crises where the heavyweight member states do not want to act. Blaming the UN was easy for those who were responsible for its inaction. Passing the buck to the African Union was another favorite resort to sophistry.

The Report of the UN Commission of Inquiry on the Darfur Violence provided an example of the world body and the United Sates each acting their parts in a coordinated show of egregious disingenuousness. The report documented violations of international human rights by "people who might have acted with genocidal intentions"; yet the situation was not a genocide, although it was definitely "war crimes." But the United States did not like the International Criminal Court (ICC), fearing that some of its own human rights violations, particularly in Iraq, might make it liable to prosecution. It therefore did not favor the UN suggestion that Darfur war crimes should be brought to the ICC, suggesting instead that a special tribunal might be set up in Arusha on the model of the Rwanda tribunal.

Off the record, everyone worried about naming names in an eventual prosecution because the perpetrators of the Darfur war crimes were the same people who, according to the January 9, 2005, "peace agreement," were now supposed to implement the Nairobi settlement and turn Sudan into a brave new world of peace and prosperity.

The African Union's Moment

Once the OAU had decided to shed its skin and be reborn as the African Union (AU), it had known that it would be judged, both by its member states and by the broader international community, on the basis of its competence in conflict management. Darfur was the first major crisis to face the organization since its transformation, and its commission chairman, Alpha Konare, and the AU chairman in 2004–2005, President Olusegun Obasanjo of Nigeria, knew that the moment of truth had arrived.

But the financial provisions under which the AU operated were highly unrealistic. Its 2003 budget had been a meager $43 million and out of this the member states had neglected to pay $26 million. This did not prevent Konare from requesting $1.7 billion for a "strategic plan" for the AU, which was to have its own peace fund, a pan-African parliament (based in South Africa), a court of justice, and even a standing army. When the dreaming stopped, the Addis Ababa-based organization finally settled for a budget of $158 million, with $63 million financed by obligatory payments and another $95 million by "voluntary contributions."

In the short term, the estimated cost of a peacekeeping operation in Darfur—nearly $250 million—had to be financed entirely by foreign donors. In many ways they were only too glad to contribute. Brussels promised $110 million and others, including Washington and the UN, pledged the rest. The AU decided to send 132 observers to Western Sudan, with 300 troops whose mandate would be restricted to protecting the observers.

It also declared that in its opinion, this was not ethnic cleansing in Darfur. This was to be a recurrent problem for the AU: in many ways it has not stopped being the "heads of state trade union," which President Julius Nyerere of Tanzania had denounced in 1978. Afraid of Darfur's potential for splintering the organization between Arabs and black Africans, Konare tried his best to minimize the racial angle of the crisis. Worse, he systematically refused to condemn Khartoum or even to put the responsibility for the massacres squarely on the janjaweed. For the AU, Darfur remained a case of mass murder without any known perpetrators, and Khartoum was even discreetly advised on how to "handle the whites."

Obasanjo had offered 2,000 Nigerian troops, but only a fraction of them were going to be sent as part of the AU contingent. Khartoum's minister of the interior, Abd-er-Rahim Mohamed Hussein, one of the two or three most powerful figures in the government, retorted, "We will not tolerate the presence of any foreign troops, whatever their nationality." In Khartoum's usual style this meant, "We will accept foreign troops: all that matters is their nationality and their mandate."

Khartoum would be satisfied on both accounts, leading it to accept what it had at first so vociferously rejected. The troops would all be African. And their mandate—peacekeeping alone being acceptable—was satisfactory both for the Western countries, which were let off the hook easily, and for Khartoum, which was getting an impotent and probably mute witness to its "good faith."

As for the AU, it was also satisfied: it had been allowed to play in the big boy's league and would not have to pay for the privilege. "Africa" would be at the forefront of the Darfur crisis and any accusation of impotence or limitation of means would be beamed back at the donors.

In a way not completely unlike that of the UN, the AU has been scheduled for a "Mission Impossible." It is supposed to substitute itself for the coalition of the unwilling, to stop what it is only mandated to observe, to operate on a shoestring, and to keep the pretense of serious international involvement for its tight-fisted sponsors. Predictably, all it has achieved is a token presence.

The Usual Explanations

Once the principle of some kind of foreign intervention was decided, even one as limited as that given to the AU, the problem of "genocide" came back to the fore, not so much as a media term but as a legal label with potential consequences for international proceedings and criminal sanctions.

The number of victims is not a key factor in deciding whether large-scale killings constitute a genocide or not. But numbers are relevant, first in themselves (the magnitude of what the targeted group has suffered) and secondly because of their real or potential impact on world opinion. In the case of Darfur, however, numbers of victims have been both extremely difficult to compute and the object of fierce differences of opinion.

A more fundamental aspect of the problem is semantics, which not only goes to the heart of the matter but illuminates the way Darfur has been dealt with by the international community. Four types of explanations have been offered for the Darfur violence. The first is that it is an explosion of tribal conflicts exacerbated by drought. This has been usually (but not always) the Sudanese government's explanation.

Second, it is explained as a counterinsurgency campaign gone badly wrong because the government has used inappropriate means to fight back the insurrection. This is roughly the position of the Darfur specialist Alex de Waal and a number of Western governments. De Waal does not use the argument to exonerate Khartoum. But the Western governments adopting this position usually minimize Khartoum's responsibility, preferring to talk of "errors."

A third explanation posits a deliberate campaign of "ethnic cleansing," with the Sudanese government trying to displace or eliminate "African" tribes in order to replace them by "Arab" ones that it feels would be more supportive of "Arab" rule in Khartoum. Finally, there is the genocide hypothesis, supported by evidence of systematic racial killings.

The "ethnic conflict" explanation has to be looked at technically, not ideologically. Ethnic tensions and problems have existed in Darfur for a long time, though not along the lines of the present conflict. This is an essential point that makes Darfur not unlike Rwanda. Tensions between Tutsi and Hutu were already present when the first Europeans arrived in the 1890s. However, they had never been globalized in the way that occurred during the 1994 genocide. Ethnic tensions can slip into violence, but they involve local weaponry, do not present a relentless and systematic character, and do not entail large-scale cooperation from the administration.

When Darfur villages were bombed and strafed by government aircraft, this was not the work of spontaneously violent local nomads. When the janjaweed were organized into coordinated military units and assigned to camps they shared with the regular army, it was not possible to characterize what was happening as spontaneous violence. Ethnic tensions in Darfur were and still are real, and recurring droughts have made them worse. But they of themselves were not sufficient to unleash the violence we have seen. They were the raw material, not the cause.

Nevertheless, Khartoum has systematically resorted to this and other similar "explanations" in order to deny its involvement in the massacres. The problems of Darfur are caused by "bandits, not rebels"; in any case these bandits are "just a little gang, incapable of standing up to the regular army"; as for the janjaweed, they are "a bunch of thieves," just like the rebels. Actually, the rebels and the janjaweed are the same thing. There is "no rebellion in Darfur, just

a conflict among specific tribes. The government has not armed any militia. The propaganda in the West is trying to exaggerate what is happening." A list of such quotations would be almost endless.

If one discounts these unlikely "explanations," then what of the "counterinsurgency gone wrong?" In many ways, this is true, but is it the whole picture and, specifically, is it an excuse of some kind? Technically, Darfur is a bad case of poorly conceived counterinsurgency carried out with completely inadequate means. A "clean" counterinsurgency may even be impossible if a guerrilla movement has arisen from deep-seated economic, social, and cultural grievances.

But beyond this question of "counterinsurgency gone wrong," there is another point that causes the problem to slip into another dimension. In many ways the 1980s were a period of permanent counterinsurgency, when Arabs in Khartoum looked on the "African" tribes in Darfur as the enemy. The fact that the pace of the violence slowed down somewhat during the 1990s did not change that basic outlook. The state of ethnic relations resulting from frantic ideological manipulations of that period remained a permanent threat to non-Arabs in the province. Thus, any armed movement initiated by the non-Arab tribes of Darfur was like a red rag waved before the eyes of an excited bull.

Here again the parallel with Rwanda is striking. When Tutsi rebels entered Rwanda in October 1990 they probably did not realize the degree of danger they were creating for the other Tutsi living inside the country. In an atmosphere charged with racism an armed rebellion by the "inferior" group is fraught with enormous danger for the civilians of that group.

Indeed, counterinsurgency in Darfur could perhaps only have gone wrong. This was not "counterinsurgency" organized by a government trying to restore law and order. It was an answer with arms by a racially and culturally dominant group to the insurrection of a racially and culturally subject group. The hope that repression could be limited to combatants was completely unrealistic.

The Big-G Word

The two other explanations, "ethnic cleansing" and "genocide," are closely related. As a rough differentiation we could take "ethnic cleansing" to mean massive killings of a certain section of the population in order to frighten the survivors away and occupy their land but without the intent of killing them all. "Genocide" is more difficult to define. The December 1948 International Convention on the Prevention and Punishment of Crimes of Genocide says that what constitutes genocide is "deliberately inflicting on the group conditions of life calculated to bring about its physical destruction *in whole or in part.*"

Blaming the UN was easy for those who were responsible for its inaction.

I personally used another definition in my book, *The Rwanda Crisis*—namely, a coordinated attempt to destroy a racially, religiously, or politically predefined group in its entirety. I am attached to the notion of an attempt at *total* obliteration because it has a number of consequences that seem to be specific to a "true" genocide. First, the numbers tend to be enormous because the purge is thorough. Second, there is no escape. In the case of a racially defined group, the reason is obvious, but if the group is religiously defined no conversions will be allowed. And if it is politically defined, no form of submission will save its members.

Finally, the targeted group will retain for many years after the traumatic events a form of collective paranoia that will make even its children live with an easily aroused fear. This is evident among the Armenians, the Jews, and the Tutsi. But it is present also in less obviously acute forms in groups such as the North American Indians, French Protestants, and Northern Irish Catholics. It is this "fractured consciousness" that makes future reconciliation extremely difficult.

If we use the December 1948 definition it is obvious that Darfur is a genocide, but if we use the definition I proposed in my book on Rwanda, it is not. At the immediate existential level this makes no difference; the horror experienced by the targeted group remains the same, no matter which word we use. But this does not absolve us from trying to understand the nature of what is happening.

And whether the "big-G word" is used or not appears to make a considerable difference in terms of international reaction. It is a measure of the jaded cynicism of our times that we seem to think that the killing of 250,000 people in a genocide is more serious, a greater tragedy, and more deserving of our attention than that of 250,000 people in nongenocidal massacres.

The reason seems to be the overriding role of the media coupled with the mass-consumption need for brands and labels. Things are not seen in their reality but in their capacity to create brand images, to warrant a "big story," to mobilize television time high in rhetoric. "Genocide" is big because it carries the Nazi label, which sells well. "Ethnic cleansing" is next best (though far behind) because it goes with Bosnia, which was the last big-story European massacre. But simply killing is boring, especially in Africa.

The notion of "ethnic cleansing," implying that the Sudanese government has been trying to displace African tribes in order to give their land to "Arabs," was at first not backed by any evidence other than the shouts hurled at victims by the perpetrators themselves. The perpetrators might hope for such an outcome from their massacres, but such a policy probably was not clearly thought out in Khartoum.

It is possible, however, that in a diffuse and decentralized way there has been a deliberate attempt to "Arabize" Darfur. The few instances of "Arabs" settling on the land abandoned by the African peasants do not seem very convincing. The "Arabs" are mostly nomads who do not appear to be much interested in becoming agriculturalists. But they are desperate for pastureland, made more and more scarce by the southward movement of the desert. Blacks in Darfur might be dying in part so that camels and sheep can graze where men used to cultivate.

A Strange Ballet

As for the most prominent use of the word "genocide" in connection with Darfur, Secretary of State Powell seems to have based his thinking on the December 1948 definition when he said on September 9, 2004, that in his opinion Darfur was a genocide. Other spokesmen for world opinion danced a strange ballet around the big-G word. President Bush declared: "Our conclusion is that a genocide is under way in Darfur." British Foreign Minister Chris Mullin was more prudent, merely saying that a genocide "might have taken place." The spokesman for the French Foreign Ministry limited himself to saying that there had been "massive violations of human rights," while Walter Lindner, for the German Foreign Affairs Ministry, said that this was "a humanitarian tragedy . . . with a potential for genocide." In the end none of them went beyond talk. The UN, the AU, and the humanitarians were left holding the bloody babies.

This leaves open the question of "intent," which was at the center of the UN Commission of Inquiry's decision not to call Darfur a genocide. The commission wrote that there was "not sufficient evidence to indicate that Khartoum had a state policy intended to exterminate a particular racial or ethnic group," a definition that moved away from that of December 1948, but which in itself is acceptable.

However, the semantic play ended up supporting an evasion of reality. The notion that this was probably not strictly speaking a "genocide" seemed to satisfy the commission that things were not really too bad. Conclusions about "war crimes" could have serious consequences, but that would require translating them into ICC indictments.

From Bad to Worse?

What is the present situation in Darfur? It is bad and fast deteriorating. The massive humanitarian effort undertaken during 2004 enabled over 2 million people to survive in internal-displaced-person camps, precariously perched on the edge of death. But this effort is now seriously undermined because the means that the international community is ready to put into African catastrophes are limited. The drought now playing havoc with the economies of Tanzania, Kenya, Somalia, and parts of Ethiopia will require money, and that money is largely being culled out of the Darfur budget.

This financial shrinkage is occurring at a time when violence in Darfur is again on the rise. The fact that the AU is completely impotent has given a feeling to both the janjaweed and the rebels that they need not bother about the military tourists in their midst. As a result, the guerrillas have stepped up military operations and the janjaweed have gone back to attacking the civilian population, albeit on a smaller scale than in 2004.

In addition, Darfur is suffering spillover from what might be called "the Chadian war of succession." Curiously enough this was triggered, if not caused, by Darfur. The Zaghawa tribe, which lives on both sides of the Chad border, was one of those targeted by the janjaweed. President Deby of Chad is a Zaghawa but he chose to ally himself with Khartoum in helping the repression because some of his personal enemies had joined the rebellion on the Sudanese side.

This somewhat paradoxical alliance caused many Chadian Zaghawa to side against Deby, and he now faces a full-fledged insurgency. And most of the rebels belong not only to Deby's clan but even to his own family. In mid-March they attempted a second coup against him (the first had taken place in May 2005), and then took refuge in Darfur when they failed. Deby now accuses Khartoum of helping his rebellious relatives in order to punish him for abandoning the repression camp.

Whatever the reality of the accusations and counter-accusations currently flying between Khartoum and Ndjamena, the result is a translation of Chad's civil strife into Darfur, as if the martyred province had not suffered enough. In response, the UN has proposed replacing the inefficient AU monitors with European or NATO forces. But, since such forces could be efficient in stopping the violence, the Sudanese government has blocked the proposal by all available means—including the setting up of bogus "terrorist" organizations that "threatened" to kill UN representative Jan Pronk and the US chargé d'affaires in Khartoum.

In the face of this blackmail, the international community has backed down and prolonged the AU's impotent mandate until the end of this year. Short of a military intervention such as that of a UN force firmly equipped with sufficient guns and a clear mandate to use them, the Darfur tragedy will continue to unfold. And the cry of "never again" heard after the Rwandese genocide will ring hollowly as "once again."

GÉRARD PRUNIER is director of the French Center for Ethiopian Studies in Addis Ababa. His latest book is *Darfur: The Ambiguous Genocide* (Cornell University Press, 2005), from which this essay draws.

From *Current History*, Vol. 15, No. 691, May 2006, pp. 195–202. Copyright © 2006 by Current History, Inc. Reprinted with permission.

Banning the Bomb

A New Approach

WARD WILSON

In July of 1945, U.S. president Harry Truman wrote in his diary, "It is certainly a good thing for the world that Hitler's crowd or Stalin's did not discover this atomic bomb. It seems to be the most terrible thing ever discovered, but it can be made the most useful." Terrible and useful. For sixty years, people have focused on the terrible aspects of nuclear weapons. They have made films about nuclear war, detailed the horrors of Hiroshima and Nagasaki, and imagined the end of life on earth. In those sixty years, on the other hand, people have rarely talked seriously about the usefulness of nuclear weapons. Do they really win wars? Are they effective threats? Fear—engendered by real and imagined cold war dangers—constrained real inquiry. Absorbed by images of destruction, most people didn't ask practical questions. But it turns out that the area that we've explored the most—the terribleness of nuclear weapons—is not the key to understanding them. The key is investigating whether or not they are really useful.

I am not urging the familiar argument that nuclear weapons are too dangerous to be useful; I am suggesting that even if one could use them with impunity, nuclear weapons would still have little practical value. Sixty years of experience, recent reevaluations of the track record of nuclear weapons, and reinterpretations of Hiroshima and Nagasaki based on new research make it possible to argue that there are very few situations in which nuclear weapons are useful. It might, in fact, be possible to demonstrate that nuclear weapons are functionally the equivalent of biological and chemical weapons: powerful and dangerous weapons, but with very few real applications. And therefore it might also be possible to make the case that—as with chemical and biological weapons—there are practical, prudential reasons for banning nuclear weapons.

Current Strategies

To date, two related strategies have been used to oppose the use of nuclear weapons: the horror strategy and the risk strategy. The former relies on moral feelings and tries to persuade people that using nuclear weapons is too immoral to contemplate. The latter relies on calculations of the possibility that a small war could become an all-out nuclear war and tries to persuade people that the danger is too great.

Those who use the horror strategy often make Hiroshima and Nagasaki the centerpiece of their case. They try to drive home the immorality of using nuclear weapons by forcing their listeners to experience vicariously the horror of these cities. Doctors increased the emotional impact of this approach in the 1980s by talking unflinchingly and in detail about the medical consequences of nuclear attacks.

The risk strategy has been more widely embraced than the horror strategy. Vividly given a story line by Nevil Shute in *On the Beach* (a novel later made into a movie in which a nuclear war extinguishes all human life), it has remained a staple of antinuclear argument, used by radicals and sober policymakers alike.

Jonathan Schell updated and expanded the risk strategy in *The Fate of the Earth.* Schell eschewed the normal tack of emphasizing the risks of escalation, arguing instead that an all-out nuclear war might lead to the destruction of all life on earth. So it didn't matter how big or small the risk of escalation was, the consequences were so terrible that no amount of risk was worth running. In 1983, Carl Sagan and four others further buttressed Schell's case with evidence suggesting that severe climatic disruption, dubbed "nuclear winter," could be triggered by a nuclear war.

Sound as their reasoning might be, both these strategies have weaknesses. The horror argument's weakness is that in a crisis necessity almost always trumps morality. People will say, "Yes, it's wrong. But we have to do it. We have no other choice." If the Bomb seems likely to be militarily effective most people will decide to use it, even if they know it is wrong to do so.

The risk strategy has been eroded by the end of the cold war, which led to lowered tensions and significantly reduced the likelihood of nuclear escalation. Another key—but often overlooked—change is the end of "extended deterrence"—the threat by the United States and the Soviet Union to respond to attacks on their client states with nuclear counterattacks. At one time, all of Europe, all of Latin America, some of Asia, and even parts of Africa were covered by extended deterrence. With the collapse of the cold war client-state system, many nations are now out from under the nuclear umbrella. It is now possible for the United States to attack, say, Syria, with nuclear weapons without the threat of a nuclear response from Russia. As the risk of escalation has decreased, the strength of the risk argument has also decreased.

Bigger Is Not Better

It is often said that every weapon that man has invented has been used in war. This statement misses the point. The important issue is not whether this or that weapon has ever been used, it is whether such a weapon—once tried—has become a fixture in the arsenals of warlike nations. Horrible weapons have been imagined and tried. But are they still used?

Consider the Paris Gun. Built by the Germans in World War I, it was more than 90 feet long, weighed 256 tons, and moved on rails. It fired a 210-pound projectile more than 80 miles. Often confused with its smaller cousin, the large mortar called "Big Bertha," in its day it was the largest cannon ever built. It was a terrifying weapon. From March until August of 1918, the Germans used it to rain shells down on Paris without warning. The Parisians were bewildered and terrified. In all, the Paris Gun fired about 360 shells, killing 250 people and wounding 620.

Only a handful of other superguns have since been built (Schwerer Gustav and V3 among them). Their impact on the wars in which they participated was minimal. Today, nations do not race to build their own superguns. African nations, torn by strife, do not try to trade their oil or diamond resources for superguns bought from arms dealers. There are no angry diatribes in liberal papers about the horror of these weapons and the necessity of banning them.

"But of course this is so," someone might say, "because these weapons were not very effective." And that is the point. Decisions about acquiring or banning weapons are not based on their horribleness but on their ability or inability to help win wars.

There are four general ways that nuclear weapons might be used: in a war intended to exterminate an opponent, in a war of coercion, as a threat, and to create terror. For two of these categories—coercion and threats—it is relatively easy to show that nuclear weapons are not ideal weapons and, in some circumstances, are so seriously mismatched to the task at hand as to be useless.

On the other hand, nuclear weapons are admirably suited for wars of extermination. If you have decided on a war in which your goal is to annihilate your opponent, nuclear weapons are your best choice. In this case it is necessary to argue not that the weapons wouldn't be useful, but that such wars are morally wrong. This is not a demanding task. No case can be made that the capability to wage a war of annihilation is valuable or necessary. And this moral judgment is borne out by the practical experience of history: the actual number of wars of extermination is small. (Wars of extermination are distinct from genocide or other murderous actions within a country's own boundaries.) A careful review of human history unearthed only one clear case, the Third Punic War.

The vast majority of wars are wars of coercion. The conventional wisdom has been that nuclear weapons are decisive in this kind of war. After all, they won the war in the Pacific. But when examined closely, the presumption of decisiveness evaporates. Recent reinterpretations of the Japanese surrender call into question the notion that the bombings of Hiroshima and Nagasaki were in any way connected with that decision. The Soviet intervention radically altered the strategic situation and was the decisive event.

The power to destroy cities is not the power to win wars. Freeman Dyson makes this point vividly in an example drawn from the Falklands War. Someone had said loosely about the war that if the British had wanted to they could have "blown Buenos Aires off the map." This was true, but Dyson points out that the British would still have had to send soldiers to re-conquer the Falklands. And destroying Buenos Aires would probably have made the Argentine soldiers defending the islands fight more fiercely. Or the British could have nuked the Falklands themselves, but that would have destroyed the islands. The British abstained from using nuclear weapons not because they have admirable restraint, but because there was no practical application for the weapons.

Sixty years of experience with nuclear weapons does not support the notion that they are singularly useful to their possessors. Despite its nuclear arsenal, the United States was fought to a draw in Korea, lost a war in Vietnam, did not stop genocides in Cambodia or Rwanda, and is currently mired in conflict in Iraq. Despite its sizable nuclear arsenal, the Soviet Union suffered humiliation in its own guerrilla war in Afghanistan. Nuclear nations have fought many wars, but these supposedly powerful weapons have not played a decisive role in any of them.

Nuclear weapons do not appear to be suited to the battlefield. This inutility has already been ratified by two of the most authoritative bodies in a position to make a judgment: the military establishments of the United States and the Soviet Union. If tactical nuclear weapons were really militarily useful, would these two military establishments have allowed almost all tactical weapons to be retired in the 1980s?

Nuclear weapons are also of questionable effectiveness in attacks on economic targets. Most economic targets are roughly building-sized, and with today's precision-guided munitions, conventional weapons are more than adequate. Nuclear weapons, on the other hand, require destruction of an area many times larger than the target. What is the point of destroying a quarter of a city in order to knock out an oil refinery? It is true that a large-scale nuclear attack could effectively shatter a nation's economic infrastructure, but at what point does this become a war of extermination?

Diplomatic Influence

When the United States first got nuclear weapons, there were high hopes that they would provide not just military might, but international influence as well. Truman, when he talked about nuclear weapons being "useful" in the diary entry quoted above, was probably thinking of the upcoming negotiations he faced with the Soviet Union over the shape of the post–World War II world. His secretary of state, James F. Byrnes, told him with a touch of euphoria that nuclear weapons would probably allow the United States to "dictate our own terms after the war." Byrnes returned from the bargaining table a chastened man. The Soviets, he reported ruefully afterward, "are stubborn, obstinate, and they don't scare." Perhaps this is not surprising. Joseph Stalin said in a 1946 interview in *Pravda,* "Atomic bombs are meant to frighten those with weak nerves."

The U.S. nuclear monopoly did not prevent communist domination of Eastern Europe in the years after the Second World War. It did not prevent the Berlin Crisis of 1948. It did not prevent the communist takeover of China in 1949. Of course, any threat will work some percentage of the time—some people scare easily. The question is, are nuclear weapons reliable tools of coercion? Clearly not.

Some people argue that nuclear weapons have kept the United States and other nations safe by deterring nuclear war. This is difficult to prove. Imagine a man who says that the lucky penny he keeps on his dresser has prevented nuclear war. When you ask for proof, he says, "Well, I've kept that penny on the dresser for sixty-two years and there's been no war, so it must be working!" Nuclear weapons may provide crucial safety and security, although it is hard to imagine how dangerous weapons that cannot be defended against are the best means of providing safety. Another—perhaps more certain—way to prevent nuclear war is to ban nuclear weapons.

Of What Use Today?

Another way to assess the usefulness of nuclear weapons is to think about the role they might play in a crisis today. Imagine, for example, that the North Koreans used a nuclear weapon to attack Seoul or Tokyo. The United States, Russia, Great Britain, France, or China would all be in a position to retaliate against Pyongyang. Some might argue that this would be the right way to deter future nuclear attacks against cities. But wouldn't a far more practical deterrent be for the United States, Russia, and China to form an alliance, invade North Korea, and set up a new government? Nuking Pyongyang only punishes the innocent. North Korea's leaders would surely have left the city shortly before the North Korean nuclear strike was launched. Nuking Pyongyang kills North Korean civilians, who, because they live under a dictatorship, have no responsibility for the decision to attack. Rogue states that use nuclear weapons are unlikely to be democratic states, and because what nuclear weapons do best is kill people, nuclear weapons will never be well suited to punishing such a regime.

Many people believe that the most likely use of nuclear weapons in the next few years (barring a war in the Middle East or the Asian subcontinent) is a terrorist attack against a city. Terrorists, whose aim is to coerce political change by irregular attacks on innocents, are the people most likely to imagine that nuclear weapons are useful. On the other hand, it is difficult to imagine nuclear deterrence against terrorists. Imagine that a nuclear bomb hidden in a cargo container is detonated in Baltimore Harbor. What effective nuclear retaliation options are there? It would be very difficult to identify the attackers. But even assuming that a terrorist group takes responsibility—say, al-Qaeda—how can nuclear weapons be used to redress this evil? Would you use a nuclear weapon against a city in Pakistan in which you think Osama bin Laden is hiding? Again, the vast majority of those who die will be innocent, and if faulty intelligence leads you to attack the wrong city you risk punishing *only* the innocent.

A good deal of energy has been devoted to imagining circumstances in which nuclear weapons would be exactly the right weapons to use. But why is it necessary to imagine unlikely or outlandish scenarios in order to justify these weapons?

The current U.S. administration supports research into developing "bunker buster" nuclear weapons that could destroy targets deeply buried or secreted in caves. There are two telling objections to such a weapon. First, as with most applications of nuclear weapons, conventional weapons already provide a fairly extensive bunker buster capability. Nuclear bunker busters would only extend existing capabilities a few hundred meters (to three hundred meters below the surface at most). It is within the capabilities of almost any enemy simply to dig deeper. The second is that the intelligence necessary for such a strike is unimaginable. Even with the sophisticated technology currently available to the U.S. government, for example, we were unable to identify chemical and biological facilities in Iraq, a country with barren, cloud-free, best-case topography. This is an indication of how hard it is to locate secret facilities. And we were looking for facilities on the surface.

The current administration also imagines that mini-nukes would be useful. These are weapons with roughly a third the destructive power of the bomb that destroyed Hiroshima—about the same destructive power that was deployed in the conventional raids against Japanese cities in the summer of 1945. Why build a nuclear weapon with an end result you can already achieve using conventional weapons?

In this connection, the size of nuclear weapons raises a question. Early on in the nuclear age, physicists warned that there was no theoretical limit to the size of hydrogen bombs. The Soviets tested a bomb with a yield of roughly fifty-two megatons in 1962. Larger bombs could have been built. Yet they have not been. In fact, the size of nuclear warheads in the U.S. and Russian arsenals has been shrinking. At one time one megaton (or larger) warheads were common, but today the yield of an average warhead in the U.S. strategic arsenal is only about a third of a megaton. How can nuclear bombs be shrinking if the greater the destructive power the greater the military usefulness? If nuclear weapons are useful, why is it that the trend is toward making them more like conventional weapons?

Benefits of Banning the Bomb

The benefits of a total ban are clear. The chief benefit is that it protects us against the danger that people are currently most concerned with in connection with these weapons: use by a terrorist group against a city. By banning nuclear weapons you substantially decrease the chances that they will fall into the hands of rogue states or terrorist organizations. The only reason that the director of the Pakistani nuclear project was able to sell nuclear technology to the North Koreans is that proliferation had gained such widespread acceptance. The more nations that have nuclear weapons, the more likely someone is to put them into the hands of irresponsible people. (As I write this in

October 2006, North Korea has just tested a nuclear weapon. The international reaction serves as a strong reminder that it is important to keep nuclear weapons out of the hands of unstable leaders.)

Any international ban would have to include careful monitoring of all formerly nuclear nations and inspection of nuclear power reactors. (If nuclear nations are unwilling to give up their weapons entirely, perhaps each could warehouse a small stockpile under UN administration in their own countries. The weapons could be retrieved by their owner, but only by publicly breaking the treaty.) With no military weapons floating around, and access to nuclear power monitored and controlled by international organizations, building a rogue bomb or stealing one becomes almost impossible.

None of the arguments sketched here is the final word on the usefulness of nuclear weapons. There is considerable work still to be done. The Hiroshima argument needs to be more thoroughly researched. The case against city attacks needs to be strengthened with historical examples. And along with work on each of its parts, a systematic treatment of the entire subject is needed. But it should be clear from the limited treatment here that there is enough substance in the approach to merit further work.

In 1775, Edmund Burke rose in Parliament to oppose the use of force against the American colonies. Burke believed strongly that the application of force was not the best way to bind the colonies to the British Empire. Burke said that he opposed force not because it was an "odious" instrument of policy but because it was a "feeble" one. His assertion must have been especially surprising because the British army and navy at that time were the most powerful in the world. Using force, he argued, could intimidate and coerce, but raw power alone would not create obedience in the colonies. In some situations brute force is less effective (or more "feeble") than other means.

It may seem paradoxical to think of them as "feeble," but I want to make something of the same argument about nuclear weapons. The strongest arguments against the use of nuclear weapons are not those that demonstrate that they are horrible or dangerous (although they are certainly both), but those that show that they aren't very useful. Weapons, like tools, are situational: their "power" is measured not by their raw force but by the extent to which their capabilities match the circumstances. A jackhammer is a very powerful tool; it's not much help in repairing a watch. A howitzer is of no use underwater; a shotgun blast doesn't help where stealth is required; a knife has little effect at a thousand yards. It's not the size of the bang, it's the match between the situation at hand and the weapon's capabilities. In most military situations, conventional weapons are better suited to the task at hand than nuclear ones. Only in blowing up cities are nuclear weapons singularly well suited to a task. This is an objective, however, that only terrorists pursue enthusiastically.

If there are hardly any circumstances in which nuclear weapons are militarily useful, and if it seems likely that the more nations that have nuclear arsenals the more likely the weapons are to fall into the hands of terrorists or madmen, then it makes practical sense to ban them.

WARD WILSON is an independent scholar living in Trenton, N.J. He is currently at work on a book about the military usefulness of destroying cities throughout history. He writes regularly at www.rethinking nuclearweapons.org.

UNIT 6

Cooperation

Unit Selections

34. **Europe as a Global Player: A Parliamentary Perspective,** Hans-Gert Poettering
35. **The Grameen Bank,** Muhammad Yunus
36. **Geneva Conventions,** Steven R. Ratner
37. **Is Bigger Better?,** David Armstrong

Key Points to Consider

- Itemize the products you own that were manufactured in another country.

- What recent contacts have you had with people from other countries? How was it possible for you to have these contacts?

- Do you use the Internet to interact with people in other countries?

- How do you use the World Wide Web to learn about other countries and cultures?

- Identify nongovernmental organizations in your community that are involved in international cooperation (e.g., Rotary International).

- What are the prospects for international governance? How do trends in this direction enhance or threaten American values and constitutional rights?

- What new strategies for cooperation can be developed to fight infectious disease, terrorism, international narcotics trafficking and other threats?

- How can conflict and rivalry be transformed into meaningful cooperation?

Student Web Site

www.mhcls.com

Internet References

Carnegie Endowment for International Peace
http://www.ceip.org
OECD/FDI Statistics
http://www.oecd.org/statistics/
U.S. Institute of Peace
http://www.usip.org

© Erica Simone Leeds 2007

An individual can write a letter and, assuming it is properly addressed, be relatively certain that it will be delivered to just about any location in the world. This is true even though the sender pays for postage only in the country of origin and not in the country where it is delivered. A similar pattern of international cooperation is true when a traveler boards an airplane and never gives a thought to the issue of potential language and technical barriers, even though the flight's destination is halfway around the world.

Many of the most basic activities of our lives are the direct result of governments cooperating across borders. International organizational structures, for example, have been created to eliminate barriers to trade, monitor and respond to public health threats, set standards for international telecommunications, arrest and judge war criminals, and monitor changing atmospheric conditions. Individual governments, in other words, have recognized that their self-interest directly benefits from cooperation (in most cases by giving up some of their sovereignty through the creation of international governmental organizations, or IGOs).

Transnational activities are not limited to the governmental level. There are now tens of thousands of international nongovernmental organizations (INGOs). The activities of INGOs range from staging the Olympic Games to organizing scientific meetings to actively discouraging the hunting of seals. The number of INGOs along with their influence has grown tremendously in the past 50 years.

During the same period in which the growth in the importance of IGOs and INGOs has taken place, there has also been a parallel expansion of corporate activity across international borders. Most U.S. consumers are as familiar with Japanese or German brand-names as they are with items made in their own country. The multinational corporation (MNC) is an important non-state actor. The value of goods and services produced by the biggest MNCs is far greater than the gross domestic product (GDP) of many countries. The international structures that make it possible to buy a Swedish automobile in Sacramento or a Korean television in Buenos Aires have been developed over many years. They are the result of governments negotiating treaties that create IGOs to implement the agreements (e.g., the World Trade Organization). As a result, corporations engaged in international trade and manufacturing have created complex transnational networks of sales, distribution, and service that employ millions of people.

To some observers, these trends indicate that the era of the nation-state as the dominant player in international politics is passing. Other experts have observed these same trends and have concluded that the state system has a monopoly of power and that the diverse variety of transnational organizations depends on the state system and, in significant ways, perpetuates it.

In many of the articles that appear elsewhere in this book, the authors have concluded their analysis by calling for greater international cooperation to solve the world's most pressing problems. The articles in this section provide examples of successful cooperation. In the midst of a lot of bad news, it is easy to overlook the fact that we are in the midst of international cooperation and that basic day-to-day activities in our lives often directly benefit from it.

Article 34

A Filled Balance

Europe as a Global Player
A Parliamentary Perspective

HANS-GERT POETTERING

In the 28 years since the European Parliament was first elected, it has developed from a largely advisory forum into a full-fledged branch of Europe's legislature. Since the Single European Act of 1986 and the Maastricht Treaty of 1992, the role of the European Parliament in EU decision-making has increasingly changed from one of marginality to one of centrality. Today, members of the European Parliament share law-making powers with the Council of Ministers across many policy areas. The Parliament has truly come of age.

The advent of co-decision between the Parliament and the Council has made the Parliament a major actor in the EU legislative process. The Parliament has become an integral part of a new European political system, in which the vast majority of decisions require explicit approval of the Parliament. Whether it be the liberalization of transport, regulation of financial markets, limits on carbon emissions, or product standards and consumer protection, the decisions of the Parliament are now as important as those of member states in setting EU law.

In recent years, our work as members of the Parliament has shaped and advanced European integration in many fields. We pushed forward the process of EU enlargement when there was reticence in some other quarters. The single market and the single currency would never have occurred without the early and sustained advocacy of Euro-parliamentarians. The political majority in the European Parliament is now critical in determining who is chosen as president of the European Commission. Furthermore, as a result of parliamentary pressure, foreign and security policy has become an integral part of EU activity.

When I first became a member of the European Parliament in 1979, the individual sovereign states guarded their own foreign and security policies, making the policy area something of a taboo subject at the supranational level. This disunity, however, changed in the mid-1980s, when the Single European Act formalized modest arrangements for "European political cooperation." The Maastricht Treaty converted them into a formal Common Foreign and Security Policy, for the first time raising the possibility of a European defense. Today, more than a dozen EU military and policing missions can be found throughout the world. While deployment of EU troops or police forces outside the European Union was unheard of in 1979, it is a daily reality in 2007.

As the European Union becomes more involved in world affairs and as domestic integration deepens, it becomes more important that the European institutions function as effectively and democratically as possible. These objectives can most effectively be obtained through the ratification of the European constitutional treaty. We need the reforms espoused by the constitution to successfully fulfill our role in EU and world affairs.

European integration has gone through cycles of crisis and self-doubt in the past, but it has usually emerged stronger as a result. When the European Defense Community failed in 1954, it subsequently took less than three years to reach an agreement on the Rome Treaties. When the first effort to establish a common currency failed during the 1970s, the experience of further monetary crises pointed to the continuing necessity for a full economic and monetary union, a logic that led to the adoption of the euro in 2002. While the difficulties in securing ratification of the European constitutional treaty by all member states have been a blow to the development of the European Union, I believe that they can be overcome, just as European integration has cleared previous obstacles that initially seemed insurmountable in its 50-year history.

One clear lesson from the recent ratification crisis is that there is a need to connect more closely European citizens with the project of European integration. Some of the citizens of France and the Netherlands who voted against the constitutional treaty in referenda in the summer of 2005 did so because they regarded the European Union as insufficiently coherent, democratic, or transparent. Yet ironically, the constitutional treaty actually includes many of the changes that are necessary to strengthen democracy, coherence, and transparency in the Union. For example, it extends the mandate of the president of the European Council, gives the European Parliament even greater legislative power, clarifies the competences of the

Union, and simplifies the types of legislative action—all in an effort to improve the overall consistency, clarity, and accountability of EU institutions.

The foreign policy component of the constitutional treaty is especially important. Only an effective and democratic European Union along the lines foreseen in the constitutional treaty can be a credible actor in the world, and furthermore, a reliable partner for the United States. Though commentators like to distinguish between "soft" and "hard" power, I would prefer to distinguish between coherence and incoherence in foreign policy-making. The truth is that even though decision-making at the EU level is now integral to determining the foreign policy of the member states—and the global presence of the European Union is already an important reality in world affairs—the Union as such is not in the position to act coherently in its own right. This limitation stems in varying degrees from the Union's legal status, the institutional division between the Council and the Commission, and the Union's lack of free-standing military resources. The provisions of the constitutional treaty, which establish the post of European foreign minister and create a European external action service, are important for the emergence of a more comprehensive and credible EU foreign policy.

Responsible political leadership in the European Union is rightly committed to putting these provisions into practice. So far, the constitutional treaty has been ratified by two-thirds of the European Union's 27 member states. It is also supported by the vast majority of members of the European Parliament. Our common objective is to implement at least the core propositions enshrined in the treaty—the key substance of the original text—before the next elections to the European Parliament in June 2009.

Europe and Globalization

A constitutional treaty will make it easier for Europe to address the pressing issues of our time, at home and abroad. Globalization poses new challenges to European policymakers in the economic sphere and in many other fields. Europe has been slower in taking full advantage of the opportunities of globalization than the United States, let alone China or India. But the European Union has been fully aware that just as globalization brings new opportunities, as it empowers individuals and expands the global market, creating billions of new consumers, it simultaneously requires changes in European citizens' attitudes toward job security, welfare, and most importantly, investment in human capital through education and life-long learning. The majority of citizens in the European Union would resist any form of globalization that undermined the principles of human dignity, but this outcome need not materialize. The market dynamic can and should continue to be underpinned by a safety net for the weaker members of European society. This is an essential principle of a social market economy.

In a way, European integration has been, and continues to be, an anticipated form of regional globalization. It has been driven, by and large, by political decisions designed to support the freedom and cohesion of European societies, to facilitate the creation of a single European market, and to provide a greater measure of legal certainty to activities in the European sphere. It is based on supranational law and therefore offers a sort of framework in which a free market can flourish to the benefit of more citizens. Based on this experience, we believe that globalization will progress most smoothly if it goes hand in hand with some legal rules—not ones that undermine the forces of the market, but rules that safeguard the interests of citizens, both as consumers and producers.

Projecting Stability into the World

To date, globalization has too often left out important parts of the world community, notably in the Arab world and sub-Saharan Africa. As both these regions are physically proximate to Europe, we are particularly sensitive to this situation. In fact, it is both a strategic and a moral obligation that we pay more attention to what is taking place in these regions. Poverty, insecurity, and fear can easily produce a dangerous combination of illegal migration, fanaticism, and violence.

The European Union is now the largest donor of development aid in the world. Some critics claim that this assistance is some kind of compensation for the legacy of European colonialism in lesser-developed countries. I think it emphasizes instead Europe's firm desire to be a constructive partner in building a better world.

Europe's political leaders and institutions are determined to fight terrorism and any form of political violence. We are gravely concerned about an ideology of Islamic radicalism that includes the use of violence as a means to succeed in its political and religious goals. We absolutely condemn terror in the name of politics or religion, and we are concerned that the continuation of any form of radical Islamic terror will undermine the chances of a dialogue among cultures that is more vital today than ever.

Europe is an immediate neighbor of the Arab world. The bulk of immigrants into the European Union originate from northern Africa and sub-Saharan Africa, with Spain being the biggest recipient. Muslims have become the second largest religious group in the Union, representing around 3.5 percent of the total population. Mosques are a common sight all over Europe. In our position, a cross-cultural dialogue is crucial. By the nature of our situation and our history, the European Union is absolutely determined to guarantee a peaceful cohabitation of Christians, Muslims, Jews, and all other religious, secular, and atheist people. We can only do this on the basis of mutual respect.

An important component of the emerging foreign policy of the European Union is the effort to project stability into the immediate neighborhood of the Union and into the wider world. The recent enlargement of the European Union was a spectacular example of the success of that policy: the prospect of EU membership played an important part in ensuring the democracy and prosperity of the former Soviet republics and client states which are now safely members of a democratic European family. An enlarged European Union has recently developed a complex web of policies to stabilize its immediate surroundings and to promote peace and affluence beyond its borders. Our partnerships with Russia and other Eastern European countries that are non-EU member states are designed to build a more stable relationship with that part of Europe's neighborhood.

Likewise, the European Union is part of the "Quartet" along with the United States, the United Nations, and Russia that designed the Road Map for Peace in the Middle East. Many obituaries have been written for this Quartet process. But in the end, I believe, a comprehensive solution to the vexing Middle East conundrum will have to follow the main elements of the established Road Map and, in fact, will need the commitment of the Quartet countries. We want a comprehensive, equitable, and lasting peace that recognizes the right of existence of both Israel and a viable Palestinian state. The Euro-Mediterranean Partnership—in which the European Parliament plays a leading role—is an important vehicle for bringing all European countries together with the Arab coastal states of the Mediterranean and with Israel.

Transatlantic Partnership

Rising to the challenge of globalization also requires deeper transatlantic cooperation. Most major global issues we face cannot be resolved solely by the actions of either the European Union or the United States. In general, when we cannot reach agreement across the Atlantic on major global challenges, policy simply fails to be enacted at the international level and the credibility of the Western world decreases. In order to resolve key issues from climate control to global terrorism, the European Union and the United States must be active partners in a common endeavor.

The ties that bind the United States and the European Union are deeply rooted. We are each other's largest economic partners, whether in terms of trade, capital flows, inward investments, or jobs. Ownership of many of our companies is now in effect vested jointly in the hands of both US and EU citizens. Our great universities cooperate actively. There is a regular, intense exchange of ideas, emails, and visitors across the Atlantic. At a political level, however, there is still much to be done. We have the achievements of the NATO Treaty, we have our regular EU-US summits and parliamentary exchanges, but we have no systematic framework within which to organize our overall relations. As early as 1962, President John F. Kennedy proposed a transatlantic treaty broadening the bases for our relationship for this very reason.

In the absence of such a framework, we can still work positively together on a common agenda. The current German presidency of the Council has already declared that strengthening transatlantic relations, particularly in the economic sphere, is one of its major external policy priorities. Chancellor Angela Merkel has talked of promoting "ever-closer economic cooperation" across the Atlantic, signaling that she particularly wants to see progress toward an EU-US Transatlantic Economic Partnership, based on some variant of a "Transatlantic Market." The latter concept is not a free-trade area or a customs union; rather, it is in effect a single market, in which EU and US technical standards, regulatory régimes, and competition policies would progressively converge. The idea has long been advocated in resolutions of the European Parliament. Indeed, it is a good example of how the Parliament has shifted the policy agenda, in this case, by going out in front of the member-state governments.

The concept of a transatlantic single market has, for the first time, been picked up by the president of the European Commission, José Manuel Barroso, in Brussels, and by the US president and administration in Washington. It is an idea whose time has come. Legislators in the European Parliament, together with senators and congressmen on Capitol Hill, will need to be closely involved. If Parliament and Congress are to approve the result and make all the legislative changes necessary to implement it, it is sensible that we be partners from the start in its design, negotiation, and delivery.

Maintaining the "Atlantic Civilization"

The future of European integration and of a strong transatlantic partnership are important political objectives and key components in maintaining our "Atlantic civilization." The European Union is developing new scenarios to advance both greater unity and stronger Euro-American relations. The German presidency of the Council currently is attempting to identify methods and timelines for achieving each. As a result, there is now a very serious possibility that Europe will overcome the crisis over the ratification of the European constitutional treaty and emerge strengthened by this process. The European Union needs the substance of the reforms enshrined in the treaty, not only to better manage its affairs as a union of 27 or more member states, but also to confront the new and pressing policy challenges posed by globalization and to discharge its responsibilities in the world. Equally, there is an increasing likelihood that we will see significant progress toward a closer transatlantic partnership, at least in the economic sphere, with the concept of a barrier-free single market across the Atlantic firmly on the agenda. These twin achievements would represent major stepping stones toward building a less dangerous and more prosperous world.

HANS-GERT POETTERING, MEP, is President of the European Parliament.

The Grameen Bank

A small experiment begun in Bangladesh has turned into a major new concept in eradicating poverty.

Muhammad Yunus

Over many years, Amena Begum had become resigned to a life of grinding poverty and physical abuse. Her family was among the poorest in Bangladesh—one of thousands that own virtually nothing, surviving as squatters on desolate tracts of land and earning a living as day laborers.

In early 1993 Amena convinced her husband to move to the village of Kholshi, 112 kilometers (70 miles) west of Dhaka. She hoped the presence of a nearby relative would reduce the number and severity of the beatings that her husband inflicted on her. The abuse continued, however—until she joined the Grameen Bank. Oloka Ghosh, a neighbor, told Amena that Grameen was forming a new group in Kholshi and encouraged her to join. Amena doubted that anyone would want her in their group. But Oloka persisted with words of encouragement. "We're all poor—or at least we all were when we joined. I'll stick up for you because I know you'll succeed in business."

Amena's group joined a Grameen Bank Center in April 1993. When she received her first loan of $60, she used it to start her own business raising chickens and ducks. When she repaid her initial loan and began preparing a proposal for a second loan of $110, her friend Oloka gave her some sage advice: "Tell your husband that Grameen does not allow borrowers who are beaten by their spouses to remain members and take loans." From that day on, Amena suffered significantly less physical abuse at the hands of her husband. Today her business continues to grow and provide for the basic needs of her family.

Unlike Amena, the majority of people in Asia, Africa and Latin America have few opportunities to escape from poverty. According to the World Bank, more than 1.3 billion people live on less than a dollar a day. Poverty has not been eradicated in the 50 years since the Universal Declaration on Human Rights asserted that each individual has a right to:

A standard of living adequate for the health and well-being of himself and of his family, including food, clothing, housing and medical care and necessary social services, and the right to security in the event of unemployment, sickness, disability, widowhood, old age or other lack of livelihood in circumstances beyond his control.

Will poverty still be with us 50 years from now? My own experience suggests that it need not.

After completing my Ph.D. at Vanderbilt University, I returned to Bangladesh in 1972 to teach economics at Chittagong University. I was excited about the possibilities for my newly independent country. But in 1974 we were hit with a terrible famine. Faced with death and starvation outside my classroom, I began to question the very economic theories I was teaching. I started feeling there was a great distance between the actual life of poor and hungry people and the abstract world of economic theory.

I wanted to learn the real economics of the poor. Because Chittagong University is located in a rural area, it was easy for me to visit impoverished households in the neighboring village of Jobra. Over the course of many visits, I learned all about the lives of my struggling neighbors and much about economics that is never taught in the classroom. I was dismayed to see how the indigent in Jobra suffered because they could not come up with small amounts of working capital. Frequently they needed less than a dollar a person but could get that money only on extremely unfair terms. In most cases, people were required to sell their goods to moneylenders at prices fixed by the latter.

This daily tragedy moved me to action. With the help of my graduate students, I made a list of those who needed small amounts of money. We came up with 42 people. The total amount they needed was $27.

I was shocked. It was nothing for us to talk about millions of dollars in the classroom, but we were ignoring the minuscule capital needs of 42 hardworking, skilled people next door. From my own pocket, I lent $27 to those on my list.

Still, there were many others who could benefit from access to credit. I decided to approach the university's bank and try to persuade it to lend to the local poor. The branch manager said, however, that the bank could not give loans to the needy: the villagers, he argued, were not creditworthy.

I could not convince him otherwise. I met with higher officials in the banking hierarchy with similar results. Finally, I offered myself as a guarantor to get the loans.

In 1976 I took a loan from the local bank and distributed the money to poverty-stricken individuals in Jobra. Without exception, the villagers paid back their loans. Confronted with this evidence, the bank still refused to grant them loans directly. And so I tried my experiment in another village, and again it was successful. I kept expanding my work, from two to five, to 20, to 50, to 100 villages, all to convince the bankers that they should be lending to the poor. Although each time we expanded to a new village the loans were repaid, the bankers still would not change their view of those who had no collateral.

Because I could not change the banks, I decided to create a separate bank for the impoverished. After a great deal of work and negotiation with the government, the Grameen Bank ("village bank" in Bengali) was established in 1983.

From the outset, Grameen was built on principles that ran counter to the conventional wisdom of banking. We sought out the very poorest borrowers, and we required no collateral. The bank rests on the strength of its borrowers. They are required to join the bank in self-formed groups of five. The group members provide one another with peer support in the form of mutual assistance and advice. In addition, they allow for peer discipline by evaluating business viability and ensuring repayment. If one member fails to repay a loan, all members risk having their line of credit suspended or reduced.

The Power of Peers

Typically a new group submits loan proposals from two members, each requiring between $25 and $100. After these two borrowers successfully repay their first five weekly installments, the next two group members become eligible to apply for their own loans. Once they make five repayments, the final member of the group may apply. After 50 installments have been repaid, a borrower pays her interest, which is slightly above the commercial rate. The borrower is now eligible to apply for a larger loan.

The bank does not wait for borrowers to come to the bank; it brings the bank to the people. Loan payments are made in weekly meetings consisting of six to eight groups, held in the villages where the members live. Grameen staff attend these meetings and often visit individual borrowers' homes to see how the business—whether it be raising goats or growing vegetables or hawking utensils—is faring.

Today Grameen is established in nearly 39,000 villages in Bangladesh. It lends to approximately 2.4 million borrowers, 94 percent of whom are women. Grameen reached its first $1 billion in cumulative loans in March 1995, 18 years after it began in Jobra. It took only two more years to reach the $2-billion mark. After 20 years of work, Grameen's average loan size now stands at $180. The repayment rate hovers between 96 and 100 percent.

A year after joining the bank, a borrower becomes eligible to buy shares in Grameen. At present, 94 percent of the bank is owned by its borrowers. Of the 13 members of the board of directors, nine are elected from among the borrowers; the rest are government representatives, academics, myself and others.

A study carried out by Sydney R. Schuler of John Snow, Inc., a private research group, and her colleagues concluded that a Grameen loan empowers a woman by increasing her economic security and status within the family. In 1998 a study by Shahidur R. Khandker, an economist with the World Bank, and others noted that participation in Grameen also has a significant positive effect on the schooling and nutrition of children—as long as women rather than men receive the loans. (Such a tendency was clear from the early days of the bank and is one reason Grameen lends primarily to women: all too often men spend the money on themselves.) In particular, a 10 percent increase in borrowing by women resulted in the arm circumference of girls—a common measure of nutritional status—expanding by 6 percent. And for every 10 percent increase in borrowing by a member the likelihood of her daughter being enrolled in school increased by almost 20 percent.

Not all the benefits derive directly from credit. When joining the bank, each member is required to memorize a list of 16 resolutions. These include commonsense items about hygiene and health—drinking clean water, growing and eating vegetables, digging and using a pit latrine, and so on—as well as social dictums such as refusing dowry and managing family size. The women usually recite the entire list at the weekly branch meetings, but the resolutions are not otherwise enforced.

Even so, Schuler's study revealed that women use contraception more consistently after joining the bank. Curiously, it appears that women who live in villages where Grameen operates, but who are not themselves members, are also more likely to adopt contraception. The population growth rate in Bangladesh has fallen dramatically in the past two decades, and it is possible that Grameen's influence has accelerated the trend.

In a typical year 5 percent of Grameen borrowers—representing 125,000 families—rise above the poverty level. Khandker concluded that among these borrowers extreme poverty (defined by consumption of less than 80 percent of the minimum requirement stipulated by the Food and Agriculture Organization of the United Nations) declined by more than 70 percent within five years of their joining the bank.

To be sure, making a microcredit program work well—so that it meets its social goals and also stays economically sound—is not easy. We try to ensure that the bank serves the poorest: only those living at less than half the poverty line are eligible for loans. Mixing poor participants with those who are better off would lead to the latter dominating the groups. In practice, however, it can be hard to include the most abjectly poor, who might be excluded by their peers when the borrowing groups are being formed. And despite our best efforts, it does sometimes happen that the money lent to a woman is appropriated by her husband.

Given its size and spread, the Grameen Bank has had to evolve ways to monitor the performance of its branch managers and to guarantee honesty and transparency. A manager is not allowed to remain in the same village for long, for fear that he may develop local connections that impede his performance. Moreover, a manager is never posted near his home. Because of such constraints—and because managers are required to have university degrees—very few of them are women. As a result, Grameen has been accused of adhering to a paternalistic pattern. We are sensitive to this argument and are trying to change the situation by finding new ways to recruit women.

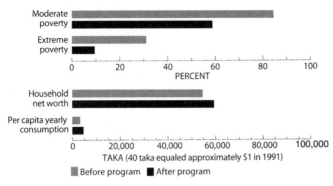

Figure 1 Household Well-Being before and after Participation in Grameen.

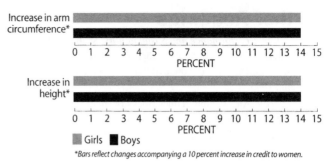

Bars reflect changes accompanying a 10 percent increase in credit to women.

Figure 2 Impact of Grameen on Nutritional Measures of Children.

Grameen has also often been criticized for being not a charity but a profit-making institution. Yet that status, I am convinced, is essential to its viability. Last year a disastrous flood washed away the homes, cattle and most other belongings of hundreds of thousands of Grameen borrowers. We did not forgive the loans, although we did issue new ones, and give borrowers more time to repay. Writing off loans would banish accountability, a key factor in the bank's success.

Liberating Their Potential

The Grameen model has now been applied in 40 countries. The first replication, begun in Malaysia in 1986, currently serves 40,000 poor families; their repayment rate has consistently stayed near 100 percent. In Bolivia, microcredit has allowed women to make the transition from "food for work" programs to managing their own businesses. Within two years the majority of women in the program acquire enough credit history and financial skills to qualify for loans from mainstream banks. Similar success stories are coming in from programs in poor countries everywhere. These banks all target the most impoverished, lend to groups and usually lend primarily to women.

The Grameen Bank in Bangladesh has been economically self-sufficient since 1995. Similar institutions in other countries are slowly making their way toward self-reliance. A few small programs are also running in the U.S., such as in innercity Chicago. Unfortunately, because labor costs are much higher in the U.S. than in developing countries—which often have a large pool of educated unemployed who can serve as managers or accountants—the operations are more expensive there. As a result, the U.S. programs have had to be heavily subsidized.

In all, about 22 million poor people around the world now have access to small loans. Microcredit Summit, an institution based in Washington, D.C., serves as a resource center for the various regional microcredit institutions and organizes yearly conferences. Last year the attendees pledged to provide 100 million of the world's poorest families, especially their women, with credit by the year 2005. The campaign has grown to include more than 2,000 organizations, ranging from banks to religious institutions to nongovernmental organizations to United Nations agencies.

The standard scenario for economic development in a poor country calls for industrialization via investment. In this "top-down" view, creating opportunities for employment is the only way to end poverty. But for much of the developing world, increased employment exacerbates migration from the countryside to the cities and creates low-paying jobs in miserable conditions. I firmly believe that, instead, the eradication of poverty starts with people being able to control their own fates. It is not by creating jobs that we will save the poor but rather by providing them with the opportunity to realize their potential. Time and time again I have seen that the poor are poor not because they are lazy or untrained or illiterate but because they cannot keep the genuine returns on their labor.

Self-employment may be the only solution for such people, whom our economies refuse to hire and our taxpayers will not support. Microcredit views each person as a potential entrepreneur and turns on the tiny economic engines of a rejected portion of society. Once a large number of these engines start working, the stage can be set for enormous socioeconomic change.

Applying this philosophy, Grameen has established more than a dozen enterprises, often in partnership with other entrepreneurs. By assisting microborrowers and microsavers to take ownership of large enterprises and even infrastructure companies, we are trying to speed the process of overcoming poverty. Grameen Phone, for instance, is a cellular telephone company that aims to serve urban and rural Bangladesh. After a pilot study in 65 villages, Grameen Phone has taken a loan to extend its activities to all villages in which the bank is active. Some 50,000 women, many of whom have never seen a telephone or even an electric light, will become the providers of telephone service in their villages. Ultimately, they will become the owners of the company itself by buying its shares. Our latest innovation, Grameen Investments, allows U.S. individuals to support companies such as Grameen Phone while receiving interest on their investment. This is a significant step toward putting commercial funds to work to end poverty.

I believe it is the responsibility of any civilized society to ensure human dignity to all members and to offer each individual the best opportunity to reveal his or her creativity. Let us remember that poverty is not created by the poor but by the institutions and policies that we, the better off, have established. We can solve the problem not by means of the old concepts but by adopting radically new ones.

Further Readings

Grameen Bank: Performance and Sustainability. Shahidur R. Khandker, Baqui Khalily and Zahed Khan. World Bank Discussion Papers, No. 306. ISBN 0-8213-3463-8. World Bank, 1995.

Give Us Credit. Alex Counts. Times Books (Random House), 1996.

Fighting Poverty with Microcredit: Experience in Bangladesh. Shahidur R. Khandker. Oxford University Press, 1998.

Grameen Bank site is available at www.grameenfoundation.org on the World Wide Web.

MUHAMMAD YUNUS, the founder and managing director of the Grameen Bank, was born in Bangladesh. He obtained a Ph.D. in economics from Vanderbilt University in 1970 and soon after returned to his home country to teach at Chittagong University. In 1976 he started the Grameen project, to which he has devoted all his time for the past decade. He has served on many advisory committees: for the government of Bangladesh, the United Nations, and other bodies concerned with poverty, women, and health. He has received the World Food Prize, the Ramon Magsaysay Award, the Humanitarian Award, the Man for Peace Award, and numerous other distinctions as well as six honorary degrees.

Geneva Conventions

They help protect civilians and soldiers from the atrocities of war. But these hard-won rules of battle are falling by the wayside: Terrorists ignore them, and governments increasingly find them quaint and outdated. With every violation, war only gets deadlier for everyone.

STEVEN R. RATNER

"The Geneva Conventions Are Obsolete"

Only in the minor details. The laws of armed conflict are old; they date back millennia to warrior codes used in ancient Greece. But the modern Geneva Conventions, which govern the treatment of soldiers and civilians in war, can trace their direct origin to 1859, when Swiss businessman Henri Dunant happened upon the bloody aftermath of the Battle of Solferino. His outrage at the suffering of the wounded led him to establish what would become the International Committee of the Red Cross, which later lobbied for rules improving the treatment of injured combatants. Decades later, when the devastation of World War II demonstrated that broader protections were necessary, the modern Geneva Conventions were created, producing a kind of international "bill of rights" that governs the handling of casualties, prisoners of war (POWs), and civilians in war zones. Today, the conventions have been ratified by every nation on the planet.

Of course, the drafters probably never imagined a conflict like the war on terror or combatants like al Qaeda. The conventions were always primarily concerned with wars between states. That can leave some of the protections enshrined in the laws feeling a little old-fashioned today. It seems slightly absurd to worry too much about captured terrorists' tobacco rations or the fate of a prisoner's horse, as the conventions do. So, when then White House Counsel Alberto Gonzales wrote President George W. Bush in 2002 arguing that the "new paradigm" of armed conflict rendered parts of the conventions "obsolete" and "quaint," he had a point. In very specific—and minor—details, the conventions have been superseded by time and technology.

But the core provisions and, more crucially, the spirit of the conventions remain enormously relevant for modern warfare. For one, the world is still home to dozens of wars, for which the conventions have important, unambiguous rules, such as forbidding pillaging and prohibiting the use of child soldiers.

These rules apply to both aggressor and defending nations, and, in civil wars, to governments and insurgent groups.

The conventions won't prevent wars—they were never intended to—but they can and do protect innocent bystanders, shield soldiers from unnecessary harm, limit the physical damage caused by war, and even enhance the chances for cease-fires and peace. The fundamental bedrock of the conventions is to prevent suffering in war, and that gives them a legitimacy for anyone touched by conflict, anywhere and at any time. That is hardly quaint or old-fashioned.

"The Conventions Don't Apply to Al Qaeda"

Wrong. The Bush administration's position since Sept. 11, 2001, has been that the global war on terror is a different kind of war, one in which the Geneva Conventions do not apply. It is true that the laws do not specifically mention wars against nonstate actors such as al Qaeda. But there have always been "irregular" forces that participate in warfare, and the conflicts of the 20th century were no exception. The French Resistance during World War II operated without uniforms. Vietcong guerrillas fighting in South Vietnam were not part of any formal army, but the United States nonetheless treated those they captured as POWs.

So what treatment should al Qaeda get? The conventions contain one section—Article 3—that protects all persons regardless of their status, whether spy, mercenary, or terrorist, and regardless of the type of war in which they are fighting. That same article prohibits torture, cruel treatment, and murder of all detainees, requires the wounded to be cared for, and says that any trials must be conducted by regular courts respecting due process. In a landmark 2006 opinion, the U.S. Supreme Court declared that *at a minimum* Article 3 applies to detained al Qaeda suspects. In other words, the rules apply, even if al Qaeda ignores them.

And it may be that even tougher rules should be used in such a fight. Many other governments, particularly in Europe, believe that a "war" against terror—a war without temporal or geographic limits—is complete folly, insisting instead that the fight against terrorist groups should be a law enforcement, not a military, matter. For decades, Europe has prevented and punished terrorists by treating them as criminals. Courts in Britain and Spain have tried suspects for major bombings in London and Madrid. The prosecutors and investigators there did so while largely complying with obligations enshrined in human rights treaties, which constrain them far more than do the Geneva Conventions.

"The Geneva Conventions Turn Soldiers into War Criminals"

Only if they commit war crimes. For centuries, states have punished their own soldiers for violations of the laws of war, such as the mistreatment of prisoners or murder of civilians. The Geneva Conventions identify certain violations that states must prosecute, including murder outside of battle, causing civilians great suffering, and denying POWs fair trials, and most countries have laws on the books that punish such crimes. The U.S. military, for example, has investigated hundreds of servicemembers for abuses in Iraq and Afghanistan, leading to dozens of prosecutions. Canada prosecuted a group of its peacekeepers for the murder of a young Somali in 1993.

Yet the idea that ordinary soldiers could be prosecuted in a foreign country for being, in effect, soldiers fighting a war is ridiculous. Yes, many countries, including the United States, have laws allowing foreigners to be tried for various abuses of war committed anywhere. Yet the risk of prosecution abroad, particularly of U.S. forces, is minuscule. Those foreign laws only address bona fide war crimes, and it is rarely in the interest of foreign governments to aggravate relations with the United States over spurious prosecutions.

The idea that the International Criminal Court could one day put U.S. commanders on trial is unlikely in the extreme. That court could theoretically prosecute U.S. personnel for crimes committed in, say, Afghanistan, but only if the United States failed to do so first. What's more, the court is by its charter dedicated to trying large-scale, horrendous atrocities like those in Sudan. It is virtually inconceivable that this new institution will want to pick a fight with the United States over a relatively small number of abuses.

"The Conventions Prevent Interrogations of Terrorists"

False. If you've seen a classic war movie such as *The Great Escape,* you know that prisoners of war are only obligated to provide name, rank, date of birth, and military serial number to their captors. But the Geneva Conventions do not ban interrogators from asking for more. In fact, the laws were written with the expectation that states will grill prisoners, and clear rules were created to manage the process. In interstate war, any form of coercion is forbidden, specifically threats, insults, or punish-

ments if prisoners fail to answer; for all other wars, cruel or degrading treatment and torture are prohibited. But questioning detainees is perfectly legal; it simply must be done in a manner that respects human dignity. The conventions thus hardly require rolling out the red carpet for suspected terrorists. Many interrogation tactics are clearly allowed, including good cop-bad cop scenarios, repetitive or rapid questioning, silent periods, and playing to a detainee's ego.

The Bush administration has engaged in legal gymnastics to avoid the conventions' restrictions, arguing that preventing the next attack is sufficient rationale for harsh tactics such as waterboarding, sleep deprivation, painful stress positions, deafening music, and traumatic humiliation. These severe methods have been used despite the protests of a growing chorus of intelligence officials who say that such approaches are actually counterproductive to extracting quality information. Seasoned interrogators consistently say that straightforward questioning is far more successful for getting at the truth. So, by mangling the conventions, the United States has joined the company of a host of unsavory regimes that make regular use of torture. It has abandoned a system that protects U.S. military personnel from terrible treatment for one in which the rules are made on the fly.

"The Geneva Conventions Ban Assassinations"

Actually, no. War is all about killing your enemy, and though the Geneva Conventions place limits on the "unnecessary suffering" of soldiers, they certainly don't seek to outlaw war. Assassinating one's enemy when hostilities have been declared is not only permissible; it is expected. But at the core of the conventions is the "principle of distinction," which bans all deliberate targeting of civilians. The boundless scope of the war on terror makes it difficult to decide who is and is not a civilian. The United States claims that it can target and kill terrorists at any time, just like regular soldiers; but the conventions treat these individuals like quasi-civilians who can be targeted and killed only during "such time as they take a *direct* part in hostilities" [emphasis mine]. The Israeli Supreme Court recently interpreted this phrase to give Israel limited latitude to continue targeted killings, but it insisted on a high standard of proof that the target had lost protected status and that capture was impossible. What standards the United States might be using—such as when the CIA targeted and killed several al Qaeda operatives in Yemen in 2002—are highly classified, so there's no way to know how much proof is insisted upon before the trigger is pulled or the button pushed.

For European countries and others who reject the idea of a "war" against terrorists to begin with, targeted killings are especially abhorrent, as international law prohibits states in peacetime from extrajudicial killings. There are very specific exceptions to this rule, such as when a police officer must defend himself or others against imminent harm. To that end, a suicide bomber heading for a crowd could legally be assassinated as a last resort. By contrast, suspected terrorists—whether planning a new attack or on the lam—are to be captured and tried.

"The Conventions Require Closing Guantánamo"

No, but changes must be made. The Geneva Conventions allow countries to detain POWs in camps, and, if someone in enemy hands does not fit the POW category, he or she is automatically accorded civilian status, which has its own protections. But none of the residents of Guantánamo's military prison qualifies as either, according to the Bush administration, thus depriving the roughly 275 detainees who remain there of the rights accorded by the conventions, such as adequate shelter and eventual release.

The possibility that detainees could remain in legal limbo indefinitely at Guantánamo has turned the issue into a foreign-relations disaster for the United States. But let's be clear—the Geneva Conventions don't require the United States to close up shop in Cuba. The rules simply insist that a working legal framework be put in place, instead of the legal vacuum that exists now.

There are several options worth consideration. The prison at Guantánamo could be turned into a pre-trial holding area where detainees are held before they are brought before U.S. courts on formal charges. (The hiccup here is that most of the detainees haven't clearly violated any U.S. law.) Alternatively, the U.S. Congress could pass legislation installing a system of preventive detention for dangerous individuals. The courts could occasionally review detainees' particular circumstances and judge whether continued detention is necessary and lawful. (The problem here is that such a system would run against 200 years of American jurisprudence.) In the end, closing Guantánamo is probably the only option that would realistically restore America's reputation, though it isn't required by any clause in the conventions. It's just the wisest course of action.

"No Nation Flouts the Geneva Conventions More than the United States"

That's absurd. When bullets start flying, rules get broken. The degree to which any army adheres to the Geneva Conventions is typically a product of its professionalism, training, and sense of ethics. On this score, U.S. compliance with the conventions has been admirable, far surpassing many countries and guerrilla armies that routinely ignore even the most basic provisions. The U.S. military takes great pride in teaching its soldiers civilized rules of war: to preserve military honor and discipline, lessen tensions with civilians, and strive to make a final peace more durable. Contrast that training with Eritrea or Ethiopia, states whose ill-trained forces committed numerous war crimes during their recent border war, or Guatemala, whose army and paramilitaries made a policy of killing civilians on an enormous scale during its long civil conflict.

More importantly, the U.S. military cares passionately that other states and nonstate actors follow the same rules to which it adheres, because U.S. forces, who are deployed abroad in far greater numbers than troops from any other nation, are most likely to be harmed if the conventions are discarded. Career U.S. military commanders and lawyers have consistently opposed the various reinterpretations of the conventions by politically appointed lawyers in the Bush White House and Justice Department for precisely this reason.

It is enormously important that the United States reaffirms its commitment to the conventions, for the sake of the country's reputation and that of the conventions. Those who rely on the flawed logic that because al Qaeda does not treat the conventions seriously, neither should the United States fail to see not only the chaos the world will suffer in exchange for these rules; they also miss the fact that the United States will have traded basic rights and protections harshly learned through thousands of years of war for the nitpicking decisions of a small group of partisan lawyers huddled in secret. Rather than advancing U.S. interests by following an established standard of behavior in this new type of war, the United States—and any country that chooses to abandon these hard-won rules—risks basing its policies on narrow legalisms. In losing sight of the crucial protections of the conventions, the United States invites a world of wars in which laws disappear. And the horrors of such wars would far surpass anything the war on terror could ever deliver.

STEVEN R. RATNER is professor of law at the University of Michigan.

Is Bigger Better?

Using market incentives, Fazle Hasan Abed built the largest antipoverty group in the world and helped pull Bangladesh out of the ashes. Now he wants to take on Africa.

DAVID ARMSTRONG

From the large glass window of his modern, well-lit and spacious offices 19 floors above Dhaka, Bangladesh, Fazle Hasan Abed, a former executive for Shell Oil, can keep tabs on nearby Korail, a dense slum of 60,000 people living in single-story mud, aluminum and bamboo shacks, some built on thin stilts over the brackish water of an urban lake. Abed, 72, has more than a little interest in the slum. The organization he founded in 1972, BRAC, the largest antipoverty group in the world, with 110,000 paid employees and a $482 million annual budget, has its hands everywhere in Korail.

Down one muddy lane a teacher trained by BRAC instructs 36 students using a BRAC-designed curriculum of Bengali, math and English. Nearby a group of women in the final month of pregnancy sit shrouded in colorful saris on the floor of a BRAC-built "birthing hut," staffed with BRAC-trained health workers, getting a lesson in prenatal nutrition. Not far away, Mosammat Anwaraan, an energetic woman in her late 50s, runs a mini real estate empire, the fruits of a 3,000 taka ($44) microloan in 1997 from BRAC. She owns 25 rooms in the slum, renting out 18 for 700 to 800 taka a month, making $2,500 a year. "I think rent will go up to 1,000 taka by next year," she says proudly.

Abed has replicated all-in-one programs like these in 1,000 urban slums and 70,000 rural villages across Bangladesh (the group was originally called the Bangladesh Rural Advancement Committee). Its microfinance program has made $4.6 billion in loans versus $6.9 billion from the better-known microlender Grameen. It runs 52,000 preschools and primary schools, with 1.5 million students. Its 68,000 health care volunteers, egged on by financial incentives, cover a population of 80 million. It operates commercial dairies, silkworm-raising centers and department stores to provide markets for the goods its poor beneficiaries produce. Says Abed, "If you want to do significant work, you have to be large. Otherwise we'd be tinkering around on the periphery."

The World Bank credits BRAC in part with what it calls the "Bangladesh paradox": Despite an impotent government (leaders of the two primary political parties are currently in jail on corruption charges), this country of 145 million people has improved significantly. According to the World Bank, the fraction of the population living in poverty (defined as below $2 a day in purchasing

power) dropped from 58% in 1992 to 40% in 2005; secondary school enrollment has climbed from 19% in 1990 to 43% today and childhood immunization from 1% in 1980 to 80% today.

In the 1980s a woman had, on average, seven kids. Today it's two.

Thirty years ago a woman had, on average, seven children. Today the fertility rate is two, thanks in large part to widespread delivery of contraceptives to the countryside, a practice pioneered by BRAC. The country's 5% annual average growth in GDP since 1990 (to $2,300 per capita) leads the World Bank to suggest that Bangladesh could join the list of "middle income" countries in ten years. To be sure, trade liberalization, garment exports and remittances from laborers abroad are vital, but the effectiveness of these macroeconomic advances are largely dependent on the kind of ground-level social progress BRAC has made.

"I don't know of any developing-world NGO [nongovernmental organization] that has been more successful," says Dr. Allan Rosenfield, dean of Columbia University's School of Public Health, who serves on the board of BRAC's U.S. arm. "Certainly in terms of the issues they work on, they're more like a minigovernment. If I were giving out Nobel Prizes, there is no doubt I would give it to Abed."

Born to a wealthy landowning family in the Bengal region of British India in 1936, Abed grew up in a household full of servants. His father was a government official. His mother, a religious woman, often brought poor villagers to the Abed home for food. He attended Glasgow University before going to London to study accounting and business. He stayed for 12 years, working as a corporate financial officer and enjoying the life of a professional expatriate: yearly drives through continental Europe, vacations in Italy, reading Western literature. In 1968 he returned to Dhaka with a prestigious job, managing Shell's accounting department.

On Nov. 21, 1970 a cyclone hit the Chittagong area in the southern part of the country, killing perhaps 500,000 people, still the deadliest cyclone on record. Abed and friends volunteered to help. "It really changed the way I look at things," Abed says.

At the time, Bangladesh was the eastern portion of the country of Pakistan, ruled over by an unsympathetic government in Islamabad. A crackdown on the pro-East Pakistan independence movement sent Abed back to London, where he raised funds for the millions of Bangladeshi refugees in India.

After a bloody war Bangladesh won its independence in 1971. Abed sold his London flat for $17,000 and returned to a country that lay in ruins. Hundreds of thousands had been killed and the economy was in tatters—soon after, Henry Kissinger famously called Bangladesh "an international basket case."

Abed and a small group of friends worked on aid projects, but he felt much of the work wasn't benefiting those who needed it most. "Poor people are poor because they are powerless," Abed says. He turned his attention to poverty relief, mapping villages into quartiles based on wealth and focusing his efforts on only those households at the bottom.

Using the proceeds of his London apartment sale, he formed BRAC in 1972. His biggest early success was reducing child mortality. In 1975, 25% of Bangladeshi children wouldn't live to see their fifth birthday; almost half of those deaths were caused by diarrhea. Abed trained groups of women to fan out into the countryside and teach others how to mix a solution of water, salt and sugar that would combat the potentially fatal loss of fluid and electrolytes. Monitors would grade the households based on how well family members did, and that grade would determine the pay of the instructors. This was an incentive-based "social entrepreneurship" program long before that phrase became common. The average worker made $40 a month, with most households scoring in the A or B range.

BRAC researchers estimate that the program, along with a government immunization initiative, has cut the mortality rate of Bangladeshi children ages 1 to 4 from 25% to 7%.

Abed vertically integrates many BRAC programs. A BRAC village organizer will first gather 20 to 30 women and extend microcredit. Many use the loans to set up small shops and grocery stores. If the women buy a cow, for example, BRAC will help them double the price they can get for milk by collecting it via refrigerated truck and bringing it to one of BRAC's 67 "chilling stations," then to BRAC's commercial dairy production center, which processes 10,000 liters of milk, yogurt and ice cream an hour, and selling it in the cities. It earns BRAC $1.7 million on sales of $13.4 million, all of which goes back into the programs.

Likewise, silkworm raising is the bottom step of another commercial market. Majeda Begum, who lives in a small village a day's drive from Dhaka, used her loan to buy silkworm eggs from BRAC, paying $3 for 50 grams. She hatches them in a tin-roofed shack behind her home. Begum feeds them by spreading mulberry leaves over the top, easy enough to collect, since BRAC has planted 20 million mulberry trees around the area to support the enterprise. She'll sell the cocoons back to BRAC for $5.75 a kilo. She earns, she figures, $370 a year, and no longer needs BRAC's loans. All three of her children, including two daughters, go to school. Without the income? "I'd probably only send my son," she says.

Vertically integrated, BRAC's businesses produce $90 million in revenue.

The silk is eventually woven into clothes and sold to Aarong, a chain of upmarket department stores BRAC owns in Bangladesh's big cities. Aarong netted $4.6 million on $28 million in sales in 2006. In all, BRAC's commercial enterprises account for some $90 million in revenue; it pulls in $116 million from its interest on microloans. BRAC still relies on donor funding for 20% of its budget.

Abed uses incentives for health programs, as well. Community health workers are asked to make home visits to 15 houses a day and can resell at a small markup common medicines, balm and birth control pills that they have bought from BRAC.

Recently health volunteers have been trained to recognize the symptoms of tuberculosis, which kills 70,000 Bangladeshis a year. Volunteers collect a sample of phlegm from suspect people and send it to a BRAC health office for testing. If it's positive, the volunteer gets 200 taka (about $2.50). Patients are given medicine free of charge but must post a $3.50 bond to ensure that they continue the six-month course of medication. "There are market incentives in everything we do," Abed says. Bangladesh has upped its cure rate of known TB cases to 90%.

BRAC has recently started targeting the 14% of women too poor to take advantage of microloans. A day's drive from Dhaka, in an un-air-conditioned BRAC field office swarming with flies, Akhtar Hossain unfurls a large sheet of brown paper on which is drawn a map of a nearby village. His house-by-house survey is meant to find "beggars and those with no land." The government is supposed to give these people a card that entitles the holder to 35 kilos of rice every three months. "But they never get it," he says. "The district official in charge of disbursing the cards gives it to people he knows."

To this group BRAC distributes cows, goats or a small plot of arable land. Haliman Khatun, who once worked as a laborer in others' homes and was paid only with small amounts of rice, shares her small shack in Pakundia with her cow, proudly showing off the space where the cow sleeps next to her own bed. She sells milk from the cow at the market but has bigger ambitions: She might sell it for the end of Eid, a Muslim holiday when livestock is slaughtered; cows can fetch a premium in the marketplace, and with that she could buy a plot of land or more goats, she says.

Abed is now bringing BRAC into Africa. The Gates Foundation has given $15 million in grants and loans to replicate BRAC's microfinance, agriculture and health programs in Tanzania, and the Nike Foundation is giving $1 million to establish designated centers for teenage girls in Tanzania. BRAC has set up organizations in the U.S. and the U.K. to bring in more charitable dollars.

It remains to be seen if BRAC can repeat the success it's had in Bangladesh. But Abed is encouraged by its track record in Afghanistan, where it set up shop in 2002. Some 180,000 women have borrowed $96 million from BRAC, and 4,000 have been trained as community health workers. When Abed sets out to do something, he does it big.

From *Forbes* Magazine, June 2, 2008, pp. 66–70. Reprinted by permission of Forbes Magazine, © 2008 Forbes Media Inc.

UNIT 7

Values and Visions

Unit Selections

38. **Humanity's Common Values: Seeking a Positive Future,** Wendell Bell
39. **And the Winner Is . . .,** Alan Wolfe
40. **Life, Religion and Everything,** Laura Sevier

Key Points to Consider

- Is it naive to speak of global issues in terms of ethics?

- What roles can governments, international organizations, and individuals play in making high ethical standards more common in political and economic transactions?

- How is the political role of women changing, and what impacts are these changes having on conflict resolution and community building?

- The consumption of resources is the foundation of the modern economic system. What are the values underlying this economic system, and how resistant to change are they?

- What are the characteristics of a leader?

- In addition to the ideas presented here, what other new ideas are being expressed, and how likely are they to be widely accepted?

Student Web Site

www.mhcls.com

Internet References

Human Rights Web
  http://www.hrweb.org
InterAction
  http://www.interaction.org

The final unit of this book considers how humanity's view of itself is changing. Values, like all other elements discussed in this anthology, are dynamic. Visionary people with new ideas can have a profound impact on how a society deals with problems and adapts to changing circumstances. Therefore, to understand the forces at work in the world today, values, visions, and new ideas in many ways are every bit as important as new technology or changing demographics.

Novelist Herman Wouk, in his book *War and Remembrance,* observed that many institutions have been so embedded in the social fabric of their time that people assumed that they were part of human nature. Slavery and human sacrifice are two examples. However, forward-thinking people opposed these institutions. Many knew that they would never see the abolition of these social systems within their own lifetimes, but they pressed on in the hope that someday these institutions would be eliminated.

Wouk believes the same is true for warfare. He states, "Either we are finished with war or war will finish us." Aspects of society such as warfare, slavery, racism, and the secondary status of women are creations of the human mind; history suggests that they can be changed by the human spirit.

The articles of this unit have been selected with the previous six units in mind. Each explores some aspect of world affairs from the perspective of values and alternative visions of the future.

New ideas are critical to meeting these challenges. The examination of well-known issues from new perspectives can yield new insights into old problems. It was feminist Susan B. Anthony who once remarked that "social change is never made by the masses, only by educated minorities." The redefinition of human values (which, by necessity, will accompany the successful confrontation of important global issues) is a task that few people take on willingly. Nevertheless, in order to deal with the dangers of nuclear war, overpopulation, and environmental degradation, educated people must take a broad view of history. This is going to require considerable effort and much personal sacrifice.

When people first begin to consider the magnitude of contemporary global problems, many often become disheartened and depressed. Some ask: "What can I do? What does it matter? Who cares?" There are no easy answers to these questions, but people need to only look around to see good news as well as bad. How individuals react to the world is not solely a function of so-called objective reality but a reflection of themselves.

As stated at the beginning of the first unit, the study of global issues is the study of people. The study of people, furthermore, is the study of both values and the level of commitment supporting these values and beliefs.

© Rob Melnychuk/Getty Images

It is one of the goals of this book to stimulate you, the reader, to react intellectually and emotionally to the discussion and description of various global challenges. In the process of studying these issues, hopefully, you have had some new insights into your own values and commitments. In the presentation of the allegory of the balloon, the fourth color added represent the *meta* component, all of those qualities that make human beings unique. It is these qualities that have brought us to this "special moment in time," and it will be these same qualities that will determine the outcome of our historically unique challenges.

Humanity's Common Values
Seeking a Positive Future

Overcoming the discontents of globalization and the clashes of civilizations requires us to reexamine and reemphasize those positive values that all humans share.

WENDELL BELL

Some commentators have insisted that the terrorist attacks of September 11, 2001, and their aftermath demonstrate Samuel P. Huntington's thesis of "the clash of civilizations," articulated in a famous article published in 1993. Huntington, a professor at Harvard University and director of security planning for the National Security Council during the Carter administration, argued that "conflict between groups from differing civilizations" has become "the central and most dangerous dimension of the emerging global politics."

Huntington foresaw a future in which nation-states no longer play a decisive role in world affairs. Instead, he envisioned large alliances of states, drawn together by common culture, cooperating with each other. He warned that such collectivities are likely to be in conflict with other alliances formed of countries united around a different culture.

Cultural differences do indeed separate people between various civilizations, but they also separate groups within a single culture or state. Many countries contain militant peoples of different races, religions, languages, and cultures, and such differences do sometimes provoke incidents that lead to violent conflict—as in Bosnia, Cyprus, Northern Ireland, Rwanda, and elsewhere. Moreover, within many societies today (both Western and non-Western) and within many religions (including Islam, Judaism, and Christianity) the culture war is primarily internal, between fundamentalist orthodox believers on the one hand and universalizing moderates on the other. However, for most people most of the time, peaceful accommodation and cooperation are the norms.

Conflicts between groups often arise and continue not because of the differences between them, but because of their similarities. People everywhere, for example, share the capacities to demonize others, to be loyal to their own group (sometimes even willing to die for it), to believe that they themselves and those they identify with are virtuous while all others are wicked, and to remember past wrongs committed against their group and seek revenge. Sadly, human beings everywhere share the capacity to hate and kill each other, including their own family members and neighbors.

Discontents of Globalization

Huntington is skeptical about the implications of the McDonaldization of the world. He insists that the "essence of Western civilization is the Magna Carta not the Magna Mac." And he says further, "The fact that non-Westerners may bite into the latter has no implications for accepting the former."

His conclusion may be wrong, for if biting into a Big Mac and drinking Coca-Cola, French wine, or Jamaican coffee while watching a Hollywood film on a Japanese TV and stretched out on a Turkish rug means economic development, then demands for public liberties and some form of democratic rule may soon follow where Big Mac leads. We know from dozens of studies that economic development contributes to the conditions necessary for political democracy to flourish.

Globalization, of course, is not producing an all-Western universal culture. Although it contains many Western aspects, what is emerging is a *global* culture, with elements from many cultures of the world, Western and non-Western.

Local cultural groups sometimes do view the emerging global culture as a threat, because they fear their traditional ways will disappear or be corrupted. And they may be right. The social world, after all, is constantly in flux. But, like the clean toilets that McDonald's brought to Hong Kong restaurants, people may benefit from certain changes, even when their fears prevent them from seeing this at once.

And local traditions can still be—and are—preserved by groups participating in a global culture. Tolerance and even the celebration of many local variations, as long as they do not harm others, are hallmarks of a sustainable world community. Chinese food, Spanish art, Asian philosophies, African drumming, Egyptian history, or any major religion's version of the Golden Rule can enrich the lives of everyone. What originated locally can become universally adopted (like Arabic numbers). Most important, perhaps, the emerging global culture is a fabric woven from tens of thousands—possibly hundreds of thousands—of individual networks of communication, influence, and exchange that link people and organizations across civilizational boundaries. Aided by electronic communications systems, these networks are growing stronger and more numerous each day.

Positive shared value: Unity.

Searching for Common, *Positive* Values

Global religious resurgence is a reaction to the loss of personal identity and group stability produced by "the processes of social, economic, and cultural modernization that swept across the world in the second half of the twentieth century," according to Huntington. With traditional systems of authority disrupted, people become separated from their roots in a bewildering maze of new rules and expectations. In his view, such people need "new sources of identity, new forms of stable community, and new sets of moral precepts to provide them with a sense of meaning and purpose." Organized religious groups, both mainstream and fundamentalist, are growing today precisely to meet these needs, he believes.

Positive shared value: Love.

Although uprooted people may need new frameworks of identity and purpose, they will certainly not find them in fundamentalist religious groups, for such groups are *not* "new sources of identity." Instead, they recycle the past. Religious revival movements are reactionary, not progressive. Instead of facing the future, developing new approaches to deal with perceived threats of economic, technological, and social change, the movements attempt to retreat into the past.

Religions will likely remain among the major human belief systems for generations to come, despite—or even because of—the fact that they defy conventional logic and reason with their ultimate reliance upon otherworldly beliefs. However, it is possible that some ecumenical accommodations will be made that will allow humanity to build a generally accepted ethical system based on the many similar and overlapping moralities contained in the major religions. A person does not have to believe in supernatural beings to embrace and practice the principles of a global ethic, as exemplified in the interfaith

declaration, "Towards a Global Ethic," issued by the Parliament of the World's Religions in 1993.

Positive shared value: Compassion.

Interfaith global cooperation is one way that people of different civilizations can find common cause. Another is global environmental cooperation seeking to maintain and enhance the life-sustaining capacities of the earth. Also, people everywhere have a stake in working for the freedom and welfare of future generations, not least because the future of their own children and grandchildren is at stake.

Positive shared value: Welfare of future generations.

Many more examples of cooperation among civilizations in the pursuit of common goals can be found in every area from medicine and science to moral philosophy, music, and art. A truly global commitment to the exploration, colonization, and industrialization of space offers still another way to harness the existing skills and talents of many nations, with the aim of realizing and extending worthy human capacities to their fullest. So, too, does the search for extraterrestrial intelligence. One day, many believe, contact will be made. What, then, becomes of Huntington's "clash of civilizations"? Visitors to Earth will likely find the variations among human cultures and languages insignificant compared with the many common traits all humans share.

Universal human values do exist, and many researchers, using different methodologies and data sets, have independently identified similar values. Typical of many studies into universal values is the global code of ethics compiled by Rushworth M. Kidder in *Shared Values for a Troubled World* (Wiley, 1994). Kidder's list includes love, truthfulness, fairness, freedom, unity (including cooperation, group allegiance, and oneness with others), tolerance, respect for life, and responsibility (which includes taking care of yourself, of other individuals, and showing concern for community interests). Additional values mentioned are courage, knowing right from wrong, wisdom, hospitality, obedience, and stability.

The Origins of Universal Human Values

Human values are not arbitrary or capricious. Their origins and continued existence are based in the facts of biology and in how human minds and bodies interact with their physical and social environments. These realities shape and constrain human behavior. They also shape human beliefs about the world and their evaluations of various aspects of it.

Human beings cannot exist without air, water, food, sleep, and personal security. There are also other needs that, although not absolutely necessary for the bodily survival of individuals, contribute to comfort and happiness. These include clothing, shelter, companionship, affection, and sex. The last, of course, is also necessary for reproduction and, hence, for the continued survival of the human species.

Thus, there are many constraints placed on human behavior, if individuals and groups are to continue to survive and to thrive. These are *not* matters of choice. *How* these needs are met involves some—often considerable—leeway of choice, but, obviously, these needs set limits to the possible.

Much of morality, then, derives from human biological and psychological characteristics and from our higher order capacities of choice and reasoning. If humans were invulnerable and immortal, then injunctions against murder would be unnecessary. If humans did not rely on learning from others, lying would not be a moral issue.

Some needs of human individuals, such as love, approval, and emotional support, are inherently social, because they can only be satisfied adequately by other humans. As infants, individuals are totally dependent on other people. As adults, interaction with others satisfies both emotional and survival needs. The results achieved through cooperation and division of labor within a group are nearly always superior to what can be achieved by individuals each working alone. This holds true for hunting, providing protection from beasts and hostile groups, building shelters, or carrying out large-scale community projects.

Thus, social life itself helps shape human values. As societies have evolved, they have selectively retained only some of the logically possible variations in human values as norms, rights, and obligations. These selected values function to make social life possible, to permit and encourage people to live and work together.

Socially disruptive attitudes and actions, such as greed, dishonesty, cowardice, anger, envy, promiscuity, stubbornness, and disobedience, among others, constantly threaten the survival of society. Sadly, these human traits are as universal as are societal efforts to control them. Perhaps some or all of them once had survival value for individuals. But with the growth of society, they have become obstacles to the cooperation needed to sustain large-scale, complex communities. Other actions and attitudes that individuals and societies ought to avoid are equally well-recognized: abuses of power, intolerance, theft, arrogance, brutality, terrorism, torture, fanaticism, and degradation.

Positive shared value: Honesty.

I believe the path toward a harmonious global society is well marked by widely shared human values, including patience, truthfulness, responsibility, respect for life, granting dignity to all people, empathy for others, kindliness and generosity, compassion, and forgiveness. To be comprehensive, this list must be extended to include equality between men and women, respect for human rights, nonviolence, fair treatment of all groups, encouragement of healthy and nature-friendly lifestyles, and acceptance of freedom as an ideal limited by the need to avoid harming others. These value judgments are not distinctively Islamic, Judeo-Christian, or Hindu, or Asian, Western, or African. They are *human* values that have emerged, often independently, in many different places based on the cumulative life experience of generations.

Human societies and civilizations today differ chiefly in how well they achieve these positive values and suppress negative values. No society, obviously, has fully achieved the positive values, nor fully eliminated the negative ones.

But today's shared human values do not necessarily represent the ultimate expression of human morality. Rather, they provide a current progress report, a basis for critical discourse on a global level. By building understanding and agreement across cultures, such discourse can, eventually, lead to a further evolution of global morality.

In every society, many people, groups, and institutions respect and attempt to live by these positive values, and groups such as the Institute for Global Ethics are exploring how a global ethic can be improved and implemented everywhere.

Principle for global peace: Inclusion.

The Search for Global Peace and Order

Individuals and societies are so complex that it may seem foolhardy even to attempt the ambitious task of increasing human freedom and wellbeing. Yet what alternatives do we have? In the face of violent aggressions, injustice, threats to the environment, corporate corruption, poverty, and other ills of our present world, we can find no satisfactory answers in despair, resignation, and inaction.

Rather, by viewing human society as an experiment, and monitoring the results of our efforts, we humans can gradually refine our plans and actions to bring closer an ethical future world in which every individual can realistically expect a long, peaceful, and satisfactory life.

Given the similarity in human values, I suggest three principles that might contribute to such a future: *inclusion, skepticism,* and *social control.*

1. The Principle of Inclusion

Although many moral values are common to all cultures, people too often limit their ethical treatment of others to members of their own groups. Some, for example, only show respect or concern for other people who are of their own race, religion, nationality, or social class.

Such exclusion can have disastrous effects. It can justify cheating or lying to people who are not members of one's own ingroup. At worst, it can lead to demonizing them and making them targets of aggression and violence, treating them as less than human. Those victimized by this shortsighted and counterproductive mistreatment tend to pay it back or pass it on to others, creating a nasty world in which we all must live.

Today, our individual lives and those of our descendants are so closely tied to the rest of humanity that our identities ought to include a sense of kinship with the whole human race and our circle of caring ought to embrace the welfare of people everywhere. In practical terms, this means that we should devote more effort and resources to raising the quality of life for the worst-off members of the human community; reducing disease, poverty, and illiteracy; and creating equal opportunity for all men and women. Furthermore, our circle of caring ought to include protecting natural resources, because all human life depends on preserving the planet as a livable environment.

2. The Principle of Skepticism

One of the reasons why deadly conflicts continue to occur is what has been called "the delusion of certainty." Too many people refuse to consider any view but their own. And, being sure that they are right, such people can justify doing horrendous things to others.

As I claimed in "Who Is Really Evil?" (*The Futurist,* March–April 2004), we all need a healthy dose of skepticism, especially about our own beliefs. Admitting that we might be wrong can lead to asking questions, searching for better answers, and considering alternative possibilities.

Critical realism is a theory of knowledge I recommend for everyone, because it teaches us to be skeptical. It rests on the assumption that knowledge is never fixed and final, but changes as we learn and grow. Using evidence and reason, we can evaluate our current beliefs and develop new ones in response to new information and changing conditions. Such an approach is essential to futures studies, and indeed to any planning. If your cognitive maps of reality are wrong, then using them to navigate through life will not take you where you want to go.

Critical realism also invites civility among those who disagree, encouraging peaceful resolution of controversies by investigating and discussing facts. It teaches temperance and tolerance, because it recognizes that the discovery of hitherto unsuspected facts may overturn any of our "certainties," even long-cherished and strongly held beliefs.

3. The Principle of Social Control

Obviously, there is a worldwide need for both informal and formal social controls if we hope to achieve global peace and order. For most people most of the time, informal social controls may be sufficient. By the end of childhood, for example, the norms of behavior taught and reinforced by family, peers, school, and religious and other institutions are generally internalized by individuals.

Principle for global peace: Skepticism.

Yet every society must also recognize that informal norms and even formal codes of law are not enough to guarantee ethical behavior and to protect public safety in every instance. Although the threats we most often think of are from criminals, fanatics, and the mentally ill, even "normal" individuals may occasionally lose control and behave irrationally, or choose to ignore or break the law with potentially tragic results. Thus, ideally, police and other public law enforcement, caretaking, and rehabilitation services protect us not only from "others," but also from ourselves.

Likewise, a global society needs global laws, institutions to administer them, and police/peacekeepers to enforce them. Existing international systems of social control should be strengthened and expanded to prevent killing and destruction, while peaceful negotiation and compromise to resolve disputes are encouraged. A global peacekeeping force with a monopoly on the legitimate use of force, sanctioned by democratic institutions and due process of law, and operated competently and fairly, could help prevent the illegal use of force, maintain global order, and promote a climate of civil discourse. The actions of these global peacekeepers should, of course, be bound not only by law, but also by a code of ethics. Peacekeepers should use force as a last resort and only to the degree needed, while making every effort to restrain aggressors without harming innocent people or damaging the infrastructures of society.

Expanding international law, increasing the number and variety of multinational institutions dedicated to controlling armed conflict, and strengthening efforts by the United Nations and other organizations to encourage the spread of democracy, global cooperation, and peace, will help create a win-win world.

Conclusion: Values for a Positive Global Future

The "clash of civilizations" thesis exaggerates both the degree of cultural diversity in the world and how seriously cultural differences contribute to producing violent conflicts.

In fact, many purposes, patterns, and practices are shared by all—or nearly all—peoples of the world. There is an emerging global ethic, a set of shared values that includes:

- Individual responsibility.
- Treating others as we wish them to treat us.
- Respect for life.
- Economic and social justice.
- Nature-friendly ways of life.
- Honesty.
- Moderation.
- Freedom (expressed in ways that do not harm others).
- Tolerance for diversity.

The fact that deadly human conflicts continue in many places throughout the world is due less to the differences that separate societies than to some of these common human traits and values. All humans, for example, tend to feel loyalty to their group, and may easily overreact in the group's defense, leaving excluded

Toward Planetary Citizenship

A global economy that values competition over cooperation is an economy that will inevitably hurt people and destroy the environment. If the world's peoples are to get along better in the future, they need a better economic system, write peace activists Hazel Henderson and Daisaku Ikeda in *Planetary Citizenship*.

Henderson, an independent futurist, is one of the leading voices for a sustainable economic system; she is the author of many books and articles on her economic theories, including most recently *Beyond Globalization*. Ikeda is president of Soka Gakkai International, a peace and humanitarian organization based on Buddhist principles.

"Peace and nonviolence are now widely identified as fundamental to human survival," Henderson writes. "Competition must be balanced by cooperation and sharing. Even economists agree that peace, nonviolence, and human security are global public goods along with clean air and water, health and education—bedrock conditions for human well-being and development."

Along with materialistic values and competitive economics, the growing power of technology threatens a peaceful future, she warns. Humanity needs to find ways to harness these growing, "godlike" powers to lead us to genuine human development and away from destruction.

Henderson eloquently praises Ikeda's work at the United Nations to foster global cooperation on arms control, health, environmental protection, and other crucial issues. At the heart of these initiatives is the work of globally minded grass-root movements, or "planetary citizens," which have the potential to become the next global superpower, Henderson suggests.

One example of how nonmaterial values are starting to change how societies perceive their progress is the new Gross National Happiness indicators developed in Bhutan, which "[reflect] the goals of this Buddhist nation, [and] exemplify the importance of clarifying the goals and values of a society and creating indicators to measure what we treasure: health, happiness, education, human rights, family, country, harmony, peace, and environmental quality and restoration," Henderson writes.

The authors are optimistic that the grassroots movement will grow as more people look beyond their differences and seek common values and responsibilities for the future.

Source: *Planetary Citizenship: Your Values, Beliefs and Actions Can Shape a Sustainable World* by Hazel Henderson and Daisaku Ikeda. Middleway Press, 606 Wilshire Boulevard, Santa Monica, California 90401. 2004. 200 pages. $23.95. Order from the Futurist Bookshelf, www.wfs.org/bkshelf.htm.

"outsiders" feeling marginalized and victimized. Sadly, too, all humans are capable of rage and violent acts against others.

In past eras, the killing and destruction of enemies may have helped individuals and groups to survive. But in today's interconnected world that is no longer clearly the case. Today, violence and aggression too often are blunt and imprecise instruments that fail to achieve their intended purposes, and frequently blow back on the doers of violence.

The long-term trends of history are toward an ever-widening definition of individual identity (with some people already adopting self-identities on the widest scale as "human beings"), and toward the enlargement of individual circles of caring to embrace once distant or despised "outsiders." These trends are likely to continue, because they embody values—learned from millennia of human experience—that have come to be nearly universal: from the love of life itself to the joys of belonging to a community, from the satisfaction of self-fulfillment to the excitement of pursuing knowledge, and from individual happiness to social harmony.

How long will it take for the world to become a community where every human everywhere has a good chance to live a long and satisfying life? I do not know. But people of [goodwill] can do much today to help the process along. For example, we can begin by accepting responsibility for our own life choices: the goals and actions that do much to shape our future. And we can be more generous and understanding of what we perceive as mistakes and failures in the choices and behavior of others. We can include all people in our circle of concern, behave ethically toward everyone we deal with, recognize that every

human being deserves to be treated with respect, and work to raise minimum standards of living for the least well-off people in the world.

We can also dare to question our personal views and those of the groups to which we belong, to test them and consider alternatives. Remember that knowledge is not constant, but subject to change in the light of new information and conditions. Be prepared to admit that anyone—even we ourselves—can be misinformed or reach a wrong conclusion from the limited evidence available. Because we can never have all the facts before us, let us admit to ourselves, whenever we take action, that mistakes and failure are possible. And let us be aware that certainty can become the enemy of decency.

In addition, we can control ourselves by exercising self-restraint to minimize mean or violent acts against others. Let us respond to offered friendship with honest gratitude and cooperation; but, when treated badly by another person, let us try, while defending ourselves from harm, to respond not with anger or violence but with verbal disapproval and the withdrawal of our cooperation with that person. So as not to begin a cycle of retaliation, let us not overreact. And let us always be willing to listen and to talk, to negotiate and to compromise.

Finally, we can support international law enforcement, global institutions of civil and criminal justice, international courts and global peacekeeping agencies, to build and strengthen nonviolent means for resolving disputes. Above all, we can work to ensure that global institutions are honest and fair and that they hold all countries—rich and poor, strong and weak—to the same high standards.

If the human community can learn to apply to all people the universal values that I have identified, then future terrorist acts like the events of September 11 may be minimized, because all people are more likely to be treated fairly and with dignity and because all voices will have peaceful ways to be heard, so some of the roots of discontent will be eliminated. When future terrorist acts do occur—and surely some will—they can be treated as the unethical and criminal acts that they are.

There is no clash of civilizations. Most people of the world, whatever society, culture, civilization, or religion they revere or feel a part of, simply want to live—and let others live—in peace and harmony. To achieve this, all of us must realize that the human community is inescapably bound together. More and more, as Martin Luther King Jr. reminded us, whatever affects one, sooner or later affects all.

WENDELL BELL is professor emeritus of sociology and senior research scientist at Yale University's Center for Comparative Research. He is the author of more than 200 articles and nine books, including the two-volume *Foundations of Futures Studies* (Transaction Publishers, now available in paperback 2003, 2004). His address is Department of Sociology, Yale University, P.O. Box 208265, New Haven, Connecticut 06520. E-mail wendell.bell@yale.edu.

This article draws from an essay originally published in the *Journal of Futures Studies 6.*

Article 39

And the Winner Is . . .

ALAN WOLFE

Human beings have never lacked for things to fight over, but for the last two millennia, they have fought the most over ideas involving the divine. Politics, technology, military capacity, and diseases have all played decisive roles in shaping history, yet it is impossible to understand the rise and fall of empires, the clash of civilizations, and the evolving balance of power without appreciating the unique fervor that religion inspires, and the speed with which new religions can spread.

Christianity, a minority sect during much of the Roman Empire, became a world religion with a vast following after the Emperor Constantine converted to it, in the fourth century A.D. Then came Islam, in the seventh century: just a hundred years after Muhammad's death, in 632, the religion he founded reached beyond the Middle East to Africa, India, and significant parts of Spain and France. The Protestant Reformation of 1517 quickly engulfed half of Europe, migrated to the New World, and fueled the Counter-Reformation in the remaining Catholic states on the Continent—by 1618, the Thirty Years' War had begun, resulting in the devastation of large swaths of western Europe and the death of some 30 percent of Germany's population. Every new outburst of religious passion, while producing ecstasy and revelation for some, has disrupted established loyalties, fueled intolerance, and led to violence between the chosen and the damned.

It may seem, at first glance, that little has changed. A recent cover story in *The Economist,* titled "The New Wars of Religion," proclaimed, "Faith will unsettle politics everywhere this century." Some scholars of religion have found new sport in predicting which religions will gain the most adherents (and upset the most applecarts) during the coming decades. Pentecostalism is one favorite candidate; it is sweeping through Latin America and Africa, already claiming some half-billion followers around the world. Catholicism is vying for the same conservative turf; Pope Benedict XVI's insistence on stricter religious teachings, though not likely to grow the Church in Boston, appears intended to win more souls in Bogotá and Brazzaville. Islam claims a fifth of the world's population, and its share is climbing quickly; it is only a matter of time, many believe, before it surpasses Christianity, which is embraced by a third of the world's population, to become the predominant faith. Hindus and Buddhists together make up 20 percent of the world's people, and high birthrates in the countries in which they are dominant suggest that this proportion will grow. Some think

that other religions will have to make room for Mormonism, an infant compared with many other faiths. (Those others will have ample time to do so—although the Church of Jesus Christ of Latter-Day Saints is growing quickly, it has just 12 million members, half in the United States.) All in all, *The Economist* forecasts, by mid-century, 80 percent of the world's people will adhere to one of the major faiths.

A lot rides on which of these predictions turn out to be true, and on how and where different religions bump up against one another. A common worry is that intense competition for souls could produce another era in which religious conflict leads to religious war—only this time with nuclear weapons. If we are really in for anything like the kind of zeal that accompanied earlier periods of religious expansion, we might as well say goodbye to the Enlightenment and its principles of tolerance.

Yet breathless warnings about rising religious fervor and conflicts to come ignore two basic facts. First, many areas of the world are experiencing a *decline* in religious belief and practice. Second, where religions are flourishing, they are also generally evolving—very often in ways that allow them to fit more easily into secular societies, and that weaken them as politically disruptive forces. The French philosopher Blaise Pascal once famously showed that it would be irrational to bet against the existence of God. It would be equally foolish, in the long run, to bet against the power of the Enlightenment. The answer to the question of which religion will dominate the future, at least politically, may well be: None of the above.

Until relatively recently, most social theorists, from Marx to Freud to Weber, believed that as societies became more modern, religion would lose its capacity to inspire. Industrialization would substitute the rational pursuit of self-interest for blind submission to authority. Science would undermine belief in miracles. Democracy would encourage the separation of church and state. Gender equality would undermine patriarchy, and with it, clerical authority. However one defined *modernity,* it always seemed likely to involve societies focused on this world rather than on some other.

But intellectual fashions are fickle, and the idea of inevitable secularization has fallen out of favor with many scholars and journalists. Still, its most basic tenet—that material progress will slowly erode religious fervor—appears unassailable. Last

October, the Pew Global Attitudes Project plotted 44 countries according to per capita gross domestic product and intensity of religious belief, gauged by the responses to several questions about faith. The pattern, as seen in the Pew study and a number of other sources, is hard to miss: when God and Mammon collide, Mammon usually wins.

Toward the right edge of the graph—in the realm of the most-prosperous countries—and at the very bottom lies western Europe, where God, if not dead, has only a faint pulse. Islam, to be sure, is increasingly prevalent in countries such as France and Great Britain, and one can also detect a slight uptick in Christian religiosity across much of the Continent in the past decade or so. But at the same time, the region's last significant pockets of concentrated religiosity are collapsing. Fifty years ago, Spain and Ireland were two of the most religious countries in Europe; now they are among the least. Not long ago, Spain was governed by a fascist dictator in close collaboration with the Catholic Church; now it allows both gay marriage and adoption by gay couples, making it as liberal as Massachusetts. Ireland once gave us, in the form of James Joyce's *Portrait of the Artist as a Young Man,* one of the most chilling depictions of damnation in world literature; these days, Dublin's churches are emptying out, and the few parishioners are apt to be Polish immigrants, most of whom presumably came to Ireland to nourish their bank accounts, not their souls.

Eastern Europe lies to the left of western Europe on the graph. Poland is of course well known for its religiosity; the Communists who governed the country for nearly half a century tried to suppress the Church but were ousted by Solidarity, in large part a faith-based movement, with the encouragement of a native-son pope. But most of the countries of eastern Europe, though poorer than their counterparts in the West, are not very different from them in religious terms. And increasing prosperity in eastern Europe may lower religiosity even more. Poland shows signs of this already. The country's outspokenly Catholic prime minister, Jaroslaw Kaczynski, who governed in collaboration with his equally devout twin brother, was defeated late last year by Donald Tusk. Tusk is far less religious in his personal life than the Kaczynskis—he was married in a civil ceremony, and held a church wedding later only to further his political career. During the election campaign, he attacked Kaczynski's ties to a right-wing, ultra-Catholic broadcasting station, and took more-liberal positions on in vitro fertilization and abortion (although he does not support legalized abortion, he opposed a Church-sponsored constitutional amendment to ban it). The first European states to fully embrace secularism did so over hundreds of years. The last holdouts appear to be making the shift in a generation.

Heading up the graph from eastern Europe in comparative religiosity, we arrive at Latin America, a region famous for its piety. Yet secular values are transforming this part of the world, too, and as they do, religiosity is declining. In 2006, Chile—one of Latin America's wealthiest nations—elected Michelle Bachelet, an openly agnostic single mother, as president. Last spring, Mexico City, the capital of the world's second-largest Catholic country, legalized early-term abortions; the law passed

in the city's legislative assembly by a vote of 46–19. One cannot ignore the rising cultural and political importance of Pentecostalism in countries ranging from Brazil to Guatemala. But neither can one ignore the growth of an increasingly secular middle class in countries such as Argentina, Colombia, and Peru.

The Asian countries surveyed are scattered around the graph, but they follow the graph's basic pattern (as do Asian countries not included in the graph). Indonesia, one of the poorest countries in the region, is up among the world's most religious ones, and has been the scene of considerable, and considerably gruesome, religious violence. China, a bit richer, is less religious (though even in poorer times, China was not generally given to religious fervor, at least not in the way that Westerners understand the term). India, China's main rival for future domination of the world economy, is also less religious than the continent's poorer countries. It does have a popular political party, the Bharatiya Janata Party, that advocates a militant and politicized form of Hinduism. But the BJP, which was part of a coalition that led the government for several years beginning in 1998, lost power in 2004 and has not recovered. Pakistan, India's poorer neighbor, shelters Osama bin Laden and turns out jihadists in droves. But its population is more moderate than many Westerners suppose: its leader, Pervez Musharraf, gets his main support from the military, not the mullahs; and the chief opposition figure, until her assassination in December, was an Oxford- and Harvard-educated woman backed by legions of well-dressed lawyers.

Among the so-called Asian Tigers—Hong Kong, Singapore, South Korea, and Taiwan—only South Korea, where Christian fundamentalism is thriving, is known for religiosity. And even there, it has been leveling off in recent years. Japan, the richest nation in Asia, is right where one would expect it to be on the religiosity scale—alongside the godless countries of western Europe.

The Middle East, of course, is the region of greatest concern to many Americans when it comes to religious fervor, for the religion in question is Islam, and Islam, we are told by conservatives of both the neo- and religious varieties, is an enemy of our way of life. Despite its oil, the Middle East is still relatively poor and only recently urbanized. No one doubts that to arrive there is to pass through the doors of devotion. When Pew asked people whether one must believe in God in order to be moral, the answers in Islamic countries were off the charts: 99 percent of Egyptians and 97 percent of Jordanians, for instance, said yes. Mathematically speaking, it is hard for societies to be more religious than that.

Much has been written about the nourishment that autocracy, on the one hand, and foreign meddling, on the other, have provided to reactionary Islamist movements in the Middle East. Worries about militant Islam often focus on Saudi Arabia, where Islamic fundamentalism really is powerful. The Saudis, moreover, use the considerable cash at their disposal to spread their version of the faith around the world. Given that 15 of the 19 September 11 hijackers were citizens of Saudi Arabia, no one should dismiss the dangers of religious fanaticism originating there.

But the Middle East is a huge area, with many forms of religious expression: the notion that Islamic fundamentalism will sweep the entire region is simply not realistic. Consider another set of data collected by Pew: among Lebanese, Turks, Kuwaitis, and Egyptians who see a struggle in their countries between modernizers and fundamentalists, a majority (or, in the case of the Egyptians, a near-majority) say that they identify with the former. It is true that Turkey, one of the world's largest Muslim countries, is governed by an Islamist party—but that party is both politically and religiously moderate (for example, it favors membership in the European Union). Dubai, one of the richest Muslim countries, is less interested in propagating radical Islam than in attracting gamblers to Las Vegas's MGM Mirage, in which it is a significant shareholder. And even in Saudi Arabia, according to a recent poll by the research organization Terror Free Tomorrow, only 15 percent of the population have a favorable view of Osama bin Laden, and 69 percent support stronger ties with the U.S.

We are left, finally, with Africa. Religiosity there is widely regarded as high, perhaps higher than in the Middle East, but it differs in character. It is in Africa where the predictions of an old-fashioned, broad-based religious revival, with all its attendant conflicts, may come closest to the mark. Much of the commentary on religion's muscle in Africa, and the consequent potential for clashing civilizations, centers on Nigeria, the continent's most populous country and one in which, Pew found, most of those who perceive a struggle between modernizers and fundamentalists put themselves in the latter camp. In recent years, 12 states in northern Nigeria have adopted sharia, or Islamic law, and created special morality police to enforce its tenets. Eliza Griswold explores Africa's religious revival, and in particular the subtleties of the contest between Christianity and Islam in Nigeria, elsewhere in this issue. Here, suffice it to say that Africa is indeed in the throes of a great awakening.

Will it endure? A hundred years ago, in *The Protestant Ethic and the Spirit of Capitalism,* Max Weber quoted the great evangelical John Wesley, the founder of the Methodist Church:

> I do not see how it is possible, in the nature of things, for any revival of true religion to continue long. For religion must necessarily produce both industry and frugality, and these cannot but produce riches. But as riches increase, so will pride, anger, and love of the world in all its branches.

In 19th-century Europe, as Weber's reference suggests, religious devotion did make people better off materially, and thereby moderated godly fervor. Just because it may have happened that way then does not mean that religion will have the same effect in the developing world now. Yet whether it is faith or some other force that stimulates economic growth in Africa (or Asia or the Middle East), growth is bound to occur, and to continue to moderate religious fervor.

You'll have noticed that I've said nothing yet about the United States. Talk about an outlier—there on the Pew chart it stands, nearly alone, as the only country in the world, apart from Kuwait, that is both wealthy and religious. Americans are not only more religious than Europeans; they are more religious than the citizens of some Latin American countries. If proof is needed that religion will remain a dominant force in history for a long time to come, the fact that the world's most affluent society is also well up among the faithful would seem to provide it. When the president says that his decision to invade another country was influenced by a call from God, or when school boards decide to include creationism in their curriculum, it appears safe to conclude that Americans are not living in the world envisioned by Marx or Freud.

But one shouldn't go overboard in describing American religiosity. For one thing, it is as shallow as it is broad: Americans know relatively little about the histories, the theological controversies, or even the sacred texts of their chosen faiths. Recent decades have seen the rise of the Christian right in the United States, but they have also witnessed the seemingly inexorable advance of secular ideals, such as personal choice and pluralism, that blossomed in the 1960s. Some signs indicate that the Christian right may be losing steam, or at least moderating, as a political force. Nonbelief, meanwhile, is increasing: not only are atheist manifestos selling in large numbers, but the percentage of those who express no religious preference to pollsters doubled between 1990 and 2001, to 15 percent.

The most important religious phenomenon in the United States, however, has nothing to do with the number of atheists. It concerns another trend that, like modernization, is changing the trajectories of religion worldwide: the creation and spread of a free religious marketplace, which partly (though by no means completely) revives religious devotion wherever it reaches, but also tends to moderate the religions offered within it.

Religious monopolies or near-monopolies, such as state-sponsored churches, generally throttle religious practice over time, especially as a country becomes wealthier; the European experience amply demonstrates this. Lacking any incentive to innovate, churches atrophy, and their congregations dwindle. But places with a free religious marketplace witness something very different: entrepreneurs of the spirit compete to save souls, honing their messages and modulating many of their beliefs so as to appeal to the consumer. With more options to choose from, more consumers find something they like, and the ranks of the religious grow.

The key precondition for this sort of marketplace is the presence of rudimentary secular values. This may sound odd, since the secular has long been thought the opposite of the religious; the First Amendment to the U.S. Constitution, the 1905 French law establishing *laïcité,* or the removal of religion from public affairs, and the creation of modern Turkey were once seen as the replacement of religious orthodoxy by Enlightenment principles. Secularism is still commonly understood in this way: a secular society is viewed as one with large numbers of freethinkers choosing science over superstition and reason over revelation.

But secularism is not the opposite of belief; nonbelief is. Indeed, secularism has religious, specifically Christian, roots; it renders unto Caesar what is Caesar's, while leaving to God what properly belongs in his realm. John Locke argued as much in *A Letter Concerning Toleration,* first published in 1689: genuine salvation, he wrote, can never be achieved through governmental coercion.

In contemporary societies influenced by Lockean ideals, then, religion's priority of belief and secularism's commitment to individual rights are not in opposition; rather, they complement each other. It was once thought that the First Amendment was written to protect public life from the depredations of religious orthodoxy. It is now commonly accepted that the Founders also separated church and state in order to protect religion from government.

So what happens to religions that find themselves with many competitors? Consider what is occurring within the growing American evangelical movement. It has built megachurches that meet the needs of time-pressed professionals by offering such things as day-care centers, self-help groups, and networking opportunities. Its music owes more to Janis Joplin than to Johann Sebastian Bach. Its church officials learn more from business-school case studies than from theological texts. And its young people—well, as the children of parents who have gone through a born-again experience, they are not likely to be as obedient as the evangelical leader James Dobson wants them to be. Having opted to grow on secular terms, American evangelicalism is becoming less hostile to liberal ideas such as tolerance and pluralism. New efforts to take it in directions sympathetic to environmentalism and social justice are a direct result of the maturing of the faith, which followed from earlier decisions to make the movement more appealing to large numbers of Americans, especially the young.

Does the pattern hold outside America? After all, it is often said that the promulgation of secular values and lifestyles, one result of globalization, is prompting a reactionary religious backlash. There is some truth to this argument, but it misses the bigger picture. Most of the religious revivals we are seeing throughout the world today complement, and ultimately reinforce, secular developments; they are more likely to encourage moderation than fanaticism.

Let's look at how global commerce is affecting religion in the developing world. Religious leaders are using advanced media technologies to propagate their message, bringing new religious options and interpretations even to many remote areas. At the same time, globalization is drawing people into the cities, where they must fend for themselves in an unfamiliar environment; in these circumstances, people begin to look to religion not for instruction in traditional ways of life, but as a means of coming to terms with new experiences. Both developments weaken the hold that local, insular religions have on their adherents, and also make it harder for governmental or clerical authorities to restrict religious choice.

Although Jihad may be at war with McWorld, most other forms of religious enthusiasm, including most forms of Islam, are not.

How does this lead to moderation? It doesn't always— rejectionist religious strains can certainly prosper, at least for a time, during periods of intense dislocation. Still, although Jihad may be at war with McWorld, most other forms of religious enthusiasm, including most forms of Islam, are not.

Various versions of the prosperity movement are attracting followers in developing countries, as well as in poorer areas of the United States, precisely because they value success in this world as much as holiness in another. These movements can be rightly accused of theological thinness, but not of adherence to old-fashioned doctrine. Their goal is not to question the modern world's riches but to bring them within the reach of more people. And once this dynamic is set in motion, it tends to gather momentum. As Eliza Griswold points out, the success of the Pentecostal Gospel of Prosperity in Nigeria has prompted the creation of a new Islamic organization focused on economic empowerment, which already has 1.2 million members in Nigeria alone.

In our time, as in Locke's, forcible conversion does not work very well, if at all. One does not spread the good news of the Lord through the bad news of war. As religious leaders recognize that they are more likely to swell their ranks through persuasion than through coercion, they find themselves accepting such secular ideas as free will and individual autonomy. And even religions that are culturally dominant and closely linked with the state must worry about holding on to the allegiance of the young, as well as retaining the loyalties—and the money— of those who have moved abroad and been exposed to religious pluralism and tolerance. As one part of the world becomes modern, those parts it touches also gain exposure to modern ideas. Few places remain where old-fashioned, rigidly dogmatic forms of religion are isolated.

One can see intimations of a pluralistic, American-style religious revival around the world. In Europe, a moderating of fundamentalist extremism, in the name of religious revivalism, may well be under way. Americans worried about the clash of civilizations tend to focus on those forms of Islam called *salafist,* a generic term meant to include those who wish to restore the Muslim faith to the purity it presumably possessed during the era of the Prophet Muhammad. Perhaps they should focus more attention on Muslim religious leaders like Amr Khaled, an Egyptian televangelist now living much of the year in England. Combining idealistic themes of self-empowerment with prosperity movement themes of self-improvement, Khaled appeals to young people in ways that are neither strictly modern nor strictly fundamentalist. So does Mustafa Hosni, a young Egyptian whose YouTube videos bring messages of self-fulfillment and spiritual renewal to jeans-clad Muslims in both Europe and the Middle East. These secularly influenced forms of Islamic revivalism may not draw huge masses into the streets, but they are exceptionally influential among the well-off, ambitious, and upwardly mobile Muslims who will be leading their countries in the future.

The pattern is similar virtually everywhere we look. Latin Americans are leaving Catholicism because they want the sense of personal empowerment that Pentecostal forms of worship can provide. The preacher and bestselling author Rick Warren is invited to Africa because his ideas about the purpose-driven life, read in the United States as a guide to getting one's personal act together, can be read in that part of the world as encouraging wider, bourgeois virtues of thrift and responsibility. In this light, Pope Benedict's decision to steer Catholicism in a more conservative, traditional direction—a move that effectively forfeits the Church's future in the developed world in order to expand its appeal in developing regions—seems like a winner only in the short run.

Even in Nigeria, there are signs of accommodation, as Lydia Polgreen of *The New York Times* wrote in a recent report from Kano, one of the states that adopted sharia. The harsher aspects of Islamic law have not been implemented there, and Christians, many of whom had fled the region, are beginning to return. "*Shariah* needs to be practical," a civil servant in Kano told Polgreen. "We are a developing country, so there is a kind of moderation between the ideas of the West and traditional Islamic values. We try to weigh it so that there is no contradiction." Those who worry about religious revivals in the world today usually pose an either/or choice between religion and secularism. In reality, the two can work together.

Religious peace will be the single most important consequence of the secular underpinning of todays religious growth. All religions tend to be protective of their traditions and rituals, but all religions also change depending upon the cultural practices of the societies in which they are based. Protestantism and secularism have always had close ties: as noted, Locke was drawing on a specifically Protestant sensibility when he wrote in defense of secular ideals. Other religions in secular environments have shown themselves quite willing to adopt Protestant notions about how faith should be practiced in order to gain or retain adherents. During the Second Vatican Council, in the early 1960s, the Catholic Church accepted the idea of religious liberty. Jews in the United States find themselves organized into denominations—Reform, Conservative, Orthodox—in ways that borrow from Protestant traditions. Despite the attention paid to what once were hotbeds of extremism like the North London Central Mosque in Finsbury Park, significant numbers of Muslims in both North America and western Europe are turning their mosques into all-purpose religious institutions and accepting innovations in gender equality foreign to the practice of Islam in the non-secular past.

What about religions in non-secular environments—can they find ways to live in peace with one another? If not, we have a pretty good idea of what will happen: the Sunni-Shia wars in Iraq, and everyday life in the occupied territories, provide examples enough. Yet because so much of the world is now, if not secular, then moving toward secularization, the sort of accommodation recently seen in Kano may ultimately take hold in other developing areas as well.

The world will never be rid of fanaticism; globalization is just as capable of disseminating extreme ideas as it is of advancing moderation. But fanaticism should not be confused with religious intensity. One can pray passionately to God and lead an otherwise balanced life, just as one can be monomaniacal about things having nothing to do with the divine.

And religious leaders prone to fanaticism are likely to find that the price of using force to spread God's word, or to try to monopolize it, will be a greatly diminished hold on the future. Moreover, the future may come sooner than we think. We have seen how rapidly religion has spread in the past, claiming adherents from competing faiths before the competition knew what hit them. Both secularism and secularly inspired ways of being religious are spreading just as rapidly—maybe even more so. Historians may one day look back on the next few decades, not as yet another era when religious conflicts enveloped countries and blew apart established societies, but as the era when secularization took over the world.

ALAN WOLFE is the director of the Boisi Center for Religion and Public Life at Boston College.

Life, Religion and Everything

Biologist and author Rupert Sheldrake believes that the world's religions have a crucial role in restoring the earth's ecological balance. Laura Sevier meets the man trying to broker a better relationship between God, man, science and the natural world.

LAURA SEVIER

A long, low drone fills the air. We are all chanting the same sound: OOOOOOOHHHHHHHH. Whistling overtones start to ring out above the group sound and then a lone female voice sings out:

Where I sit is holy

Holy is the ground

Forest mountain river listen to my sound

Great spirit circling all around.

The voice then invites everyone to join in and we sing this verse seven or eight times. Then there is silence.

It's not often you attend a talk given by an eminent scientist that begins with a session of Mongolian overtone chanting followed by a Native American Indian song about the holiness of the earth. It's especially surreal given that we're sitting on neat little rows of chairs in a Unitarian Church in Hampstead, in London.

I was there to listen to renowned English biologist Rupert Sheldrake talk about how the world's religions can learn to live with ecological integrity. The chanting, it appears, is the warm-up act, led by Sheldrake's wife, Jill Purce, a music healer.

So far so extraordinary, but then Sheldrake is no ordinary man. A respected scientist from a largely conventional educational background, he's devoted much of the past 17 years of his life to studying the sort of phenomena that most 'serious' scientists dismiss out of hand, such as telepathy, our 'seventh sense'. But religion? Given the current trend for militant atheism within science, I'm amazed. Besides, isn't religion incompatible with science? Not according to Sheldrake, an Anglican Christian. 'One of my main concerns is the opening up of science. Another is exploring the connections between science and spirituality,' he says.

His take on religion—and science—is refreshingly unorthodox precisely because it factors in a crucial new element:

nature. 'The thrust of my work is trying to break out of the mechanistic view of nature as inanimate, dead and machine-like.' In fact his 1991 book *The Rebirth of Nature: the Greening of Science and God* (Inner Traditions Bear & Company, £11.99) was devoted to showing 'how we can once again think of nature as alive'—and sacred.

The Sacred Earth

Our culture seems to have lost touch with any idea of the land as being alive and sacred and anyone who considers it to be so is often branded a tree-hugging hippie and treated with ridicule or suspicion. Land is mostly valued purely in economic terms. Yet no value is attributed to the irreplaceable benefits derived from the normal functioning of the natural world, which assures the stability of our climate, the fertility of our soil, the replenishment of our water.

Our culture seems to have lost any idea of the land being alive and sacred, and values it only in economic terms.

Religion has, until recently, remained pretty quiet on the issue.

As Edward Goldsmith wrote in the *Ecologist* in 2000, mainstream religions have become increasingly 'otherworldly'. They have 'scarcely any interest' in the natural world at all. Traditionally, religion used to play an integral role in linking people to the natural world, imbuing people with the knowledge and values that make caring for it a priority. 'Mainstream religion' Goldsmith wrote 'has failed the earth. It has lost its way, and needs to return to its roots.'

So if the world's religions are to play a part in saving what remains of the natural world, they not only need to return to their roots but also to confront the threat and scale of the global ecological crisis we now face. This means being open to a dialogue with science. 'No religions, when they were growing up, had to deal with our present situation and ecological crisis,' says Sheldrake. 'People thought they could take the earth more or less for granted. Certainly the idea that human beings could transform the climate through their actions was unheard of. This is a new situation for everybody, for religious people and scientists, for traditional cultures and modern scientific ones. We're all in this together.'

Environmental Sin

'Religion and Ecology' is now a subject of serious academic study. The Forum on Religion and Ecology at Yale University, for example, recently explored the ecological dimension of all the major world religions. The ongoing environmental crisis has sparked a 'bringing together' of the world's religions in a series of interreligious meetings and conferences around the world on the theme of 'Religion, Science and the Environment', exploring the response that religious communities can make. These brought together scientists, bishops, rabbis, marine biologists and philosophers in a way that, according to Sheldrake, 'really worked'.

Within many religions, including all branches of Christianity, there's an attempt to recover that sense of connection with nature. 'There's a lot going on,' says Sheldrake, 'even within the group seen as lagging the furthest behind—the American Evangelicals, who are somewhat retrogressive in relation to the environment.'

Some evangelicals who believe in the Rapture and think the world is soon to end have expressed the view that there's no point in attempting to save the environment because it's all going to be discarded like a used tissue.

But a more environmentally friendly view is held by the Evangelical Environmental Network (EEN), a group of individuals and organisations including World Vision, World Relief and the International Bible Society. An Evangelical Declaration on the Care of Creation, its landmark credo published in 1991, begins: 'We believe that biblical faith is essential to the solution of our ecological problems. . . . Because we worship and honour the Creator we seek to cherish and care for the creation. Because we have sinned, we have failed our stewardship of creation. Therefore we repent of the way we have polluted, distorted or destroyed so much of the Creator's work.'

It then commits to work for reconciliation of people and the healing of suffering creation.

The belief that environmental destruction is a sin isn't a new concept. The spirituality of native American Indians, for instance, is a land-based one. In this culture, the world is animate, natural things are alive and everything is imbued with spirit.

Nature informs us and it is our obligation to read nature as you would a book, to feel it as you would a poem.

In the words of John Mohawk, native American chief: 'The natural world is our Bible. We don't have chapters and verses; we have trees and fish and animals . . . The Indian sense of natural law is that nature informs us and it is our obligation to read nature as you would a book, to feel nature as you would a poem, to touch nature as you would yourself, to be part of that and step into its cycles as much as you can.'

Most importantly, environmental destruction is seen as a sin.

Loss of the Sacred

The question is, how did we lose the sacred connection with the natural world? Where did religion and culture go wrong? According to Sheldrake, the break began in the 16th century. Until then there were pagan festivals, such as May Day, that celebrated the seasons and the fertility of the land; there were nature shrines, holy wells and sacred places.

But with the Protestant Reformation in the 16th century there was an attempt by the reformers, who couldn't find anything about these 'pagan' practices in the Bible, to stamp them out. In the 17th century the Puritans brought a further wave of suppression of these things—banning, for example, Maypole dancing (Maypoles being a symbol of male fertility). 'There was a deliberate attempt to get rid of all the things that connected people to the sacredness of the land and it largely succeeded,' says Sheldrake.

Another factor he believes severed our connection is the view of nature as a machine. 'From the time of our remotest ancestors until the 17th century, it was taken for granted that the world of nature was alive, that the universe was alive and that all animals were not only alive but had souls—the word "animal" comes from the word "anima", meaning soul. This was the standard view, even within the Church. Medieval Christianity was based on an animate form of nature—a kind of Christian animism.'

But this model of a living world was replaced by the idea of the universe as a machine, an idea that stems from the philosophy of Rene Descartes. Nature was no more than dead matter and everything was viewed as mechanical, governed by mathematical principles instead of animating souls.

'This mechanistic view of nature,' Sheldrake says, 'is an extremely limiting and alienating one. It forces the whole of our understanding of nature into a machine metaphor—the universe as a machine, animals and plants as machines, you as a machine, the brain as a machine. It's a very man-centred metaphor, as only people make machines. So looking at nature in this way projects one aspect of human activity onto the whole of nature.'

Hinduism

- The Vedas (ancient Hindu scriptures) describe how the creator god Vishnu made the universe so that every element is interlinked. A disturbance in one part will upset the balance and impact all the other elements.
- Three important principles of Hindu environmentalism are *yajna* (sacrifice), *dhana* (giving) and *tapas* (penance).
- *Yajna* entails that you should sacrifice your needs for the sake of others, for nature, the poor or future generations.
- *Dhana* entails that whatever you consume you must give back.
- *Tapas* commends self-restraint in your lifestyle.
- Mother Earth is personified in the Vedas as the goddess Bhumi, or Prithvi.
- Hindu businessman Balbir Mathur, inspired by his faith, founded Trees for Life (www.treesforlife.org), a non-profit movement that plants fruit trees in developing countries, to provide sustainable and environmentally-friendly livelihoods.

Islam

- Allah has appointed humankind *khalifah* (steward) over the created world.
- This responsibility is called *al-amanah* (the trust) and Man will be held accountable to it at the Day of Judgment.
- The Qur'an warns against disturbing God's natural balance: 'Do no mischief on the earth after it hath been set in order' (7:56).
- Shari'ah (Islamic law) designates *haram* zones, used to contain urban development in protection of natural resources, and *hima,* specific conservation areas.
- The Islamic foundation for ecology and environmental sciences www.ifes.org.uk publishes a newsletter called *Eco Islam* and organised an organic *iftar* (the evening meal during Ramadan) in 2006.
- In 2000, IFEES led an Islamic educational programme on the Muslim-majority island of Misali, in response to the destruction to the aquatic ecosystem by over-fishing and the use of dynamite in coral reefs. The environmental message based on the Qur'an initiated sustainable fishing practices.

Judaism

- The Torah prohibits harming God's earth: 'Do not cut down trees even to prevent ambush, do not foul waters, or burn crops even to cause an enemy's submission' (Devarim 20:19)
- It teaches humility in the face of nature: 'Ask the beasts, and they will teach you; the birds of the sky, and they will tell you; or speak to the earth and it will teach you; the fish of the sea, they will inform you' (Job 12:7-9)
- The Talmudic law *bal tashchit* (do not destroy) was developed by Jewish scholars into a series of specific prohibitions against wasteful actions.
- The Noah Project (www.noahproject.org.uk) is a UK-based Jewish environmental organisation, engaged in hands-on conservation work, and promoting environmental responsibility by emphasising the environmental dimensions of Jewish holidays such as Tu B'Shevat (New Year of the Trees).

Christianity

- Genesis gives a picture of God creating the heavens and earth—and when it was all finished, 'God saw all that he had made, and it was very good.' (1:31) Having made man, he 'put him in the Garden of Eden to work it and take care of it' (2:15).
- Romans 8:19-22 has been interpreted as a message of redemption for the environment, calling on Christians to work towards the time when 'the creation itself will be liberated from its bondage to decay'.
- At the UN Rio Earth Summit in 1992, the World Council of Churches formed a working group on climate change. Their manifesto expresses a concern for justice towards developing countries, who are disproportionately affected by climate change, to future generations and to the world.
- www.christian-ecology.org.uk represents Churches Together in Britain and Ireland. It includes links and a daily prayer guide with references both to the Bible and to scientific and news data. Operation Noah is the climate change campaign.

Buddhism

- Buddhist religious ecology is based on three principles: nature as teacher, as a spiritual force, and as a way of life.
- Buddhists believe that nature can teach us about the interdependence and impermanence of life, and that living near to and in tune with nature gives us spiritual strength.
- Buddha commended frugality, avoiding waste, and non-violence.
- Buddhists believe that man should be in harmonious interaction with nature, not a position of authority.
- Philosopher Dr Simon James, based at Durham University, has studied the Buddhist basis of environmentalism and virtue ethics. A spiritually enlightened individual shows compassion, equanimity and humility—qualities that are intrinsic to an environmentally friendly lifestyle.
- The Zen Environmental Studies Institute (www.mro.org/zesi) in New York runs programmes in nature study and environmental advocacy, informed by Zen Buddhist meditation.

Baha'ism

- Bahá'u'lláh, founder of the Baha'i faith and regarded as a messenger from God, stated 'nature is God's Will and is its expression in and through the contingent world' (the Tablets of Baha'u'llah).
- Baha'is believe that the world reflects God's qualities and attributes and therefore must be cherished.
- The Baha'i Office of the Environment states: 'Baha'u'llah's promise that civilisation will exist on this planet for a minimum of 5,000 centuries makes it unconscionable to ignore the long-term impact of decisions made today. The world community must, therefore, learn to make use of the earth's natural resources . . . in a manner that ensures sustainability into the distant reaches of time.'
- The Barli Rural Development Institute in India was inspired by Baha'i social activism. It has trained hundreds of rural women in conservation strategies such as rainwater harvesting and solar cooking.
- www.onecountry.org is the newsletter of the Bahai international community.

It is this view, he says, that led to our current crisis. 'If you assume that nature is inanimate, then nothing natural has a life, purpose, or value. Natural resources are there to be developed, and the only value placed on them is by market forces and official planners. And if you assume that only humans are conscious, only humans have reason, and therefore only humans have true value, then it's fine to have animals in factory farms and to exploit the world in whatever way you like, and if you do conserve any bit of the earth then you have to conserve it with human ends in mind. Everything is justified in human terms.'

The mechanistic theory has become a kind of religion that is built into the official orthodoxy of economic progress and, through technology's successes, is now triumphant on a global scale. 'So,' says Sheldrake, 'this combination of science, technology, secular humanism and rationalism—all these philosophies that dominate the modern age—open the way for untrammelled exploitation of the earth that is going on everywhere today.'

The Living Universe

It seems like a pretty bleak vision. But there is an alternative: to allow our own experience and intuition to help us see nature and the universe as alive. 'Many people have emotional connections with particular places associated with their childhood, or feel an empathy with animals or plants, or are inspired by the beauty of nature, or experience a mystical sense of unity with the natural world,' Sheldrake says. 'Our private relationship with nature presupposes that nature is alive.'

In other words, we don't need to be told by science, religion or anyone that it is alive, valuable and worthy of respect and reverence. Deep down, we can feel it for ourselves. Many people have urges to get 'back to nature' in some way, to escape the confines of concrete and head for the hills, the sea, a park or even a small patch of grass. These impulses are moving us in the right direction.

Another way forward is through new revolutionary insights within science. 'Science itself is leading us away from this view of nature as a machine towards a much more organic view of living in the world,' says Sheldrake. 'The changes are happening in independent parts of science for different reasons, but all of them are pointing in the same direction: the view of a very organic, creative world.'

The big bang theory gives a new model of the universe that is more like a developing organism, growing spontaneously and forming totally new structures within it. The concept of quantum physics has broken open many of our ideas of the mechanistic universe. The old idea of determinism has given way to indeterminism and chaos theory. The old idea of the earth as dead has given way to Gaia, the living earth. The old idea of the universe as uncreative has given way to the new idea of creative evolution, first in the realm of living things, through Darwin, and now we see that the whole cosmos is in creative evolution. So, if the whole universe is alive, if the universe is like a great organism, then everything within it is best understood as alive.

Encouraging Dialogue

This has opened up new possibilities for a dialogue between science and religion. 'These changing frontiers of science are making it much easier to see that we're all part of, and dependent on, a living earth; and for those of us who follow a religion, to see the living God as the living world,' says Sheldrake. Such insights breathe new meaning into traditional religions, their practices and seasonal festivals.

For example, all religions provide opportunities for giving thanks, both through simple everyday rituals, like saying grace, and also in collective acts of thanksgiving. These expressions of gratitude can help to remind us that we have much to be thankful for. But as Sheldrake points out, 'It's hard to feel a sense of gratitude for an inanimate, mechanical world.'

Helping people see the land as sacred again, Sheldrake maintains, is one of the major roles of religion. 'They all point towards a larger whole: the wholeness of creation and a larger story than our own individual story. All religions tell stories about our place in the world, our relation to other people and to the world in which we live. In that sense all religions relate us to the earth and the heavens.'

Sheldrake thinks we need stories: 'It's part of our nature. Science gives us stories, too—the universe story. So does TV, fiction, books.' And these stories, in his view, unify us in a way that, for instance, some New Age practices (such as personal shrines) don't. While those things have personal value, they don't have the unifying function that a traditional religion does. 'When you go to a Hindu festival or pilgrimage, you see thousands of people coming together, the whole community united by a common story or a celebration of a sacred place.'

The fascinating thing about Rupert Sheldrake is his ability to assimilate ideas from an array of different subjects that are normally kept separate, draw new connections and conclusions and open up new dialogues. He's certainly not afraid to explore new territory or use new metaphors. Thus the big bang is like 'the primal orgasm' or like 'the breaking open of the cosmic egg'.

When talking about the discovery that 95 per cent of the universe is 'dark matter' or unknown, he says, 'it is as if science has discovered the cosmic unconscious'. He embraces the idea of 'Mother Nature'—in fact he believes the old intuition of nature as Mother still affects our personal responses to it and conditions our response to the ecological crisis. 'We feel uncomfortable when we recognise that we are polluting our own Mother; it is easier to rephrase the problem in terms of "inadequate waste management".' He sees the green movement as one aspect of 'Mother Nature reasserting herself, whether we like it or not.'

One of the most significant implications of Sheldrake's worldview is that it connects people to the natural world and 'if people feel more connected to the world around them, they might be less likely to accept its destruction,' he says. Reframing our view to encompass a world that is alive also, effectively, puts humans back in our proper place in the scheme of things.

Sheldrake's scientific and philosophical investigation is fuelled by a passionate concern for all of life, and his vision of life expands to the cosmos. If the earth is alive, if the universe is alive, if solar systems are alive, if galaxies are alive, if planets are alive, then causing harm to any of these systems really is a sin; one that we have committed all too willingly for far too long.

For Further Information

Rupert Sheldrake: www.sheldrake.org

Forum on Religion and Ecology: http://environment.harvard.edu/religion—the ecological dimension of various religions

The Alliance of Religions and Conservation (ARC): www.arcworld.org

LAURA SEVIER is a freelance journalist and regular contributor to the *Ecologist*.

Test-Your-Knowledge Form

We encourage you to photocopy and use this page as a tool to assess how the articles in *Annual Editions* expand on the information in your textbook. By reflecting on the articles you will gain enhanced text information. You can also access this useful form on a product's book support Web site at *http://www.mhcls.com*.

NAME: DATE:

_____

TITLE AND NUMBER OF ARTICLE:

_____

BRIEFLY STATE THE MAIN IDEA OF THIS ARTICLE:

_____

LIST THREE IMPORTANT FACTS THAT THE AUTHOR USES TO SUPPORT THE MAIN IDEA:

_____

WHAT INFORMATION OR IDEAS DISCUSSED IN THIS ARTICLE ARE ALSO DISCUSSED IN YOUR TEXTBOOK OR OTHER READINGS THAT YOU HAVE DONE? LIST THE TEXTBOOK CHAPTERS AND PAGE NUMBERS:

_____

LIST ANY EXAMPLES OF BIAS OR FAULTY REASONING THAT YOU FOUND IN THE ARTICLE:

_____

LIST ANY NEW TERMS/CONCEPTS THAT WERE DISCUSSED IN THE ARTICLE, AND WRITE A SHORT DEFINITION:

We Want Your Advice

ANNUAL EDITIONS revisions depend on two major opinion sources: one is our Advisory Board, listed in the front of this volume, which works with us in scanning the thousands of articles published in the public press each year; the other is you—the person actually using the book. Please help us and the users of the next edition by completing the prepaid article rating form on this page and returning it to us. Thank you for your help!

ANNUAL EDITIONS: Global Issues 09/10

ARTICLE RATING FORM

Here is an opportunity for you to have direct input into the next revision of this volume.
We would like you to rate each of the articles listed below, using the following scale:

1. **Excellent: should definitely be retained**
2. **Above average: should probably be retained**
3. **Below average: should probably be deleted**
4. **Poor: should definitely be deleted**

Your ratings will play a vital part in the next revision.
Please mail this prepaid form to us as soon as possible.
Thanks for your help!

RATING	ARTICLE	RATING	ARTICLE
	1. A Special Moment in History		22. Drugs
	2. Can Extreme Poverty Be Eliminated?		23. Ensuring Energy Security
	3. The Ideology of Development		24. The Power and the Glory
	4. The Rise of the Rest		25. Nuclear Now!: How Clean, Green Atomic Energy Can Stop Global Warming
	5. Feminists and Fundamentalists		26. Life After Peak Oil
	6. The Century Ahead		27. Terrorist Rivals: Beyond the State-Centric Model
	7. Africa's Restless Youth		28. The Long March to Be a Superpower
	8. Still Hungry: One Eighth of the World's People Do Not Have Enough to Eat		29. What Russia Wants
	9. Pandemic Pandemonium		30. Lifting the Veil: Understanding the Roots of Islamic Militancy
	10. Deflating the World's Bubble Economy		31. A Mideast Nuclear Chain Reaction?
	11. The Great Leap Backward?		32. The Politics of Death in Darfur
	12. Water of Life in Peril		33. Banning the Bomb: A New Approach
	13. Ocean 'Dead Zones' Spreading Worldwide		34. Europe as a Global Player: A Parliamentary Perspective
	14. Cry of the Wild		35. The Grameen Bank
	15. Globalization and Its Contents		36. Geneva Conventions
	16. It's a Flat World, After All		37. Is Bigger Better?
	17. Why the World Isn't Flat		38. Humanity's Common Values: Seeking a Positive Future
	18. The Case against the West: America and Europe in the Asian Century		39. And the Winner Is . . .
	19. A Bigger World		40. Life, Religion and Everything
	20. The Lost Continent		
	21. Promises and Poverty		

ABOUT YOU

Name   Date

_____

Are you a teacher? ❏ A student? ❏
Your school's name

_____

Department

_____

Address   City   State   Zip

_____

School telephone #

_____

YOUR COMMENTS ARE IMPORTANT TO US!

Please fill in the following information:
For which course did you use this book?

_____

Did you use a text with this ANNUAL EDITION? ❏ yes ❏ no
What was the title of the text?

_____

What are your general reactions to the Annual Editions concept?

_____

Have you read any pertinent articles recently that you think should be included in the next edition? Explain.

_____

Are there any articles that you feel should be replaced in the next edition? Why?

_____

Are there any World Wide Web sites that you feel should be included in the next edition? Please annotate.

_____

May we contact you for editorial input? ❏ yes ❏ no
May we quote your comments? ❏ yes ❏ no